Teaching Young Adult Literature Today

Teaching Young Adult Literature Today

Insights, Considerations, and Perspectives for the Classroom Teacher

Judith A. Hayn and Jeffrey S. Kaplan

ROWMAN & LITTLEFIELD PUBLISHERS, INC.
Lanham • Boulder • New York • Toronto • Plymouth, UK

Published by Rowman & Littlefield Publishers, Inc.
A wholly owned subsidiary of The Rowman & Littlefield Publishing Group, Inc.
4501 Forbes Boulevard, Suite 200, Lanham, Maryland 20706
http://www.rowmanlittlefield.com

10 Thornbury Road, Plymouth PL6 7PP, United Kingdom

British Library Cataloguing in Publication Information Available

Library of Congress Cataloging-in-Publication Data

Teaching young adult literature today : insights, considerations, and perspectives for the classroom teacher / edited by Judith A. Hayn and Jeffrey S. Kaplan.
pages cm
Summary: "Teaching Young Adult Literature Today introduces the reader to what is current and relevant in the plethora of good books available for adolescents. This smart collection by literary experts illustrates how teachers can help their students become lifelong readers by simply introducing them to smart, insightful, and engaging books"— Provided by publisher.
Includes bibliographical references and index.
ISBN 978-1-4422-0719-6 (hardback) — ISBN 978-1-4422-0720-2 (paper) — ISBN 978-1-4422-0721-9 (electronic) (print)
1. Young adult literature—Study and teaching. 2. Teenagers—Books and reading—United States. I. Hayn, Judith, 1944- editor of compilation. II. Kaplan, Jeffrey S., 1951- editor of compilation.
PN1008.8.T44 2012
809'.892830712—dc23 2011043226

™ The paper used in this publication meets the minimum requirements of American National Standard for Information Sciences—Permanence of Paper for Printed Library Materials, ANSI/NISO Z39.48-1992.

Printed in the United States of America

In Memory
Robert L. Hayn
1942–1994

In Memory
James Kaplan
1924–2006

Contents

Introduction

We conceived the idea for this text at a National Council of Teachers of English convention a few years ago during a meeting of the Conference on English Education's Commission on the Study and Teaching of Adolescent Literature. We are sadly aware of the lack of documented research concerning the effectiveness of using adolescent literature with teachers, with students, and with preservice students. Those of us who believe in the genre constitute a small but vociferous band of zealots who desire to spread our enthusiasm to our colleagues in English education and to other educators.

The effort to accomplish this is further complicated because we seem to have an identity crisis in naming the subject area. What is adolescent literature? What is young adult literature (YAL)? Do they differ? Do we use the terms interchangeably? We think we do the latter. The terms are driven by the audience; books written specifically for an adolescent, for a young adult, or for teens fit our definition. We believe also that these books generally have a young protagonist who deals with issues that other young people face or might have to face, no matter the setting.

Additionally, adolescent literature is anything that young adults *choose* to read. Several of the authors in this text discuss what teens do read, and this brings us to another caveat. Publishers market to the teen audience, and they label books as young adult specifically for that purpose.

Our intent in this text is to provide an overview of the adolescent/YAL field by first looking in section I at where young adult literature has been. Hayn and Nolen introduce the study of young adult literature as both an art form and a teaching tool in its infancy. As an emerging field of inquiry, however, young adult literature struggles for legitimacy and prestige in the humanities. The authors of this chapter issue a call to educational researchers to shift the focus of current YAL research from teaching the content (text analysis research) to that of student learning in the classroom (empirical research). Then in chapter 2, Kaplan demonstrates that with the advent of technology and the ascendancy in popular culture of the triumphs and tragedies of teen life, the very nature and content of young adult literature has changed since its infancy in the 1950s and 1960s, when the baby boomers were just coming of age and the works of J. D. Salinger (*Catcher in the Rye,* 1951), William Golding (*Lord of the Flies,* 1954), Harper Lee (*To Kill a Mockingbird,* 1960), and S. E. Hinton (*The Outsiders,* 1967) were populating the bookshelves of English teachers and teenagers alike. Finally, Elliott-Johns presents an analysis and discussion of various perspectives in current research related to adolescent literature and teacher education, specifically teacher education that prepares teachers to successfully work with adolescents in school settings. Like the other three authors, she advocates further research, especially studies that raise the profile of YAL in literacy teacher education, access opportunities for projects that assist and inform the field, and research studies that enable us to better understand how and what young people read.

Section II examines where YAL is now—the current status of the field. In chapter 4, Bull leads off with a discussion of how teachers can avoid common obstacles to the use of YAL and make use of the valuable resources available. She looks at the obstacles of overemphasis on the classics, high-stakes testing, and scripted curriculum, and she worries about possible challenges and censorship. She then offers access to quality YAL hints, as well as professional instructional resources. In the next chapter, Kelley, Wilson, and Koss discuss the current status of motivation to read among middle schoolers and share results of studies they have conducted with disengaged readers about their motivation to read. Survey data and interview responses shed light on how educators can engage these disenfranchised readers. They add a list of Web resources of YAL that appealed to the disengaged readers in the study.

In chapter 6, Hill untangles the complex messages that three dystopian series for young adults convey to adolescent readers about their present and their future. He offers insights into *The Giver, Uglies,* and *The Hunger Games* as illustrative of novels that offer ominous futures. He asserts that through witnessing futuristic societies no one would want to inhabit, readers can imagine and begin to build toward a future they desire. Hill advocates including these series in their entirety in the high school curriculum and offers classroom applications for each to engage readers before, during, and after reading.

In chapter 7, Renzi, Letcher, and Miraglia question the absence of lesbian, gay, bisexual, transgender, and questioning (LGBTQ) young adult literature in secondary classrooms, when it is such an important issue in our society. They cite the research that illustrates the severity of bullying and harassment, plus emotional and physical problems our LGBTQ students encounter. They affirm that why we read, why we learn, and how we learn are all subject to a political viewpoint, and including LGBTQ-themed literature in the classroom is certainly a political action. By beginning with small steps, questioning existing curricula, and introducing texts chosen for the particular school environment, teachers can begin to combat the homophobic environment of our nation's schools. The authors offer a rich assortment of quality LGBTQ texts for teachers to use as selections for classroom inclusion.

In chapter 8, extending the definition of multiculturism to any group that has been marginalized, Hayn and Burns consider diversity to include race, gender, ethnicity, language of origin, ability, age, social class, religion, sexual orientation, and disabilities. They offer rationales for teachers to become more aware of multiculturism in their curriculum as they outline results of the 2010 Census and its impact on our students. They suggest texts that address each of the above areas of diversity, beyond those that are LGBTQ.

In chapter 9, Hazlett provides guidelines for educators to use in selecting quality YAL for classrooms while balancing these with curriculum requirements. Anthologies are generally similar, but selection of YAL is determined by personal, subjective choices; the titles that are read by students in school vary widely. She offers suggestions for finding titles that are older or otherwise used infrequently. Providing another way to expand text selections in chapter 10, Ward, Young, and Day present a contemporary look at novels that blur boundaries among literary genres. Through text analysis and author interviews, they offer insights into the works of Patrick Carman, Gene Luen Yang, Margarita Engle, and Gary Paulsen, who share their thoughts about the books they have created and the audience for whom they were written.

In chapter 11, Bickmore takes a look at the recent phenomenon of mainstream authors who publish YAL titles, choosing three authors in each of two categories. James Patterson, Ridley Pearson, and Carl Hiaasen are the first group and are best-selling authors for adult audiences. Sherman Alexie, Michael Chabon, and Joyce Carol Oates, the second group, represent authors who have achieved literary acclaim.

This section ends with Stover and Bach demonstrating how YAL might serve as a catalyst for community service and activism while enhancing student learning. They focus on the use of YAL in conjunction with a variety of strategies that all fall under the umbrella of a larger "activism" concept, which includes service-learning. They identify five topics that are important in today's society and discuss several YAL texts along with classics that could result in students taking action.

The final section focuses on where YAL might be going. In chapter 13, Sheehy and Clemmons advocate pairing YAL with technology as an innovative and engaging way to teach curriculum standards across all content areas, not just in English language arts classrooms. They maintain that YAL has an inherent ability to draw attention to critical concepts in all content areas as well as the adolescent experience. Using the emerging framework of technological, pedagogical, and content knowledge (TPACK), they share multiple examples of interactive technologies combined with a range of YAL titles, all aligned with standards.

Parsons and Hundley, in chapter 14, focus on adolescent readers who have grown up surrounded by digital media and consumer stories and narratives in a variety of digital formats, as well as traditional print books. They believe that the landscape of adolescent readers' textual world situates story in a broad, connected environment of which traditional texts are a small part. They discuss contemporary YAL that responds to the changing expectations of digital-generation readers, who expect the blurring of the boundaries between page and screen.

The final chapter in our text continues this look at the future. Blasingame addresses the needs of the "digital natives" who inhabit our classrooms; they turn to Facebook, Twitter, and iPhones to participate in a cyber community. He asserts that YAL also comes naturally to teens, who see themselves in the characters and problems addressed in these texts. Classrooms that enable students to engage with YAL through the use of technology are meeting the needs of the twenty-first-century global citizen, as well as meeting curriculum standards. He describes the experiences of secondary classroom teachers who are using video games, wikis, Twitter, YouTube, iPads, smartphones, and other technological tools to help their students engage with text.

We hope you find our text of value in preparing English language arts teachers to adopt YAL as a component of their curriculum. We strove to help you find compelling arguments for so doing, as well as providing texts and classroom practice that would enable it. We invite you to join us in support of the study and teaching of adolescent literature.

Section I

WHERE HAS YAL BEEN?

1

Young Adult Literature: Defining the Role of Research

Judith A. Hayn and Amanda L. Nolen

> Because [works of young adult literature] are about adolescents and for adolescents, they put students at the center of the learning experiences we devise. Because they illustrate for young readers what literature can be, moving them and revealing to them how literature builds knowledge and perspective, they use our time effectively.
>
> —Gary M. Salvner (2000, pp. 96–97)

DEFINING TERMS

What is adolescent literature? Is it different from young adult literature (YAL)? What is teen fiction? Juvenile fiction? Why are there different words for the same genre? The answer lies perhaps in evolution, and not all of us who advocate the genre agree on the terminology. The Library of Congress still categorizes it with Juvenile Fiction, which is certainly anachronistic. The two journals that are the primary publishing venues for the genre, *The ALAN Review* (ALAN serving as the acronym for the Assembly on Literature for Adolescents of the National Council of Teachers of English) and *SIGNAL* (the acronym for the Special Interest Group of Adolescent Literature of the International Reading Association), both use *adolescent literature*. Yet YALSA (the Young Adult Library Services Association, affiliated with the American Library Association) favors *young adult literature*. What is the discerning advocate to do?

Pam B. Cole (2009), in her text *Young Adult Literature in the 21st Century*, asserts the following: "Given the negative connotations of the words *adolescent* and *teens*, most experts agree upon *young adult* literature" (p. 49). While this reasoning may be arguable, the latter term does seem to permeate the field, a phenomenon perhaps related to marketing. However, this chapter's purpose is to investigate the status of research in the genre. Difficulty ensues when searching databases where both classifications are used, so isolating the search to either adolescent or young adult literature limits the findings. For example, a recent troll of the ERIC database revealed that using the search term *adolescent literature* paired with *research* yielded 413 hits, while switching to *young adult literature* generated only 64. If YAL and adolescent literature suffer from an identity crisis, then studying the genre becomes difficult.

We agree with Salvner (2000), whose quote opens this chapter, and take the stance that educators who believe in the use of YAL need support and validation for their position with a solid body of research drawn from the field. That the need for this is vital is evident as illustrated in the following anecdote: One of the authors of this chapter heard about a conversation at a recent Conference on English Education summer meeting where a colleague was asked to explain the value of young adult literature after his session on the topic. If English educators still question its validity in the curriculum, in classrooms, and in teacher education, the significance of a research basis emerges as vital (Hayn, Kaplan, & Nolen, 2011).

TARGETING THE PROBLEM

Little empirical research exists about the transaction that occurs when young adult literature is taught in a classroom setting (Christenbury, 2007; Wilhelm, 2008; Zirinsky & Rau, 2001). We know much about what good books are available, but we know little about what actually happens when teens read young adult novels. It is important that we encourage researchers in the field to shift their lens from an empirical study of the text itself to an empirical study of the *user* of the text. The user in this sense could be a teacher of the text, a student being taught the text, or simply a person enjoying the text.

One explanation of the unbalanced nature of the research is that the study of young adult literature is new compared to other, more established genres, and researchers are just getting to know this emerging body of literature (Kaplan, 2006, 2007, 2008, 2010). Thus, there is a need for rigorous empirical research of young adult literature that addresses these and similar questions:

- What transactional occurrences happen between teacher and students?
- What transactional occurrences happen between students and students?
- What transactional occurrences happen between readers and texts?

The intent of this chapter is to call attention to what little is known about these phenomena and to identify where more research needs to be done. This is a call to arms for researchers and teachers alike to begin the next phase in the empirical study of literature for teens. Teachers, academics, and researchers need to know what happens in a classroom setting when young people read adolescent novels (Moje & Hinchman, 2004; Probst, 2004; Ruggieri, 2007). We call for a research agenda around a field that is emerging, prolific, and vital for the academic, social, and emotional development of young people. The Commission on the Study and Teaching of Adolescent Literature, under the auspices of the National Council of the Teachers of English, was established in the early 1990s, specifically to develop and nurture a solid body of empirical evidence of the curricular uses and impact of young adult literature on adolescent student populations. Our analysis of the field over the first decade of the twenty-first century suggests that while small inroads have been made in the commission's research agenda, much more is needed.

EXAMINING THE STATUS OF THE RESEARCH

We embarked on an article analysis covering peer-reviewed journals from the time period 2000 through 2010 to identify the research that has been published that focuses on young adult literature. Through EBSCO*host*, we used Academic Search Complete, a multidisciplinary academic database that provides access to more than nine thousand academic journals, the MLS Directory of Periodicals, and the MLA International Bibliography. We limited our search to the subject terms young adult literature and adolescent literature, requiring only peer-reviewed sources from 2000 through 2010. The query resulted in 382 items. Of these, 346 were editorials, book reviews, teaching strategies, bibliographies, author interviews, and text analyses. Only 36 articles (9.4 percent) were empirical studies focusing on the user of the text, rather than on the text itself. These studies varied in method of inquiry, unit of analysis, and topic of study. Two journals, *The ALAN Review* and the *Journal of Adolescent & Adult Literacy*, housed 50 percent of the articles, with seven and eleven articles, respectively. *The ALAN Review* is a peer-reviewed journal published by the Assembly on Literature for Adolescents of the National Council for Teachers of English. The journal contains articles on young adult literature, its application in the classroom, and current research trends in the field of young adult literature. The *Journal of Adolescent & Adult Literacy* is published specifically for teachers and contains classroom strategies, curriculum ideas, and reflections on literacy trends for those working with adolescent and adult readers. The remainder of the articles included in our analysis were sparsely distributed across eleven other journals, with one article apiece. These journals spanned several disciplines including qualitative research, reading research, childhood development, and educational technology. A full list of the articles including their citation information is included in table 1.1.

Table 1.1. The Empirical Articles Resulting from the Young Adult/Adolescent Literature Article Analysis

Article	*Method of Inquiry*	*Topic of Inquiry*	*Population of Inquiry*
Baurain, B. (2007). Small group multitasking in literature classes. *English Language Teachers Journal, 61*(3), 237–245.	Quantitative	Reading behaviors	High school students
Bean, T., & Moni, K. (2003). Developing students' critical literacy: Exploring identity construction in young adult fiction. *Journal of Adolescent & Adult Literacy, 46*(8), 638–649.	Qualitative	Social issues	High school students
Bean, T., & Rigoni, N. (2001). Exploring the intergenerational dialogue journal discussions of a multicultural young adult novel. *Reading Research Quarterly, 36*(3), 232–248.	Qualitative	Response patterns	College students; high school students
Daisey, P. (2010). Secondary preservice teachers remember their favorite reading experiences: Insights and implications for content area instruction. *Journal of Adolescent & Adult Literacy, 53*(8), 678–687.	Qualitative	Teacher reflections	Preservice teachers
George, M. (2008). Comparing middle grade teachers' and middle grade students' reactions to Newbery Award winners. *The ALAN Review, 36*(1), 55–65.	Qualitative	Response patterns	Teachers
Gibbons, L., Dail, J., & Stallworth, B. J. (2006). Young adult literature in the English curriculum today: Classroom teachers speak out. *The ALAN Review, 33*(3), 53–61.	Survey	Teacher attitudes toward merit of young adult literature	English teachers
Gill, D. (2000). A national survey of the use of multicultural young adult literature in university courses. *The ALAN Review, 27*(2), 48–50.	Survey	Multicultural issues	College faculty
Glasgow, J. N. (2001). Teaching social justice through young adult literature. *English Journal, 90*(6), 54–61.	Qualitative	Social issues	College students; high school students
Glazier, J., & Seo, J. (2005). Multicultural literature and discussion as mirror and window? *Journal of Adolescent & Adult Literacy, 48*(8), 686–700.	Qualitative	Social and cultural issues	High school students
Godina, H., & McCoy, R., (2000). Emic and etic perspectives on Chicana and Chicano multicultural literature. *Journal of Adolescent & Adult Literacy, 44*(2), 172–179.	Qualitative	Cultural issues	Teachers
Groenke, S. L. (2008). Missed opportunities in cyberspace: Preparing preservice teachers to facilitate critical talk about literature through computer-mediated communication. *Journal of Adolescent & Adult Literacy, 52*(3), 224–233.	Qualitative	Online platform as a forum for discussion	Teachers; middle school students

Groenke, S. L., & Paulus, T. (2007). The role of teacher questioning in promoting dialogic literary inquiry in computer-mediated communication. *Journal of Research on Technology in Education, 40*(2), 141–164.	Quantitative	Online platform as a forum for discussion	Preservice teachers; middle school students
Hazlett, L., Johnson, A. B., & Hayn, J. A. (2009). An almost young adult literature study. *The ALAN Review, 37*(1), 48–53.	Quantitative	Teacher attitudes toward merit of young adult literature	Teachers
Hebert, T., & Kent, R. (2000). Nurturing social and emotional development in gifted teenagers through young adult literature. *Roeper Review, 22*(3), 167–171.	Quantitative	Social and emotional development	Gifted high school students
Hill, C. (2009). Birthing dialogue: Using *The First Part Last* in a health class. *The ALAN Review, 37*(1), 29–34.	Survey	Social issues	High school students
Hooper, R. (2006). The good, the bad, and the ugly: Teachers' perception of quality in fiction for adolescent readers. *English in Education, 40*(2), 55–70.	Survey	Teacher attitudes toward merit and uses of young adult literature in the classroom	Teachers
Houge, T. T., & Geier, C. (2009). Delivering one-to-one tutoring in literacy via videoconferencing. *Journal of Adolescent & Adult Literacy, 5*(2), 153–163.	Quantitative	Teaching young adult literature through distance education	High school students
Johnson, D. (2010). Teaching with authors' blogs: Connections, collaborations, creativity. *Journal of Adolescent & Adult Literacy, 54*(3), 172–180.	Qualitative	Teaching young adult literature using online social media	High school students
Johnson, H. (2000). "To stand up and say something": "Girls Only" literature circles at the middle level. *New Advocate, 13*(4), 375–389.	Qualitative	Gender and social issues	Middle school students
Kaplan, J. (2007). Recent research in young adult literature: Three predominant strands of study. *The ALAN Review, 34*(3), 53–60.	Action research	Social issues	Incarcerated males; preservice teachers
Kornfeld, J., & Prothro, L. (2005). Envisioning possibility: Schooling and student agency in children's and young adult literature. *Children's Literature in Education, 36*(3), 217–239.	Qualitative	Social issues	Middle school students

(continued)

Table 1.1. *(continued)*

Article	*Method of Inquiry*	*Topic of Inquiry*	*Population of Inquiry*
Kottke, S. (2010). RSVPs to reading: Gendered responses to the permeable curriculum. *The ALAN Review, 37*(3), 8–22.	Qualitative	Reading behaviors	Middle school students
Lewis, C., Ketter, J., & Fabos, B. (2001). Reading race in a rural context. *Qualitative Studies in Education, 14*(3), 317–350.	Qualitative	Social and cultural issues	Teachers
Louie, B. (2005). Development of empathetic responses with multicultural literature. *Journal of Adolescent & Adult Literacy, 48*(7), 568–578.	Qualitative	Social , cultural, and political issues	High school students
Ma'ayan, H. (2010). Erika's stories: Literacy solutions for a failing middle school student. *Journal of Adolescent & Adult Literacy, 52*(8), 646–654.	Qualitative	Reading behaviors	Middle school students
Meixner, E. (2006). Teacher agency and access to LGBTQ young adult literature. *Radical Teacher, 76*, 13–19.	Action research	Social and gender issues	Librarians
Onofrey, K. A. (2006). "It is more than just laughing": Middle school students protect characters during talk. *Journal of Childhood Education, 20*(6), 207–217.	Qualitative	Reader response theory	Middle school students
Paul, D. G. (1999). Images of black females in children's/adolescent contemporary realistic fiction. *Multicultural Review, 8*(2), 34–65.	Qualitative	Gender and cultural issues	High school students
Rothbauer, P., & McKechnie, L. E. F. (2000). The treatment of gay and lesbian fiction for young adults in selected prominent reviewing media. *Collection Building, 19*(1), 15–16.	Quantitative	Social and cultural issues	Journal editors/ reviewers
Singer, J. Y., & Smith, S. A. (2003). The potential of multicultural literature: Changing understanding of self and others. *Multicultural Perspectives, 5*(2), 17–23.	Qualitative	Multicultural issues	College students
Stallworth, B. J., Gibbons, L., & Fauber, L. (2008). It's not on the list: An exploration of teachers' perspectives on using multicultural literature. *Journal of Adolescent & Adult Literacy, 49*(6), 478–489.	Mixed methods	Multicultural issues	Teachers
van Schooten, E., de Glopper, K., & Stoel, R. (2004). Development of attitudes toward reading adolescent literature and literacy reading behavior. *Poetics, 32*(5), 343–386.	Quantitative	Reading behaviors	High school students
Vyas, S. (2004). Exploring bicultural identities of Asian high school students through the analytic window of a literature club. *Journal of Adolescent & Adult Literacy, 48*(1), 12–23.	Qualitative	Multicultural issues	High school students
Zywica, J., & Gomez, K. (2008). Annotating to support learning in the content areas: Teaching and learning science. *Journal of Adolescent & Adult Literacy, 52*(2), 155–164.	Quantitative	Reading behaviors	High school students

OVERVIEW OF PEER-REVIEWED JOURNAL ARTICLES

Methods of Inquiry

The thirty-six articles included in this analysis represented a variety of research methods and epistemologies. The majority of the studies (n=19, 55 percent) were qualitative in nature, with case study being the most favored research design. Eight studies used a quantitative design and only one study used a mixed-method design. Four studies conducted survey research, while another two studies described their approach as action research that utilized both qualitative and quantitative measures.

The variety of methods used in this small sample of articles includes innovative and imaginative data collection and analysis strategies. For example, Glazier and Seo (2005) used ethnographic and sociolinguistic methods to analyze data obtained when observing discussions prompted by multicultural young adult texts in a suburban high school. They found that the use of multiple texts might help create a global perspective, along with improving intercultural and intracultural understanding. Johnson (2000) observed "Girls Only" literature circles to study the phenomenon of girls falling silent in the classroom and the detrimental effect on their learning. Another example of an ambitious study was by Houge and Geier (2009), who examined the use of videoconferencing in one-on-one literacy tutoring in which young adult novels were used by teacher education candidates working with adolescents in ten states. The quality and diversity of these studies provide a broad methodological base from which the young adult literature field can continue to grow.

Topics of Inquiry

The studies we examined also varied by topic of inquiry. Topics included adolescent attitudes about complex social issues, multiculturism, platforms for instruction or interaction, reading behaviors or response patterns, and teachers' knowledge and uses of young adult literature in the classroom. The most prevalent theme centered on how adolescents approached complex and sometimes sensitive social issues using young adult literature. These issues included gender issues (Johnson, 2000; Meixner, 2006; Sutherland, 2005), abstract issues of power and oppression (Glasgow, 2001; Johnson, 2000; Kaplan, 2007), and controversial issues, including teen pregnancy and sexuality (Hill, 2009; Rothbauer & McKechnie, 2000).

Another important topical theme was using young adult literature to address multicultural themes and attitudes of adolescents (Glazier & Seo, 2005; Godina & McCoy, 2000; Louie, 2005; Stallworth, Gibbons, & Fauber, 2008; Vyas, 2004). Gill (2000) surveyed college professors regarding their attitudes about the use of multicultural texts in their adolescent literature classes. He examined syllabi to determine which adolescent literature authors are taught, including the absence of non-American authors. In another article on the topic, Lewis, Ketter, and Fabos (2001) included themselves in an ethnographic study that examined how discussions of multicultural young adult literature among white rural teachers were shaped by constructs of racial identity. Finally, Vyas (2004) explored bicultural identities of seven Asian high school students in a literature club that focused on the importance of students making personal connections to the literature they read.

Reading behaviors of adolescents, including reader response patterns (Bean & Rigoni, 2001; George, 2008; Onofrey, 2006; Singer & Smith, 2003), were frequently addressed across the studies. In an original format for research presentation, Kottke (2010) compared gender choices for academic and extracurricular self-selected reading materials among sixth graders during one school year. His entire article is presented in graphic novel format, using John Dewey as a commentator throughout.

The remaining themes represented in the sample of articles were the use of various technology platforms to engage adolescents around young adult literature (Groenke, 2008; Groenke & Paulus, 2007; Houge & Geier, 2009) and teachers' attitudes toward young adult literature as curriculum (Daisey, 2010; Hazlett, Johnson, & Hayn, 2009; Hooper, 2006). Gibbons, Dail, and Stallworth (2006) surveyed English teachers who regularly use young adult literature to discover their conclusions about literary merit, issues of time and crowded curriculum, and potential with struggling and reluctant readers. George (2008) examined the data collected over four years of field notes and transcript discussions from faculty-student book clubs in two New York City middle schools. Not surprisingly, teachers often began by studying stylistic elements of the seven Newbery Award winners, while students responded to characters in terms of believability.

Populations of Inquiry

The studies included in this analysis used a variety of sampling measures and criteria. More than half of the articles (n=22) used middle or high school students as the sole or primary population of inquiry. The remainder of the studies included samples from college student populations including preservice teachers, K–12 teachers, college faculty, or any combination of populations. For example, Groenke and Paulus (2007) paired university preservice teachers with middle school students to discuss young adult literature in online chat rooms and discovered that teaching strategies, along with responding, were necessary. Singer and Smith (2003) examined two different university teacher education groups involved in discussions of the same young adult text. One group consisted of undergraduate private university teacher education students, while the other group included students in a children's literature class at a large urban public university. The authors found that what the readers brought to a text (e.g., culture) was of major importance in determining how they responded.

Shifting the Lens

Finally, two articles clearly exemplify the transition from text analysis to the person engaging the text as the focus of inquiry. First, Rothbauer and McKechnie (2000) considered how thirty-two novels for young adults that feature gay and lesbian characters were treated in 158 interviews with librarians. They concluded that gay and lesbian literature stands separate from young adult literature as a category. Second, Paul (1999), although outside our ten-year window, discussed the messages transmitted to black girls via children's and adolescent books with female protagonists used in schools and published between 1985 and 1990. The researcher used triangulated reader response, content analysis, and contextual recording through coded inferences to reach conclusions.

By looking at the results of what has been studied, advocates of young adult literature can use this emerging evidence for the value and uses of young adult literature in curriculum design. This evidence could convince those who doubt the efficacy of young adult literature in English language arts education. The number of studies we were able to identify that focused on the user of the text was small in comparison to the field of study, but the diversity of methods, topics, and impact implies that this is a rich and viable area of inquiry for those interested in young adult literature as a field of study.

A CALL TO THE FIELD

Fallon (2006) took educational researchers to task for not empirically investigating and producing persuasive, trustworthy evidence about how to best prepare teachers. He concluded his article as follows:

> Advocates of teacher education programs within institutions of higher education cannot promote them effectively with a predominance of logical propositions and moral argument. In the end, dependable relationships between the interventions of teacher education programs and the learning of pupils taught by teachers who have been subject to those interventions must be reliably demonstrated with convincing evidence. (p. 152)

Just as he lamented the quality of the research being produced by those in the field, the findings of this study reflect a similar scarcity of persuasive empirical evidence around young adult literature as curriculum.

It is important to note that none of the empirical articles we found that examine adolescent literature used sophisticated statistical or qualitative analysis. All remained at the descriptive level rather than an inferential level for the quantitative studies or a conceptual level for the qualitative studies. For example, educational researchers who use hierarchical modeling procedures communicate that they understand the nested structure of educational data. One cannot simply examine educational outcomes without contextualizing students' performance and behavior in situ—within the classroom (teacher effects), within a school, within a community, and so on. In the same vein, educational researchers who employ a qualitative case study design could rely on embedding phenomena within the case and make comparisons across cases (Yin, 2009). Complex time-series designs allow for the rich explanation of the multifaceted patterns across multiple sets of variables over time. How teachers and students engage over young adult literature and how that genre can be used not only in instruction but also in assessment practices creates a rich research agenda that requires equally complex strategies and designs.

Fallon's concerns echoed the research agenda developed by the Commission on the Study and Teaching of Adolescent Literature to develop a robust body of evidence as to the impact of this genre on the teaching and learning of adolescents. We echo Fallon's call to educational researchers to use the might of our situated expertise to produce persuasive and trustworthy empirical evidence that will lead to an increased understanding of the complex nature of using young adult literature to improve student success, both in and out of the classroom.

REFERENCES

Bean, T., & Rigoni, N. (2001). Exploring the intergenerational dialogue journal discussions of a multicultural young adult novel. *Reading Research Quarterly, 36*(3), 232–248.

Christenbury, L. (2007). *Retracing the journey: Teaching and learning in an American high school.* New York: Teachers College Press.

Cole, P. B. (2009). *Young adult literature in the 21st century.* New York: McGraw-Hill.

Daisey, P. (2010). Secondary preservice teachers remember their favorite reading experiences: Insights and implications for content area instruction. *Journal of Adolescent & Adult Literacy, 53*(8), 678–687.

Fallon, D. (2006). The buffalo upon the chimneypiece. *Journal of Teacher Education, 57*(2), 139–154.

George, M. (2008). Comparing middle grade teachers' and middle grade students' reactions to Newbery Award winners. *The ALAN Review, 36*(1), 55–65.

Gibbons, L., Dail, J., & Stallworth, B. J. (2006). Young adult literature in the English curriculum today: Classroom teachers speak out. *The ALAN Review, 33*(3), 53–61.

Gill, D. (2000). A national survey of the use of multicultural young adult literature in university courses. *The ALAN Review, 27*(2), 48–50.

Glasgow, J. N. (2001). Teaching social justice through young adult literature. *English Journal, 90*(6), 54–61.

Glazier, J., & Seo, J. (2005). Multicultural literature and discussion as mirror and window? *Journal of Adolescent & Adult Literacy, 48*(8), 686–700.

Godina, H., & McCoy, R. (2000). Emic and etic perspectives on Chicana and Chicano multicultural literature. *Journal of Adolescent & Adult Literacy, 44*(2), 172–179.

Groenke, S. L. (2008). Missed opportunities in cyberspace: Preparing preservice teachers to facilitate critical talk about literature through computer-mediated communication. *Journal of Adolescent & Adult Literacy, 52*(3), 224–233.

Groenke, S. L., & Paulus, T. (2007). The role of teacher questioning in promoting dialogic literary inquiry in computer-mediated communication. *Journal of Research on Technology in Education, 40*(2), 141–164.

Hayn, J. A., Kaplan, J. S., & Nolen, A. (2011). Young adult literature research in the 21st century. *Theory into Practice, 50*(3), 176–181.

Hazlett, L., Johnson, A. B., & Hayn, J. A. (2009). An almost young adult literature study. *The ALAN Review, 37*(1), 48–53.

Hill, C. (2009). Birthing dialogue: Using *The First Part Last* in a health class. *The ALAN Review, 37*(1), 29–34.

Hooper, R. (2006). The good, the bad, and the ugly: Teachers' perception of quality in fiction for adolescent readers. *English in Education, 40*(2), 55–70.

Houge, T. T., & Geier, C. (2009). Delivering one-to-one tutoring in literacy via videoconferencing. *Journal of Adolescent & Adult Literacy, 5*(2), 153–163.

Johnson, H. (2000). "To stand up and say something": "Girls Only" literature circles at the middle level. *New Advocate, 13*(4), 375–389.

Kaplan, J. (2006). Dissertations on adolescent literature: 2000–2005. *The ALAN Review, 33*(2), 51–59.

Kaplan, J. (2007). Recent research in young adult literature: Three predominant strands of study. *The ALAN Review, 34*(3), 53–60.

Kaplan, J. (2008). Perception and reality: Examining the representations of adolescents in young adult fiction. *The ALAN Review, 36*(1), 42–49.

Kaplan, J. (2010). Doctoral dissertations (2008–2009): A review of research on young adult literature. *The ALAN Review, 37*(2), 54–58.

Kottke, S. (2010). RSVPs to reading: Gendered responses to the permeable curriculum. *The ALAN Review, 37*(3), 8–22.

Lewis, C., Ketter, J., & Fabos, B. (2001). Reading race in a rural context. *Qualitative Studies in Education, 14*(3), 317–350.

Louie, B. (2005). Development of empathetic responses with multicultural literature. *Journal of Adolescent & Adult Literacy, 48*(7), 568–578.

Meixner, E. (2006). Teacher agency and access to LGBTQ young adult literature. *Radical Teacher, 76*, 13–19.

Moje, E., & Hinchman, K. (2004). Culturally responsive practices for youth literacy learning. In T. Jetton & J. A. Dole (Eds.), *Adolescent literacy research and practice* (pp. 321–350). New York: Guilford Press.

Onofrey, K. A. (2006). "It is more than just laughing": Middle school students protect characters during talk. *Journal of Childhood Education, 20*(6), 207–217.

Paul, D. G. (1999). Images of black females in children's/adolescent contemporary realistic fiction. *Multicultural Review, 8*(2), 34–65.

Probst, R. E. (2004). *Response and analysis: Teaching literature in the secondary school* (2nd ed.). Portsmouth, NH: Heinemann.

Rothbauer, P., & McKechnie, L. E. F. (2000). The treatment of gay and lesbian fiction for young adults in selected prominent reviewing media. *Collection Building, 19*(1), 15–16.

Ruggieri, C. (2007). Making connections with contemporary literature. *English Journal, 96*(4), 112–113.

Salvner, G. M. (2000). Time and tradition: Transforming the secondary English class with young adult novels. In V. R. Monsea & G. M. Salvner (Eds.), *Reading their world: The young adult novel in the classroom* (pp. 85–99). Portsmouth, NH: Boynton/Cook–Heinemann.

Singer, J. Y., & Smith, S. A. (2003). The potential of multicultural literature: Changing understanding of self and others. *Multicultural Perspectives, 5*(2), 17–23.

Stallworth, B. J., Gibbons, L., & Fauber, L. (2008). It's not on the list: An exploration of teachers' perspectives on using multicultural literature. *Journal of Adolescent & Adult Literacy, 49*(6), 478–489.

Sutherland, L. (2005). Black adolescent girls' use of literary practice to negotiate boundaries of ascribed identity. *Journal of Literacy Research, 37*(3), 365–406.

Vyas, S. (2004). Exploring bicultural identities of Asian high school students through the analytic window of a literature club. *Journal of Adolescent & Adult Literacy, 48*(1), 12–23.

Wilhelm, J. D. (2008). *"You gotta BE the book": Teaching engaged and reflective reading with adolescents* (2nd ed.). New York: Teachers College Press.

Yin, R. K. (2009). *Case study research: Design and methods* (4th ed.). Thousand Oaks, CA: Sage.

Zirinsky, D., & Rau, S. (2001). *A classroom of teenaged readers: Nurturing reading processes in senior high English*. New York: Addison Wesley Longman.

2

The Changing Face of Young Adult Literature

What Teachers and Researchers Need to Know to Enhance Their Practice and Inquiry

Jeffrey S. Kaplan

"Read this!"

In front of me was Madeleine L'Engle's *A Wrinkle in Time*.

It was 1977, and I was teaching the seventh grade.

And one of my students was urging me to read this acclaimed classic.

I did not know *A Wrinkle in Time* (the story of a family who searches for their father lost in a space/time warp), nor did I know much about young adult literature.

So, at her insistence, I read it, and I am very glad I did.

Young adult literature (books for the teen reader) has changed considerably since the publication of L'Engle's *A Wrinkle in Time* (1962). There are now more books than ever that speak honestly and openly about the lives of young people. Madeleine L'Engle's books, and others—J. D. Salinger's *The Catcher in the Rye* (1951), William Golding's *Lord of the Flies* (1954), Harper Lee's *To Kill a Mockingbird* (1960), S. E. Hinton's *The Outsiders* (1967), Robert Lipsyte's *The Contender* (1967), and Paul Zindel's *The Pigman* (1968)—did much to change the dynamic of adolescent reading.

More importantly, the groundbreaking works of Robert Cormier—*The Chocolate War* (1974), *I Am the Cheese* (1977), and *After the First Death* (1979)—elevated the notion of what young adult literature can and should be. His unblemished look at adolescence—like that of his predecessors—jolted the notion of what teens were like and more importantly, what they would like to read. No longer were teens stuck with reading only the classics (McLaren, 1998). The high school literary canon—those long novels with teenage characters, but primarily written for adults, or at least advanced readers (works like Charles Dickens's *David Copperfield* [1850],

Mark Twain's *Tom Sawyer* [1876] and *Huckleberry Finn* [1884], Stephen Crane's *The Red Badge of Courage* [1895], and George Orwell's *Animal Farm* [1945])—was suddenly challenged by contemporary fare. In the last fifty years, teen readers have seen unfold before their eyes the very essence of narratives that speak in a language all their own—the voice of confused yet questioning young adults (Kaplan, 2010).

Despite all the recent social, environmental, and technological changes, young people are still interested, above all, in their own lives. From contemporary realistic fiction to fantasy, adolescents are always looking for stories (in books, videos, movies) to answer the timeless question, "Who am I and who am I supposed to be?" (Hayn, Kaplan, & Nolen, 2011). Questions of self-identity and self-discovery continue to underlie narratives for teens, and no matter the literary style or genre, young people often find comfort and solace in engaging reads that attempt to define their journey toward self-understanding (Bach, Choate, & Parker, 2011; Huck, Hepler, Hickman, & Kiefer, 1997).

Thus this chapter will explore the ever-unfolding universe of young adult literature. Everything from realistic fiction to fantasy will be examined to illustrate how much the style and content of narrative fiction for young people has changed in the last fifty years and how this trend continues to unfold. Particular attention will be paid to the changing nature of contemporary realistic fiction, multicultural literature, romance literature, gay and lesbian literature, dystopian science fiction literature, paranormal romance literature, graphic novels, technology-infused fiction, literature infused with religious overtones, crossover novels, and verse novels. For one thing we know for sure: young adult literature changes as quickly as teens do themselves (Kaplan, 2006, 2007, 2008).

CONTEMPORARY REALISTIC FICTION

As long as there are teenagers, there will be drama. Who is going out with whom? Who is wearing what? Who is hot? And who is not? These are all questions that occupy the minds and hearts of adolescents almost everywhere, and if they do not, then at some point in their lives, they certainly will. All young people are curious about who they are, how they fit in, and, more importantly, how they are perceived by others.

Hence, the world of contemporary realistic fiction occupies a very special place in the lives of young adults—especially for those who are avid readers. In adolescent novels, teens wrestle with issues large and small, struggling to determine the rightness of their decisions and the meaning of their journey (Bach, Choate, & Parker, 2011; Philion, 2009). As they contemplate their uncertain lives, they worry about their appearance, their feelings, their attitudes, their parents, their siblings, their fate, and their happiness. For all of life's unexpected twists and turns underscore their very well-being, marking for many young adults their first true and palpable pains of human existence (Buehler, 2009; Capella, 2010).

Coming-of-age novels have been and continue to be popular among adolescents. From J. D. Salinger's *The Catcher in the Rye* (1951) to Laurie Halse Anderson's *Speak* (1999), young people continue to find solace in smart contemporary reads about the agony of growing up in a world in which they are often confused, misunderstood, and sometimes victimized (Christenbury, 2006).

Today, though, for young adult books, nothing is taboo. Years ago, the anonymous novel *Go Ask Alice* (1971), which speaks openly and honestly about teenage drug addiction, sparked considerable controversy because of its frank portrayal. Yet if it were published for the first time today, its blunt language and discussion of sex and drugs would hardly be noticed.

Instead, nowadays, contemporary young adult realistic fiction covers every conceivable concern that teenagers face in their lives (Sturm & Michel, 2009; Veit & Osada, 2010). From the trauma of rape and incest to the agony of recognizing one's sexual identity, books for young adults are a haven and respite for adolescents to read about what is real and self-evident in their lives. Whereas years ago "inappropriate language" was the hallmark of books for teens, today books that speak of horrible but all-too-realistic truths—such as self-mutilation, laceration, and abuse—are the books that are most often questioned; yet they remain popular with teens who identify all too well with these brutal accounts of human existence (Cart, 1996).

Most notably, Todd Strasser's chilling documentary novel *Give a Boy a Gun* (2000) illustrates vividly the changing landscape of the problem novel. Here we read the story of the growing anger and hatred of two teenagers, Gary and Brendan, who dream of taking revenge on the teens who have bullied them and then, sadly, transform that venom into a mind-blowing reality. Other novels dealing with bullying and violence in an equally compelling style include Ron Koerge's verse novel *The Brimstone Journals* (2001), James Howe's *The Misfits* (2001), Nancy Garden's *Endgame* (2006), C. G. Watson's *Quad* (2007), Diane Tullson's *Lockdown* (2008), and Jennifer Brown's *Hate List* (2009).

Speaking of violence, self-inflicted wounds are a popular topic in books for teens. One of the first young adult novels dealing with the growing phenomenon of cutting—where teens inflict punishment on their own skin by cutting themselves—is Shelley Stoehr's *Crosses* (1991). Similarly, suicide—long considered taboo in young adult literature for fear of influencing young readers to do the same—has become a topic of discussion with the enormous success of Jay Asher's *Thirteen Reasons Why* (2007). In this gripping read, a teenager leaves audiocassettes explaining her suicide.

Finally, there's Laurie Halse Anderson's *Twisted* (2007), which explores with honesty and compassion the inexplicable and shocking death of a young boy at his own hands.

What is certainly new, though, is a topic that early young adult novelists could hardly have imagined—cyberbullying. Angry and anonymous are the key ingredients of the narratives of teens who go online to inflict pain deliberately on others without being forced to see its effect. Laura Ruby's *Good Girls* (2006) and Shana Norris's *Something to Blog About* (2008) are two recent entries to illustrate this most serious phenomenon.

Naturally, modern times bring modern problems, and what could be more contemporary than the specter of terrorism? After September 11, 2011, many young adult books appeared—both fiction and nonfiction—that dealt with the fear of the threat of violent death at the hands of fanatics—especially foreign-born. Most notably, Joyce Maynard's crossover novel *The Usual Rules* (2003), Francine Prose's *Bullyville* (2007), and David Levithan's *Love Is the Higher Law* (2009) are all strong books for young adults that deal with life in a world where unsuspecting victims fall prey to harsh and unrelenting terror (M. Roberts, 2010).

Thus contemporary realistic fiction remains a steadfast presence on teen bookshelves. Ever changing, ever imposing, teens can read about their greatest fears and hopes, depicted with often unabashed honesty and earnestness (Gross, Goldsmith, & Carruth, 2008; Koss & Teale, 2009; Monseau & Salvner, 2001). As noted young adult author and critic Michael Cart (2010a) remarks, young adult novels remain popular because teens, even at a tender age, know instinctively that life "even at its darkest, can hold the promise of hope and positive change—especially when we read about it with open minds and hearts, with intellectual attention and emotional empathy" (p. 35).

MULTICULTURAL LITERATURE

Multicultural literature has also changed considerably in the past fifty years. What was once a novelty in publishing, especially for young people, has now become a major force in the lives of young adult readers. Today, in books for teens, it is not unusual to find stories populated with characters who are remarkably different from their readers in both race and culture, as authors everywhere bring their own background into play. In addition, young adult novels with diverse characters, places, and issues remain popular because they validate the lives of adolescents who read them (Meminger, 2011). In the stories they read, young people often see, for the first time, characters who look and act just like them—providing a comfort and understanding that, for many, only literature can illustrate (Johnson, 2011).

Clearly, the sudden emergence of multicultural literature, especially in children's and young adult literature, was a direct outgrowth of the civil rights movement in the United States in the 1950s and 1960s. The landscape of books for teens was changed by Maya Angelou's *I Know Why the Caged Bird Sings* (1969), Alice Childress's *A Hero Ain't Nothin' But a Sandwich* (1973), Virginia Hamilton's *M. C. Higgins, the Great* (1974), Mildred Taylor's *Roll of Thunder, Hear My Cry* (1976), and later Rosa Guy's *Friends* (1995) and Walter Dean Myers's *Monster* (1999).

And although the life and culture of African Americans remains—despite great progress—a prominent civil rights issue, the multicultural movement was reenergized in the 1980s by Latinos, Native Americans, Asian Americans, women, people with disabilities, and people with varying sexual preferences (Gavigan & Knutts, 2010; Wolk, 2009). In addition, the topic of immigration has spurred many good reads for teens. Books that depict the lives of contemporary teens of diverse backgrounds, like Sandra Cisneros's *The House on Mango Street* (1983), Gary Soto's *The Afterlife* (2003), and Gene Luen Yang's *American Born Chinese* (2006), are an indication of the healthy future of young adult multicultural literature.

In fact, the importance of multicultural literature in the lives of all adolescents becomes even more significant when we consider how quickly American society is changing. Undergoing the most radical population change in its history, the United States now reflects a diversity that is becoming even more blended than separate (Baer & Glasgow, 2010). And with this ever-increasing and changing American population, America's children now, more than ever, need to cultivate an understanding of the world that considers with wide-open acceptance both the uniqueness and the specialness of their own culture as well as the cultures of others (Baer & Glasgow, 2010; Cassidy, Valadez, Garrett, & Barrera, 2010). Multicultural literature teaches the value of diversity, the importance of racial tolerance, and the power of artistic transformation (Cassidy et al., 2010).

More importantly, today, the changing face of multicultural literature has made considerable progress in helping adolescents (and teachers) move away from the practice of using stories about Caucasian and European Americans as the only literary canon suitable and required for adolescents; instead, multicultural literature has given significant voice and credibility to readings and narratives in which the characters and events represent other traditions and perspectives are nontraditional. Simply, the other has become the norm (Nilsen & Donelson, 2009; Wopperer, 2011).

ROMANCE LITERATURE

Publishers are keenly aware that too much of a good thing is sometimes just that—too much of a good thing. So, betting that young people wanted something more than another "problem novel," literary agents and publishers began in the 1990s to pitch conventional romance novels aimed at the teen market—resulting in many wildly popular book series aimed at adolescent girls, such as *Wildfire, Sweet Dreams, Young Love, First Love, Wishing Star, Caprice,* and *Sweet Valley High*. Highly questioned as to their legitimacy as "real literature" by librarians and feminists alike, these books—generally about rich middle-class teens with rich middle-class problems—became, as suspected, enormously popular among adolescents (especially teen girls) and helped establish a marketing genre that continues to flourish to this day (W. Glenn, 2008).

Such popular fare has grown to include three prominent teen series (among many)—*Gossip Girl* (von Ziegesar, 2002), *The A-List* (Dean, 2003), and *The Insiders* (Minter, 2004). Each of these popular teen serial reads features a similar group of central figures—wealthy upper-middle-class teenagers who have everything money can buy and then some. While the intricacies of the plots differ, the themes of these urban romance novels among socially elite teens remains the same—that wealth leads to entitlement. Yes, empty relationships might be the norm, but social class and lots of money trump despair and isolation.

Thus, following the popularity of the *Sweet Valley High* series in the 1980s, publishers tapped into the social milieu credo that "rich" is the desired social status and "conspicuous consumption" is the preferred lifestyle—even for those who have very little (W. Glenn, 2008). As the narrator in this and similar series—the *Au Pairs* series (de la Cruz, 2005), the *Summer Boys* series (Abbott, 2009), and the *Clique* series (Harrison, 2010)—suggests, even though their parents are absent and the teens themselves stab each other in the back, trying to fit in at all costs is the rule, and wealth is what matters most in the end (W. Glenn, 2008).

GAY AND LESBIAN LITERATURE

It has been more than four decades since the publication of John Donovan's young adult novel *I'll Get There. It Better Be Worth the Trip* (1969), a breakthrough work about gay teens. Although well received at the time, it has since been fairly criticized for its stereotypical portrayal of homosexuality. Since then, though, literature for gay and lesbian teens has changed profoundly, providing a more rounded portrait of teenagers caught in the throes of defining their sexual identity (Blackburn & Smith, 2010; Cart & Jenkins, 2004).

Slowly and gradually, though, as the world has become more accepting—or at least more open and aware of young adults who are LBGTQ—books for teens have begun to address the notion of homosexuality and respect for individual differences with greater certainty and rectitude (Hazlett, Sweeney, & Reins, 2011). For unfortunately, many early gay-themed novels—like Isabelle Holland's *The Man without a Face* (1972), Lynn Hall's *Sticks and Stones* (1972), and Sandra Scoppettone's *Trying*

Hard to Hear You (1974)—left readers with the impression that being gay led to dire consequences (Cart, 2010b; Crisp, 2009).

Later, though, more affirming gay-themed books took hold—notably, Nancy Garden's *Annie on My Mind* (1982), Aidan Chambers's *Dance on My Grave* (1982), Ann Heron's *One Teenager in Ten* (1983), and Sasha Alyson's *Young, Gay, and Proud* (1985), to name a few. In fact, *Annie on My Mind* is a novel that has never been out of print and is probably the singular work to change the course of gay-themed literature aimed at young adults. This story—of two high school girls who fall in love—continues to receive praise for being both an engaging read and a positive representation of gay life.

Truly, the 1990s represented a turning point in the publication of young adult novels dealing with gay and lesbian themes (Wickens, 2011). Nancy Garden followed *Annie on My Mind* with *Lark in the Morning* (1991) and *Good Moon Rising* (1996), two compelling and rounded portraits of gay individuals. Similarly, M. E. Kerr published *Deliver Us from Evie* (1994), about a boy with a lesbian sister, which was followed by *Dive* (1994) by Stacey Donovan, *The Necessary Hunger* (1997) by Nina Revoyr, *The House You Pass on the Way* (1997) by Jacqueline Woodson, *Girl Walking Backwards* (1998) by Bett Williams (who intended the novel for an adult audience, though it was popular among teens), *Hard Love* (1999) by Ellen Wittlinger, and *Dare Truth or Promise* (1999) by Paula Boock. All are early, precedent-setting books dealing openly about what it is like to be a gay teenager.

Today, fortunately, there are more books than ever dealing with gay and lesbian themes. As the public attitude toward homosexuality has grown more accepting, gay individuals—both adults and teens—are portrayed in books as individuals living lives, integrated inside a larger community, and not isolated, separate and alone (Blackburn & Smith, 2010; Greenblatt, 2011). Some noteworthy titles with stories in this vein are Chris Crutcher's *Athletic Shorts: Six Short Stories* (1989) and *Angry Management: Three Novellas* (2009), *Baby Be-Bop* (1995) by Francesca Lia Block, *The Perks of Being a Wallflower* (1999) by Stephen Chbosky, the *Rainbow* trilogy (2001–2005) by Alex Sanchez, and *Impulse* (2007) by Ellen Hopkins.

Finally, one significant indication that gay young adult novels have gained greater acceptance is the fact that since 1999, many such books have won awards—including the highly respected American Library Association's Best Books for Young Adults Award, a recognition that specifically went to Alex Sanchez's *Rainbow Boys* (2001) and David Levithan's *Boy Meets Boy* (2005).

DYSTOPIAN SCIENCE FICTION LITERATURE

Following the success of Suzanne Collin's *The Hunger Games* (2008), young adult literature has seen a dramatic surge in dystopian novels. Dystopia, defined in the classic sense, is a counter-vision of the world where a twisted vision of perfection is imposed upon a populace. To be sure, dystopian literature has always been prevalent in young adult fiction—George Orwell's *Animal Farm* (1945) and *1984* (1949), Ray Bradbury's *Fahrenheit 451* (1953), Lois Lowry's *The Giver* (1993)—but now, it seems more than ever, young people are aware of how regimented their daily lives are.

Especially their daily lives. Whether at school or at home, young people live with restrictions—some real, some fanciful—that define what they can and cannot do. So naturally, when confronted with alternative realities—worlds that they can easily define and perhaps subvert or change—they are attracted to these fanciful notions. Young people are also keenly aware that they live in a world in which since September 11, 2001, there has been an increase in inexplicable violence and unmitigated terror. Hence, readers have noticed the popularity of stories and novels in which the lead characters confront a world that has seemingly been turned upside down (Stallworth, 2006).

Some well-received dystopian young adult novels that depict a world gone mad and unrecognizable include M. T. Anderson's *Feed* (2002), Scott Westerfield's *Uglies* trilogy (2005–2007), Paolo Bacigalupi's *Ship Breaker* (2010), Catherine Fisher's *Incarceron* series (2010), Caragh M. O'Brien's *Birthmarked* trilogy (2010, 2011), James Dashner's *The Maze Runner* trilogy (2011), Cameron Stracher's *The Water Wars* (2011), Megan McCafferty's *Bumped* (2011), Veronica Roth's *Divergent* trilogy (2011), Lauren DeStefano's *The Chemical Garden trilogy* (2011), and David Patneaude's *Epitaph Road* (2011). All of these strong reads depict alternative worlds where the rules of the game have been dramatically altered—sometimes for the better, but far more often for the worse.

PARANORMAL ROMANCE LITERATURE

To be sure, one of the most appealing genres for teens (and for many adults) is paranormal romance literature. Here the real blends with the unreal, as fantastic elements are integrated into an alternate version of reality, often involving witches, ghosts, vampires, demons, werewolves, and/or humans with psychic abilities. Prevalent in many paranormal adventures are stories of time travel, usually involving futuristic and/or extraterrestrial romances (Kokkola, 2011; Silver, 2010).

Fantasy, naturally, has always been popular with readers, especially teens. Tolkien's trilogy, *The Lord of the Rings* (1954–1955), and J. K. Rowling's *Harry Potter* series (1997–2007) are considered the two seminal publications in the realm of fantasy appealing to teen readers. Other fantasy writers, like Ursula Le Guin (*Earthsea* trilogy, 1968–1972), Terry Brooks (*The Sword of Shannara* trilogy, 1977–1985), and William Sleator (*House of Stairs*, 1991), garnered much early attention with their smart reads infused with varying degrees of fantasy and hyperrealism that teen readers found equally engaging.

Today, supernatural fantasy has been eclipsed by an explosive number of stories about vampires and/or werewolves. Young people (and adults) cannot seem to get enough books where dark and dangerous adolescents turn out to be brooding half-animal–half-teenagers who both love and prey upon other teens. Popular young adult books include Stephenie Meyer's wildly popular *Twilight* (2005–2008) series, followed by Jennifer Lynn Barnes's *Raised by Wolves* series, Colleen Houck's *Tiger's Curse* series, Lauren Kate's *Fallen* series, P. C. Cast's *House of Night* series, Maggie Stiefvater's *Wolves of Mercy Fall* series, Rachel Caine's *Morganville Vampire* series, Jenna Black's *Faeriewalker* series, L. J. Smith's *Vampire Diaries*, Ellen Schreiber's *Vampire Kisses* series, and Aprylinne Pike's *Laurel* series. All these series depict the public fascination with what I call "dangerous kids"—adolescents who thrive on the bad because they love tempting fate and fortune. These works appeal to young people's desire to see the mysterious; they reflect the appeal to adolescents of the dark side of human nature.

GRAPHIC NOVELS

In discussing contemporary literature, one cannot dispute the ever-growing popularity of graphic novels—especially for teens. Graphic novels (essentially, fancy comic books) have long had a foothold in the publishing industry (they were quite popular in Europe long before the United States) and now with their abundant presence on the American market, teens and librarians have embraced them wholeheartedly (Carter, 2007; Ward & Young, 2011).

With the awarding of the Pulitzer Prize to Art Spiegelman for his noted holocaust memoirs *Maus I: A Survivor's Tale: My Father Bleeds History* (1986), followed by his *Maus II: A Survivor's Tale: And Here My Troubles Began* (1991), the graphic novel established itself as a presence in American literature. Told vividly in black and white, this haunting comic-book portrayal of life under the Nazis continues to shape the growth and dynamism of the ever-evolving graphic novel, especially for adolescents. Similarly, two equally successful graphic novels—Neal Gaiman's *The Sandman: A Game of You* (1989–1996), about a young witch who leads a group of women on a quest to destroy the "evil Cuckoo," and Alan Moore and Dave Gibbons's *Watchmen* (1986), a compelling story of an exploration of a post-Hiroshima world—have had a considerable impact on the growth and popularity of graphic novels for the adolescent reader (Carter, 2011).

Within the genre of graphic novels, it must be noted that there are several types that readers can enjoy—including history, biography, classic adaptations, and science information—but teen fiction is still by far the most popular (Carter, 2007). Graphic novels popular among teen readers include Frank Miller's *Batman: The Dark Knight Returns* (1997), Brian Bendis and Mark Bagley's *Ultimate Spider-Man: Power and Responsibility* (2002), Marjane Satrapi's *Persepolis: The Story of a Childhood* (2003), Peter Sanderson's *X-Men: The Ultimate Guide* (2003), Bryan Lee O'Malley's *Scott Pilgrim* series (2004–2010), Gene Luen Yang's *American Born Chinese* (2006), and Bill Willingham's *Fable* series. All are vivid in design, color, and narrative (Rabey, 2010).

Manga, the Japanese form of the graphic novel, has also proven enormously successful among young and old alike. Its highly stylized nature continues to make inroads in how stories are told and visualized and is especially appreciated by readers who enjoy the visuals as much as the words. In fact, in Japan, people of all ages read manga—like graphic novels, it includes every conceivable genre: action-adventure, romance, sports and games, historical drama, comedy, science fiction and fantasy, mystery, horror, sexuality, and nonfiction as well (Goldstein & Phelan, 2009).

The origin of manga is traced back to a young doctor named Osamu Tazuka, who at the close of World War II began to write and draw *Diary of Ma-chan*. Tazuka was known as the "god of manga"; present-day manga drawings can be traced to his artistic style. In fact, in postwar Japan, the popularity of manga grew considerably, because it was both inexpensive and accessible (Nilsen & Donelson, 2009).

Produced in both black-and-white and color, these fully developed stories are often produced as sequels, leaving readers to follow the escapades of their favorite heroes and heroines in multiple volumes. And their popularity has naturally spawned live-action and animated films that are frequented by their many fans, young and old alike.

For teens, fortunately, there are a plethora of manga titles and series to be enjoyed. Most notably, there is the *Dragonball* series by Akira Toriyama (1984–1995; a boxed set was published in 2009), Rumiko Takahashi's *Inuyasha* series (1996–2008), Tite Kubo's *Bleach* series (2001–present), Natsuki Takaya's *Fruits Basket* series (1999–2006), Masashi Kishimoto's *Naruto* series (1999–present), and Ai Yazawa's *Nana* series (2000–present). These and many other manga titles are all relished by young adults for their stark and stylized features in both design and storytelling.

TECHNOLOGY AND THE YOUNG ADULT NOVEL

Young adult novels, as you can readily surmise, have changed considerably with the increasing presence of technology in our lives. No longer are authors and publishers confined to the space of a single page, but they can and do manipulate stories so that readers may take alternative paths toward satisfying endings. Through the magic of cyberspace, readers can now link to designated websites and explore alternative avenues of expression and narrative that portend to take readers on a journey that is far more fantastical (and often, more realistic) than a single read (George, 2011; Groenke & Maples, 2010).

Today, it is not uncommon for many books geared for adolescent readers to venture into universes where only computer graphics and technology wizardry can make the seemingly unreal into part and parcel of the story. Linking to alternative venues in cyberspace, teen readers can begin to explore alternative narrative pathways or, at the very least, venues where the story is enhanced by a cyberspace presence. Such reads tap into the "technology punk" generation—a generation raised on reading where the use of multiplatforms (links to websites and other venues) is both commonplace and expected (Peowski, 2010).

For example, K. A. Applegate's *Everworld* (1999) is a twelve-part series about high school students' adventures into ancient mythology; it has an accompanying website, complete with story details and interactive elements. Similarly, Erin Hunter's *Warriors: The New Prophecy* series (2005), Anthony Horowitz's horror series *The Gatekeepers* (2005), and P. J. Haarsma's *Softwire* series (2006) are a just a few of the many books aimed specifically at the teen audience and accompanied by Web platforms for additional opportunities in reading and gaming. Naturally, the possibilities are endless. I suspect that as technology continues to evolve, so too will technology-infused books for the adolescent reader.

RELIGION AND THE YOUNG ADULT NOVEL

One field that does not garner much attention but still deserves consideration is the presence of religion—or at least, religious overtones—in young adult novels. To be sure, serious books about the role of religion in the lives of adolescents do not get considerable play in mainstream culture. Such narratives—however strong and rich they may be—are not valued as commercial fare unless they are accompanied by elements of fantasy and/or horror that make them more economically viable (Hodges, 2010; Stephens, 2007).

Nevertheless, with the ever-increasing popularity of both contemporary realistic novels and the more fantastical and paranormal romances, religion and religious themes have made their presence known in adolescent novels and undoubtedly will continue to do so. Such reads—sometimes serious, always heartfelt—are real and vital attempts to connect with young people in an area that is often close to their well-being but not easily accessible because of many publishers' reluctance to go there. ("Will it sell?")

Still, we cannot overlook the good books for young adults with religious overtones that do exist and inspire their own following. For example, the *Clearwater Crossing* series (1998) by Laura Peyton Roberts highlights a diverse group of teenagers who come to terms with a multitude of dilemmas that compel them to rely on each other and their respective faiths. Also, Lurlene McDaniel, an avid young adult author, directs her readers to the importance of both secular and religious values in many of her works, including the noteworthy *Angels Watching over Me* (1996) and *Angel of Hope* (2000). Or there's *The Singing Mountain* (1998) by Sonia Levitin, in which a Jewish teen decides to join an Orthodox Jewish yeshiva (school) when visiting Israel—producing an internal conflict for both his parents and the teen himself.

Questioning one's faith is a popular theme in many current young adult novels. In Ilene Cooper's *Sam I Am* (2004), young Sam's mother is Christian, his father Jewish—and Sam is torn about his own questions of faith and practice. Similarly, in Will Weaver's *Full Service* (2005), a teen, once a devoted member of a closely knit religious community, leaves for a job in another town and there questions many of the tenets of his own faith. And in Han Nolen's *When We Were Saints* (2003), a young teen explores his own spiritual identity as he witnesses his grandfather's sudden death.

Religious fanaticism is also a prominent theme in young adult literature. Joining a religious cult and following fanatical leaders is the subject of many young adult novels, beginning with these two precedent-setting early books: Richard Peck's *The Last Safe Place on Earth* (1995) and Margaret Peterson Haddix's *Leaving Fishers* (1997). Both speak of young people who fall prey to uncompromising so-called religious leaders. Also, *Faith Wish* (2003) by James Bennett tells the tale of a young teen who is drawn to a charismatic religious cult leader until she finds herself having his child. Similarly, in Judy Waite's *Forbidden* (2006), brainwashed teen Elinor must work through her inner conflict between her parents' religious cult and her own sexual abuse at the hands of religious leaders.

Issues of life and death within a religious context arise in many contemporary young adult novels. In Gary Soto's *The Afterlife* (2003), Jacqueline Woodson's *Behind You* (2004), and Gabrielle Zevin's *Elsewhere* (2005), the central characters are dead and, in their own distinctive narrative voice, are observing the lives of family and friends. Perched in their afterlife, these soul-searching newly departed teens try to make sense of their own life—the choices they made, their values and beliefs—while simultaneously reflecting on the people they left behind. In this same vein, another interesting read is Adele Griffin's *Where I Want to Be* (2005), an exploration of two sisters, one alive and one dead, who are both coming to terms with the loss of the other.

Finally, some of the more noteworthy novels about young people wrestling with religious ideals and principles include Sarah Littman's *Confessions of a Closet Catholic* (2005), Nikki Grimes's *Dark Sons* (2005), Robin Brande's *Evolution, Me, and Other Freaks of Nature* (2007), Jacqueline Woodson's *Feathers* (2007), Paula Jolin's *In the Name of God* (2007), Yann Martel's *Life of Pi* (2001), Helen Hemphill's *Long Gone Daddy* (2006), and Matthue Roth's *Never Mind the Goldbergs* (2005). All of these distinguished works indicate the continued vitality of books for teens that demonstrate how young people cope with the eternal questions of life and death (Krasner & Zollman, 2010; Lesesne, 2003, 2006).

CROSSOVER NOVELS

A fascinating trend in the publication and growth of young adult literature is the advent of crossover novels—books that appeal to both teens and adults. Three big crossover series—J. K. Rowling's *Harry Potter*, Stephenie Meyer's *Twilight*, and Suzanne Collins's *The Hunger Games*—began this sudden surge and are duly recognized not only for their literary appeal but also for their ability to generate sales among teens and adults alike.

Clearly, this welcome change in young adult literature sales has resulted in adults buying books for kids and, inadvertently, becoming readers of the very same young adult book themselves. Unsuspectingly, they learn that books considered primarily for the teenage audience are often universal in their themes and engaging in their reads—hence, their crossover appeal (Benedetti, 2011).

Some of the more recent crossover novels include many genres and styles. M. T. Anderson's two-volume *The Astonishing Life of Octavian Nothing, Traitor to the Nation* (2006, 2008), *The Game of Sunken Places* (2004), and *The Empire of Gut and Bone* (2011) are all popular reads for adults who enjoy historical journeys. Similarly, Libba Bray's gothic fantasy novels *A Great and Terrible Beauty* (2003), *The Sweet Far Thing* (2007), *Going Bovine* (2009), and *Beauty Queens* (2011) appeal (like so many others in the same genre) to teens and adults alike who enjoy reads enriched with vampires and the occult. And then there is Cassandra Clare's best-selling *Mortal Instruments* series, including *City of Bones* (2007), which continues to charm readers with equally mysterious stories of urban fantasy.

Naturally, we cannot forget adults and teens who prefer more realistic fare. Sarah Dessen's chick-lit romance *That Summer* (1996) and *Someone Like You* (1998) began a series of reads that have done exceptionally well among all ages, but especially teen girls. Dessen's novels feature strong, young, middle-class women with family and relationship troubles, emphasizing an appeal to readers who prefer a more down-to-earth approach to understanding life's everyday problems.

Another popular crossover novelist is Scott Westerfield. Known for his dystopic series—*Uglies* (2005a), *Pretties* (2005b), *Specials* (2006), and *Extras* (2007)—Westerfield has seen many of his books fall into the hands of eager adults and teens. Challenging our notion of what is good and true in a world that praises physical beauty above all, Westerfield consistently produces a good read.

And last, but certainly not least, is Markus Zusak's *The Book Thief* (2006), a multiple award–winning book about a young girl living in Munich, Germany, during World War II. There, in the shadow of the Nazis, she learns to read by sharing stolen books with the Jewish man hidden in their house. This work, as well as the popularity of crossover books by Carl Hiaasen, Joyce Carol Oates, John Grisham, James Patterson, and many others, continues to revive a book market that often suffers from sluggish sales and Internet competition.

VERSE NOVELS

Finally, one of the growing trends in young adult literature is the rise of the verse novel. Mel Glenn is credited with one of the first books for teens written in verse, a work titled *Class Dismissed: High School Poems* (1982). Characteristically, a verse novel tells a story in poetry, often in the first person and with a single narrator. This genre—specialized in form, yet popular with teens who like their reads quiet and nuanced—has found a foothold with many prominent young adult authors.

A number of young adult novels have seen their stature elevated by the presence of a story form in free verse. Most notably, Karen Hesse's *Out of the Dust* (1997), a story set in the Oklahoma Dust Bowl during the Great Depression, and her equally compelling *Aleutian Sparrow* (2003), a tale of the internment of Aleutian Islanders in American camps during World War II, have been well received by teens. In addition, Virginia Euwer Wolff's *Make Lemonade* (1993) and her National Book Award–winning sequel *True Believer* (2001), as well as Ellen Hopkins's ever-popular series—*Crank* (2004), *Burned* (2006), *Glass* (2007a), *Identical* (2007b), *Impulse* (2007c), and *Tricks* (2009)—are all about the tough and often grim reality of teenage urban life, and all have found a following among young adult readers.

Similarly, one cannot discuss books told in verse and written with teens in mind without mentioning acclaimed author Nikki Grimes. Her *Bronx Masquerade* (2002) and *A Girl Named Mister* (2010) both speak in poetic form to the vagaries of a teen life interrupted by life's hard turns.

Lesser known but equally impressive are Stephanie Hemphill's *Wicked Girls: A Novel of the Salem Witch Trials* (2010), which follows her Printz Honor Book *Your Own, Sylvia: A Verse Portrait of Sylvia Plath* (2007), two bold verse novels based on historical figures; Jame Richards's *Three Rivers Rising: A Novel of the Johnstown Flood* (2010), a novel in verse that uses the 1889 Johnstown flood to explore class divisions and social mores in a moving portrait of four fictional families; and Sherry Shahan's *Purple Daze* (2011), a retelling of life in the turbulent antiwar, peace-loving 1960s told in free verse.

Finally, young people who enjoy verse novels will find these good reads as well: Malorie Blackman's *Cloud Busting* (2004), the story of an unlikely friendship between two young boys; Tayna Stone's *A Bad Boy Can Be Good for a Girl* (2006), a poetic tale of peer pressure; Steven Herrick's *By the River* (2006), about coming of age in a small Australian town; Kristen Smith's *The Geography of Girlhood* (2006); Judith Ortiz Cofer's *Call Me Maria* (2004), about growing up in inner-city New York; Ann Turner's *Hard Hit* (2006), about a boy's love for his dying father; and Patricia McCormick's *Sold* (2006), a first-person account, told in short poetic vignettes, about a thirteen-year-old girl sold into prostitution in modern-day Calcutta. Truly, poetic novels for teen readers have come of age.

CONCLUSION

With the ever-increasing influence of a youth-saturated media culture, the marketing of books, movies, and music to young people seems to be more popular than ever. Teens—with technology at their fingertips—seem to have more free time on their hands to explore the world in all its complexities. Time, speed, and convenience are on their side, leaving ample room to find new avenues to share their enthusiasm for adventurous escapades into new and fantastical worlds and even more sobering ventures into the harsh light of day.

Knowing this, teachers, authors, and enthusiasts of young adult literature continue to push a genre of books that seems to have no conceivable bounds and/or saturation. Young people, publishers know, will always be on a journey to find themselves, and their exploration, however gruesome or unbelievable as it may be, will always find new and fertile ground in the realm of the arts (Wilhelm, 2008; V. K. Williams, 2011). Whether in graphic novels or in more traditional literature, adolescents will search for the words and pictures that portend to define them, no matter how disturbing the image may be. Equally important, young people will always reach beyond their grasp, hoping that their self-proclaimed journey toward enlightenment will result in new meanings for themselves and the world in which they live.

And rest assured, young adult literature will be there every step of the way.

REFERENCES

Abbott, H. (2009). *Summer boys* series. New York: Scholastic.

Alyson, S. (Ed.). (1985). *Young, gay, and proud*. Boston: Alyson.

Anderson, L. H. (1999). *Speak*. New York: Farrar, Straus & Giroux.

Anderson, L. H. (2007). *Twisted*. New York: Viking/Penguin.

Anderson, M. T. (2002). *Feed*. Cambridge, MA: Candlewick Press.

Anderson, M. T. (2004). *The game of sunken places*. New York: Scholastic.

Anderson, M. T. (2006). *The astonishing life of Octavian Nothing, traitor to the nation*. Volume 1: *The pox party*. Cambridge, MA: Candlewick Press.

Anderson, M. T. (2008). *The astonishing life of Octavian Nothing, traitor to the nation*. Volume 2: *The kingdom on the waves*. Cambridge, MA: Candlewick Press.

Anderson, M. T. (2011). *The empire of gut and bone*. New York: Scholastic.

Angelou, M. (1969). *I know why the caged bird sings*. New York: Random House.

Anonymous. (1971). *Go ask Alice*. New York: Simon & Schuster.

Applegate, K. A. (1999). *Everworld* series. New York: Scholastic.

Asher, J. (2007). *Thirteen reasons why: A novel*. New York: Razorbill.

Bach, J., Choate, L., & Parker, B. (2011). Young adult literature and professional development. *Theory into Practice, 50*(3), 198–205.

Bacigalupi, P. (2010). *Ship breaker*. New York: Little, Brown.

Baer, A. L., & Glasgow, J. N. (2010). Negotiating understanding through the young adult literature of Muslim cultures. *Journal of Adolescent & Adult Literacy, 54*(1), 23–32.

Bendis, B., & Bagley, M. (2002). *Ultimate Spider-Man: Power and responsibility*. New York: Marvel Comics.

Benedetti, A. (2011). Not just for teens. *Library Journal, 136*(11), 40–43.

Bennett, J. (2003). *Faith wish*. New York: Holiday House.

Blackburn, M. V., & Smith, J. M. (2010). Moving beyond the inclusion of LGBT-themed literature in English language arts classrooms: Interrogating heteronormativity and exploring intersectionality. *Journal of Adolescent & Adult Literacy, 53*(8), 625–634.

Blackman, M. (2004). *Cloud busting*. New York: Doubleday.

Block, F. L. (1995). *Baby be-bop*. New York: HarperCollins.

Boock, P. (1999). *Dare truth or promise*. Boston: Houghton Mifflin.

Bradbury, R. (1953). *Fahrenheit 451*. New York: Ballantine.

Brande, R. (2007). *Evolution, me, and other freaks of nature*. New York: Knopf.

Bray, L. (2003). *A great and terrible beauty*. New York: Delacorte Press.

Bray, L. (2007). *The sweet far thing*. New York: Delacorte Press.

Bray, L. (2009). *Going bovine*. New York: Delacorte Press.

Bray, L. (2011). *Beauty queens*. New York: Delacorte Press.

Brooks, T. (1977). *The sword of Shannara*. New York: Random House.

Brooks, T. (1982). *The elfstones of Shannara*. New York: Ballantine.
Brooks, T. (1985). *The wishsong of Shannara*. New York: Ballantine.
Brown, J. (2009). *Hate list*. New York: Little, Brown.
Buehler, J. (2009). Ways to join the living conversation about young adult literature. *English Journal, 98*(3), 26–32.
Capella, D. (2010). Kicking it up beyond the casual: Fresh perspectives in young adult literature. *Studies in the Novel, 42*(1/2), 1–10.
Cart, M. (1996). *From romance to realism: Fifty years of growth and change in young adult literature*. New York: HarperCollins.
Cart, M. (2010a). A literature of risk. *American Libraries, 41*(5), 32–35.
Cart, M. (2010b). A new literature for a new millennium? The first decade of the Printz Awards. *Young Adult Library Services, 8*(3), 28–31.
Cart, M., & Jenkins, C. A. (2004). *The heart has its reasons: Young adult literature with gay/lesbian/queer content, 1969–2004*. Lanham, MD: Scarecrow Press.
Carter, J. B. (Ed.). (2007). *Building literacy connections with graphic novels: Page by page, panel by panel*. Urbana, IL: National Council of Teachers of English.
Carter, J. B. (2011). Graphic novels, web comics, and creator blogs: Examining product and process. *Theory into Practice, 50*(3), 190–197.
Cassidy, J., Valadez, C., Garrett, S., & Barrera, E. (2010). Adolescent and adult literacy: What's hot, what's not. *Journal of Adult & Adolescent Literacy, 53*(6), 448–456.
Chambers, A. (1982). *Dance on my grave*. New York: Amulet Books.
Chbosky, S. (1999). *The perks of being a wallflower*. New York: Pocket Books.
Childress, A. (1973). *A hero ain't nothin' but a sandwich*. New York: Coward-McCann.
Christenbury, L. (2006). *Making the journey: Being and becoming a teacher of English language arts*. Portsmouth, NH: Heinemann.
Cisneros, S. (1983). *The house on Mango Street*. Houston, TX: Arte Publico Press.
Clare, C. (2007). *The mortal instruments*. Book 1: *City of bones*. New York: McElderry/Simon & Schuster.
Cofer, J. O. (2004). *Call me Maria: A novel*. New York: Orchard Books.
Collins, S. (2008). *The hunger games*. New York: Scholastic.
Cooper, I. (2004). *Sam I am*. New York: Scholastic.
Cormier, R. (1974). *The chocolate war*. New York: Pantheon.
Cormier, R. (1977). *I am the cheese*. New York: Pantheon.
Cormier, R. (1979). *After the first death*. New York: Pantheon.
Crane, S. (1895). *The red badge of courage*. New York: D. Appleton & Co.
Crisp, T. (2009). From romance to magical realism: Limits and possibilities in gay adolescent fiction. *Children's Literature in Education, 40*(4), 333–348.
Crutcher, C. (1989). *Athletic shorts: Six short stories*. New York: Greenwillow/HarperCollins.
Crutcher, C. (2009). *Angry management: Three novellas*. New York: Greenwillow Books.
Dashner, J. (2011). *The death cure* (*Maze runner* trilogy). New York: Delacorte Press.
Dean, Z. (2003). *The A-list*. Boston: Little, Brown.
De la Cruz, M. (2005). *Au Pairs* series. New York: Simon & Schuster.
Dessen, S. (1996). *That summer*. New York: Orchard Books.
Dessen, S. (1998). *Someone like you*. New York: Viking.
DeStefano, L. (2011). *The chemical garden* trilogy. Book 1: *Wither*. New York: Simon & Schuster.

Dickens, C. (1850). *David Copperfield*. London: Bradbury & Evans.
Donovan, J. (1969). *I'll get there. It better be worth the trip*. New York: Harper & Row.
Donovan, S. (1994). *Dive*. New York: Dutton Children's Books.
Fisher, C. (2010). *Incarceron* series. New York: Dial Books.
Gaiman, N. (1989–1996). *The sandman* series. New York: DC Comics.
Garden, N. (1982). *Annie on my mind*. New York: Farrar, Straus & Giroux.
Garden, N. (1991). *Lark in the morning*. New York: Farrar, Straus & Giroux.
Garden, N. (1996). *Good moon rising*. New York: Farrar, Straus & Giroux.
Garden, N. (2006). *Endgame*. Orlando, FL: Harcourt.
Gavigan, K. W., & Knutts, S. (2010). Using children and young adult literature in teaching acceptance and understanding of individual differences. *Delta Kappa Gamma Bulletin, 77*(2), 11–16.
George, M. (2011). Preparing teachers to teach adolescent literature in the twenty-first century. *Theory into Practice, 50*(3), 182–189.
Glenn, M. (1982). *Class dismissed! High school poems*. New York: Clarion.
Glenn, W. (2008). Gossiping girls, insider boys, A-list achievement: Examining and exposing young adult novels consumed by conspicuous consumption. *Journal of Adolescent & Adult Literacy, 52*(1), 34–42.
Golding, W. (1954). *Lord of the Flies*. New York: Coward-McCann.
Goldstein, L., & Phelan, M. (2009). Are you there, God? It's me, manga: Manga as an extension of young adult literature. *Young Adult Library Services, 7*(4), 32–38.
Greenblatt, E. (2011). Literature from the heart. *Journal of LBGT Youth, 8*(1), 99–102.
Griffin, A. (2005). *Where I want to be*. New York: Putnam.
Grimes, N. (2002). *Bronx masquerade*. New York: Dial.
Grimes, N. (2005). *Dark sons*. New York: Hyperion.
Grimes, N. (2010). *A girl named Mister*. Grand Rapids, MI: Zondervan.
Groenke, S. L., & Maples, J. (2010). Young adult literature goes digital: Will teen reading ever be the same? *The ALAN Review, 37*(3), 38–44.
Gross, M., Goldsmith, A., & Carruth, D. (2008). What do young adult novels say about HIV/AIDS? A second look. *Library Quarterly, 78*(4), 397–418.
Guy, R. (1995). *Friends*. New York: Laurel-Leaf.
Haarsma, P. J. (2006). *The softwire: Virus on Orbis 1*. Somerville, MA: Candlewick Press.
Haddix, M. P. (1997). *Leaving Fishers*. New York: Simon & Schuster.
Hall, L. (1972). *Sticks and stones*. Chicago: Follett.
Hamilton, V. (1974). *M. C. Higgins, the great*. New York: Macmillan.
Harrison, L. (2010). *The clique* series. New York: Little, Brown.
Hayn, J., Kaplan, J. S., & Nolen, A. (2011). Young adult literature research in the twenty-first century. *Theory into Practice, 50*(3), 176–181.
Hazlett, L. A., Sweeney, W. J., & Reins, K. J. (2011). Using young adult literature featuring LGBTQ adolescents with intellectual and/or physical disabilities to strengthen classroom inclusion. *Theory into Practice, 50*(3), 206–214.
Hemphill, H. (2006). *Long gone daddy*. Asheville, NC: Front Street.
Hemphill, S. (2007). *Your own, Sylvia: A verse portrait of Sylvia Path*. New York: Knopf.
Hemphill, S. (2010). *Wicked girls: A novel of the Salem witch trials*. New York: Balzer & Bray.

Heron, A. (1983). *One teenager in ten: Writings of gay and lesbian youth*. Boston: Alyson.
Herrick, S. (2006). *By the river*. Asheville, NC: Front Street.
Hesse, K. (1997). *Out of the dust*. New York: Scholastic.
Hesse, K. (2003). *Aleutian sparrow*. New York: McElderry.
Hinton, S. E. (1967). *The outsiders*. New York: Viking/Penguin.
Hodges, G. (2010). Reasons for reading: Why literature matters. *Literacy, 44*(2), 60–68.
Holland, I. (1972). *The man without a face*. Philadelphia: Lippincott.
Hopkins, E. (2004). *Crank*. New York: Simon & Schuster.
Hopkins, E. (2006). *Burned*. New York: Simon & Schuster.
Hopkins, E. (2007a). *Glass*. New York: Simon & Schuster.
Hopkins, E. (2007b). *Identical*. New York: Simon & Schuster.
Hopkins, E. (2007c). *Impulse*. New York: Simon & Schuster.
Hopkins, E. (2009). *Tricks*. New York: McElderry.
Horowitz, A. (2005). *The gatekeepers*. Book 1: *Raven's gate*. New York: Scholastic.
Howe, J. (2001). *The misfits*. New York: Atheneum.
Huck, C., Hepler, S., Hickman, J., & Kiefer, B. (Eds.). (1997). *Children's literature* (6th ed.). Boston: McGraw-Hill.
Hunter, E. (2005). *Warriors: The new prophecy* series. New York: HarperCollins.
Johnson, A. B. (2011). Multiple selves and multiple sites of influence: Perceptions of young adult literature in the classroom. *Theory into Practice, 50*(3), 215–222.
Jolin, P. (2007). *In the name of God*. New Milford, CT: Roaring Press.
Kaplan, J. (2006). Dissertations on adolescent literature: 2000–2005. *The ALAN Review, 33*(2), 51–59.
Kaplan, J. (2007). Recent research in young adult literature: Three predominant strands of study. *The ALAN Review, 34*(3), 53–60.
Kaplan, J. (2008). Perception and reality: Examining the representations of adolescents in young adult fiction. *The ALAN Review, 36*(1), 42–49.
Kaplan, J. (2010). Doctoral dissertations (2008–2009): A review of research on young adult literature. *The ALAN Review, 37*(2), 54–58.
Kerr, M. E. (1994). *Deliver us from Evie*. New York: HarperCollins.
Kishimoto, M. (1999–present). *Naruto* series. San Francisco: VIZ Media.
Koerge, R. (2001). *The brimstone journals*. Cambridge, MA: Candlewick Press.
Kokkola, L. (2011). Virtuous vampires and voluptuous vamps: Romance conventions reconsidered in Stephenie Meyer's *Twilight* series. *Children's Literature in Education, 42*(2), 165–179.
Koss, M. D., & Teale, W. H. (2009). What's happening in YA literature? Trends in books for adolescents. *Journal of Adolescent & Adult Literacy, 52*(7), 563–572.
Krasner, J., & Zollman, J. W. (2010). *Are you there God?* Judaism and Jewishness in Judy Blume's adolescent fiction. *Shofar: An Interdisciplinary Journal of Jewish Studies, 29*(1), 22–47.
Kubo, T. (2001–present). *Bleach* series. San Francisco, CA: Viz Media.
Lee, H. (1960). *To kill a mockingbird*. Philadelphia: Lippincott.
Le Guin, U. (1968). *The Earthsea cycle*. Book 1: *A wizard of Earthsea*. Berkeley, CA: Parnassus Press.

Le Guin, U. (1971). *The Earthsea cycle.* Book 2: *The tombs of Atuan.* New York: Atheneum.
Le Guin, U. (1972). *The Earthsea cycle.* Book 3: *The farthest shore.* New York: Atheneum.
L'Engle, M. (1962). *A wrinkle in time.* New York: Farrar, Straus & Giroux.
Lesesne, T. S. (2003). *Making the match: Finding the right book for the right teen at the right time.* New York: Stenhouse.
Lesesne, T. S. (2006). *Naked reading: Uncovering what tweens need to become lifelong readers.* New York: Stenhouse.
Levithan, D. (2005). *Boy meets boy.* New York: Knopf/Random House.
Levithan, D. (2009). *Love is the higher law.* New York: Knopf.
Levitin, S. (1998). *The singing mountain.* New York: Simon & Schuster.
Lipsyte, R. (1967). *The contender.* New York: Harper & Row.
Littman, S. (2005). *Confessions of a closet Catholic.* New York: Dutton/Penguin.
Lowry, L. (1993). *The giver.* Boston: Houghton Mifflin.
Martel, Y. (2001). *Life of Pi.* New York: Harcourt.
Maynard, J. (2003). *The usual rules.* New York: St. Martin's Press.
McCafferty, M. (2011). *Bumped.* New York: Balzer & Bray.
McCormick, P. (2006). *Sold.* New York: Hyperion.
McDaniel, L. (1996). *Angels watching over me.* New York: Bantam.
McDaniel, L. (2000). *Angel of hope.* New York: Random House.
McLaren, P. (1998). Culture or canon. *Harvard Educational Review, 58*(2), 33–38.
Meminger, N. (2011). Getting diverse books into the hands of teen readers: How do we do it? *Young Adult Library Services, 9*(3), 10–13.
Meyer, S. (2005). *Twilight.* New York: Little, Brown.
Meyer, S. (2006). *New moon.* New York: Little, Brown.
Meyer, S. (2007). *Eclipse.* New York: Little, Brown.
Meyer, S. (2008). *Breaking dawn.* New York: Little, Brown.
Meyers, W. D. (1999). *Monster.* New York: HarperCollins.
Miller, F. (1997). *Batman: The dark knight returns.* New York: DC Comics.
Minter, J. (2004). *The insiders.* New York: Bloomsbury.
Monseau, V., & Salvner, G. (Eds.). (2001). *Reading their world: The young adult novel in the classroom.* Portsmouth, NH: Boynton/Cook-Heineman.
Moore, A., & Gibbons, D. (1986). *Watchmen.* New York: DC Comics.
Nilsen, A., & Donelson, K. (2009). *Literature for today's young adults* (8th ed.). Boston: Pearson.
Nolen, H. (2003). *When we were saints.* San Diego: Harcourt.
Norris, S. (2008). *Something to blog about.* New York: Amulet Books.
O'Brien, C. M. (2010–2011). *The birthmarked* trilogy. New York: Roaring Brook Press.
O'Malley, B. L. (2004–2010). *Scott Pilgrim* series. Portland, OR: Oni Press.
Orwell, G. (1945). *Animal farm.* London: Secker & Warburg.
Orwell, G. (1949). *1984.* London: Secker & Warburg.
Patneaude, D. (2011). *Epitaph road.* New York: Egmont.
Peck, R. (1995). *The last safe place on earth.* New York: Delacorte Press.
Peowski, L. (2010). Where are all the teens? Engaging and empowering them online. *Young Adult Library Services,* 8(2), 26–28.
Philion, T. (2009). The age of ______? Using young adult literature to make sense of the contemporary world. *Young Adult Library Services, 7*(4), 46–49.

Prose, F. (2007). *Bullyville*. New York: HarperTeen.
Rabey, M. (2010). Historical fiction mash-ups: Broadening appeal by mixing genres. *Young Adult Library Services, 9*(1), 38–41.
Revoyr, N. (1997). *The necessary hunger: A novel*. New York: Simon & Schuster.
Richards, J. (2010). *Three rivers rising: A novel of the Johnstown flood*. New York: Knopf.
Roberts, L. P. (1998). *The Clearwater Crossing* series. New York: Bantam.
Roberts, M. (2010). Teaching young adult literature. *English Journal, 100*(2), 125–128.
Roth, M. (2005). *Never mind the Goldbergs*. New York: PUSH/Scholastic.
Roth, V. (2011). *Divergent* trilogy. New York: Katherine Tegen Books.
Rowling, J. K. (1997– 2007). *Harry Potter* series. London: Bloomsbury.
Ruby, L. (2006). *Good girls*. New York: HarperTempest.
Salinger, J. D. (1951). *The catcher in the rye*. Boston: Little, Brown.
Sanchez, A. (2001–2005). *Rainbow* trilogy. New York: Simon & Schuster.
Sanderson, P. (2003). *X-Men: The ultimate guide*. New York: DK Publishing.
Satrapi, M. (2003). *Persepolis: The story of a childhood*. New York: Pantheon.
Scoppettone, S. (1974). *Trying hard to hear you*. New York: Harper & Row.
Shahan, S. (2011). *Purple daze*. Philadelphia: Roaring Press.
Silver, A. (2010). Twilight is not good for maidens: Gender, sexuality, and the family in Stephenie Meyer's *Twilight* series. *Studies in the Novel, 42*(1/2), 121–138.
Sleator, W. (1991). *House of stairs*. New York: Dutton/Penguin.
Smith, K. (2006). *The geography of girlhood*. New York: Little, Brown.
Soto, G. (2003). *The afterlife*. Orlando, FL: Harcourt.
Spiegelman, A. (1986). *Maus I: A survivor's tale: My father bleeds history*. New York: Pantheon.
Spiegelman, A. (1991). *Maus II: A survivor's tale: And here my troubles began*. New York: Pantheon.
Stallworth, B. J. (2006). The relevance of young adult literature. *Educational Leadership, 63*(7), 59–63.
Stephens, J. (2007). Young adult: A book by any other name . . . Defining the genre. *The ALAN Review, 35*(1), 34–42.
Stoehr, S. (1991). *Crosses*. New York: Delacorte Press.
Stone, T. (2006). *A bad boy can be good for a girl*. New York: Wendy Lamb.
Stracher, C. (2011). *The water wars*. Naperville, IL: Sourcebook.
Strasser, T. (2000). *Give a boy a gun*. New York: Simon & Schuster.
Sturm, B. W., & Michel, K. (2009). The structure of power in young adult problem novels. *Young Adult Library Services, 7*(2), 39–47.
Takahashi, R. (1996–2008). *Inuyasha* series. San Francisco: Viz Media.
Takaya, N. (1999–2006). *Fruits basket* series. Tokyo: Hakusensha.
Taylor, M. (1976). *Roll of thunder, hear my cry*. New York: Dial/Penguin.
Tolkien, J. R. R. (1954–1955). *The lord of the rings* trilogy. London: George Allen & Unwin.
Toriyama, A. (2009). *Dragonball box set* (Volumes 1–16). San Francisco: Viz Comics.
Tullson, D. (2008). *Lockdown*. Victoria, BC: Orca.
Turner, A. (2006). *Hard hit*. New York: Scholastic.
Twain, M. (1876). *The adventures of Tom Sawyer*. Chicago: American Publishing.
Twain, M. (1884). *The adventures of Huckleberry Finn*. London: Chatto & Windus.

Veit, F., & Osada, F. (2010). Absolutely true experiences of two new librarians: The importance of popular literature in educating young adult librarians. *Young Adult Library Services, 8*(4), 11–13.
von Ziegesar, C. (2002). *Gossip girl.* Boston: Little, Brown.
Waite, J. (2006). *Forbidden.* New York: Atheneum.
Ward, B. A., & Young, T. A. (2011). Reading graphically: Comics and graphic novels for readers from kindergarten through high school. *Reading Horizons, 50*(4), 283–295.
Watson, C. G. (2007). *Quad.* New York: Razorbill.
Weaver, W. (2005). *Full service.* New York: Farrar, Straus & Giroux.
Westerfield, S. (2005a). *Uglies.* New York: Simon & Schuster.
Westerfield, S. (2005b). *Pretties.* New York: Simon & Schuster.
Westerfield, S. (2006). *Specials.* New York: Simon & Schuster.
Westerfield, S. (2007). *Extras.* New York: Simon & Schuster.
Wickens, C. M. (2011). Codes, silences, and homophobia: Challenging normative assumptions about gender and sexuality in LGBTQ young adult literature. *Children's Literature in Education, 42*(2), 148–164.
Wilhelm, J. D. (2008). *"You gotta BE the book": Teaching engaged and reflective reading with adolescents* (2nd ed.). New York: Teachers College Press.
Williams, B. (1998). *Girl walking backwards.* New York: St. Martin's Griffin.
Williams, V. K. (2011). Building and evaluating juvenile collections in academic libraries. *College and Undergraduate Libraries, 18*(1), 58–76.
Wittlinger, E. (1999). *Hard love.* New York: Simon & Schuster.
Wolff, V. E. (1993). *Make lemonade: A novel.* New York: Scholastic.
Wolff, V. E. (2001). *True believer.* New York: Atheneum/Simon & Schuster.
Wolk, S. (2009). Reading for a better world: Teaching for social responsibility with young adult literature. *Journal of Adolescent & Adult Literacy, 52*(8), 664–673.
Woodson, J. (1997). *The house you pass on the way.* New York: Delacorte Press.
Woodson, J. (2004). *Behind you.* New York: Putnam.
Woodson, J. (2007). *Feathers.* New York: Putnam.
Wopperer, E. (2011). Inclusive literature in the library and the classroom. *Knowledge Quest, 39*(3), 26–34.
Yang, G. L. (2006). *American born Chinese.* New Milford, CT: Roaring Brook Press.
Yazawa, A. (2000–present). *Nana* series. San Francisco: Viz Media.
Zevin, G. (2005). *Elsewhere.* New York: Farrar, Straus & Giroux.
Zindel, P. (1968). *The pigman.* New York: Harper & Row.
Zusak, M. (2006). *The book thief.* New York: Random House.

3

Literacy Teacher Education Today and the Teaching of Adolescent Literature

Perspectives on Research and Practice

Susan E. Elliott-Johns

DEFINING ADOLESCENT LITERATURE

The term *adolescent literature* refers here to books written for a target audience of young people between twelve and eighteen years old. Another distinction between adolescent literature and young adult literature (YAL) is often made, with some young adult audiences extending from sixteen years of age into the early twenties (Galda & Graves, 2007). These age ranges represent a broad spectrum of reading abilities, levels of maturity, interests, and aptitudes common to adolescents. Knowledge of the depth and breadth of YAL titles available will assist teachers in effectively meeting students' needs and interests.

Stephens (2007) suggests a clear-cut answer to the questions "What characterizes a book as Young Adult? What makes it different from its Children's or Grownup relatives?" (p. 40). He offers his own definition to teachers of adolescents:

> As I see it, the label "Young Adult" refers to a story that tackles the difficult, and oftentimes adult, issues that arise during an adolescent's journey toward identity, a journey told through a distinctly teen voice, that holds the same potential for literary value as its "Grownup" peers. (pp. 40–41)

The complexity of adolescents' literate lives documented in current research demonstrates that the kinds of sophisticated literacy activities adolescents engage in outside the classroom need to be more widely represented in classroom contexts (Alvermann, Hinchman, Moore, Phelps, &

Waff, 1998; Brozo, Walter, & Placker, 2002; Flores-Gonzalez, 2002; Lankshear & Bigum, 1999; Lankshear & Knobel, 2003; Sanford, 2002; Smith & Wilhelm, 2006; Worthy, 1998).

Literacy teacher education that acknowledges contemporary research on adolescents and offers opportunities to critically explore quality adolescent literature is needed if we are to successfully engage adolescent students in school literacy learning experiences and extend traditional approaches to communicating understanding.

CURRENT TRENDS IN LEARNING TO TEACH ADOLESCENT LITERATURE

Perspectives on trends in YAL have significant implications for teachers and teacher education as more vibrant discussion resonates around this topic and the study of YAL is taken more seriously. Drawing on current research and practice, three critical issues emerge: (1) why teach YAL?, (2) the classics versus YAL, and (3) teachers as readers of YAL. All three warrant increased attention, clarification, and understanding if teacher educators and teachers are to be effective as teachers of YAL in contemporary classrooms.

Why Teach YAL?

Increasingly, teachers can select well-written young adult titles to effectively engage contemporary students in reading, to get them to care about reading, and as a result, to motivate them and develop more positive attitudes toward reading (Carter, 2007; Lesesne, 2010; Wilhelm, 2008). Research shows that YAL is what adolescent students are purchasing and reading *outside* of school (Bach, 2009; Koss & Teale, 2009; Renaissance Learning, 2009; Reno, 2008; Schieble, 2009; Smith & Wilhelm, 2006). Young people read these books because they can relate to the characters, the stories, the settings, and the issues that characters experience; they also gain a sense that their own voice matters. Similarly, students in school often find it difficult to engage with classic texts. Groenke and Scherff (2010) suggest,

> While we believe—like Della DeCourcy, Lyn Fairchild, and Robin Follet, authors of *Teaching* Romeo and Juliet: *A Differentiated Approach* (2007)—that "all students should have access to Shakespeare" (p. 1), we also know that the esoteric language, need for intensive teacher guidance and explanation, and seeming lack of relevance to today's popular culture are reasons why adolescent readers struggle to engage with classic texts. (p. 8)

Teachers who offer students some choice about what they read and make available a wide range of titles relevant to twenty-first-century lives contribute to building more confident, capable, thoughtful readers who readily engage with texts—during classroom instruction and independent reading.

The Classics versus YAL

The perceived lack of literary merit in YAL selections is often linked to teachers' perspectives on whether to teach *either* classics *or* YAL. Carol Jago (2004) suggests, "There is an art to choosing books for students. First I look for literary merit. Without this, the novel will not stand up to scrutiny or be worth the investment of classroom time" (p. 47). However, in the context of the increasing quality and sophistication of texts written and illustrated for young adults, this argument is becoming less convincing. Lesesne (2010) makes a compelling case for re-considering the rigors of YA literature:

> From its earliest incarnations, YA literature has suffered from a misconception that it is somehow less literary than *real* literature. Junior novel, teen lit, adolescent book: even these early terms for the literature carry negative connotations. I am willing to bet that you have encountered this apparent prejudice against using contemporary literature in the classroom, particularly for classroom study. I think those folks who would denigrate using YA literature fail to see that it has structure, style, and substance. It is worthy of scrutiny in the classroom. (p. 4)

Groenke and Scherff (2010) make the case for YAL taking a central place in the English curriculum and no longer being relegated to "independent reading" time. They explore and recommend numerous titles for whole-class, mixed-ability learners, making clear which titles would go back on the bookshelf for independent reading (and why). Rigorous differentiated instruction, using *both* classics and young adult selections according to students' needs and interests, is regarded as a solution to the either/or dichotomy. Essential knowledge of alternative selections, teaching practices that promote the wide range of literature available, and a genuine recognition of the need for *access* to quality literature will help bridge this divide (Groenke & Scherff, 2010).

Teachers as Readers of YAL

Harste (2010) reminds us, "Like everything else, we as teachers cannot do for children what we cannot first do ourselves" (p. 39). Teachers (and teacher educators) must be knowledgeable and enthusiastic about available titles, award winners, themes, and forms within the genre and also be prepared to articulate how and why they are teaching YAL. In order to do this, as well as model processes of fluent, effective reading, teachers need to gain insider perspectives by reading the books presented to their students. As a result, a wider range of quality adolescent literature will reach the hands of adolescents, and teachers will become increasingly confident about the merits of teaching with YAL.

Effective teacher education nurtures *teachers as readers*. Teacher candidates must understand the powerful influence one can have as a practicing teacher who actually reads the books assigned to students—and the titles students are reading voluntarily on their own time. A critical first step is designing innovative courses that promote and extend literacy as social practice—for example, reading widely and deeply (across curriculum areas); talking about books; learning how to make informed choices in the context of differentiated instruction; and modeling the knowledge, skills, and habitual reading necessary to forge interpersonal connections through thought-provoking conversations about reading. It is insufficient to display recommended YAL resources in class. Teachers of adolescents who keep up to date with research and practice, who model knowledge and uses of quality titles, motivate others to do the same.

PERSPECTIVES ON TEACHER EDUCATION AND THE TEACHING OF YAL

Tracing the Progress of Research on Teaching

Grossman (2001) comments on the significance of the first chapter on research on the teaching of literature to be included in the *Handbook of Research on Teaching*: "If this first chapter is not to be the last, researchers and teachers of literature alike will need to make their voices heard in the debate over the place of literature in and out of school" (p. 429). Recently, there has been renewed interest in literacy instruction for adolescents, and a flurry of publications extolling best practices for classroom teachers have appeared (Gallagher, 2004; Hill Campbell, 2007; Peterson & Swartz, 2008; Unrau, 2008; Wood & Blanton, 2009). Works that directly address issues related to teaching adolescent literature are still limited, but this too is changing (Groenke & Scherff, 2010). The *Handbook of Adolescent Literacy Research* (Christenbury, Bomer, & Smagorinsky, 2009) suggests key challenges facing the field, but even here, discussions of teacher preparation are extremely limited. A number of chapters explore how literacy looks from the point of view of young people themselves and highlight students' frequently overlooked strengths and capabilities as well as needs. But where are the voices of preservice teachers and teacher educators? What have we learned about *their* strengths, capabilities, and needs? The following discussion of related research seeks to explore both of these questions.

Research in Teacher Education

Research in teacher education is still not prolific in the literature, and studies of adolescent literacy teacher education are no exception. Adolescent literacy teacher preparation and development has far to go—although there is a historical legacy on which to build (Alvermann & Moore, 1991). But as Anders (2008) writes, "The state of literacy teacher education is bleak" (p. 343). In 2007, the International Reading Association commissioned a study (Risko, Cummins Roller, Bean, Block, & Anders, 2007) to review research in teacher education. Only seventy-five studies were identified that met trustworthiness criteria for investigations related to the preparation of reading teachers. Of those, eleven studies focused on content area reading, with no studies that could be considered as "adolescent literacy" teacher preparation. Furthermore, none of the studies emphasized issues of diversity or made any apparent attempt to help transition future teachers to the classroom. When studies of this nature are located, they tend to explore methods, best practices, processes, and procedures for instruction. Anders, Hoffman, and Duffy (2000) introduced their review of teacher education research as follows:

> [Reading teacher education] . . . has received little attention from the reading research community. Reading researchers have attended to the reading process, drawing inferences and conducting studies to test their theories. Relatively few researchers have asked questions about the processes teachers go through as they learn and continue to learn to teach reading. (p. 719)

A comparison of results from two surveys of twenty-five leaders in the field of literacy education used to construct the "What's Hot and What's Not?" list of topics for 2010 and 2011 (Cassidy, Ortlieb, & Shettel, 2011) shows adolescent literacy as one of the "very hot" topics on both lists, with at least 75 percent of respondents in agreement in both 2010 and 2011. In results from both the 2010 and 2011 surveys, at least 50 percent of respondents were also in agreement that (preservice) teacher education for reading was *not* a hot topic, but 75 percent of all respondents were in agreement that it *should* be. The results of these surveys reflect some increased attention to adolescent literacy in the field, but an ongoing lack of attention to related teacher education.

In a detailed analysis of the "What's Hot" topics (Cassidy, Valadez, Garrett, & Barrera, 2010), the authors indicate that adolescent literacy first appeared on the survey in 2001 and attained status as a "very hot" topic in 2006 (Cassidy, Garrett, & Barrera, 2006). In 2011, the improvement in scores on standardized tests of early readers in the United States is credited to targeted additional funding initiatives for younger learners, while scores for secondary-level students have remained unchanged. One wonders, therefore, what teacher education in reading might look like should additional funding be made available for teachers of adolescents; some indications can perhaps be gleaned from the work of Cassidy, Ortlieb, and Shettel (2011):

> Thus, because in 2011, adolescent literacy, comprehension, core learning/literacy standards, and RTI are "very hot," now seems the ideal time to involve literacy coaches, offer professional development, and facilitate learning communities in secondary schools to train classroom teachers in the use of content area literacy strategies and Response to Intervention. (p. 7)

In the event of additional funding being made available to support learning in the higher grades, it is hoped that secondary school literacy teacher education is not to be more about "training" teachers to assist students in succeeding on standardized tests. A preferable approach would be to consider preservice education and ongoing professional development opportunities that enable teachers to be knowledgeable about the literature and how to teach (and develop) secondary school reading. Outcomes of offering a wide range of literature selections to adolescent students that they are both able and motivated to read have been seen to result in improved scores on those standardized tests (Allington, 2001; Gallagher, 2009; Kavanaugh, 2010) as opposed to "killing" reading altogether (Gallagher, 2009).

Literacy Teacher Education and YAL

A review of literature, taking into account more than thirty years of research and practice (1980–2010), resulted in very few sources related to teacher education. As Bean and Harper observed (2004), teacher education and adolescent literacy are two fields of study that have "not had much intellectual contact" (p. 392), and the situation does not appear to have significantly changed.

Several citations pertaining to "children's literature" were excluded to maintain the focus on adolescent literacy teacher education. One such study, while of particular relevance to literacy teacher education in Canada (Jobe, 1989), focused mainly on the reasons for the increased attention being paid to children's literature by the teaching profession. However, Jobe includes literature for young adults in the description and comparison of courses for teachers across the country: "Demands are being placed on the universities and colleges to provide more up-to-date courses, and it is obvious that literature for children and young adults is becoming more of a vital component in the education of teachers in Canada" (p. 65). Similarly, many research studies into literacy teacher education were more concerned with student teachers' understandings of literacy learning and teaching as a result of their program (Bainbridge & Macy, 2008) than with the role of learning to teach adolescent literature in teacher preparation. Consequently, studies of this nature were also excluded.

Hayn, Kaplan, and Nolen (2011) surveyed research in adolescent literature over a ten-year period, 2000–2010. Further reference to their findings is found in chapter 1 of this text. Equally limited in number (possibly due to the added search term "teacher education"), studies selected for discussion here offer some significant insights and suggest many potential points of departure for future research and teaching.

Nugent (1983) draws attention to whether "pedagogy for" or "study of" adolescent literature was the focus of courses for teachers in universities and colleges following a national survey conducted by Abrahamson (1981). The distinction between whether courses for teachers deal primarily with *methods* of teaching adolescent literature or with the *study* of adolescent literature is an important one for teacher educators, as decisions on this issue will inevitably influence the nature of the entire course. While concluding that not much time in classes appeared to have been spent studying adolescent literature as literature, many of the assignments did require students to write short critical or analytical papers. "Thus, although not overtly stated, these courses require literary analysis skills" (p. 108). Nugent expressed disappointment with the apparent lack of attention to studying adolescent literature, posing questions that could well have been asked by advocates of YAL today:

> What happened to the *study* of adolescent literature in the course content? Where is any indication in this survey that adolescent literature is viewed as literature? No responses suggested that author's style, literary techniques, or criticism were included within this course. My original disappointment in this survey stems from seeing this as a weakness in adolescent literature courses. If we as teachers view this literature as worthwhile, why do we avoid studying it as literature? (p. 108)

Nugent's questions still have implications for teacher education today. Consider, how are beginning teachers being introduced to thinking about YAL as "literature"? How are experienced teachers being supported in their professional learning and development of programs for adolescents in contemporary classrooms?

Opportunities for preservice teachers to familiarize themselves with a wide range of Canadian authors of young adult literature were the focus of a course described by McQuirter Scott (2004). McQuirter Scott's course assisted junior/intermediate (grades 4–10 in Ontario) preservice teachers in increasing their awareness of Canadian authors of YAL. Course assignments on Canadian authors were found to greatly enhance the preservice teachers' knowledge of young adult literature, and an emphasis on relationships among the novels read in presentations and culminating assignments (e.g., an author study comparing writers' techniques across novels studied; a thematic study identifying a key theme in the novels; or a cross-curricular study linking components of the novels with other content areas such as social studies, science, or the arts) also addressed relevant pedagogical content. After graduating, preservice teachers reported that coursework they had completed (e.g., many novels read and written papers or creative, collaborative presentations) was valuable when purchasing resources for their classrooms.

A national U.S. survey of the use of multicultural young adult literature in university courses (Gill, 2000) examined professors' responses to questions about the number of novels used in courses, the gender and race of the authors, and questions utilizing a four-point Likert scale exploring attitudes about the importance and relevance of multicultural literature. Course syllabi used in methods courses were also collected in order to identify the novels and authors being taught and to see if they fit into a broad definition of "multicultural" literature. Findings indicated that the professors were allowing students to self-select texts (thus allowing for more reader flexibility and encouraging the exploration of more types of YA novels) and were trying to balance authors chosen by gender. Many minority writers were included in assigned course readings, and newer YA novels were selected alongside older titles. The concept of multicultural literature was seen as valued, but respondents agreed that it is "undervalued and overlooked in teacher preparation" (p. 50). In conclusion, Gill raises a very interesting point about the "dearth" of non-American writers in the course readings and poses a significant question (especially relevant if professors believed, as they said they did, that multicultural literature is often too narrowly defined by race): Why are more cultures originating beyond the United States not included in course content?

Complex challenges associated with encouraging *all* teachers to consider themselves teachers of literacy seem to be particularly characteristic in teachers of adolescents, and "literature for the content areas" was highlighted in one paper documenting a university's attempts to provide a course that encourages teacher candidates from all content areas to become active teachers of reading (Carroll, Froelich, & Steadman, 2009). Designed to acquaint preservice teachers with the structures, strategies, and approaches to teaching reading in the content areas, this course involves both pedagogy and explorations of literature selections. Ongoing development and updating of course syllabi, teacher candidates' reactions to the changes, and future directions for research and teaching clearly indicated the successful integration of pedagogy and literature in this multisemester program.

Reports of a general decline in the reading skills of young adults reflected in assessment data from 1992 to 2003 (National Center for Education & Statistics, 2005; National Endowment for the Arts, 2004) prompted Stotsky (2010) to conduct a survey of more than four hundred English teachers in grades 9, 10, and 11 in public schools across the United States in order to discern (a) what literature teachers in standard and honors courses are assigning and (b) the characteristics of literary study in secondary English classrooms.

Stotsky suggests a potential source of this decline to be the level of difficulty of the texts that students are currently reading and makes direct links to the prevalence of YAL titles in this regard. For example, findings in a report from Renaissance Learning (2009) stated, "The Harry Potter series and other contemporary young adult fantasy series (by Stephenie Meyer in particular) are among the most widely read books by secondary school students." (A table of "Top 40 Titles" in the 2009 Accelerated Reader Database from Renaissance Learning does indeed show ten of the top sixteen most frequently read books by students in grades 9–12 to be contemporary young adult fantasies.) Stotsky's critique of books students were found to be reading therefore included their being of middle school levels of difficulty in terms of vocabulary and sentence structure, and the listing of very few nonfiction titles, arguing that

> the content of what students choose to read raises concerns about the quality and rigor of the curriculum in our public schools. It does not seem that the challenges and pleasures of reading mature works are being cultivated by the school curriculum. Nor are advanced reading skills being developed. (p. 10)

Stotsky's findings resulted in recommendations across three specific areas: K–12 curriculum and standards policies; state assessments in language arts; and undergraduate and professional preparation of prospective English teachers. For example, a more challenging language arts curriculum was recommended to meet the needs of those students in the "middle third" of academic performance in grades 7–12—in other words, those neither in the top nor the bottom third of their grade-level peers; a call for more literature and reading standards at high school levels; and a call for common assessments such as those used in high schools in British Columbia (an exit test) and Massachusetts (grade 10 tests), which were deemed "exemplary" (p. 4). It was also recommended that programs of English and reading teacher preparation should be required to emphasize both how to do and how to teach the analytical reading with assigned texts.

Arguments for and against teaching "the canon" are not exactly a new debate. More than five decades ago, Rosenblatt (1956), "the pioneer of English curriculum reform" (Nicol, 2008), suggested:

> No particular type of reading is being urged here as the panacea. There is no formula: not contemporary literature as against literature of the past, nor minor as against major works, nor even syntactically simpler as against more

> demanding works. Rather we need to be flexible, we need to understand where our pupils are in relation to books, and we need a sufficient command of books to see their potentialities in the developmental process. Our main responsibility is to help the student find the right book for growth. (p. 71)

It is, however, essential to keep in mind that the world in which we live and teach is constantly changing, and these changes— technological innovations, greater access to information and multimedia, emerging genres of literature, and increasingly diverse student and teacher populations (Nicol, 2008)—will inevitably influence learning and teaching today and into the future.

Other perspectives on learning and teaching with adolescent literature address important issues related to teacher education, including calls for teachers to acquire a substantive knowledge of quality adolescent literature and the ability to teach it successfully (proficient reading skills *and* appreciation/analytical skills). Titles traditionally acknowledged as the canon are often included as adolescent literature (Bach, 2009; Hazlett, 2009), and we need to recognize professional learning opportunities for teachers to read and discuss titles from the increasingly available body of quality young adult literature (Kaplan, 2009).

Nicol (2008) suggests that multiple issues related to the selection of literature for the high school English curriculum provide insights into the wisdom of cautiously questioning the canon. Nicol's informative and well-crafted argument both highlights calls for change (e.g., Greenbaum, 1994) and provides a rationale for caution (i.e., careful consideration of *why* class texts should change, ensuring that reasons are pedagogically sound in terms of students' future reading *and* their academic careers). A blending of texts (from both the canon and more divergent sources) that may "best suit the diverse reading interests and pedagogical concerns that exist in our English classrooms" (p. 27) is recommended. Furthermore, Nicol emphasizes that the choice of novel becomes far less important than how it is taught, citing successful examples of classroom practice where modern, innovative ways were found to work with titles from the canon, as well as with more recent literature selections.

Defenders of teaching the classics challenge YAL as not as rigorous or as less worthy of literary merit compared to works drawn from the canon (Jago, 2004). Bickmore (2008) counters, "Choosing YA literature does not have to mean providing a text of inferior quality, but it does mean that more of us should explain the craftsmanship in these novels" (p. 77), and Stephens (2007) argues that it is unfortunate that a book's literary value be judged solely on the age of its audience. Stephens points out that a careful scan of the canon results in numerous books featuring adolescent protagonists and quotes Robert Cormier from an interview with Carroll (2001): "I write to affect people. Everything is to affect the reader." Stephens (2007) offers the following conclusion:

> And that's what a quality Young Adult novel does. It takes its readers, youth and adult alike, to a place where adolescence lives on, a place where that journey toward identity continues to happen. (p. 41)

The purpose of a study conducted by Claiborne (2004) was to discover as much as possible about high school English teachers' knowledge, attitudes, and use of YAL in the classroom. YA titles being used were examined, along with teachers' opinions of using YAL in their classroom. In addition, this study looked at whether or not teachers belonged to certain professional organizations, namely the National Council of Teachers of English (NCTE) and the Assembly on Literature for Adolescents (ALAN). A survey was mailed to high school English teachers in twelve different schools (a total of 138 teachers were contacted, and 93 returned questionnaires, for a 67 percent response rate). Findings in the data indicated very little consistency in how departments promote use of YAL, and teachers' reasons for *not* using it varied widely. Of those surveyed, 73 percent did not use YAL, citing a wide variety of reasons, including the use of "classics" of YAL instead. Respondents did have specific knowledge of YAL and indicated that they have read more contemporary selections themselves. The study also revealed that most of the ninety-three respondents did not belong to one of the two professional affiliations that promote uses of YAL: thirty-eight belonged to NCTE and one to ALAN. Claiborne's study warrants replication in order to compare findings in light of the gradually elevated profile of YAL today.

SUMMARY

Returning to the questions, "Where are the voices of preservice teacher educators and preservice teachers? What have we learned about their strengths, capabilities, and needs?" it appears we haven't learned very much. Rather, the studies discussed fall into three categories, indicating that (1) incidences of research into adolescent literature remain limited (e.g., Hayn, Kaplan, & Nolen, 2011); (2) studies that examine preservice teacher education still grapple with the issues of "pedagogy for" or "study of" adolescent literature (e.g., Nugent, 1983; McQuirter Scott, 2004; Gill, 2000); and (3) other studies merge examinations of research and practice for teacher preparation and ongoing professional learning (e.g., Carroll, Froelich, & Steadman, 2009; Stotsky, 2010; Nicol, 2008; and Claiborne, 2004). Furthermore, the voices of teacher educators (and teachers) are not prolific in the literature, and all the studies cited indicate that more research is needed to inform pedagogy for teacher education and instructional practices for contemporary classrooms.

A review of eleven doctoral dissertations completed in 2008–2009 (Kaplan, 2010) further highlights the lack of academic papers on young adult works, despite the plethora of young adult novels in the last fifty years and the abundance of teachers and scholars interested in research in this area. Kaplan emphasizes the quality and substance of those that do exist and comments on the depth and understanding of these studies in "revealing how the study of books for young adults—works designed to appeal to adolescents—contributes to developing lifelong readers, critical thinkers, and book lovers everywhere" (p. 54). While studies cited in Kaplan's paper do not specifically relate to the focus topic of this chapter, there is an implicitly direct link to literacy teacher education:

> Curious as this may be, young adult literature scholars, though few in number, do stand alone for their unique perspective that recognizes the critical element in all good instruction—the ability to persuade teenagers to see the world through different eyes. What these dissertations have in common is their concentration on the remarkable insight that literature intended for young adults brings to the conversation about what matters most to young people. (p. 54)

Initial teacher education and ongoing professional learning that promote teachers' knowledge and understanding of YAL can inform and enhance learning, teaching, and research-based practices in contemporary classroom instruction for adolescents, and may even foster a greater presence of teachers' voices in the research literature in the future.

CONCLUSIONS

Kaplan (2010) notes that scholarly research papers on topics related to young adult literature are somewhat limited—and research specific to literacy teacher education and young adult literature is even more difficult to locate. We currently know very little about what constitutes an effective teacher preparation program for teaching YAL in grades 5–12.

Many informative resources published in the last few years address adolescent *literacy*, but they do not necessarily address learning and teaching with young adult literature, or assist with integrating selected YAL titles into students' learning experiences. However, the availability of resources both teacher educators and teachers can draw upon to learn more about research and practice in this area is slowly increasing; resources are often in the form of doctoral theses and other publications (e.g., journal articles or online sources and resources) that are made available through professional affiliations like ALAN (www.alan-ya.org). Initial teacher education and ongoing professional learning must be informed and enhanced by knowledge of and access to the resources available.

Recent works (Groenke & Scherff, 2010; Lesesne, 2010) address the claims that YAL selections are inferior to the classics, making compelling arguments supported by research and practice that this is not the case. The influence of this claim will be less pervasive as teachers become more aware of the depth, scope, and complexity of quality YA novels, many of which are equally capable of withstanding rigorous literary analysis as anything from the canon. If reading is truly about thinking, we must continue to defuse the either/or argument and focus on developing informed approaches to instruction, in which teachers and students select from the wide range of adolescent literature available (i.e., *both* classics and YAL) in order to meet instructional purposes at hand.

To truly know from the inside out the titles that meet their students' needs and interests, teachers must also be readers who habitually read selections designed for their students. In this way, teachers gain insider perspectives that enhance and extend their abilities to build vital interpersonal bridges in teaching, when lively and informed conversations about books are made both possible and authentic. Research-based classroom practice that engages even the most reluctant readers is supported by wide reading of research and professional literature.

No discussion of reading and adolescents today would be complete without some mention of technology and the redefining of literacy to include multiple texts and different ways of accessing those texts. In an era of multimedia, computers, SMART Boards, iPads, iPods, e-readers, and numerous other electronic devices, students' access to reading and literature include many modes in addition to print. Bird and Giles (2010) suggest,

> It is a rare sight to see a teenager without some sort of technology—text messaging, ear buds attached to an iPod, and laptops in the backpack are all part of the typical teenaged life. . . . Yet even as technology changes our perceptions and definitions of "books," students will still read, and books will still be written and published in some form. (p. 47)

Literacy teacher education for contemporary classrooms must also include coursework to prepare teachers to effectively integrate technology into instruction in order to support students' abilities to make text-to-world connections, critical thinking about that world, and multimodality (Deringer, 2003; Hill, 2003; Leu, Castek, Henry, Coiro, & McMullan, 2004; Philion, 2009; Schieble, 2009).

RECOMMENDATIONS FOR FURTHER RESEARCH

Conclusions suggest further research in three significant areas: (1) studies to raise the profile of YAL in literacy teacher education; (2) access opportunities for "knowledge mobilization" projects that assist and inform the field; and (3) research studies that enable us to better understand that how young people read is radically changing.

We still know very little about the profile of YAL in literacy teacher education, and therefore more research in this area is recommended. For example, how are the complexities of adolescent literature being addressed in preservice teacher education? How is the case being made for teachers' essential knowledge of current literature, and their abilities to select texts relevant to adolescents in contemporary classrooms? How are teacher educators promoting understanding of the need for critical, evaluative, and thoughtful selection of a wide range of reading choices? At the intersection of their personal and academic lives, how are preservice teachers being encouraged to see themselves as readers—models of proficient, effective reading—and teachers who value and make time for reading alongside their adolescent students *and* in their own lives? In-depth investigation of questions of this nature will better inform the work of teacher educators and support increased integration of the growing body of YAL into teacher education settings.

A multitude of uses of and applications for technology are second nature to our adolescent students and, increasingly, teacher candidates in faculties of education (most of whom these days would all consider themselves digital natives). Researchers and practitioners can integrate available technology into their work and improve knowledge mobilization. One such example is the Knowledge Network for Applied Education Research (KNAER), recently set up as a partnership between the Universities of Toronto and Western Ontario in Ontario, Canada, and supported and funded by the Ministry of Education. The intent is to act as a "knowledge broker" in disseminating results of applied educational research and making results more accessible to educators, researchers, and policymakers (http://www.knaer-recrae.ca).

Nontraditional research-related products (e.g., a wide range of print, audio and visual products, events, learning and teaching materials) all offer different ways to get the findings and implications of current research into the hands of school boards, principals, teachers, parents, students, and the general public. Therefore, the potential for generating more knowledge about the quality adolescent literature titles available and the rationale for using these in classroom instruction (as well as for independent reading) is exponential. By utilizing approaches to disseminating research that embrace technology, future research studies in teacher education and YAL have the potential to reach a much wider audience and facilitate the ongoing development of research-informed classroom practices in the field—locally, nationally, and internationally.

Literacy today is redefined, and adolescent students are on the cutting edge of a great deal of change and adaptation, specifically in terms of new forms of the construction of meaning and communication. More research is needed that helps teachers better understand increased uses of technology in students' everyday lives—and to find innovative ways of integrating technology into enhanced classroom practices.

More research into *how* young people are reading these days as well as *what* they are reading will inform the field and enable educators to keep current with the rapid pace of change related to technology and YAL. Ongoing research must also address the increasingly disparate literacy lives of students and their teachers and ways to tap into the potential for "bridging the new literacies with the old in ways that will gradually transform how youth express ideas and learn in schools" (O'Brien & Scharber, 2008).

If teachers are indeed to "touch the future," research in literacy teacher education must investigate approaches to teacher preparation that explore YAL, the successful integration of technology into adolescent literacy instruction, and innovative ways of more effectively sharing findings.

REFERENCES

Abrahamson, R. (1981). How adolescent literature is taught in American colleges and universities: A national survey. *English Education, 13*(4), 224–229.

Allington, R. L. (2001). *What really matters for struggling readers: Designing research-based initiatives*. New York: Longman.

Alvermann, D. E., Hinchman, K., Moore, D. W., Phelps, S., & Waff, D. (1998). *Reconceptualizing the literacies in adolescents' lives*. Mahwah, NJ: Erlbaum.

Alvermann, D. E., & Moore, D. W. (1991). Secondary schools. In R. Barr, M. Kamil, P. B. Mosenthal, & P. D. Pearson (Eds.), *Handbook of reading research* (Vol. 2, pp. 951–983). New York: Longman.

Anders, P. L. (2008). Multiple dimensions of adolescent literacy teacher education. In K. Hinchman & H. Sheridan-Thomas (Eds.), *Best practices in adolescent teacher education*. New York: Guilford Press.

Anders, P. L., Hoffman, J., & Duffy, G. (2000). Teaching teachers to teach reading: Paradigm shifts, persistent problems, and challenges. In M. Kamil, P. B. Mosenthal, P. D. Pearson, & R. Barr (Eds.), *Handbook of reading research* (Vol. 3, pp. 719–742). Mahwah, NJ: Erlbaum.

Bach, J. (2009). *Using classic young adult novels in new ways*. Paper presented at the National Council of Teachers of English, Philadelphia, PA.

Bainbridge, J., & Macy, L. (2008). Student teachers link teacher education to perceptions of preparedness for literacy teaching. *Teacher Education Quarterly, 35*(2), 65–83.

Bean, T. W., & Harper, H. J. (2004). Teacher education and adolescent literacy. In T. L. Jetton & J. A. Dole (Eds.), *Adolescent literacy research and practice* (pp. 392–411). New York: Guilford Press.

Bickmore, S. T. (2008). It is inexcusable to deny *Inexcusable* a place in the classroom. *The ALAN Review, 35*(2), 75–83.

Bird, S., & Giles, V. M. (2010). They go together—teenagers, technology, and reading. *Voices from the Middle, 17*(3), 47–48.

Brozo, W. G., Walter, P., & Placker, T. (2002). "I know the difference between a real man and a TV man": A critical exploration of violence and masculinity through literature in a junior high school in the 'hood. *Journal of Adolescent & Adult Literacy, 45*, 530–538.

Carroll, P. (2001). YA authors' insights about the art of writing. *English Journal, 90*, 104–109.

Carroll, P., Froelich, K., & Steadman, S. (2009). *Reading literature in every content area? Encouraging all teachers to be literacy teachers*. Paper presented at the National Council of Teachers of English, Philadelphia, PA.

Carter, J. B. (Ed.). (2007). *Building literacy connections with graphic novels: Page by page, panel by panel*. Urbana, IL: National Council of Teachers of English.

Cassidy, J., Garrett, S., & Barrera, E. (2006). What's hot in adolescent literacy 1997–2006. *Journal of Adolescent & Adult Literacy, 50*(1), 30–36.

Cassidy, J., Ortlieb, E., & Shettel, J. (2011). What's hot for 2011: Survey reveals a focus beyond primary grades. *Reading Today, 1*, 6–8.

Cassidy, J., Valadez, C., Garrett, S., & Barrera, E. (2010). Adolescent and adult literacy: What's hot, what's not. *Journal of Adolescent & Adult Literacy, 53*(6), 448–456.

Christenbury, L., Bomer, R., & Smagorinsky, P. (2009). *Handbook of adolescent literacy research*. New York: Guilford Press.

Claiborne, J. L. (2004). *A survey of high school English teachers to determine their knowledge, use, and attitude related to young adult literature in the classroom*. Unpublished doctoral dissertation, University of Tennessee, Knoxville.

DeCourcy, D., Fairchild, L., & Follett, R. (2007). *Teaching* Romeo and Juliet: *A differentiated approach*. Urbana, IL: National Council of Teachers of English.

Deringer, M. L. (2003). Visual responses to YAL that encourage higher-level thinking. *Voices from the Middle, 10*(4), 11–12.

Flores-Gonzalez, N. (2002). *School kids/street kids: Identity development in Latino students*. New York: Teachers College Press.

Galda, L., & Graves, M. (2007). *Reading and responding in the middle grades*. Boston: Allyn & Bacon (Pearson).

Gallagher, K. (2004). *Deeper reading: Comprehending challenging texts, 4–12*. Portland, ME: Stenhouse.

Gallagher, K. (2009). *Readicide: How schools are killing reading and what you can do about it*. Portland, ME: Stenhouse.

Gill, D. (2000). A national survey of the use of multicultural young adult literature in university courses. *The ALAN Review, 27*(2), 48–50.

Greenbaum, V. (1994). Expanding the canon: Shaping inclusive reading lists. *English Journal, 83*(8), 36–39.

Groenke, S. L., & Scherff, L. (2010). *Teaching YA lit through differentiated instruction*. Urbana, IL: National Council of Teachers of English.

Grossman, P. (2001). Research on the teaching of literature: Finding a place. In V. Richardson (Ed.), *Handbook of research on teaching* (4th ed., pp. 416–432). Washington, DC: American Educational Research Association.

Harste, J. C. (2010). Multimodality. In P. Albers & J. Sanders (Eds.), *Literacies, the arts, and multimodality*. Urbana, IL: National Council of Teachers of English.

Hayn, J., Kaplan, J. S., & Nolen, A. (2011). Young adult literature research in the twenty-first century. *Theory into Practice, 50*(3), 176–181.

Hazlett, L. A. (2009). *Once and future classics: YA literature's forgotten classics.* Paper presented at the National Council of Teachers of English Annual Convention, Philadelphia, PA.

Hill, J. (2003). *An interactive study of teachers' online discussions of young adult literature.* Unpublished doctoral dissertation, Kent State University, Ohio.

Hill Campbell, K. (2007). *Less is more: Teaching literature with short texts, grades 6–12.* Portland, ME: Stenhouse.

Jago, C. (2004). *Classics in the classroom: Designing accessible literature lessons.* Portsmouth, NH: Heinemann.

Jobe, R. (1989). Children's literature and teacher education in Canada. *Early Child Development and Care, 48,* 59–66.

Kaplan, J. (2009). *The history of the genre: Once and future classics.* Paper presented at the National Council of Teachers of English Annual Convention, Philadelphia, PA.

Kaplan, J. (2010). Doctoral dissertations (2008–2009): A review of research on young adult literature. *The ALAN Review, 37*(2), 54–58.

Kavanaugh, D. (2010). Let's stop killing reading. *Reading Today, 27*(6), 23.

Koss, M. D., & Teale, W. H. (2009). What's happening in YA literature? Trends in books for adolescents. *Journal of Adolescent & Adult Literacy, 52*(7), 563–572.

Lankshear, C., & Bigum, C. (1999). Literacies and new technologies in school settings. *Pedagogy, Culture, & Society, 7*(3), 445–465.

Lankshear, C., & Knobel, M. (2003). *New literacies: Changing knowledge and classroom learning.* Maidenhead, UK: Open University Press.

Lesesne, T. S. (2010). *Reading ladders: Leading students from where they are to where we'd like them to be.* Portsmouth, NH: Heinemann.

Leu, D. J., Castek, J., Henry, L. A., Coiro, J., & McMullan, M. (2004). The lessons that children teach us: Integrating children's literature and the new literacies of the Internet. *Reading Teacher, 57*(5), 496–503.

McQuirter Scott, R. (2004). Canadian author study: Preservice teachers engage in assignments to promote awareness of Canadian young adult literature. *Brock Education, 13*(2), 50–55.

National Center for Education & Statistics. (2005). *National assessment of adult literacy.* Washington, DC: U.S. Department of Education.

National Endowment for the Arts. (2004). *Reading at risk: A survey of literary reading in America.* Washington, DC: U.S. Department of Education.

Nicol, J. C. (2008). Questioning the canon: Issues surrounding the selection of literature for the high school English curriculum. *English Quarterly, 38*(2/3), 22–28.

Nugent, S. M. (1983). Adolescent literature: Toward a healthy balance. *English Education, 15*(2), 107–108.

O'Brien, D., & Scharber, C. (2008). Digital literacies go to school: Potholes and possibilities. *Journal of Adolescent & Adult Literacy, 52*(1), 66–68.

Peterson, S., & Swartz, L. (2008). *Good books matter: How to choose and use children's literature to help students grow as readers.* Markham, ON: Pembroke.

Philion, T. (2009). The age of ________? Using young adult literature to make sense of the contemporary world. *Young Adult Library Services (YALS), 7*(4), 46–49.

Renaissance Learning. (2009). *What kids are reading: The book-reading habits of students in American schools*. Wisconsin Rapids, WI: Renaissance Learning.

Reno, J. (2008). Generation R (R is for reader). *Newsweek*. Retrieved January 16, 2011, from http://www.newsweek.com/2008/05//13/generation-r-r-is-for-reader.html

Risko, V. J., Cummins Roller, C., Bean, R., Block, C., & Anders, P. L. (2007). *A critical review of the research on teacher preparation for reading instruction*. Newark, DE: International Reading Association.

Rosenblatt, L. M. (1956). The acid test for literature teaching. *English Journal, 45*(2), 66–74.

Sanford, K. (2002). Popular media and school literacies: Adolescent expressions. In R. Hammett & B. Barrell (Eds.), *Digital expressions: Media literacy and English language arts*. Calgary, AB: Detselig Enterprises.

Schieble, M. B. (2009). *Exploring multimodality, literacy, and learning with young adult fiction*. Unpublished doctoral dissertation, University of Wisconsin, Madison.

Smith, M., & Wilhelm, J. (2006). *Going with the flow: How to engage boys (and girls) in their literacy learning*. Portsmouth, NH: Heinemann.

Stephens, J. (2007). Young adult: A book by any other name . . . Defining the genre. *The ALAN Review, 35*(1), 34–42.

Stotsky, S. (2010). *Literary study in grades 9, 10, and 11: A national survey*. Boston: Association of Literary Scholars, Critics, and Writers.

Unrau, N. (2008). *Content area reading and writing: Fostering literacies in middle and high school cultures* (2nd ed.). Upper Saddle River, NJ: Pearson Merrill Prentice Hall.

Wilhelm, J. (2008). *"You gotta BE the book": Teaching engaged and reflective reading with adolescents*. New York: Teachers College Press.

Wood, K. D., & Blanton, W. E. (2009). *Literacy instruction for adolescents: Research-based practice*. New York: Guilford Press.

Worthy, J. (1998). "On every page someone gets killed!": Book conversations you don't hear in school. *Journal of Adolescent & Adult Literacy, 41*, 508–517.

Section II

WHERE IS YAL NOW?

4

Identifying Obstacles and Garnering Support

Young Adult Literature in the English Language Arts Classroom

Kelly Byrne Bull

Reading about the obstacles educators face when they try to add young adult literature (YAL) to their curriculum might be viewed as a cautionary tale. It is important to know what might stand in our way when we try to bring YAL into our students' classroom experiences. In fact, many of us have firsthand experience of stumbling over such obstacles on our path toward bringing great contemporary YAL to our adolescent readers. Avoiding such bumps in the road may not be possible, but it can certainly be instructional to us as we refuse to accept the status quo. Part of this chapter addresses those obstacles so that we can anticipate them. But that is not enough.

Simply knowing that issues or policies might stand in our way is insufficient. Knowing what is available to us as we try to add YAL to our curriculum is essential. For this reason, a large part of this chapter is devoted to sharing resources available to classroom teachers. Reading about such supports might be viewed as a celebratory tale, illustrating what is available to help teachers succeed in bringing YA books into their teaching. Knowing what professional resources and research are available to support our efforts is key. Getting quality YAL into our classrooms and into the hands of our adolescent readers is a worthy goal.

OBSTACLES

Maintaining the Tradition of the Classics

Traditional classics continue to fill the shelves of secondary school English departments across the country, making the most commonly taught texts those from the canon. Stallworth, Gibbons, and Fauber's 2006 survey found the following canonical works as the most frequently taught texts in high school English classes:

Harper Lee, *To Kill a Mockingbird*
F. Scott Fitzgerald, *The Great Gatsby*
Nathaniel Hawthorne, *The Scarlet Letter*
William Shakespeare, *Romeo and Juliet*
William Shakespeare, *Julius Caesar*
Arthur Miller, *The Crucible*
William Shakespeare, *Macbeth*
Mark Twain, *The Adventures of Huckleberry Finn*
George Orwell, *Animal Farm*
John Knowles, *A Separate Peace*

These classics have been taught to several generations of students, often because there are some English language arts teachers and supervisors who have a narrow view of what quality literature is: the time-tested canon of classics. Such teachers believe exposing adolescents to classic works will enable them to pass down this important cultural heritage. This belief has continued to lead many teachers and supervisors in their "advocacy for selecting texts in high school English courses . . . grounded in preserving the canon" (Tatum, 2008, p. 83). Tatum, a professional developer for English language arts curricula in high schools, laments that students are "grossly disengaged as teachers continue to teach texts emanating from a tradition of curriculum, an age-old tradition that has not evolved to pay attention to students' modern-day contexts" (p. 83).

Tatum (2008) asserts that students in middle and high school classrooms are *not* reading texts that they find meaningful, echoing that the "classics only" push results in putting obstacles in the way of adding young adult literature to the English language arts classroom. Tatum suggests using young adult literature to engage adolescents with questions that matter to them, using texts that address students' multiple identities. "Rarely are discussions involving text selection for today's adolescents anchored by consideration for their adolescent, ethnic, gender, and linguistic identities. The advocacy for selecting texts in high school English courses is often grounded in preserving the canon" (p. 83). When our students do not have opportunities to hear their voices, concerns, and dreams in the literature they are reading, they become disengaged. Our most avid readers will look beyond the four walls of the school to find meaningful texts; they will read in spite of school, not because of it. Our more reluctant readers will simply not read. In Ivey and Broaddus's (2001) *Just Plain Reading: A Survey of What Makes Students Want to Read in Middle School Classrooms,* adolescents ranked their classrooms as one of the *least likely places* to find the materials they want to read. Long-time advocate for young adult literature Don Gallo (2001) expands on this by asserting that public education in the United States teaches children "how to read in the early grades and then forces them, during their teenage years, to read literary works that most of them dislike so much that they have no desire to continue to read into their adulthood" (p. 39).

High-Stakes Testing and Scripted Curriculum

Pressure to teach the classics is not the only obstacle interfering with teachers' efforts to incorporate YAL into their classrooms. Our current climate of high-stakes testing also impedes teachers' abilities to add new YA titles to their teaching. No Child Left Behind (NCLB) has inadvertently created a chilly climate for such curricular enrichment. In response to NCLB, all states require tests to determine whether each public school is meeting Adequate Yearly Progress (AYP). Many states now also require students to pass high school exit exams before granting students diplomas. Thus, these tests have become high-stakes events for both schools and the students enrolled; accreditation and funding are linked to a school's ability to meet AYP, and the high school diploma is linked to a student's ability to pass the exit exams. In attempts to ensure that students are prepared for these state tests, many school systems have instituted additional periodic assessments that are given every few months.

Such practices, intended to raise reading scores, can actually kill students' love for reading, says Kelly Gallagher (2009), a veteran English teacher, language arts coordinator, and literacy consultant. This is what Gallagher calls *readicide.* According to Gallagher, readicide is "the systematic killing of the love of reading, often exacerbated by the inane, mind-numbing practices found in schools" (p. 2). Schools have become the coconspirators in the decline of reading for several reasons, according to Gallagher. Two of the reasons that are central to this discussion include schools acting as though they "value the development of test-takers more than the development of readers," and schools "limiting authentic reading experiences" (Gallagher, 2009, p. 5). Teachers and students alike know that instructional time is spent on what is valued, and currently our instructional time is being spent on test preparation, not on literature instruction.

Despite large amounts of instructional time spent on preparing students for the high-stakes tests, students in the United States continue to lag behind in reading proficiency and are often reluctant readers (Gallagher, 2009). The assessment data post-NCLB provides evidence of this. Biancarosa and Snow, in their 2006 report, "Reading Next—A Vision for

Action and Research in Middle and High School Literacy," document the following findings:

- Only 70 percent of high school students graduate on time with a regular diploma, and fewer than 60 percent of African American and Latino students do so (Greene & Winters, 2005).
- Approximately 32 percent of high school graduates are not ready for college-level English composition courses.
- Compared to ten years ago, significantly fewer adults demonstrate the skills necessary to perform complex and challenging literacy activities (National Center for Education Statistics, 2005).

Published just one year later, the National Endowment for the Arts produced similarly staggering findings in its "To Read or Not to Read: A Question of National Consequence" (2007):

- Fifteen- to twenty-four-year-olds spend only seven to ten minutes per day on voluntary reading—about 60 percent less time than the average American. By contrast, fifteen- to twenty-four-year-olds spend 2 to 2.5 hours per day watching TV.
- Seventeen-year-olds' average reading scores began a slow downward trend in 1992. For more than thirty years, this age group has failed to sustain improvements in reading scores.
- Reading test scores for nine-year-olds—who show no declines in voluntary reading—are at an all-time high.
- Little more than one-third of high school seniors now read proficiently.

It is the discrepancy between the last two bulleted statements that raises a red flag for me. We know that adolescent literacy is often overlooked and underfunded by governing agencies; however, in those eight years of schooling, our students are missing out. Our students are missing out on opportunities to discover and develop their own reading interests and lifelong literacy habits because of the large amounts of instructional time used to prepare them for high-stakes tests. It is this tremendous amount of instructional time devoted to test preparation that leads to other skills and content being left behind in the English language arts classroom. Classroom teachers must decide whether there is enough time and space in an already-packed English language arts curriculum to add young adult literature.

Adhering to Scripted Curriculum

Scripted curriculum, an outcome of the current high-stakes testing climate, is an obstacle for teachers who wish to add young adult literature to their instruction. Often scripted curriculum is implemented in order to meet post-NCLB federal guidelines regarding comprehensive school reform programs (Demko & Hedrick, 2010). Linking funding to reform has been an effective way to prompt school systems to purchase "scientifically based" reading programs for reading instruction. According to Dutro (2010), policies are "motivated by the economic realities of schooling, and states and districts quickly adopted programs from a short list of commercial literacy curricula known to meet the federal requirements" (p. 262).

Many such programs require tightly scripted compliance, requiring teachers to literally read from a script and follow a daily pacing guide (Lehr, 2010). As such, scripted curriculum leaves little room for the addition of new texts. Concern over how to add a new text or try out a new approach is reflected in the current research literature as well. Dickson and Costigan's 2011 article, "Emerging Practice for New Teachers: Creating Possibilities for 'Aesthetic' Readings," discusses how "trying out new approaches can mean more than overcoming the fear that a lesson might not go well; it also may involve the risk that a teacher will be 'discovered' deviating from what is 'prescribed' and somehow be reprimanded or punished" (p. 167). These preservice teachers considered how to engage adolescents in meaningful discussions surrounding relevant texts without being reprimanded by administrators. Such worries reflect a concern that Lehr (2010) refers to as backdoor censorship. Unlike direct challenges on books, backdoor censorship excludes books from the curriculum because they are not considered for adoption or inclusion in the first place.

Challenges and Censorship

Challenges and censorship are cited as concerns of teachers who would like to add YAL to their curriculum. Challenges, attempts to remove or restrict materials based on the objections of a person or group, take place in today's twenty-first-century schools, inside both the library and the classroom. Such challenges to YA books do make some English language arts teachers consider carefully whether or not to add YA books to their classroom instruction. Many teachers "fear the potential (real or imagined) problems when parents, colleagues, administrators, students, and the community disagree with the content of the literature curriculum," according to Stallworth, Gibbons, and Fauber (2006, p. 484). This represents self-censorship, according to Hill (2010), when a teacher's or librarian's fear that something "might" happen causes him or her to omit particular texts. What follows this fear is second-guessing, involving the removal, replacement, or restricting of readers' access to that book. Most worrying is that self-censorship means that teachers are not following an established review process. Cole (2009), in her book *Young Adult Literature in the 21st Century,* encourages teachers to be proactive in their choice of YAL. Cole states that teachers must understand what their school system already has in place regarding approved books and must become knowledgeable about their system's procedures for book selection and book challenges.

It is the challenges to teachers' book selections that can and sometimes do lead to the censoring of books. Censorship is the "suppression of ideas and information that certain persons—individuals, groups or government officials—find objectionable or dangerous," according to the American Library Association's Office of Intellectual Freedom (2011). Censors pressure schools, libraries, and teachers to suppress and remove information that they deem to be inappropriate for the public. In schools, censors are the groups or individuals who seek to limit students' access to books; this means that the censors believe their point of view is accurate and that other, conflicting points of view should be removed. Censorship violates the First Amendment, which protects our right to read, view, speak, and share information.

Censorship is certainly a topic that causes concern for citizens in the United States. In the last twenty years, there have been 10,415 censorship cases, violating citizens' rights to read, according to the ALA's Office of Intellectual Freedom (Hill, 2010). There are important issues at stake when censors take aim at the books English language arts teachers have selected for classroom use. Censorship violates our students' intellectual freedom, a concept central to our democratic society. Censorship questions the professionalism of teachers, casting doubt on a teacher's expertise to select texts that both align with curricular objectives and meet students' needs. Chris Crutcher, YA author and champion of readers' rights, perhaps said this best in a January 2010 e-mail conversation. When I asked him what advice he would give to teachers who want to add YA literature to their teaching but are overwhelmed by what they perceive to be obstacles in their way, Crutcher responded:

> I'd advise [teachers] to go ahead anyway. What they need to understand is that the censors are attacking them as directly, or even more directly, than they're attacking my book. These censors aren't teachers; they have none of the training or expertise of the professionals who are choosing books to add to their curriculum or their reading lists. They don't know the kids. They, for the most part, don't know child development. They know their rigid philosophies and what offends them personally.

It is a censorial spirit that prompts such attacks on both the professionalism of our teachers and the intellectual freedom of our students.

Avoiding Obstacles

Recognizing that teachers may experience obstacles when trying to add YAL to their English language arts curriculum is important. Some of these obstacles tend to be initiated by the powers-that-be within our school structures. These include maintaining the tradition of the classics, reacting to high-stakes testing, and instituting scripted curriculum. An obstacle that is typically initiated by parents is challenges to and censorship of books. However, being aware of what might stand between our students and the YAL we would have them read is simply a first step: identifying these obstacles can help us anticipate how we will confront them should they arise. Additionally, knowing what supports are available to us as we work to add YAL to our curriculum offers possibilities and potential. These supports are addressed in the remaining sections of this chapter.

SUPPORTS

Availability of High-Quality Young Adult Literature

For English language arts teachers seeking to add YAL to their curriculum, there is a wealth of high-quality contemporary literature available in multiple genres. Some of these genres include novels, short stories, poetry, graphic novels, and nonfiction. Many of these YA texts are increasingly being offered in electronic format, including audio books (CDs and Playaways), e-readers (Kindles, Nooks, and Pandigital novels), and e-reader applications for tablet computers (iPads and Galaxy tabs) and other mobile devices (Android). However, at present, most YA texts are purchased in traditional book format. In the last decade, adolescents have been one of the fastest-growing populations in the United States, and there has been a parallel "growth spurt in YAL and other reading materials targeted to teens, such as teen websites and magazines" (Koss & Teale, 2009, p. 563). With this increase in volume, educators are witnessing an increase in quality as well.

Teacher educators assert that it is the *quality* of YAL that will appeal to English language arts teachers who seek to add new titles to their teaching. Soter and Connors (2009) illustrate that current YAL is accessible and relevant, yet also has literary sophistication. They believe that YAL has "the kind of literary merit that canonical literature demonstrates" (p. 66), and they argue that YAL is stylistically complex and offers thoughtful social and political commentaries. Monseau and Salvner (2000) agree in the preface to their book, *Reading Their World: The Young Adult Novel in the Classroom*, asserting that "young adult novels have come of age and proven themselves to be literature of quality" (p. ix). High-quality literature that is accessible and relevant to adolescents' intellectual and emotional growth makes YAL appealing to today's educators.

As a measure of this literary quality, the Young Adult Library Services Association (YALSA) recognizes outstanding contributions in the field of

YAL annually. Honoring the best books for teen readers, the six literary awards established by YALSA include the Alex, Edwards, Morris, Nonfiction, Odyssey, and Printz awards. The Alex Awards are given annually to ten books written for adults that have special appeal to young adults. The Edwards Award honors an author and a specific work for significant and lasting contribution to writing for teens. The Morris Award honors a book written for young adults by a first-time, previously unpublished author. The YALSA Award for Excellence in Nonfiction honors the best nonfiction book for young adults. The Odyssey Award honors the producer of the best audiobook produced for children and/or young adults, available in English in the United States. The Printz Award honors excellence in literature written for young adults.

The YALSA website, www.yalsa.ala.org, is a source for helping teachers find quality and engaging YAL for their classrooms. This site is updated each January, announcing the award winners. This site also provides listings of award winners from past years, and it affords readers the opportunity to nominate favorite books. There are other booklists of interest to teachers, as well. These include "Amazing Audio Books for Young Adults," "Best Fiction for Young Adults," "Fabulous Films for Young Adults," "Great Graphic Novels for Young Adults," "Outstanding Books for the College Bound," "Popular Paperbacks for Young Adults," "Quick Picks for Reluctant Young Adult Readers," "Readers' Choice," and "Teens' Top Ten." To address the growing number of YA books published annually (more than two thousand titles per year in 2008), the American Library Association elected to more clearly define categories for recommended books. Before 2011, there was a Best Books for Young Adults category that included all genres. Today, discrete categories enable teachers to choose texts that better meet their curricular objectives and students' needs. For example, a teacher might consider including a nonfiction piece in the existing curriculum, and to do so, she could look directly to the Excellence in Nonfiction and Great Graphic Novels listings (yes—nonfiction in the form of a graphic novel!). This website provides teachers with a quick way to identify what currently published YAL has been recognized and recommended by professionals in the field.

Examining trends in currently published YAL, Koss and Teale's 2009 survey indicates overall trends, acknowledging some concerns about diversity and representation, but also identifying numerous titles that offer YA readers opportunities to explore different cultures, identities, and narrative structures. First, the YAL examined for this survey proved to be predominantly fiction, most often contemporary realistic fiction. Characters were mostly European American and the settings were in the United States. Although an increase in the instances of international settings and characters was observed, the characters were white and European. This is unfortunate because, as Stover (2001) aptly points out, exploring issues of identity and ethnicity across cultures is an important goal of quality literature programs. To learn about recent titles that explore cultural diversity, visit my Multicultural Young Adult Literature blog (multiculturalyaliterature.blogspot.com) and chapter 8 of this text, "Multicultural Literature: Finding the Balance." Second, Koss and Teale (2009) noted an increase in the incidence of LGBTQ (lesbian, gay, bisexual, transgender, queer/questioning) characters and characters with disabilities (for more LGBTQ texts, see chapter 7 of this text, "Out of the Closet and Into the Open"). Third, Koss and Teale noted authors' use of increasingly complex writing devices that were important parts of the narrative structure. These included flashbacks, flash-forwards, poetry, songs, and often the use of many of these devices within a single text. In all, the boom in YAL being published means more choices for teachers and their students. Making deliberate decisions to include YAL that is both inclusive of multiple ethnicities and identities and stylistically complex can ensure our students access to books that are both thoughtfully written and thought-provoking.

Availability of Professional Resources for Teaching YAL

To complement the boom in YAL currently being published, there are multiple and varied instructional resources and materials available to teachers who wish to add YAL to their curriculum. For busy classroom teachers, this is an important support because such resources provide ideas and strategies on how to fit quality YAL into classroom instruction. Print and electronic resources abound, inviting teachers to both consider methods and connect professionally with colleagues. Sometimes, knowing where to look and whom to contact can be a teacher's greatest ally in creating meaningful instructional materials and lessons. The resources described herein can be broadly classified as textbooks, trade books, professional journals, online resources, and professional organizations.

Many veteran teachers' first encounters with YAL took place in college classrooms when they were introduced to the field and *THE* textbook. Thankfully, more and more of the preservice teachers I work with have had firsthand experience reading YAL during their own high school years, not always as in-class readings but often as independent reading selections. In either case, the young adult literature textbook is a mainstay because it is complete, comprehensive, and correct. Textbooks on YAL provide literary, social, and historical perspectives and delineate multiple genres and corresponding criteria for choosing and evaluating YAL. Textbooks currently available represent both veteran voices (as evidenced in the authors' numerous revisions) and newer voices (in terms of book publications). Some of these include *Literature for Today's Young Adults* (ninth edition) by Nilsen and Donelson; *Using Young Adult Literature in the English Classroom* (fourth edition) by Bushman and Haas; *Young Adult Literature: Exploration, Evaluation, and Appreciation* (second edition) by Bucher and Hinton; *Young Adult Literature: From Romance to Realism* by Cart; *Literature and the Young Adult Reader* by Bond; and *Young Adult Literature in the 21st Century* by Cole. These comprehensive textbooks provide foundational information on the genre of YAL.

Trade books published by both professional organizations and independent presses offer teachers concrete strategies and methods on how to teach YAL in the English language arts classroom. Some trade books offer close analysis of specific YA authors such as the Scarecrow Studies in Young Adult Literature series, whose most recent publications include *Robin McKinley: Girl Reader, Woman Writer* (Perry, 2011), *John Marsden: Darkness, Shadow, and Light* (Moore, 2010), and *Donna Jo Napoli: Writing with Passion* (Crew, 2010). Another publisher, Christopher-Gordon, features ways to connect YAL with classics, offering Kaywell's most recent volumes of *Adolescent Literature as a Complement to the Classics* (2010). Other trade books offer methods for teaching specific works of particular authors, such as Heinemann's series on teaching the selected works of current YA authors, including Walter Dean Myers (Zitlow, 2007) and Chris Crutcher (Monseau & Hauschildt, 2008). Still other trade books published by professional organizations like the National Council of Teachers of English (NCTE) and the International Reading Association (IRA) detail ways in which English language arts teachers can engage their students with contemporary YAL by connecting theory with classroom practice. Some recent titles include *Teaching YA Lit through Differentiated Instruction* (Groenke & Scherff, 2010), *Building Literacy Connections with Graphic Novels: Page by Page, Panel by Panel* (Carter, 2007), and *YAL in the Classroom: Reading It, Teaching It, Loving It* (Elliott & Dupuis, 2001). Such trade books provide classroom teachers with concrete strategies and methods for incorporating YA titles into the curriculum.

Professional journals present the most recent research in the field of YAL and also supply educators with valuable ideas for selecting, teaching, and evaluating YAL. Such journals are peer-reviewed; articles submitted are monitored for accuracy and quality by knowledgeable professionals in the field. As such, professional journal articles are able to accurately reflect current research, trends, and strategies. Journals that regularly publish articles in the field of YAL include those by professional organizations such as NCTE, IRA, and ALA. NCTE publishes *English Journal* and *Voices from the Middle*. Both have columns devoted exclusively to YAL—"Off the Shelves" (in *EJ*) and "Books for Young Adolescents" (in *VM*)—and each journal also publishes full-length articles on YAL occasionally. NCTE's Assembly on Literature for Adolescents (ALAN) publishes *The ALAN Review* three times per year, focusing exclusively on issues, strategies, and trends in YAL. The International Reading Association (IRA) publishes the *Journal of Adolescent and Adult Literacy*, which has both a regular column that reviews books for adolescents and, at times, full-length articles about young adult literature. IRA also publishes *SIGNAL: The Journal of the International Reading Association's Special Interest Group Network on Adolescent Literature*, featuring articles exclusively on YAL. The American Library Association publishes *Booklist*, a journal that reviews books, media, and reference materials, and *School Library Journal* claims to be "the world's largest reviewer of books, multimedia, and technology for children and teens." Finally, *Voices of Youth Advocates* provides book reviews, booklists, and feature columns. Knowing that so many professional journals regularly feature articles and columns that contribute to the professional understandings and teaching of YAL is certainly a worthy support for teachers who seek to add YA books to their curriculum.

There are also valuable online resources available to assist teachers in choosing and using YAL for their classroom instruction. One is ReadWriteThink.org, a partnership between NCTE and IRA, which supplies materials for the English language arts classroom, including lesson plans, podcasts, calendar activities, interactive tools for students, reproducible worksheets, and links to journal articles and books. These resources are neatly divided by grade level and searchable by subject, so finding relevant YA-specific resources is easy. Other valuable resources are online booksellers like Amazon and Barnes & Noble, which offer helpful information for teachers, too. Providing professional book reviews (from well-regarded sources like *School Library Journal, Booklist, and Publishers Weekly*), "Search Inside" functions, and readability estimates for tens of thousands of in-print, out-of-print, and electronic books, online booksellers afford us valuable tools to use toward YA text selection. Another function that I have grown increasingly fond of is the "Customers Who Bought This Item Also Bought . . ." feature, because it often helps me find more books that are "read-alikes" or "next reads." A third online resource is the website TeenReads.com. Author interviews, reading lists, contests, question-of-the-month, weekly new YA releases, book clubs, and reading guides are just some of the incredibly helpful and informative resources on this site.

Two more online resources worth noting are the English Companion Ning and YAL blogs. The English Companion Ning (www.englishcompanion.ning.com) is a social network created by veteran English teacher and author Jim Burke and is described as "a place to ask questions and get help. A community dedicated to helping you enjoy your work. A café without walls or coffee: just friends." Here, there are literally tens of thousands of resources: English teachers interacting with one another, considering issues related to curriculum, instruction, and professional development. Professionals share their ideas and resources freely to improve the quality of instruction in English classrooms. Book clubs, webstitutes, forums, blogs, roundtables, and groups are available for teachers to join so that they can join in the professional conversation and collaboration, or they can read and view ongoing and past discussions. Specific to the teaching of YA literature are multiple groups (adolescent literature, teaching texts, grade-leveled teaching of English language arts), blogs (specific to literature), and book clubs (YA Lit, *Reading Ladders*). Within these specific groups, teachers can pose questions, share resources, and offer suggestions about the selection and teaching of YAL. In addition to English Companion Ning, there are dozens of top-notch blogs devoted exclusively to reviewing contemporary YAL. Reading YAL blogs provides teachers with access to an abundance of weekly reviews that give a synopsis of the plot and evaluate the style of each YA book being reviewed. Especially helpful and manageable with the online tool of a blog, is the ability to link to other books (next reads or read-alikes) and media (professionally written reviews, author websites, videos, contests, and give-aways). A few well-known YAL blogs include *Steph Su Reads* (stephsureads.blogspot.com), *PersnickitySnark* (www.persnicketysnark.com), and *Forever Young Adult* (www.foreveryoungadult.com). A favorite of mine is *Book Love* (kdkbooklove.blogspot.com), because it is hosted by one of my former students, Katie DeKoster, who started the blog as part of her course requirements for my YAL class. Katie's blog has grown and blossomed into this wonderful spot for reviewing YAL, posing teaching questions to her readers, and considering how to reach and teach adolescents. The "Follow" function on blogs enables English teachers to have easy access to updates posted on their favorite blogs simply by logging into their own blog account. In all, the blogosphere of YAL and the professional community of the EC Ning offer resources for the teaching and promotion of YAL.

Professional organizations for English language arts teachers—already mentioned throughout this chapter—provide some of the best professional development for both preservice and in-service teachers. Nationally, there are the National Council of Teachers of English (NCTE), the International Reading Association (IRA), Young Adult Services Library Association (YALSA), and Assembly on Literature for Adolescents (ALAN). Each hosts annual conventions and/or workshops where colleagues gather to share the latest research, methods, and materials for reaching and teaching adolescent readers, the readership of YAL. Each national organization also has state affiliates that provide close-to-home professional development opportunities for English teachers. Becoming an active member of these organizations is an important way to join in the professional conversations in the field of YAL. In fact, state affiliate conferences of NCTE and IRA are always eager to have those in the field write proposals and present programs featuring adolescent literacy and young adult literature. Meeting and collaborating with colleagues from across the state can help teachers form partnerships and networking opportunities that help them further their own professional growth.

YAL and Student Engagement and Motivation

Having knowledge regarding the engagement and motivation of adolescents when they read young adult literature helps provide a rationale and support for adding YAL to the English language arts classroom. Developmentally appropriate and both emotionally and cognitively accessible, YAL provides adolescents with a motivation to read (Stover, 2001). Author and educator Don Gallo (2001) concurs:

> With their engaging teenage narrators and contemporary language, their realistic and fast-moving stories told in 200 pages or less, these books attracted young teen readers desperate to understand themselves in a rapidly changing world. Sensitive adults immediately recognized the appeal of these books and the ability of their talented authors to speak in the voices of contemporary young people and to provide insights into the significant issues with which teens struggle—peer pressures, relationships with parents, physical and emotional disabilities, the threat of violence, love, death, and uncertainty about the future. (p. 39)

So, what most motivates adolescent readers in the English classroom? Free reading time, read-alouds, interesting materials, and choice, according to Ivey and Broaddus (2001). Some educators are surprised to learn the range of books that adolescents enjoy reading, including nonfiction, poetry, fiction, graphic novels, and magazines. Finding such variety is not a problem in today's bookstores and libraries, and selecting quality YA books from within particular genres is made even easier today by referring to the annual award-winners chosen by ALA and YALSA.

Should motivation and engagement matter to administrators who, at times, may seem largely concerned over test scores? Absolutely. National Assessment of Educational Progress results indicate that motivation to read leads to increased time spent reading—which, in turn, results in higher levels of reading proficiency (National Center for Education Statistics, 2011). *Reading Next* (Biancarosa & Snow, 2006) asserts that it is exactly this need to engage adolescents that our schools seem to be missing: "The proportion of students who are not engaged or motivated by their school experiences grows at every grade level and reaches epidemic proportions in high school" (p. 9). The research literature supports these assertions (Ivey & Broaddus, 2001; Lapp & Fisher, 2009; Moje, Overby, Tysvaer, & Morris, 2008; Pitcher et al., 2007). Traditional practices, say Pitcher et al., act as disincentives because they fail to take into account what motivates adolescents to read. These researchers asserted the need for adolescents to feel connected to what they are reading, and they maintained that—even at the high school level—teachers talking and sharing their enthusiasm about books can have a tremendous impact on students' reading habits and attitudes.

It is this idea of feeling connected that influences adolescents' motivation and engagement in the English language arts classroom (Lapp & Fisher, 2009; Groenke & Scherff, 2010). How can we establish classroom communities that promote and encourage adolescents' sense of belonging and connectedness? One strategy is to add YAL and structure social learning opportunities around students' choices of the YA books. Offering students choice in selecting what they read is a powerful motivator. English teachers can organize book clubs or literature circles around small groups of students' agreed-upon choices of YAL. Such collaborations afford students challenges, support, and encouragement from their peers. English teachers can also organize book-sharing groups, in which small group discussions around multiple YA texts occur. Such book-sharing opportunities lead students to make connections among texts in order to share understandings about individual books with group members (Bull, 2008). A second strategy is to share YA books with the class via book talks (presented by both the teacher and students). This provides opportunities for teachers to model their own reading enjoyment and to share new titles with the class. It also provides adolescents with opportunities to share their YA books with classmates, previewing books that their peers may then choose to read. Finally, it reinforces the idea that the classroom is a community of readers who share books and support one another in their reading. All of these give students voice and choice, encouraging adolescents' sense of belonging and motivation.

Garnering Support

For English language arts teachers who wish to add YAL to their classroom, there are important and helpful supports available. First, high-quality contemporary young adult literature is widely available. Vast and varied genres that appeal to even the choosiest readers include fiction, nonfiction, short stories, poetry, and graphic novels. Choosing quality YAL has become easier, too, with numerous ways to preview texts and read reviews published both professionally (by NCTE, IRA, ALAN, and YALSA) and individually (by teachers, students, and bloggers of YAL). Second, theoretically driven and practice-based texts written by educators offer concrete suggestions and strategies for busy teachers about how to incorporate YA titles into their classroom instruction. Third, the research literature on motivation and engagement supports the idea of providing adolescents with YAL in order to meet their interests and match their cognitive and emotional growth. All of these, when considered together, seem to offer a reasonable argument: Add YA titles to the English language arts classroom in order to offer adolescents choice and promote engagement.

Young adult literature can address multiple instructional goals: relate to students' interests, increase motivation, help striving readers build literacy skills, and address time constraints of a crowded curriculum (Stallworth, Gibbons, & Fauber, 2006). Stover (2001) says this well: "While helping teachers meet all the secondary goals of reading programs, the use of YAL uniquely promotes its primary goal: the creation of lifelong readers" (p. 134). Young adult literature also holds the potential to broaden adolescents' vision of self and the world, providing an avenue for reflection and a means for personal development (Groenke & Scherff, 2010). With such supports available, it seems we can overcome obstacles, and we can put quality YAL into the hands, hearts, and minds of our adolescent readers.

REFERENCES

ACT. (2005). *Crisis at the core: Preparing all students for college and work.* Retrieved from http://www.act.org/research/policymakers/pdf/crisis_report.pdf

American Library Association. (2011). Office of Intellectual Freedom. About banned and challenged books. Retrieved from http://www.ala.org/ala/issuesadvocacy/banned/aboutbannedbooks/index.cfm

Biancarosa, C., & Snow, C. E. (2006). *Reading next—A vision for action and research in middle and high school literacy: A report to Carnegie Corporation of New York* (2nd ed.). Washington, DC: Alliance for Excellent Education.

Bond, E. (2011). *Literature and the young adult reader.* New York: Allyn & Bacon.

Bucher, K., & Hinton, K. (2009). *Young adult literature: Exploration, evaluation, and appreciation* (2nd ed.). New York: Prentice Hall.

Bull, K. (2008). Within, among, and outside of the texts: Preservice teachers reading young adult literature. Retrieved from http://gradworks.umi.com/32/94/3294812.html

Bushman, J., & Haas, K. (2005). *Using young adult literature in the English classroom* (4th ed.). New York: Prentice Hall.

Cart, M. (2010). *Young adult literature: From romance to realism.* Chicago: American Library Association.

Carter, J. (2007). *Building literacy connections with graphic novels: Page by page, panel by panel.* Urbana, IL: National Council of Teachers of English.

Cole, P. (2009). *Young adult literature in the 21st century.* New York: McGraw-Hill.

Crew, H. (2010). *Donna Jo Napoli: Writing with passion.* Lanham, MD: Scarecrow Press.

Demko, M., & Hedrick, M. (2010). Teachers become zombies: The ugly side of scripted reading curriculum. *Voices from the Middle, 17*(3), 62–64.

Dickson, R., & Costigan, A. (2011). Emerging practice for new teachers: Creating possibilities for "aesthetic" readings. *English Education, 43*(2), 145–170.

Dutro, E. (2010). What "hard times" means: Mandated curricula, class-privileged assumptions, and the lives of poor children. *Research in the Teaching of English, 44*(3), 255–291.

Elliot, J., & Dupuis, M. (2001). *Young adult literature in the classroom: Reading it, teaching it, loving it.* Newark, DE: International Reading Association.

Gallagher, K. (2009). *Readicide.* Portland, ME: Stenhouse.

Gallo, D. (2001). How classics create an aliterate society. *English Journal, 90*(3), 33–39.

Gibbons, L. C., Dail, J. S., & Stallworth, B. J. (2006). Young adult literature in the English curriculum today: Classroom teachers speak out. *The ALAN Review, 33*(3), 53–61.

Gill, D. (2000). A national survey of the use of multicultural young adult literature in university courses. *The ALAN Review, 27*(2), 48–50.

Glenn, W. J., King, D., Heintz, K., Klapatch, J., & Berg, E. (2009). Finding space and place for young adult literature: Lessons from four first-year teachers engaging in out-of-school professional induction. *The ALAN Review, 36*(2), 6–17.

Greene, J., & Winters, M. (2005). Getting ahead by staying behind: An evaluation of Florida's program to end social promotion. *Education Next, 6*(2), 65–69.

Groenke, S., & Scherff, L. (2010). *Teaching YA lit through differentiated instruction.* Urbana, IL: National Council of Teachers of English.

Hill, R. (2010). The problem of self-censorship. *School Library Monthly, 27*(2), 9–12.

Ivey, G., & Broaddus, K. (2001). "Just plain reading": A survey of what makes students want to read in middle school classrooms. *Reading Research Quarterly, 36*(4), 350–377.

Kaywell, J. (2010). *Adolescent literature as a complement to the classics: Addressing critical issues in today's classrooms.* Norwood, MA: Christopher-Gordon.

Knickerbocker, J., & Rycik, J. (2002). Growing into literature: Adolescents' literary interpretation and appreciation. *Journal of Adolescent & Adult Literacy, 46*(3), 196.

Koss, M., & Teale, W. (2009). What's happening in YA literature? Trends in books for adolescents. *Journal of Adolescent & Adult Literacy, 52*(7), 563–572.

Lapp, D., & Fisher, D. (2009). It's all about the book: Motivating teens to read. *Journal of Adolescent & Adult Literacy, 52*(7), 556–561.

Lehr, S. (2010). Literacy, literature, and censorship: The high cost of No Child Left Behind. *Childhood Education, 87*(1), 25–34.

Moje, E., Overby, M., Tysvaer, N., & Morris, K. (2008). The complex world of adolescent literacy: Myths, motivations, and mysteries. *Harvard Educational Review, 78*(1), 107–154.

Monseau, V., & Hauschildt, P. (2008). *Teaching the selected works of Chris Crutcher.* Portsmouth, NH: Heinemann.

Monseau, V., & Salvner, G. (Eds.). (2000). *Reading their world: The young adult novel in the classroom.* Portsmouth, NH: Boynton/Cook–Heinemann.

Moore, J. (2010). *John Marsden: Darkness, shadow, and light.* Lanham, MD: Scarecrow Press.

National Center for Education Statistics (NCES). (2005). *A first look at the literacy of America's adults in the 21st century.* Washington, DC: U.S. Government Printing Office.

National Center for Education Statistics (NCES). (2011). *The nation's report card: National Assessment of Educational Progress at grades 4, 8, and 12, 2010.* (NCES 2011-467). Washington, DC: U.S. Department of Education.

National Endowment for the Arts. (2007). *To read or not to read: A question of national consequence.* Washington, DC: U.S. Department of Education.

Nilsen, A., & Donelson, K. (2012). *Literature for today's young adults* (9th ed.). Upper Saddle River, NJ: Pearson.

Perry, E. (2011). *Robin McKinley: Girl reader, woman writer.* Lanham, MD: Scarecrow Press.

Pitcher, S., Albright, L., DeLaney, C., Walker, N., Seunarinesingh, K., Mogge, S., et al. (2007). Assessing adolescents' motivation to read. *Journal of Adolescent & Adult Literacy, 50*(5), 378–396.

Salvner, G. M. (2000). Time and tradition: Transforming the secondary English class with young adult novels. In V. R. Monseau & G. M. Salvner (Eds.), *Reading their world: The young adult novel in the classroom* (2nd ed.) (pp. 85–99). Portsmouth, NH: Boynton/Cook–Heineman.

Samuels, B. (1983). Young adult novels in the classroom? *English Journal, 72*(4), 86–88.

Santoli, S., & Wagner, M. (2004). Promoting young adult literature: The other real literature. *American Secondary Education, 33*(1), 65–73.

Soter, A., & Connors, S. (2009). Beyond relevance to literary merit: Young adult literature as "literature." *The ALAN Review, 37*(1), 62–67.

Stallworth, B., Gibbons, L., & Fauber, L. (2006). It's not on the list: An exploration of teachers' perspectives on using multicultural literature. *Journal of Adolescent & Adult Literacy, 49*(6), 478–489.

Stover, L. T. (2001). The place of young adult literature in secondary reading programs. In B. O. Ericson (Ed.), *Teaching reading in high school English classes* (pp. 115–138). Urbana, IL: National Council of Teachers of English.

Tatum, A. (2008). Overserved or underserved? A focus on adolescents and texts. *English Journal, 98*(2), 82–85.

Zitlow, C. (2007). *Teaching the selected works of Walter Dean Myers.* Portsmouth, NH: Heinemann.

5

Using Young Adult Literature to Motivate and Engage the Disengaged

Michelle J. Kelley, Nance S. Wilson, and Melanie D. Koss

> *Bridge to Terabithia* was the most interesting book I have recently read. It is by far my favorite book . . . because it was just really mysterious.

Most teachers would be excited to have a sixth grader share this comment. It is hopeful; she appears to be an engaged reader. However, closer examination of her reading habits revealed she was actually a disengaged reader. Lucky for her, she had teachers who recognized this and were armed and ready for the challenge of getting her to engage in a book. Although a number of books were suggested based on her interests in relationships and adventure, she was immediately drawn to Katherine Paterson's *Bridge to Terabithia,* and she couldn't put it down. While it was the only title she read that school year, she enjoyed it, thus beginning her journey as a reader.

Other students are not as fortunate. Statistics estimate that eight million fourth through twelfth graders struggle to read on grade level (National Center for Education Statistics, 2003). This academic failure can lead to emotional, social, and community concerns. Many of the nation's current literacy problems stem from students' lack of reading skills and strategy knowledge. We are particularly concerned that students are not engaged in the reading process outside of school-related activities. This lack of engagement negatively affects reading motivation (Ivey, 1998; Libsch & Breslow, 1996; Moje, Young, Readence, & Moore, 2000) and contributes to aliteracy among adolescents (Alvermann, 2003). Research has shown that students, even students who like to read, tend to read less as they progress from early elementary to middle school (O'Brien & Dillion, 2008; Yankelovich and Scholastic, 2006). As social and technological advances continue to raise the need for literacy skills, the literacy development of adolescents is of vital importance (Biancarosa & Snow, 2004). Unfortunately, being capable and competent, like the sixth grader in our opening quote, does not ensure literacy success because children must also be motivated in order to successfully engage in the reading process.

WHAT CHARACTERISTICS DISTINGUISH AN ENGAGED READER FROM A DISENGAGED READER?

As educators, we are always looking for ways to engage our students in reading a wide variety of texts. Not only do we want to pass on our love of reading, we also recognize that there is a powerful link between the time students spend reading and their reading achievement (Cunningham & Stanovich, 1997; Guthrie, Wigfield, Metsala, & Cox, 1999). Some students may be proficient readers, but they simply do not choose to read. Many students appear to read but in actuality are faking it (Kelley & Clausen-Grace, 2006). How do we identify these readers in our classrooms?

The engaged reader has confidence, is metacognitive, and understands how reading impacts future learning. According to Guthrie and Wigfield (2000), engaged readers seek to understand and are tenacious when faced with obstacles. They are motivated to read by personal goals and interests, are knowledgeable regarding what they read, are strategic when comprehending, and approach literacy as a social process (Bereiter & Scardamalia, 1989; Guthrie, McGough, Bennett, & Rice, 1996). If students can monitor and understand their reading and reading strategies, they can become more confident in their identities as readers, and in turn effectively implement strategies more often (Bandura, 1989; Bransford, Brown, Cocking, Donovan, & Pellegrino, 2000).

In contrast, disengaged readers rarely elect to read, even if they are capable. Disengaged readers often exhibit avoidance behaviors or employ coping mechanisms that allow them to put forth minimal effort to complete a reading task (Kelley & Clausen-Grace, 2006). One thing is clear—being a competent reader does not necessarily equate to being an engaged reader. Even though many fake readers work hard to appear to be reading, we can usually pick them out after observing them in the reading process (Kelley & Clausen-Grace, 2008). Far less, though, is known about what motivates these readers and how best to engage them in the reading process. Therefore, knowing what motivates them is of particular interest to educators and a major focus of this chapter.

WHAT IS MOTIVATION AND HOW CAN WE MEASURE IT?

Motivation is highly complex and influenced by many factors; overall, it is an internal driving force to do something. Wigfield and Guthrie (1997) suggested that reading motivation is multifaceted or multidimensional, which has been confirmed in a subsequent study (Baker & Wigfield, 1999). Wigfield (1997) identified three major motivational categories:

1. Competence and efficacy: the belief that one can and the willingness to tackle challenging tasks
2. Purposes for reading: intrinsic and extrinsic reasons
3. Social purposes for reading: the influence of family and peers

Baker and Wigfield (1999) substantiated these categories, determining that there "are clusters of children with different motivational characteristics." They suggested that educators not pigeonhole readers as having low or high motivation, but rather understand that children "have a mixture of motivational characteristics" and, correspondingly, will react differently to each teacher's "motivational strategies" (p. 470). Their findings demonstrate the importance of identifying what motivates each reader and what teachers can do to thwart disengagement.

The "expectancy-value" theory of motivation (Eccles, 1983) asserts that motivation is impacted by one's expectation of failure or success and the value placed on a particular task. Gambrell, Palmer, Codling, and Mazzoni (1996) applied this theory to reading by developing the Motivation to Read Profile (MRP) for elementary-aged children. The MRP assesses motivation in two areas, a student's self-concept and the value a student places on reading, and includes two instruments, a reading survey and a conversational interview. The survey includes twenty items on a four-point response scale and can be group administered; the interview is given individually and provides detailed information on a student's individual reading motivation related to narrative, informational, and general reading.

More recently, Pitcher et al. (2007) revised the MRP for use with adolescents, known as the Adolescent Motivation to Read Profile (AMRP). The language used in the MRP survey was revised to reflect how adolescents talk, and interview questions were expanded to include probes related to using electronic resources, identifying enjoyable schoolwork, and reading and writing independently. Pitcher et al. (2007) used the AMRP with adolescents, finding:

- a discrepancy between in-school and out-of-school literacy
- the use of multiple literacies
- the influence of family and friends on reading
- the influence of instructional methods
- the importance of choice in reading and learning

Both Gambrell et al. (1996) and Pitcher et al. (2007) recommended that teachers use these instruments to plan "developmentally appropriate instruction" (Pitcher et al., 2007, p. 395) that is meaningful to students.

WHAT MAKES MIDDLE SCHOOLERS UNIQUE?

Middle school students are young adolescents in the midst of rapid and significant developmental changes: physically, intellectually, and emotionally (Caskey & Anfara, 2007). Physical development is most prominent, as their bodies transform from childhood to adulthood. Intellectual development is less obvious but just as profound (Caskey & Anfara, 2007). Students are developing the ability to be metacognitive and independent in their thoughts, as they are eager to learn about things they find useful and interesting (Kellough & Kellough, 2008). Their emotional development craves independence as they seek to form a personal identity (Caskey & Anfara, 2007). As adolescents mature, their interests and needs begin to shift, thus impacting their literacy development.

WHAT IS THE CURRENT STATE OF MOTIVATION TO READ AMONG ADOLESCENTS?

In light of the physical and physiological changes among young teens, as well as issues with engagement, we investigated the current level of motivation and interests of middle school students related to reading. By employing the AMRP with middle school students, coupled with our own experiences, we explored the question, "What motivates disengaged readers and what can you do as a teacher to motivate and engage these readers?"

Two sets of middle school students were surveyed: one at a mid-sized suburban public school (Kelley & Decker, 2009), and a second at a small suburban private school. Both groups of students were given the survey portion of the AMRP to determine overall reading motivation and evaluate reader self-concept and the value they place on reading.

At both schools we found that both gender and grade accounted for significant differences in students' value of reading. Females had a higher motivation to read than males, and sixth and seventh graders had higher levels than eighth graders (Kelley & Decker, 2009). Females valued reading more than males, and as the grade level increased, students' overall value for reading decreased. Additionally, females had a slightly higher self-concept than males (Kelley & Decker, 2009).

Since both gender and grade accounted for the difference in students' value of reading, we looked at what might have caused the difference. First, females reported sharing good books with friends some of the time, while males did not. Second, females noted that knowing how to read well was very important, while males thought it was only "sort of" important. Finally, subscores were examined in terms of the overall motivation to read in a composite score. Self-concept contributed more to students' overall motivation to read than did value. This finding corroborated existing data showing that students' self-concepts as readers were higher than their value of reading (Kelley & Decker, 2009). Overall results indicated a lack of motivation; therefore, we wanted to know more about the types of books, authors, and characters these students did and would read.

WHAT IS THE CURRENT STATE OF MOTIVATION TO READ AMONG DISENGAGED ADOLESCENTS?

Since we wanted to learn what disengaged readers like about reading, we interviewed students from both school settings. At the mid-sized school, interviewees were obtained through identification by homeroom teachers using an observational checklist. The checklist asked observers to tally when students were overtly disengaged (e.g., out of seat, talking, flipping pages, and looking around the room). Behaviors were totaled, and this established the pool of less engaged readers to be interviewed. In contrast, all students at the small private school were interviewed. The AMRP interview protocol was utilized to uncover students' reading preferences.

Reading Preferences/Book Selection

Reading preferences included students' reading habits and their motives for reading. These disengaged students did read, both for pleasure and/or for educational purposes, but they read primarily school-related texts. Every student noted a text they had read in school. At the mid-sized school, these were texts read during a mandatory homeroom reading program. At the small school, with no mandatory program, these were texts read during English class. Regardless of setting, the students' reasons for reading and reading preferences showed that students were influenced by both internal and external factors.

Internal Factors

Internal factors related to student perceptions of the book itself and included plot (genre and series inclinations), author, and personal connections to text content. Having choice of reading material was also considered an internal factor, and almost all students said they chose what they read without assistance. Their reading selection process was significantly driven by their interests related to author and genre and their background knowledge.

> I don't really read the newspaper that much, but the war going on . . . I've read the newspaper about that. That's about it. [I learned] that many soldiers are

> dying over there. It's our soldiers over there and they're giving their lives for us so we cannot get attacked. (eighth grader)

As is evident above, the student read the newspaper to gather more information regarding the war due to a personal interest. The role of personal interest was a recurring theme throughout students' descriptions of what motivated them to read.

We asked students to identify the genre, settings, and characters to determine the types of texts that appealed to them. Most students preferred to read realistic fiction and fantasy/science fiction, followed by mystery; these findings are consistent with a recent content analysis of trends found in young adult literature (Koss & Teale, 2009). When asked about setting or characters, students reported that the age of the characters and/or the time period of the text were not important, yet closer examination revealed that students preferred characters their own age.

In order to gain more detailed knowledge about students' preferences, we asked them what they liked about the books that they did read. They recognized aspects of books they liked, such as books being interesting, full of action, or mysterious. The following quotes demonstrate what students enjoyed about the books they read:

> The characters were close to my age and experienced some of the pain I have, but they experienced it in more extreme conditions. (eighth grader, S. E. Hinton's *The Outsiders*)

> I love the idea that kids can do what they need to do when they want. (eighth grader, James Patterson's *Maximum Ride*)

It was clear that these students hit on a key aspect of what makes YA realistic fiction appealing to students—the ability of a student to find a character he or she can relate to and can identify with some of the character's experiences (Koss, 2009a, 2009b).

A deeper analysis of the interview data demonstrated that these students had definite opinions regarding the qualities of a good book, centering on three key ideas: stories must build readers' interest; they must contain relatable characters; and they must be "interesting."

First, a story must capture the readers' interest relatively early in the reading process. Students shared the following regarding what builds interest in a book:

> When it [the story] jumps right into the good part of the book and I don't have to read the boring parts first. (sixth grader)

> When it [the story] captures you in the beginning and throughout the rest of the book. (seventh grader)

> I love books that confuse at first, and only start to make sense at the middle. (seventh grader on mystery books)

These quotes demonstrate that students did not want to wait to see what exciting things might happen; they wanted the books to grab them right away. They wanted to read books that made them think about what was happening and what was going to happen next.

Second, the students felt that books must contain relatable characters. A few of their comments about relatability include "being able to connect to the characters" and "being able to put yourself in their [the characters'] position and your heart beats faster just feeling what they feel." Students were interested in reading about characters that were like them. Considering that adolescence is a time of constant change, students preferred to read about characters who were wrestling with the same conscious and subconscious identity issues that they themselves were experiencing.

Finally, students wanted to read books they found interesting. They wanted books that had "interesting settings, story lines, and characters," good descriptions, and good stories. In addition, students defined books as "interesting because they have a lot of action" (seventh grader). Throughout their responses, students described books that were interesting as descriptive and telling a cohesive story. The way a story often meets these characteristics is through the portrayal of relatable characters and engaging beginnings.

In summary, students' perception of a good book included an emphasis on fiction, with an engaging beginning, relatable characters, and something that interests them.

External Factors

External factors influencing students' book selections include their active involvement in the reading process and their interaction with significant others who model reading as a noteworthy and engaging endeavor. Interview probes revealed that all students identified a specific individual who played an important role in their reading decisions, including family members, teachers, and friends.

For many disengaged readers, school was the only place they reported engaging in reading, even after the definition of reading expanded to include multiliteracies. Although all the students from the mid-sized public school identified a book they were reading during homeroom—a mandatory program—the data was quite different in regard to reading at home. Only half of the students said they *ever* read at home. Thus, many of the readers would not be reading independently at all if not for the time provided in school. At the small school, students reported little reading outside of school as well; thus, their reading was predominantly limited to what was assigned by the teacher.

From these disengaged readers, we learned the types of books that interest them, the power of the adult as an external factor for reading, and the role of the school as the centerpiece of a student's reading.

LESSON LEARNED: MOTIVATING DISENGAGED READERS

From these interviews it would appear that many of the above-quoted readers had clear understandings of what engaged them in reading. They were able to identify books, characters, and genres that were of interest. However, the fact that reading outside of school was rarely indicated, we felt that it would be helpful to identify teaching suggestions to support the disengaged middle school reader:

1. Create a classroom climate conducive to literacy.
2. Integrate authentic reading practices throughout the school day.
3. Get to know your students.
4. Be knowledgeable about and provide students access to a wide variety of texts.

Create a Classroom Climate Conducive to Literacy

> When we group read. I really enjoy that. So, it's like the whole class participating . . . it gives everybody a chance to participate. I enjoy that group reading. (eighth grader, female)

Creating a safe, comfortable, literacy-rich classroom environment is one of the most important factors to motivate students to read. If your classroom is filled with various reading materials, if those materials are valued and highlighted in lessons and activities throughout the day, if you model a love of and interest in reading, and if you give your students ample opportunity to explore and interact with books, the vibe of your classroom will be one in which students feel encouraged and excited about reading.

Your classroom should look and feel inviting in a literary way. Investing in a classroom library, having visual displays highlighting reading, and establishing a reading area can help create a climate conducive to literacy. One idea is to use bulletin boards to showcase favorite authors, award winners, and/or student-suggested texts. Involving students in creating these bulletin boards will help create synergy around books.

How you integrate reading into your classroom can send both subtle and overt messages that reading is valued. The modeling of a teacher who is passionate about reading and shares books can be one of the most useful ways of turning students into readers. If a child sees a significant adult in his or her life as an engaged reader, one who shares the excitement of reading rather than just teaching it because he or she must, reading can be viewed in a different light. When students see their teacher reading a variety of materials for a variety of purposes, a classroom environment is created in which students with different reading abilities feel comfortable engaging in reading.

We recognize that students have a variety of reading abilities and that some struggling readers may feel uncomfortable with other students seeing them struggle. A safe classroom environment is also one of support, in which learners with different strengths and abilities feel comfortable and encouraged to explore reading materials for interest and practice because the focus is on a love of reading, rather than only to learn. The classroom should be a place where students are supported and given the opportunity to take risks with different types and levels of texts.

Integrate Authentic Reading Practices throughout the School Day

We know school days are packed with required curricular elements and that it is difficult to fit in additional activities, but we feel it is crucial that books and reading take a central role. Integrating reading by sharing texts, talking about texts, and encouraging students to talk about texts makes reading an acceptable and natural part of the day. Ways to entice students to read include integrating structured independent reading time, conducting booktalks, reading aloud, encouraging frequent library visits, and holding special reading events such as author days or author visits.

Integrate independent reading into your regular classroom instruction. Our studies demonstrated that school is often the only place where disengaged readers read. Using structured independent reading supports these students as they read independently. Whether in the form of Reading Workshop (Atwell, 1998) or the more focused R^5: Read, Relax, Reflect, Respond, and Rap (Clausen-Grace & Kelley, 2007; Kelley & Clausen-Grace, 2008), students who engage in supported independent reading during the school day obtain benefits that come from reading, such as increased reading achievement (Guthrie, Wigfield, Metsala, & Cox, 1999) and larger vocabularies (Anderson & Nagy, 1992).

The teacher should also be reading during this time. Teachers can serve as reading mentors. The research done by Yankelovich and Scholastic (2006) found that teachers were a significant source of reading suggestions. Students are often intrigued by a book a teacher is visibly reading. Encourage different faculty members to identify a favorite book and perhaps photograph them holding that book and display the photograph in the media center or post it outside each classroom.

Booktalks are another effective way of encouraging reading for pleasure (Bodart, 2002). Booktalks allow you to present books you think your students might want to read in a quick and upbeat manner (Bodart, 2002; Lesesne, 2003, 2006). Throughout the day, hold up a few titles and give brief marketing talks to catch students' attention with the goal of getting students aware of titles of interest. Not only can teachers do the booktalks, students can as well.

> Sometimes, I go by what my friends tell me. So if they say it is a really good book, I go "OOOuuu" and she will tell me about some parts, and then she tells me she's not going to tell me the surprise ending because it's really good. So I go, "Okay," and once I go through a book my mom says, "Cindy, it's time to go to sleep." I go, "No wait, can I finish this?" And when I see a sequel, I'm like, "I got to read this!" (sixth grader, female)

Readers often select texts based on the recommendations of peers, demonstrating that book sharing is a powerful motivator. When students enjoy a book, have them give a booktalk to their classmates. Often one student's excitement about a title can lead others to want to read that same title. Excitement for student booktalks can be generated when they are held at an anticipated time of the day. Students will want to want to share new titles and thus will be encouraged to read more. "My Favorite Books" or "My Recommended Reading" charts created by students can also provide a valuable resource.

Student-created book displays are also motivating. Rather than traditional book reports, encourage students to create media projects such as "wanted" posters, newspapers, or postcards to display books they enjoyed reading and want to share with others. Creating new book covers is also an effective activity, as students often feel a book's cover does not accurately represent the content.

> Well, in Ms. M's class we had this book report thing, where we could make Wanted Posters and stuff like that. Some kids talked about some of the books that they read and some of those were really good, like I don't remember the names right now but they sounded good. (eighth grader, female)

Another way to capture students' attention is by reading aloud. Students are never too old to be read to. Reading aloud engages students in a text they might not have picked independently and provides a voice for literature. Two techniques can be used: reading aloud a whole book to students a few chapters at a time, or reading aloud just the beginning or a particularly juicy bit, and then putting the book down for students to grab at will. Daily read-alouds can be at a certain time of day that students anticipate.

Once the booktalks and read-alouds have enticed your students, the next step is to provide your students access to the books. Having a large classroom library and arranging frequent library trips are a few suggestions.

Another useful resource is the website Goodreads (http://www.goodreads.com), an online social media website designed to help you and your students record books you've read or want to read as well as your personal reviews, to share books and suggestions with others, and to join online book discussion groups. Your class or even your whole school can create a Goodreads group and use it as an online database for posting and discussing books.

Once authentic reading practices are integrated into your school day, your students will have opportunities to engage with books. The next step is finding them the right books to read. Student choice is key. The role of choice in reading engagement has been well established (Ivey, 1998; Schraw, Flowerday, & Reisetter, 1998), and although choice was not explicitly identified as a factor for most of our middle school readers, it should not be ignored. We can help students with their choices by getting to know both the students and their personal interests, and by knowing a variety of texts and resources.

Get to Know Your Students

> Well the book I just finished yesterday was *There's a Girl in my Hammerlock*. It's from Jerry Spinelli. That was an interesting book, and I am trying to finish all of the Jerry Spinelli books by the end of this year. I think I'm on nine right now. I read *Maniac Magee*, that book really caught my attention because I was in running. And I guess I could associate with him, because he runs everywhere he goes, and I pretty much run everywhere I go. (seventh grader, male)

This student's teacher took the time to get to know her students, and as a result, she was able to match one nonreader to a book he wanted to read because he found the topic relatable and interesting. This interest led him to want to read other books by the same author. Once considered a disengaged reader, this student was able to, with support, find an author and set of books that he enjoyed. Since book selection is integral to the success of any independent reading approach and a key ingredient to reading engagement, matching students to texts they can and want to read is an important skill.

The easiest way to get to know your students is to simply ask them about their lives and interests. By creating a classroom environment that displays the importance of books to successful learning experiences, you will encourage your students to open up and share what they like and don't like. This will give you, as a teacher, insights about what topics they might want to read about. You will also want to acquire their literacy histories. What genres and authors have they read? What is their attitude toward literacy activities? Several instruments have been designed to find out this information, such as interest inventories and attitude surveys.

Be Knowledgeable about and Provide Students Access to a Wide Variety of Texts

> My Critical Thinking teacher gets me into books. When she tells us a book she makes us get excited. Like she'll tell us some parts of the books, and if I like it, I'll read it. (sixth grader, male)

In a survey by SmartGirl and YALSA (2005), the majority of teen respondents said that they would read more if they knew about more good books to read. Once you get to know your students and they know they will be supported and given time to read texts of their choice during the school day, the door is open for you to suggest titles and reading materials you think may be of interest.

As a teacher, a great skill is to be knowledgeable about authors, series, and genres that appeal to adolescents, especially new and popular titles your students are reading. This does not mean you have to read every new book that is published, but rather that you are cognizant of trends in adolescent literature and know resources to keep current on this information. Children's literature listservs, websites targeted for teachers or students, author and illustrator personal websites, blogs, and social media pages are all useful tools for you to use to find out what children are reading.

There are a variety of listservs devoted solely to the discussion of children's literature topics and issues. One popular, high-traffic listserv is child_lit. This listserv is the place for talking about all things relating to children's literature and is populated by scholars, authors, and other children's literature enthusiasts. Additional suggested listservs are adbooks and middle_school_lit (see appendix for Web addresses).

Many websites provide valuable information for finding titles of books to read, learning more about authors, or finding ideas on how to use books authentically in the classroom. Some sites, such as Carol Hurst's Children's Literature Site or the Children's Literature Comprehensive Database, are developed primarily for teacher use and provide thematic book lists, lesson plans and ideas, and even lexile levels. Other websites are developed with children and adolescents in mind. Providing your students with a list of some of these websites is a great way for them to use the Internet and even social networking to start finding out and talking about the books that they read and enjoy.

The Book Report Network consists of a group of age-specific websites that provide information related to book content, such as reviews and author interviews, and interactive elements such as questions, contests, and polls. One of their sites, teenreads.com, is a wonderful resource for learning the latest on new titles, authors, and happenings in the world of middle school literature. Targeted to teens, teenreads.com provides teens with not only book reviews and book lists, but insider scoops like access to chapters of not-yet-released titles, in-depth author interviews, book contests, and online author interaction. Teens can also chat and network with other teens about the books they love.

Based on the research showing that boys don't read, author Jon Scieszka created Guys Read, a Web-based literacy program devoted to boys. This interactive website includes book reviews and book suggestions on boy-centered topics such as war, wrestling, space, and humor; a guys-only blog; and special projects designed to help promote literacy development among boys.

Other teen-targeted websites include Young Adult Books Central, a site that provides links to author interviews, biographies, book lists, Web pages, contests, book trailers for upcoming titles and related children's literature news. Another extremely popular site is Reading Rants! Out of the Ordinary Teen Booklists! Browse this site for updates on the latest and greatest new teen titles. Thematic booklists and up-to-date book reviews are posted, but what makes this site unique is the ability for teens to post their own opinions on existing reviews and to write reviews of their own.

Also encourage students to check out the websites, Facebook and Myspace pages, and/or blogs of their favorite authors.

FINAL THOUGHTS

Although our findings cannot be generalized to all disengaged readers, our encounters with the reluctant middle school readers who participated in this study have convinced us that engaging students with adolescent literature requires a multipronged approach—creating a comfortable classroom environment conducive to literacy (Clary, 1991; Ivey, 1998), integrating reading in authentic ways throughout the school day, getting to know your students, and being knowledgeable about available literature and providing students with access to these texts (Ivey, 1998). Similar to Pitcher et al. (2007), we found discrepancies between students' in-school and out-of-school reading. For most of our disengaged readers, school is the only place they read.

We do not believe that simply requiring students to read independently at home is enough. Our students' book selections, like those of Pitcher et al. (2007), were influenced by friends, family, and teachers, as well as the different teaching methods employed in the classroom. We emphasize the importance of the role the classroom teacher must play both in helping students find books that entice them to read, and in providing a framework for reading within the classroom.

As we look toward the future and the texts that our students read, we recommend that teachers celebrate the mulitiliteracies of this generation of students (Pitcher et al., 2007). Consider online texts students read, including magazines and blogs, and their use of new technologies such as iPads, Kindles, and Nooks. Ask them about the digital texts and technologies they engage with, and have them tell you what and how they're reading. As we look toward the future, we must look to our students and the texts that motivate them to read, rather than limiting ourselves to traditional texts.

APPENDIX

Listservs/E-mail Groups on Children's and Young Adult Literature

Adbooks (http://groups.yahoo.com/group/adbooks)

This listserv is devoted to talking about young adult literature. This group holds the annual JHunt book award contest.

Child_lit (http://www.rci.rutgers.edu/~mjoseph/childlit/about.html)

This listserv is the place for talking about all things relating to children's literature and is populated by scholars, authors, and other children's literature enthusiasts.

Middle_school_lit (http://groups.yahoo.com/group/middle_school_lit)

A group focused on discussing literature specifically for the middle grades. They work on the Middle Hall of Fame, a core collection of quality middle school literature.

Websites for the Teacher

American Folklore (http://www.americanfolklore.net)

Folklore galore is available at the American Folklore website. Retellings of myths, legends, North American and Native American folktales, tall tales, and other traditional tales from across the United States are shared.

Carol Hurst's Children's Literature Site (http://www.carolhurst.com)

This website is a complete collection of books and resources about children's literature. Book lists, reviews, and lesson ideas are provided and organized by themes, professional areas of interest, subject matter, curricular area, and grade level.

Children's Literature Comprehensive Database
(http://www.childrenslit.com)

This (subscription required) online database contains book reviews from major reviewer outlets including *The ALAN Review*, *VOYA*, *Kirkus*, and *BookList*. Subscription includes reading level programs, multiple book search features, curriculum tools, and links to author and illustrator webpages and WorldCat information.

The Children's Literature Web Guide (http://people.ucalgary.ca/~dkbrown)

The Children's Literature Web Guide provides a list of Internet resources related to books for children and young adults. The site includes discussion boards, award lists, best-seller lists, author website links, readers' theater scripts, journals, teacher and parent resources, and children's literature organizations.

Cynthia Leitich Smith's Author Web Page with Children's and YA Literature Resources (http://www.cynthialeitichsmith.com)

Cynthia's personal author website, plus author interviews, resource links, and so much more.

Goodreads (http://www.goodreads.com)

Goodreads is an online social media website designed to help you and your students record books you've read or want to read as well as your personal reviews, share and suggest books to others, and join online book discussion groups. Perfect for a class or school to set up.

Read Kiddo Read (http://www.readkiddoread.com/home)

Another resource designed to help children find books of interest, Read Kiddo Read has book reviews, summaries, related text suggestions, and online activities. Free subscription includes additional content such as teacher lesson plans, author interviews, and links to other resource pages.

Web English Teacher—Children's Literature and YA Literature (http://www.webenglishteacher.com/childlit.html; http://www.webenglishteacher.com/ya.html)

This site is full of information and teaching resources for English teachers. The two URLs provided are links to resources on a large number of children's or young adult authors and illustrators. Also available are lesson plans and resources spanning the English curriculum.

Young Adult Books Central (http://www.yabookscentral.com)

This website provides links to author interviews, biographies, book lists, and Web pages, as well as contests, book trailers for upcoming titles, and related children's literature news.

Websites Targeted to Students

Bookwink (http://www.bookwink.com)

Bookwink is a site completely devoted to video booktalks across a wide range of topics developed specifically for children in 3rd through 8th grade.

Giggle Poetry (http://www.gigglepoetry.com/index.aspx)

Giggle Poetry is "the self-proclaimed number one fun poetry site for kids on the Web!" Teacher resources are available, including tips for teaching children to write and enjoy poetry and oodles of poetry for children to read, rate, and enjoy.

Guys Read (http://www.guysread.com)

Based on the research that boys don't read, author Jon Scieszka created Guys Read, a Web-based literacy program devoted to boys. This interactive website includes book reviews and suggestions for books on boy-centered topics such as war, wrestling, space, and humor; a guys-only blog; and special projects designed to help promote literacy development among boys.

Kidsreads.com (http://kidsreads.com)

Kidsreads is an interactive website created to help children find information about their favorite authors and books. In addition to book reviews and author information, games, trivia, and contests are also regularly added and changed.

Readergirlz (http://www.readergirlz.com)

This website is part resource and part social media. The site's mission is to promote teen literacy; teens are encouraged to sign in, talk about their favorite books, link to Facebook and Myspace author and book pages, and recommend books to others.

Reading Rants! Out of the Ordinary Teen Booklists! (http://www.readingrants.org)

This is the site to browse for updates on the latest and greatest new teen titles. Thematic booklists and up-to-date book reviews are posted, but what makes this site unique is the ability for teens to both post comments and their own opinions on existing reviews and to write reviews of their own.

Teen Ink (www.teenink.com)

An online teen literary magazine, website, and book links for teens written by teens. Completely teen-created content.

Teenreads.com (www.teenreads.com)

Targeted to teens, teenreads.com provides teens with not only book reviews and book lists but also insider scoops like access to chapters of not-yet-released titles, in-depth author interviews, book contests, and online author interaction. Teens can also chat and network with other teens about the books they love.

REFERENCES

Alvermann, D. E. (2003). Seeing themselves as capable and engaged readers: Adolescents and re/mediated instruction. Retrieved September 24, 2009, from http://www.learningpt.org/pdfs/literacy/readers.pdf

Anderson, R. C., & Nagy, W. E. (1992). The vocabulary conundrum. *American Educator, 16*(4), 14–18, 44–47.

Atwell, N. (1998). *In the middle: New understandings about writing, reading, and learning* (2nd ed.). Portsmouth, NH: Boynton/Cook.

Baker, L., & Wigfield, A. (1999). Dimensions of children's motivation for reading and their relations to reading activity and reading achievement. *Reading Research Quarterly, 34*, 452–477.

Bandura, A. (1989). Regulation of cognitive processes through perceived self-efficacy. *Developmental Psychology, 25*, 729–735.

Bereiter, C., & Scardamalia, M. (1989). Intentional learning as a goal of instruction. In L. B. Resnick (Ed.), *Knowing, learning, and instruction* (pp. 361–392). Hillsdale, NJ: Erlbaum.

Biancarosa, C., & Snow, C. E. (2004). *Reading next—A vision for action and research in middle and high school literacy: A report to Carnegie Corporation of New York.* Washington, DC: Alliance for Excellent Education.

Bodart, J. R. (2002). *Radical reads: 101 young adult novels on the edge*. Lanham, MD: Scarecrow Press.

Bransford, J. D., Brown, A. L., Cocking, R. R., Donovan, S. V., & Pellegrino, J. W. (Eds.). (2000). *How people learn: Brain, mind, experience, and school.* Washington, DC: National Academy Press.

Caskey, M. M., & Anfara, V. A., Jr. (2007). Research summary: Young adolescents' developmental characteristics. Westerville, OH: National Middle School Association. Retrieved April 20, 2009, from http://www.nmsa.org/Research/ResearchSummaries/DevelopmentalCharacteristics/tabid/1414/Default.aspx

Clary, L. M. (1991). Getting adolescents to read. *Journal of Reading, 34*, 340–345.

Clausen-Grace, N., & Kelley, M. (2007). You can't hide in R[5]: Restructuring independent reading to be more strategic and engaging. *Voices in the Middle, 14*(3), 38–50.

Cunningham, A. E., & Stanovich, K. E. (1997). Early reading acquisition and its relation to reading experience and ability ten years later. *Developmental Psychology, 33*, 934–945.

Eccles, J. (1983). Expectancies, values, and academic behaviors. In J. T. Spence (Ed.), *Achievement and achievement motives* (pp. 75–146). San Francisco: Freeman.

Gambrell, L. B., Palmer, B. M., Codling, R. M., & Mazzoni, S. A. (1996). Assessing motivation to read. *Reading Teacher, 49*(7), 518–533.

Guthrie, J. T., & Wigfield, A. (2000). Engagement and motivation in reading. In M. L. Kamil, P. B. Mosenthal, P. D. Pearson, & R. Barr (Eds.), *Handbook of reading research* (Vol. 3, pp. 403–422). Mahwah, NJ: Erlbaum.

Guthrie, J. T., Wigfield, A., Metsala, J., & Cox, K. (1999). Motivation and cognitive predictors of text comprehension and reading amount. *Scientific Studies of Reading, 3*(3), 231–256.

Guthrie, J. T., McGough, K., Bennett, L., & Rice, M. E. (1996). Concept-oriented reading instruction to develop motivational and cognitive aspects of reading. In L. Baker, P. Afflerbach, & D. Reinking (Eds.), Developing engaged readers in school and home communities (pp. 165–190). Mahwah, NJ: Erlbaum.

Ivey, G. (1998). Discovering readers in the middle level school: A few helpful clues. *NASSP Bulletin, 82*, 48–56.

Kelley, M. J., & Clausen-Grace, N. (2006). R[5]: The SSR makeover that transformed readers. *Reading Teacher, 60*, 148–159.

Kelley, M. J., & Clausen-Grace, N. (2008). *R[5] in your classroom: A guide to differentiating independent reading and developing avid readers.* Newark, DE: International Reading Association.

Kelley, M. J., & Decker, E. (2009). The current state of motivation to read among middle school students. *Reading Psychology, 30*(5), 466–485.

Kellough, R. D., & Kellough, N. G. (2008). *Teaching young adolescents: Methods and resources for middle grades teaching* (5th ed.). Upper Saddle River, NJ: Pearson Merrill Prentice Hall.

Koss, M. D. (2009a). One new trend in YA literature: Novels with multiple narrative perspectives. *SIGNAL, 32*(1), 14–21.

Koss, M. D. (2009b). Young adult novels with multiple narrative perspectives: The changing nature of YA literature. *The ALAN Review, 36*(3), 73–80.

Koss, M. D., & Teale, W. H. (2009). What's happening in YA literature? Trends in books for adolescents. *Journal of Adolescent & Adult Literacy, 52*(7), 563–572.

Lesesne, T. S. (2003). *Making the match: Finding the right book for the right teen at the right time.* New York: Stenhouse.

Lesesne, T. S. (2006). *Naked reading: Uncovering what tweens need to become lifelong readers.* New York: Stenhouse.

Libsch, M. K., & Breslow, M. (1996). Trends in non-assigned reading by high school seniors. *NASSP Bulletin*, 111–116.

Moje, E. B., Young, J. P., Readence, J. E., & Moore, D. (2000). Reinventing adolescent literacy for new times: Perennial and millennial issues. *Journal of Adolescent & Adult Literacy, 43*, 400–410.

National Center for Education Statistics. (2003). *Nation's report card: Reading 2002.* Washington, DC: U.S. Government Printing Office. Retrieved from http://nces.ed.gov/pubsearch/pubinfo.asp?pubid=2003521

O'Brien, D. G., & Dillion, D. R. (2008). The role of motivation in engaged reading of adolescents. In K. A. Hinchman & H. K. Sheridan-Thomas (Eds.), *Best Practices in Adolescent Literacy Instruction* (pp. 99–113). New York: Guilford Press.

Pitcher, S. M., Albright, L. K., DeLaney, C. J., Walker, N. T., Seunarinesingh, K., Mogge, S., et al. (2007). Assessing adolescents' motivation to read. *Journal of Adolescent & Adult Literacy, 50*(5), 378–396.

Schraw, G., Flowerday, T., & Reisetter, M. F. (1998). The role of choice in reader engagement. *Journal of Educational Psychology, 90,* 705–714.

SmartGirl. (2005). Teen read week 2005. Retrieved September 16, 2006, from http://www.smartgirl.org/reports/5100284.html

Wigfield, A. (1997). Children's motivation for reading and reading engagement. In J. T. Guthrie & A. Wigfield (Eds.), *Reading engagement: Motivating readers through integrated instruction.* Newark, DE: International Reading Association.

Wigfield, A., & Guthrie, J. T. (1997). Relations of children's motivation for reading to the amount and breadth of their reading. *Journal of Educational Psychology, 89,* 420–432.

Worthy, J., Moorman, M., & Turner, M. (1999). Why what Johnny likes to read is hard to find in school. *Research Quarterly, 34*(1), 12–27.

Yankelovich and Scholastic (2006). *The kids and family reading report.* Retrieved August 20, 2007, from www.scholastic.com/aboutscholastic/news/readingreport.htm

6

Dystopian Novels

What Imagined Futures Tell Young Readers about the Present and Future

Crag Hill

> Young people handle dystopia every day: in their lives, their dysfunctional families, their violence-ridden schools. They watch dystopian television and movies about the real world where firearms bring about explosive conclusions to conflict.
>
> —Lois Lowry, quoted in Hintz and Ostry (2003a)

TRAUMATIC YET TANTALIZING FUTURES

By the droves, adolescent readers—and, for many of the dystopian novels discussed in this chapter, adult readers (*The Hunger Games* series is sweeping across college campuses)—fearlessly transport themselves into disquieting futures that seem but a few missteps away from the world just outside the covers of the books they are reading. But these are not escapist novels, places to go to forget one's troubles; these are stories that turn a glaring eye on many of the problems we now face as humans. These are novels that exhort their readers to make changes before it is too late. What follows are glimpses of a few of them.

In the not-too-distant future of M. T. Anderson's *Feed* (2002), the populace is online virtually twenty-four hours a day. If you have sufficient credit, you can buy anything you want at any time. If you like the pair of pants your friend is wearing, all you need to do is glance at them and your computer feed, fed directly into your stream of thought, will tell you how much they cost and place the order for you. Your feed will subsequently be flooded with enticing advertisements for similar products and/or accessories. You can chat with your friends, too, whenever you want, no matter where you are (you will never need a keyboard again), by simply transmitting your thoughts into the feed.

Get into trouble at school, get on the bad side of your parents, and you may be unwound in the world of Neal Shusterman's *Unwind* (2007). Having failed to settle our differences over the issue of abortion, the United States has suffered a second civil war. The war ends with a compromise: In place of abortion, children between the ages of thirteen and eighteen, if unwanted by their parents or deemed delinquent by the state, can be retroactively aborted, or unwound, their body parts systematically harvested for those needing transplants. Yet, because all body parts are utilized and the unwound therefore become a vital part of the living, the public believes that technically they have not died.

In James Dashner's *The Maze Runner* (2009), a virulent disease spawned by increasing sun flare activity has killed millions of humans and laid much of the earth to waste. The ozone is destroyed. Go outside and you can be severely burned. Scientists, desperate to save the human race, create a grueling mental and physical test in which boys are imprisoned in a maze to observe how they work together to solve the life-threatening puzzle. Scientists hope the boy or boys who can crack the maze and escape will have the intelligence and motivation to develop a cure for the disease. But first they have to figure out who is on their side, if anyone.

Three series, the novels I will focus on in this chapter, have been particularly arresting for my high school and college students over the last ten years. In the first novel of Lois Lowry's *The Giver* series (1993), humans have created a highly structured world with stable families; children are safe wherever they go, and every citizen has a valued role in the community, one determined through careful observation of one's interests and abilities. The physical and emotional pain that often troubles our current lives is essentially absent. But for all these gains, many of the things that enrich our existence have been eradicated or suppressed.

In the opening of Scott Westerfeld's *Uglies* (2005a), physical appearance is paramount. The authorities have developed an operation that builds perfect bodies and faces, with everyone undergoing the pretty operation on their sixteenth birthday. Following the operation, the new pretties are free to party until they start training for the important jobs they are guaranteed in the community. Violence is unheard of, and there is no competition between cities for resources. Yet you discover that with this beauty and security comes an unsettling uniformity.

In Suzanne Collins's *The Hunger Games* trilogy (2008–2010), following a brutal civil war, the Capitol dictates what other districts can do economically and socially. The Capitol, in fact, possesses the power to force districts to give up two children each year to a game extravagantly staged for the

Capitol's entertainment in which only one child survives. Inhabitants are required to watch the Games, forced to witness as two of their young neighbors are likely to be killed each year. Dehumanization of all the vanquished districts is almost complete.

These hypothetical futures are relentlessly disturbing, yet adolescent readers are not giving up or giving in. They read these novels so intently they reluctantly close them at the end of sustained silent reading. They are compelled to go on; they want to find out what will happen next; they want to fight their way to a hopeful end. For the classroom today, it is critical that teachers provide the space for students to read and process the implications of these dystopian novels. As teachers, we must understand why students are fascinated with these stories, helping them find ways to think through the issues they raise. We must help them find answers to the questions they keep asking: What can I do to prevent such a world? How can we survive? How can we remain human?

AN OVERVIEW: DYSTOPIA DEFINED

A dystopia is a futuristic society in which a system has been constructed to allay the ills that pervade our present, such as poverty and overpopulation. On the surface this system, through advanced technology and/or other means, appears to benefit the populace, but on closer examination citizens are worse off. Distinguishing dystopian literature from science fiction, Booker (1994) contends that dystopian fiction

> constitutes a critique of existing social conditions or political systems, either through the critical examination of the utopian premises upon which those conditions and systems are based or through the imaginative extension of those conditions and systems into different contexts that more clearly reveal their flaws and contradictions. (p. 3)

Dystopian novels provide the aperture to view our present, providing "fresh perspectives on problematic social and political practices that might otherwise be taken for granted or considered natural and inevitable" (p. 3).

For Hintz and Ostry (2003), "Dystopias are . . . precise descriptions of societies, ones in which the ideals for improvement have gone tragically amok" (p. 3). They suggest that dystopian literature appeals to young readers because "the 'growing pains' of a society moving toward utopia or away from dystopia are framed as synonymous with adolescent growth itself, and the development of agency" (p. 10). Bleak though the future may be, young readers, who may feel unempowered in the present, can rehearse the role of liberator, saving the world from the maelstrom of destruction adults have set in motion.

Dystopian narratives have been a staple in American and British literature for more than a century. H. G. Wells's *The Sleeper Wakes* (1899), Charlotte Perkins Gilman's *Herland* (1915) (debatably the first feminist dystopia), Aldous Huxley's *Brave New World* (1932), Ayn Rand's *Anthem* (1938), George Orwell's *1984* (1949), Ray Bradbury's *Fahrenheit 451* (1953), Margaret Atwood's *The Handmaid's Tale* (1985), and Orson Scott Card's *Ender's Game* (1985), among others, have established themselves as classics within the genre, many currently included in the literature curriculum at the secondary and college levels. Read voraciously by teenagers and adults, the novels discussed below should also be seriously considered for inclusion into secondary language arts classes, especially as the centerpieces of units that explore agency at the individual and societal level.

A COMMON THEME: AGENCY AND COMMUNITY

Since Lois Lowry's *The Giver* (1993) offered adolescent readers a compelling, portentous world through which to explore their relationship to society, a spate of dystopian and postapocalyptic novels have propelled the young adult literature market. Dystopian novels such as Margaret Peterson Haddix's *Among the Hidden* (1998), Rodman Philbrick's *Last Book in the Universe* (2000), Nancy Farmer's *The House of the Scorpion* (2002), Cory Doctorow's *Little Brother* (2008), and Patrick Ness's *The Knife of Never Letting Go* (2008) deliver complex messages to their adolescent readers about their present and future. These cautionary tales expose readers to possible futures dominated by repressive governments assembled after military or environmental disasters, futures constricted by physical and intellectual uniformity, flawed solutions to today's problems. In positing ominous futures, these novels spotlight the present, proposing to readers that the freedoms they now enjoy may not be as permanent as they seem. By witnessing futuristic societies no one would want to inhabit, adolescent readers can imagine a future they desire, envisioning a present that can begin to build toward that future.

Personal agency, the capability to initiate and direct one's actions for specific purposes, figures prominently in these novels. For each of the narrative's teenaged protagonists, there is no greater principle than to act in ways that improve their lives and the lives of others. These novels implore readers to preserve the power over their own lives, but they also illustrate that such power is gained primarily through the concerted actions of a community, however large or small. As determined as an individual can be, lasting change cannot be accomplished alone.

A typical coming-of-age trope in young adult literature depicts teenagers, in response to pressure from parents, teachers, and peers, taking significant steps toward adulthood by making choices on their own terms with full awareness of the positive and negative consequences. Adolescent characters then attain adulthood when the choices they make not only arise out of their own individuation but also contribute to their community. The *Giver*, *Uglies*, and *Hunger Games* series add a layer to this trope, demonstrating that once teenaged protagonists perceive how government manipulates their lives, they must resist that control despite the peril to their own safety and the safety of their communities, or forever lose their autonomy. They learn that through their own actions joined with the actions of other citizens, they can overcome the tyranny of the state.

I argue that the following novels should be included in the high school curriculum. I argue, in addition, that these series—which have proven to be quick reads for my students of all ability levels—should be taught in their entirety. As I have witnessed for *The Hunger Games* at both the high school and university level, while the first novel is being discussed, many students in class have already read the second and often the third novels and are biting their tongues in order not to give anything away about the sequels. In the next three sections, I outline how agency plays out in these popular series and offer classroom applications to engage readers before, during, and after reading.

THE GIVER SERIES

The villages of Lois Lowry's *The Giver* (1993), *Gathering Blue* (2000), and *Messenger* (2004) have risen out of the ashes of a nuclear war. These societies—seemingly unconnected, determined in their insularity to protect themselves—have organized in an attempt to prevent the kinds of problems that led to the wide devastation. In *The Giver*, Jonas's society has dissolved economic classes. Every citizen is employed and every job is valued, with birth mothers and laborers on a par with Jonas's mother, who works in the Department of Justice. The government distributes the goods necessary to live comfortably—food, clothing, housing, and bicycles, the main mode of transportation; there are no have-nots. Sexual cravings have been medicinally eliminated; emotions such as anger and depression are effectively absent; pain, physical and psychological, is virtually unknown. On the societal level, competitiveness has been neutralized, and children conditioned from a very young age not to boast. Everything has its time, the lives of citizens unfolding with little uncertainty: from naming of children to assignment of vocations, to applying for marriage and children, to retirement in the Home of the Old, and, finally, to the honor of release.

But shadows stir beneath the veneer of equanimity. Surveillance is omnipresent, with the government monitoring all activities. Jonas, training to be the next Receiver, the keeper of the community's memories, is privy to what the populace has given up: sensual experience, the lessons of important historical events, and the perception of color (the world is now experienced in black and white). To Jonas, the greatest loss, however, is the loss of love, of intimacy. When he learns that release is not retirement to a carefree life elsewhere but rather euthanasia, he is distraught. Citizens, including Gabriel, a colicky infant, can be released without recourse. With his teacher's consent, Jonas resolves to flee the village with Gabriel, discharging the painful feelings and memories he had received back into the community. His destination is unknown, but Jonas knows that to enjoy the intimacy of love, one must also accept suffering. He forfeits one of the village's foremost positions to give the citizens a greater degree of self-determination.

Unlike Jonas's society, the Council of Guardians in *Gathering Blue* shuns technological development. Peasants scratch out a subsistence living; power and plenty reside in the Council Edifice, which reaps all it can from the labor of its serfs. Protecting itself from future cataclysmic events, this village also organizes itself in ways that squelch competition. Full employment exists—if people cannot fulfill a job, they are taken to the Field, where people believe beasts carry them away, never to be heard from again—yet quality of life is minimal: residents have shelter and food to eat, but no one can stockpile much of anything; when one dies of the diseases that periodically ravage the village, gardens are raided, huts dismantled or burned, clothing and other goods squirreled away by neighbors.

The only way to rise above this chronic poverty is to possess a gift utilized in the Gathering, an annual village ritual when the Ruin Song is recited to remind the citizens of the terrible world the state now shields them from. With her gift of embroidery, Kira repairs the Singer's robe and fills the gaps with new illustrations; Thomas the Carver possesses the gift of carving used to fashion the staff with which the Singer measures the song's pace; and Jo, with the gift of singing, trains to eventually replace the Singer. In the course of her training, Kira uncovers the brutality of the Council, who may have killed Thomas's and Jo's parents to take custody of the talented children. In the end, Kira ponders whether to stay and create change within this repressive society or to escape. Like Jonas, Kira opts to help her community with complete awareness of the consequences of her decision. Choosing to remain, in concert with Thomas and Jo, she will begin to tell a more optimistic story.

Messenger weaves together the worlds of *The Giver* and *Gathering Blue*. Jonas has become Leader of Village, a utopian community founded as a haven for outcasts from other societies, a place free of strife, every resident working for the good of all. Kira's father, once thought to be dead, plays a leading role in Village. Matty, the quintessential street urchin who befriends Kira and, in *Gathering Blue*, leads her blind father to Kira's village to meet her, becomes the messenger of Village, delivering messages from the Leader to outlying villages. As Village begins to veer toward xenophobia, deciding to close its borders to any new immigrants, the surrounding forest comes to malevolent life—rocks sharpen and throw themselves at Matty as he delivers his messages, and roots and branches choke and stab.

Having healed a frog's severed leg and resuscitated a deceased dog with his touch, Matty, now confident that his gift is healing, pours his body and spirit into the earth, certain that only he can save Village. In giving up his life to heal the hatred of Forest and Village, to restore peace, Matty has made the ultimate selfless choice.

Practical Classroom Applications

Before Reading: Three-Corner Debate

Ask students to write about what—if anything—they would give up (e.g. personal property, civil rights, lifestyle) in exchange for absolute safety (absence of crime, serious injury, emotional/physical abuse, and poverty), full employment for a lifetime, and social equality. Choose a student to share what he or she would give up and write it as a statement on the board (e.g., "I would give up my driver's license"). Ask students to sort themselves into three groups: (1) agree with statement, (2) disagree with statement, and (3) maybe agree/disagree. Begin the debate by calling on the "agree" group to provide a persuasive rationale in support of the statement. Then, ask the "disagree" group to rebut the rationale. Before returning to the agree group to respond to the rebuttal, ask if anyone in the "maybe agree/disagree" group has been persuaded to move to either the agree or disagree group. If not, ask someone from the maybe agree/disagree group to voice their position (why they neither agree nor disagree). Continue to debate by taking turns between the three groups. To ensure depth of argument, allow ten minutes before moving to another statement or until the points begin to be repetitive. Make time for at least five statements to be debated. As closure, ask students to write an exit slip about the most persuasive point they heard in the debate in favor of or against giving up something in exchange for safety, full employment, or social equality. Later, after reading the first few chapters of *The Giver*, read a selection of these writings to see if any of the students' choices played out in the novel.

During Reading: Compare/Contrast *The Giver* and *Gathering Blue*

Compare/contrast the way the village in *Gathering Blue* has structured itself to protect its citizens from the destructive consequences of a global war to the way the village in *The Giver* has been organized. In writing and/ or small group or whole class discussion, ask students to consider these questions: Who is in charge of the village? How do those in power in both novels share and/or withhold that power? What choices do citizens have in terms of employment? What is their quality of life (e.g., food, shelter, free time)? In what ways are citizens informed or not informed of the larger world around them? Which village would you prefer to live in? Why?

After Reading: Extending the Ending

Have students write a new chapter—individually or in small groups—in which Jonas returns to his native village. Have him enter into dialogues with the Giver, his parents, and his friends. Before writing, think about these questions: What happened when the memories he was carrying were let loose back into the village? How did people respond to Jonas's escape from the village? What has the village learned from these events? In what ways have they changed or not changed? Do they now experience pain and other emotions previously repressed? Do they still euthanize old people and unwanted children? Do they have more contact with other villages?

Another chapter option could be to write the scene in which Jonas and Gabriel are rescued from the snowstorm after their escape in *The Giver*. What do his rescuers know about the village he is fleeing? How do they take Jonas in? What are his first impressions of his new village? Does he want to contact his native village? What would he want to tell them? What kind of changes would he want them to make to the way they live? What would they have to do for him to consider returning?

Alternatively, these new chapters could be written as scripts. The scenes could then be rehearsed and performed or filmed for the class.

THE *UGLIES* SERIES

In Scott Westerfeld's *Uglies* series, cities are self-contained city-states. Carefully limiting population and consumption of natural resources, the sole commerce that cities exchange is the surgical technology for transforming uglies into pretties, including the medically induced brain lesions that repress individual initiative. These cities appear to be paradise; racism, sexism, jealousy, and crime are nonexistent—these thoughts, feelings, and actions engineered away by the surgical procedures that give everyone what humans most covet: perfect faces, perfect bodies, perfect social lives. Young pretties have no decisions greater than what to wear to the next party in New Pretty Town, and what and how much to drink; they cannot even imagine choices of larger import.

Only a few people know about the lesions and their suppression of free will: Maddy and Az—two doctors who quit pretty society for the wilderness when they found out about the lesions—and their wild-born son, David. When Tally is sent into the wild by Dr. Cable, inventor of the lesions, to locate and betray The Smoke, home to a growing number of runaway uglies, she becomes convinced that the use of lesions to control the populace is too high a price to pay for the physical and psychological comfort of being pretty. After she inadvertently alerts the police force, the Specials, to the location of The Smoke, having set off the tracking pendant when she tries to destroy it in a campfire, and the village is wiped out, its residents killed or captured, she chooses to act in the interests of others. Tally hazards her own life to rescue some of the captives from the Specials' compound, and when her friend Shay, now a pretty, is mentally incapable of giving consent, she volunteers to undergo the debilitating pretty operation in order to test the drug Maddy has developed to dissolve the lesions and restore agency.

Though Tally makes many selfless decisions throughout the series, more difficult and perilous decisions than any of her peers, she is conflicted and self-critical. She believes Dr. Cable has coerced her to choose her side in the battle between the city and the Smokies, first by postponing her pretty operation until she found and betrayed The Smoke. Yet as she experienced the Smokie way of life in *Uglies* (2005a)—living communally at a subsistence level—she decided to remain ugly for the rest of her life, giving up the mindless hedonism of New Pretty Town. In *Pretties* (2005b), she believes her motivation to find Maddy in the wilderness to help her friend Zane, with whom she split the experimental pills, his health deteriorating as a result of only taking half of the cure, was self-serving. It is her resolve, however, to be "bubbly," to be able to think clearly, to express her free will, that inspires her peers to do likewise and to escape the city. In *Specials* (2007), as Tally and Shay, now Specials themselves, track a group of runaway pretties, the Crims, to Diego, a city being liberated from the lesions, Tally believes her affection for Zane again is the driving force for her actions. Tally indeed acts in her self-interest, yet she also exhibits considerable concern for others.

In all three novels, Tally's journeys into the wild stimulate her growth. In *Uglies*, she determines to stay with the Smokies in the mountains, persuaded that their lifestyle, though not without its problems, was a more ethical one. In *Pretties*, her long, rugged escape with Zane allows her to cure herself, to seize control of her will despite the presence of the invasive lesions, to permanently think herself as "bubbly." In *Specials*, Tally's arduous journey to Diego motivates her to circumvent the Special operation forced on her by Dr. Cable. Ultimately, Tally achieves freedom of choice and elects to roam the wild with David, ready to spring into action when they determine the cities are following the doomed steps of the Rusties too closely. Through the arc of the trilogy, Dr. Cable's power shrinks while Tally's expands. Unlike Dr. Cable, who used her strength and intelligence to subdue the people of the city without their knowledge and volition, Tally resolves to exercise her power for the betterment of others during her lifetime and to protect the earth for future generations.

Practical Classroom Applications

Before Reading: Predicting Setting and Characters

Ask students to predict in writing what kinds of natural and/or man-made disasters could end the way we currently live our lives. In the wake of these disasters, what will happen to our cities? What will happen to the forests, rivers, and mountains, to the wildlife? How will the survivors rebuild to prevent the same kinds of disasters from happening again? Based on these writings, have students in groups envision a model city three hundred years after the ecological disasters they predicted. How will these cities handle water? How will they feed their citizens? How will they dispose of individual and industrial waste? What will education consist of? Have each group present these ideas to the class, making sure to highlight any details that match up with the depiction of the cities in the series. Post the similarities on the board as the beginning details for the setting of *Uglies*.

To make predictions of characters, ask students to leaf through a variety of magazines—entertainment, sports, news—searching for the perfect male and perfect female face. Ask students to write what makes these faces perfect; then, in small groups, discuss what qualities make them perfect and what would happen if everyone had them. What would daily life be like? What would young people be interested in? What social problems might be eased? What new social problems might arise? Ultimately, what would be gained or lost with such alterations to the human body?

During Reading: Protecting the Natural World

In the *Uglies* series, cities leave the natural world outside their boundaries essentially untouched. As an extension of the "before reading" exercise, ask students what they would consider eliminating in their current lives in terms of the demands they make on the environment (e.g., driving to school, purchasing the latest electronic device, eating fast food). Have them spend at least one class period researching the cost of these activities or products on the environment. Questions to consider: Where do these products come from? What natural resources are used in their production? Then have students prepare a two- or three-minute speech about why they would eliminate this activity or product from their lives, supporting their points with their research on the costs of these products to the environment. Following the speeches, discuss in small groups or as a whole class what activities or products could realistically be reduced or removed from our lives.

In what ways as individuals can we make our cities more self-sustaining? In what ways can individuals in concert with groups of other individuals ensure we sustainably manage the consumption of our natural resources?

After Reading: Making Comics

At the end of *Specials*, Tally Youngblood still possesses the superhuman reflexes, strength, and senses she received from Dr. Cable's special operation. Ask students to script and draw (or use a comic program such as Comic Life) a four-to-eight-page comic that shows Tally and David fighting against out-of-control development. Show them intervening in the clear-cutting in Diego or similar events. How will they not only stop that kind of development but also convince the citizens of these cities to preserve the environment? Because they cannot respond to all of this activity with physical force, what kinds of practices will they try to implement to teach citizens to design self-sustaining civic projects?

THE HUNGER GAMES TRILOGY

At the start of Suzanne Collins's *The Hunger Games* (2008), the Capitol, victors in a massive civil war now decades past, holds a monopoly on resources, both natural and human. Maintaining airtight control of information, the Capitol wields its power to subjugate the other districts physically and psychologically, employing the Hunger Games, a nationally televised extravaganza devised by the Capitol, to remind the other districts of the Dark Days when their rebellion was crushed. Each district surrenders its resources to enhance the utopian lifestyle of the Capitol. Citizens in districts like District 12, a destitute coal-mining region, barely eke out a living, forcefully discouraged from supplementing their meager livelihoods by hunting or other means. On the fringes of the Capitol's authority, however, Katniss and Gale hunt for game outside the electrified fences, which they trade for other goods. It is these trips beyond the grasp of the Capitol, analogous to Tally's journeys, that plant the seed for Katniss's resistance, for the freedom she ultimately wins, the right to conduct her own life on its own terms.

But first Katniss must survive the Games. As one of two tributes from District 12, Katniss must find a way to defeat the tributes from the other districts, or die as part of the macabre entertainment for the Capitol. Intensely independent—Katniss has been the caretaker of her household since her father's death in a mining accident, her mother being incapacitated by grief—Katniss outwits the tributes from the other districts in the battle royale because of her woodsman's skills along with her determination to spite the Capitol, to win or die by her own methods. She forces the Gamemakers to back down when she and Peeta, the other District 12 tribute, threaten to kill themselves with poisonous berries. As the Games must have a winner, both Katniss and Peeta are declared victors. Their victory, however, viewed by the entire country, was a serious affront to the authority of President Snow and the Capitol.

In *Catching Fire* (2009), Katniss's worldview begins to shift from a focus on herself to a commitment toward others, though initially she does not recognize those who are working with her for the greater good, including her mentor Haymitch. As a result of her defiant actions in the Hunger Games, Katniss has become a reluctant symbol for the downtrodden districts, instigating them to revolt in whatever ways they can. But these protests have brutal consequences. As she and Peeta take their victory tour through the districts, Katniss witnesses displays of solidarity followed by the Capitol's swift and ruthless response. Desperate to end Katniss's growing influence, the Capitol invokes the right to stage Quarter Quell, reaping tributes from the pool of surviving winners from previous Hunger Games, to kill off those who could foster an uprising. By the conclusion of *Catching Fire,* Katniss accepts her symbolic role as the mockingjay, joining an alliance of districts, including District 13, once thought to have been annihilated, to fight for the end to the Capitol's rule. Like Jonas, Kira, Matty, and Tally, Katniss is willing to put her life on the line to create change for the good of the community.

In *Mockingjay* (2010), as a result of playing a major role in weakening the power of the Capitol, Katniss earns the dubious right to publicly execute President Snow in retribution for the Capitol's atrocities. But other events intervene, forcing Katniss to make difficult choices, none of them unequivocally right or wrong. To assuage the fury of the other districts, District 13, the new Capitol, plans to hold the Hunger Games one more time, now featuring tributes from the Capitol. In reaction, Katniss chooses to assassinate the new president, Coin, instead—Snow is trampled in the aftermath—accomplishing a larger goal: snapping the cycle of ritualized violence that has gripped her world. Despite her role in liberating the country, Katniss is dismayed at her actions. No longer needed as a symbol or a leader in any other capacity, suffering excruciating nightmares, Katniss retreats to the ruins of District 12, where she tries to find meaning in her life. Finally, after many years in the company of Peeta, Katniss begins to recover and starts a family. To endure the terrors of her nightmares, afraid that any pleasure she experiences in life could be snatched away at any time, Katniss composes a list "of every act of goodness [she has] seen someone do" (p. 390). By compiling such a record, Katniss contextualizes her own actions, coming to terms with what she has done and become, and in doing so boosts her fragile sense of morality.

Practical Classroom Applications

Before Reading: Simulations of the Reaping and the Games

Simulate a reaping from Katniss's impoverished district. Divide the class into families of three or four, one or two adults and two children. Assign families equally to three economic classes: subsistence (father unemployed, missing, or deceased; members hunt, gather, and barter on the black market to try to make ends meet), worker (father employed in the local industry, able to bring home a consistent salary, but there is no compensation if he is injured or sick and unable to work), or merchant (relatively well-to-do; have more than enough to meet the needs of the family, but do not feel secure enough to share their relative wealth with families in need).

For each child in the family, put their names on five slips of paper and put them in a jar. The subsistence class can elect to supplement their family income by putting more slips into the reaping—they receive bread for a week for three additional slips for each child. The working class can also supplement their family income by putting in one more slip for each child, for which they will receive bread for two weeks. Pull the name of one male and one female. Repeat the reaping ten times. How many times were those from the subsistence class picked? How many times were the other two classes picked? Discuss the implications of these results.

To provide a sense of what happens to the children in the Games, organize a simulation. As students enter the classroom circle (move all desks to the side), hand them a playing card (evenly divided between clubs, spades, hearts, and diamonds). To represent those lost at the beginning of the Games, in the melee at the cornucopia, declare all those with diamonds out of the game (thirty-two students down to twenty-four). For round 2, have students meet in six groups of four. Have them count the money they have in their possession. The group with the least is out of the game (down to eighteen players). In round 3, draw a target on the board. Have students make paper airplanes and try to hit the target. The four whose airplanes are farthest from the target are out of the game (down to fourteen). For round 4, ask students to draw a map of the school in two minutes. Eliminate the four least accurate maps (down to ten). For the next round, give students a riddle to solve, eliminating those who can't solve the riddle in one minute. At this time, those eliminated in the first four rounds can decide to give one or more of the remaining players some object that will protect them (clothing, first aid, a hiding place for one round, etc.). This item protects the player from elimination during the next round. In the next round, arrange a foot race. Eliminate all but two (unless one or more of the players has been given protection). For the last round, have the students do push-ups. The person who does the most in two minutes is the winner. If needed, create more rounds. Essentially, the simulation should represent the strength, skills, wit, and luck needed to survive the Games. A follow-up discussion could focus on what students thought and felt as they eliminated their peers or were eliminated. How could they prepare for these kinds of life-or-death Games?

During Reading: News/Sports Writing, Editorials

Ask students to write newspaper articles or scripts for broadcast news or sports that describe the events during the Games for the citizens of the Capitol. These articles/scripts could report the events from an overall perspective, or they could focus on one character and describe what they have been doing in the Games and how they are holding up. What strategies are they taking to be competitive? How are they protecting themselves? What kind of techniques are they employing as they hunt the others? These articles/scripts should include comments about the events from the citizens of the Capitol. Another option would be to write an editorial in favor of one of the contestants, urging readers to sponsor this contestant to improve his or her chances of winning. The editorial should highlight what qualities make this contestant worthy of sponsorship.

After Reading: Interviews with Key Participants

Have students script interviews with Peeta, Katniss, Haymitch, and others twenty-five years after the final Games. Questions to consider: What do they remember about the Games? What do they wish they could forget? What did they learn about humanity during these Games? What are they or others doing to make sure something like the Games never happens again? In what ways has life improved since the end of the Games and the defeat of the Capitol? These interviews could be rehearsed and videotaped with documentary scenes spliced in (e.g., footage from the Games could be acted out or clips could be taken from movies such as *Lord of the Flies* and other films).

CONCLUSION

Why do the above dystopian novels have such appeal for adolescent readers and why should we teach them? Zipes (2003) conjectures:

> We are living in very troubled times. More than ever before, we need utopian and dystopian literature. . . . These kinds of literary works emanate from a critique of "postmodern," advanced technological societies gone awry—and from a strong impulse for social change. (p. ix)

These novels suggest to readers that ordinary teenagers such as Jonas, Tally, and Katniss "can take power into their own hands and create better worlds for themselves" (Zipes, 2003, p. xi). Hintz and Ostry (2003b) argue that utopian and dystopian literature teaches young readers about social organization, instructing them "to view their society with a critical eye, sensitizing or predisposing them to political action" (p. 7). By encountering the colossal dysfunctions of potential societies through their imagination, adolescent readers prepare "for a more sustained consideration of the nature of justice and other elements of ideal social life" (p. 9). By witnessing the absence of agency, readers measure "the value of every individual to the community, as well as the need to keep society from dismantling individual rights" (p. 9). These novels advocate that readers hold on fiercely to their independence and, fortified by relationships with others who share their vision, work for social, political, and economic parity during their lifetimes. In critiquing our present, these futuristic worlds foreground what we cannot lose lest we be lost forever.

Johnson, Kleismit, and Williams (2002), Hintz and Ostry (2003b), Hintz (2003), and Zipes (2003) argue that dystopian novels champion free will, teenaged protagonists creating change in their lives when adults have failed to make a difference. In cooperation with the Giver, Jonas pulls the veil of repression from his society, forcing its citizens to live again with the full range of human emotions. When Kira chooses to remain in her village, she positions herself, along with Thomas and Jo, to seize the village's narrative from the Guardians. Matty gives more than any other character, his life, to heal the fear and anger tearing apart his world. With other courageous teenaged characters, Tally, forgoing the comforts that technology had fashioned for humans, fights against a group of adults who have decided that mind control is an acceptable vehicle to maintain peace, their struggle returning self-determination to millions of people. Benefitting from Peeta, Haymitch, and other adult supporters throughout the *Hunger Games* series, Katniss spearheads a drastic revision of her world, challenging its use of violence to subdue those who do not agree.

In all these novels, teenaged protagonists manifest their abilities and motivation to transform their societies; they selflessly apply their agency to fight for what they believe is right.

Adolescents are well aware of the problems in our world: the threat of annihilation by war, environmental degradation, the pervasiveness of poverty, inequitable access to education and healthcare resources, and many others. Uncertain about how their lives will unfold in the future, readers of young adult dystopian fiction learn that their world can be drastically different. Through systemic government intervention and/or scientific manipulation, personal safety and health may be enhanced, differences between people—physical, social, economic—made less so. Yet these seemingly attractive advances may have unfathomably adverse effects. In view of these novels, young readers can imagine the world they would want to live in, then begin to find ways to create that world.

When students study novels such as those discussed above, participating in conversations about their present and how it may lead to a desirable or undesirable future, they are challenged to live not only in the present but in the light—or dark—of their future. Studying these novels will not only tap into what students are independently reading by the ream, but also engage adolescents in the core of their beings at a time when they are just beginning to envisage ways to live a meaningful life. We cannot miss the opportunity to connect our students to what is possible through the power of their freely exercised imaginations.

REFERENCES

Anderson, M. T. (2002). *Feed.* Cambridge, MA: Candlewick Press.
Atwood, M. (1985). *The handmaid's tale.* Boston: Houghton Mifflin.
Booker, M. K. (1994). *Dystopian literature: A theory and research guide.* Westport, CT: Greenwood Press.
Bradbury, R. (1953/1996). *Fahrenheit 451.* New York: Ballantine.
Card, O. S. (1985). *Ender's game.* New York: Tor.
Collins, S. (2008). *The hunger games.* New York: Scholastic.
Collins, S. (2009). *Catching fire.* New York: Scholastic.
Collins, S. (2010). *Mockingjay.* New York: Scholastic.
Dashner, J. (2009). *The maze runner.* New York: Delacorte Press.
Doctorow, C. (2008). *Little brother.* New York: Tor Teen.
Farmer, N. (2002). *The house of the scorpion.* New York: Atheneum.
Gilman, C. P. (1915/1998). *Herland.* Mineola, NY: Dover.
Haddix, M. P. (1998). *Among the hidden.* New York: Simon & Schuster.
Hintz, C. (2003). "Joy but not peace": Zilpha Keatley Snyder's *Green-sky trilogy.* In C. Hintz & E. Ostry (Eds.), *Utopian and dystopian writing for children and young adults* (pp. 107–117). New York: Routledge.
Hintz, C., and Ostry, E. Interview with Lois Lowry, author of *The Giver.* (2003a) In C. Hintz and E. Ostry (Eds.), *Utopian and dystopian writing for children and young adults* (pp. 196–199). New York: Routledge.
Hintz, C., and Ostry, E. (Eds.). (2003b). *Utopian and dystopian writing for children and young adults.* New York: Routledge.
Huxley, A. (1932/1998). *Brave new world.* New York: Perennial Classics.
Johnson, A. B., Kleismit, J. W., & Williams, A. J. (2002). Grief, thought, and appreciation: Re-examining our values amid terrorism through *The Giver. The ALAN Review, 29*(3), 15–19.
Lowry, L. (1993). *The giver.* New York: Laurel-Leaf.
Lowry, L. (2000). *Gathering blue.* New York: Laurel-Leaf.
Lowry, L. (2004). *Messenger.* New York: Laurel-Leaf.
Ness, P. (2008). *The knife of never letting go.* Somerville, MA: Candlewick Press.

Orwell, G. (1949/1961). *1984*. New York: Signet Classics.
Philbrick, R. (2000). *Last book in the universe.* New York: Scholastic.
Rand, A. (1938/1995). *Anthem*. New York: Signet Classics.
Shusterman, N. (2007). *Unwind*. New York: Simon & Schuster.
Wells, H. G. (1899/2000). *The sleeper wakes.* Lincoln, NE: Bison Books.
Westerfeld, S. (2005a). *Uglies*. New York: Simon & Schuster.
Westerfeld, S. (2005b). *Pretties*. New York: Simon & Schuster.
Westerfeld, S. (2007). *Specials*. New York: Simon & Schuster.
Zipes, J. (2003). Utopia, dystopia, and the quest for hope. In C. Hintz & E. Ostry (Eds.), *Utopian and dystopian writing for children and young adults*. New York: Routledge.

7

Out of the Closet and Into the Open

LGBTQ Young Adult Literature in the Language Arts Classroom

Laura A. Renzi, Mark Letcher, and Kristen Miraglia

With a quick scan through the TV channels on any given night, society at large would seem to be an accepting, welcoming place—open homosexual relationships on prime-time television shows; news stories about the parents of students bullied for veering from the normal, socially accepted, heterosexual, hormone-filled teenager or the parents of a transgender kindergartener fighting for the child's rights in school; and the occasional retired professional athlete "coming out" to the world.

The students in our nation's schools are watching *Glee* and *Skins*, both of which prominently portray lesbian, gay, bisexual, transgender, and questioning (LGBTQ) characters, relationships, and themes. Other popular culture texts include Katy Perry's "Firework" and Beyoncé's "All the Single Ladies" music videos, which include a same-gender kiss and a transgender dancer respectively. Although there have been same-gender kisses before, à la Britney Spears and Madonna, or the Jennifer Aniston–Winona Ryder kiss on a *Friends* episode, these recent music videos and television sitcoms don't simply forefront these LGBTQ acts; they are a part of the story message of the video or show. They are a part of the community, not a showpiece. These shows portray an accepting attitude toward LGBTQ characters; however, there is conflicting information indicating that the culture our adolescents experience within our nation's schools is not as accepting as mass media would have us believe.

THE PROBLEM

According to the Gay, Lesbian, and Straight Education Network (GLSEN), there is a problem in our nation's schools: hostile school environments where students who identify as LGBTQ are bullied, assaulted, isolated, do worse in academics, and overall are singled out for their sexuality or gender expression. According to the GLSEN School Climate Survey (2009),

- 88.9 percent of students heard "gay" used in a negative way
- 72.4 percent heard other homophobic language frequently
- 61.1 percent felt unsafe at school
- 84.6 percent were verbally harassed at school because of their sexual orientation
- 62.4 percent did not report the harassment, believing staff would take little or no action

Although this survey reported no dramatic change from the survey GLSEN conducted in 1999, it is not enough to say that our schools aren't getting worse. "Schools nationwide are hostile environments for a distressing number of LGBT students—almost all of whom commonly hear homophobic remarks and face verbal and physical harassment and even physical assaults because of their sexual orientation or gender expression" (Gay, Lesbian, and Straight Education Network, 2010). The 2009 survey reported LGBTQ students' belief that teachers and staff would do nothing to help them, which is just as horrifying as the idea of these students being singled out in the first place. This speaks to the hostile environment that the GLSEN survey revealed, an environment forged by students, faculty, staff, parents, and community.

An extremely important positive finding from the 2009 GLSEN survey is that schools that have active Gay-Straight Alliances (GSAs) and/or supportive inclusive curricula were seen as less hostile to LGBTQ students. An inclusive curriculum, according to the survey, included positive representations of LGBTQ people in multiple areas within the school curriculum. These representations were seen in health classes, history classes, and English classes (Gay, Lesbian, and Straight Education Network, 2009). According to the survey findings, in schools with inclusive curricula:

- students were more likely to report that their classmates were somewhat or very accepting of LGBTQ people
- students heard fewer homophobic remarks
- less than half (42.1 percent) of students felt unsafe because of their sexual orientation

- less than a fifth (17.1 percent) of LGBTQ students had missed school in the past month (compared to 31.6 percent of other students)
- LGBTQ students had a greater connectedness to their school community than other students

In everyday society, conversation about "don't ask, don't tell" or "gay marriage" is widespread, so why is it that LGBTQ young adult literature can't find its place in our nation's secondary classrooms? The language arts classroom is an obvious place to begin this inclusive curriculum (or continue it, for some) by bringing positive representations of LGBTQ people into the classroom. When speaking about what literature can do, Robert Probst (2006) states, "Literature offers us the opportunity to come to understand better the possible range of human experience, to see our lives and the world more clearly" (p. 47). As teachers of literature, but more importantly as teachers of students, we all know the power of literature. Helping students find meaning, a connection to something outside of their own individual world, is amazing. We look for the opportunity, we plan for it, and when it happens in the classroom we remember the exact moment. Langner (1995) reminds us that literature is a way to explore possibilities and help students find themselves, imagine others, value difference, and search for social justice. Literature is used to explore students' responses to the world (Purves, Rogers, & Soter, 1990), and it has the "power to transport us to unexplored worlds and allows us—at least as long as the book lasts—to become other than who we are" (Jago, 2000, p. 7). Wilhelm (1997) reminds us that "literature offers the possibility for so much more. Literature is transcendent; it offers possibilities; it takes us beyond space, time, and self; it questions the world as it is and offers possibilities for the way it could be. It offers a variety of views, visions, and voices that are so vital to a democracy" (p. 38). The power of literature to encourage imagination and change lives has been a consistent notion throughout the years.

Literature reflects our lives and our place in society, but it can also make us painfully aware of reality; the reality is that some of our students' lives are invisible, nonexistent, or just plain ignored. LGBTQ young adult literature provides an opportunity for LGBTQ students to see themselves, to look into a mirror (Bishop, 1992), and to reflect on their lives. And yet, in spite of the popular culture images of LGBTQ issues mentioned at the beginning of this chapter, young adult literature that reflects these images and issues back to young readers is conspicuously absent from our nation's secondary classrooms. Literature often pushes ahead of society, reflecting the future of what could be. The increased occurrence of LGBTQ characters in young adult literature who are accepted, loved, and fully engaged members of society shows the reader a society that could be—

a society that should be. Cart and Jenkins (2006) would categorize this new wave of texts as Queer Consciousness/Community.

A BRIEF HISTORY OF LGBTQ THEMES IN YOUNG ADULT LITERATURE

As young adult literature (YAL) has developed as a field of literature, one group of adolescents who have struggled to gain exposure in print have been LGBTQ teens. As in adult fiction, adolescent titles with LGBTQ themes and characters are not a recent phenomenon. Thankfully, these works are becoming more prevalent today.

Prior to the 1960s, examples of gay and lesbian characters in literature for young people were extremely rare. Incidental treatment of homosexuality can be found in Maureen Daly's *Seventeenth Summer*, published in 1942, and J. D. Salinger's *Catcher in the Rye*, published in 1951. The scenes with homosexual themes in each novel are brief, and while noteworthy, they hardly constitute a movement toward more inclusive literature for LGBTQ adolescent readers.

The gay liberation movement is often seen as officially beginning in June 1969 with the Stonewall riots, in which a police raid on a Greenwich Village gay bar incited the patrons to fight back for the first documented time in history. Gays had always been a visible presence beforehand, but this event was the catalyst for a sudden eruption of activity. The year 1969 also saw the publication of what is widely considered to be the first YA novel to deal with homosexuality in a frank and open manner. John Donovan's *I'll Get There. It Better Be Worth the Trip* follows Davy, a lonely thirteen-year-old who, after his grandmother's death, must move to Manhattan to live with his estranged mother. Davy's friendship with a boy from his new school begins to turn more than platonic; their reaction to their budding romance conveys guilt and shame. Davy's dog is even killed by a car earlier in the novel, an event that Davy views as punishment for his deviance from the socially accepted norm. At the novel's end, the boys agree that "the important thing is not to do it again" (p. 188). The idea of homosexuality being directly associated with misfortune, or even death, became a prominent theme in the few YA titles that dealt with homosexuality in the years following the publication of Donovan's novel.

The year 1976 saw the publication of Rosa Guy's *Ruby*, the first YA novel with an arguably lesbian character. High school seniors Ruby and Daphne develop a strong relationship throughout the novel, but in the end Daphne denies her lesbian feelings, in order to maintain heterosexuality; Ruby's sexual orientation, however, remains unclear. Still, with no major characters dying by book's end, the treatment of LGBTQ characters and themes in *Ruby* can be viewed as forward progress for LGBTQ adolescent literature.

Guy's sensitive portrayal of a lesbian couple helped pave the way for Nancy Garden's 1982 novel, *Annie on My Mind*. The high school seniors in this novel, Annie and Liza, struggle with their feelings for each other, but they ultimately accept that their love is real and cannot be denied. While the novel does feature secondary characters with strong homophobic reactions to the couple, Garden's novel is an important landmark in LGBTQ literature because of the way it depicts the powerful and enduring love between the characters. In addition, Annie and Liza remain a couple at the end of the novel despite the obstacles in their way.

Homosexuality became tinged with an even darker specter in the 1980s as AIDS began to ravage the gay community. The first YA novel to deal with AIDS was M. E. Kerr's *Night Kites*, published in 1986, five years after the official discovery of the disease. Kerr presents a sensitive and, even to this day, extremely brave depiction of a gay man who contracts AIDS and returns home to die. Narrated by his younger brother, Erik, *Night Kites* remains one of the most believable narratives of AIDS suffering. While AIDS prompted a great deal of adult literature on the subject, few YA titles tackled the disease in its early days, aside from Kerr's novel, Ron Koertge's *The Arizona Kid* (1988), and Theresa Nelson's *Earthshine* (1994).

Perhaps encouraged by the publication of Kerr's novel, the 1980s saw a greater number of YA titles dealing with LGBTQ issues. Norma Klein's *Breaking Up* (1980) features a gay parent, and Gary Bargar's *What Happened to Mr. Forster?* (1981) is set in the 1950s, when a gay sixth-grade teacher resigns due to parental pressure. *Jack*, written by A. M. Homes in 1989, depicts a young man trying to maintain a normal life in the face of his parents' divorce, after learning that the reason for the divorce was his father's homosexuality. Francesca Lia Block's *Weetzie Bat* (1989), which spawned several later novels, presented an unabashedly upbeat and quirky view of love in many forms, through a magical realist lens.

Novels such as Homes's and Block's laid the groundwork for the 1990s and an even greater number of YA titles dealing with LGBTQ issues. While many books in this decade still only tangentially dealt with these themes (i.e., homosexuals were minor characters), several notable titles broke new ground. In 1994, Marion Dane Bauer edited *Am I Blue? Coming Out from the Silence*, the first collection of LGBTQ short stories. Chris Crutcher introduced Angus Bethune in his 1991 short story collection, *Athletic Shorts*. Angus lives with two gay parents, without any apparent trauma or problems as a result. Through Angus's love for his parents, and their new partners, Crutcher showed readers that LGBTQ teens, or heterosexual teens with LGBTQ parents, could indeed lead stable and rewarding lives. Jacqueline Woodson's *From the Notebooks of Melanin Sun* (1995) dealt with an African American teen's coming to grips with his mother's lesbianism and her relationship with a white woman. M. E. Kerr continued to address LGBTQ topics, with the 1994 release of *Deliver Us from Evie*, a rich, well-drawn lesbian love story set in rural Missouri, concluding with the lovers leaving town, alive and still a couple. As the 1990s ended, two works were published that still stand as strong representations of what teen LGBTQ literature can accomplish: Stephen Chbosky's *The Perks of Being a Wallflower*, and Ellen Wittlinger's *Hard Love*, both published in 1999. When read alongside works from earlier decades, it is clear that LGBTQ young adult literature had come a long way, particularly in the way Charlie, in Chbosky's novel, simply accepts the revelation that his friend Patrick is gay, without significant drama or angst.

The beginning of the twenty-first century saw an increased rate of publication for LGBTQ-themed titles in the field of YAL, as well as several landmark works. David Levithan's *Boy Meets Boy* (2003) is significant for the ways in which he disrupts the idea of a heteronormative society and moves beyond a call for tolerance for LGBTQ teens, imagining a world in which acceptance is the norm rather than the exception. Julie Anne Peters's *Luna: A Novel*, published in 2004, was the first YA novel to feature a transgender main character.

Bisexuality has become a more prevalent theme in recent years, though not overly so. Titles that address bisexuality, or possible bisexuality, include Garret Freymann-Weyr's *My Heartbeat* (2002), Brent Hartinger's *Geography Club* (2003), Lauren Myracle's *Kissing Kate* (2003), Maureen Johnson's *The Bermudez Triangle* (2004), Sara Ryan's *The Rules for Hearts* (2007), and Julie Anne Peters's *Rage: A Love Story* (2009). In some of these titles, the question of a character's sexual orientation is never fully resolved, and perhaps that's the way it should be. Sexual identity can be a fluid construction, affected by personality, peers, and societal influences, so it is encouraging that YAL reflects this. At the same time, there is room for much more exploration of identity-questioning in YAL.

A clear reflection of LGBTQ young adult literature's increased quantity and quality has been the establishment in 2010 of a Children and Young Adult Literature area of the American Library Association's Stonewall Awards, given annually to the best LGBTQ publications in the previous year. Top honors for 2010 and 2011, given to Nick Burd's *The Vast Fields of Ordinary* (2009) and Brian Katcher's *Almost Perfect* (2009), respectively, demonstrate not only that LGBTQ young adult literature has progressed rapidly in its relatively short history, but also that it represents some of the most daring and well-written literature within adolescent literature.

IN THE CLASSROOM

This dramatic increase in publication rates is wonderful news, but these texts are still finding it hard to gain access to young adults through school libraries and secondary English classrooms. The reticence of preservice and in-service teachers to include LGBTQ texts in the classroom has been well documented (Blackburn & Buckley, 2005; Clark & Blackburn, 2009; Steffel & Renzi-Keener, 2009). The concerns of retribution, censorship, and/or push back from the students and community are real concerns, but as the GLSEN report reveals, the welfare of our students is at stake.

Articles about LGBTQ young adult literature's literary merit and impassioned pleas to include this literature in classrooms have been published in scholarly journals (Banks, 2009; Cart, 2004; Cart & Jenkins, 2006; Hayn & Hazlett, 2011); however, there have been few articles that actually look at LGBTQ texts or themes being included in the high school English curriculum. Vicki Greenbaum's "Literature Out of the Closet: Bringing Gay and Lesbian Texts and Subtexts Out in High School English" was published in 1994 in *English Journal*. Greenbaum, as a closeted English teacher, began to question the traditional texts taught in her classroom. She challenged the heteronormative readings of these texts, and her students responded as "entire classes began to notice the often ignored (or tip-toed around) moments" in *Catcher in the Rye* and *The Glass Menagerie* (p. 72). This example of inclusive teaching is not alone, but they are few and far between.

In the 2009 special edition of *English Journal* dedicated to sexual identity and gender expression, Clark and Blackburn's review of the literature titled "Reading LGBT-Themed Literature with Young People: What's Possible?" focused on LGBTQ texts' use in schools. Although it is telling that there were only a handful of studies and articles reviewed in this piece, this article does give an idea about the texts that are being taught and the ways in which they are being presented in both middle and high school classrooms. This review found that "across the classrooms [studied], students were free and even empowered to maintain a homophobic position" (p. 27). As Clark and Blackburn point out, the assumption that students are homophobic only reinforces the heteronormative attitude and environment in many of our nation's schools. If we as teachers approach the material and our classrooms assuming students to be either LGBTQ themselves or supportive allies, we can disrupt the heterosexual norm and begin to question *why* students are homophobic rather than reinforcing these homophobic attitudes.

As educators, we (the authors) realize this is a risky proposition, but there is an inherent political action to teaching. Why we read, why we learn, and how we learn are all subject to a political viewpoint, and including LGBTQ-themed literature in the classroom is certainly a political action. There has to be a conscious choice on the part of the teacher to examine the heteronormative environment of the school and to include LGBTQ ideas, themes, and literature in the classroom to battle the homophobia that pervades our schools. To teach a text with LGBTQ themes and characters without combating the homophobia in a school reinforces the validity and social acceptance of this homophobic environment. Without a conscious choice or adequate examination of one's own actions and language, a teacher contributes to the homophobic environment of the school and classroom.

GETTING STARTED

As earlier discussed, bringing these texts into the classroom is not only possible but also necessary (Clark & Blackburn, 2009). But we have also seen that if it is not done correctly, bringing LGBTQ texts into the classroom reinforces the homophobic environment found in our nation's schools. In looking for a particular text that fits into the classroom and touches on the LGBTQ issue, we find quite a range of texts that address a myriad of issues. However, bringing in an LGBTQ text just for the sake of bringing in an LGBTQ text can cause more harm than good. Students who are questioning or identify as LGBTQ could begin to feel (or continue to feel) alienated, and a teacher could mistakenly teach students that one specific type of person is the embodiment of this sexual identity, thereby reinforcing existing stereotypes.

As the GLSEN survey found, an LGBTQ-inclusive curriculum provides the best results in combating the homophobic and heteronormative environment of the schools, as well as in creating an environment where LGBTQ students feel comfortable in the classrooms. In the English language arts classroom, LGBTQ characters need to be part of a critical literacy approach to reading and discussing literature. The classroom must be an environment free from judgment and also a place safe for questions and discussion. The texts used in the classrooms must represent various perspectives; if just one book is used, there is danger of students believing that all LGBTQ characters, and thus all LGBTQ people, fall into one category. As is the case with all characters and people, there are multiple perspectives, races, languages, religions, home lives, and living situations. A variety of experiences must be represented in the books chosen for the English language arts classroom.

The inclusion of LGBTQ characters in the classroom through the use of literature should not be reactionary. If a text is brought into the classroom after a student comes out, after a bullying incident, or after a media story, the danger is that anyone in your classroom who self-identifies could be seen with pity or sympathy instead of being seen as just another student in the classroom, drawing undue attention and possible harm to that student. The inclusion of LGBTQ texts and conversations needs to be a planned, discussed part of the curriculum; a coherent and consistent message from the administration and faculty must be present to combat homophobia in the schools.

For those who don't know where to start or who fear the retribution in your school district, start with questioning. Take an honest look at the literature and readings that you have students work with in your classroom. What types of conversations occur around this literature? What questions do you or your students pose? What do these readings say about sexuality? What do they say about gender? If the answers to these questions lead to the realization that the classroom curriculum and discussions reinforce the heteronormative structure of society, then this is a place for teachers to begin to raise questions with their students, and also with their colleagues.

Two wonderful resources for teachers, "An LGBT/Queer Glossary," by Becca Chase and Paula Ressler, and "LGBT-Inclusive Language," by Michael Weinberg, provide a foundation for common language use and a beginning place for examination of the teaching environment. These articles were published in the 2009 special edition of *English Journal* dedicated to sexual identity and gender expression. The authors explain and discuss LGBTQ-acceptable wording and phrases to be used when discussing literature, individuals, and other LGBTQ topics with students. In an inclusive environment, such language would be implemented at all times.

A second place for teachers to begin is with the existing curriculum and a critical approach. Viewing literature through a literary lens (historical, feminist or gender studies, queer theory, etc.) provides an opportunity to step outside of the reader (and the classroom) and ask questions of the literature that provides new ways of looking at society. In Robert Cormier's *The Chocolate War* (1974), for example, if we look through a gender perspective, how is power distributed throughout the text? What gender roles do each of the characters adopt within the power hierarchy? What stereotypical gender roles are seen? In asking these questions, students are asked to examine the power structure, not through the eyes of the adults, the school gang, and everyone else, but to think about how the power structure was implemented and why it persists. As will be discussed later in this chapter, *The Chocolate War* does not contain any LGBTQ characters, but it does offer the possibility of questioning traditional gender roles and power, which is a good place to start.

If a whole class LGBTQ text is not possible at this time, literature circles and choice texts are two ways to give LGBTQ texts a place in your classroom. In both of these instances, a teacher can not only provide students an opportunity for choice, but also allow for what Clark and Blackburn (2009) call for—an opportunity to read LGBTQ texts for enjoyment and pleasure.

After looking at your curriculum, faculty should determine the general environment of the school, in terms of LGBTQ acceptance and inclusion. This could answer some of the questions that were raised when looking at the curriculum, and it will also put your teaching and your rationale for bringing LGBTQ texts in the classroom into focus. For the purposes of categorization, we have identified four potential categories. These categories are fluid; you may find yourself in one category, your students in another, and your community in yet another. These categories are meant as a place to start: (1) hostile environment, (2) ignorant/open, (3) open/accepting, and (4) open. The basic definitions of each category are provided below; each category refers not only to the general environment of the school but also to the treatment of LGBTQ topics and characters. For each category there are suggested texts that would work in each environment, but these are only suggestions. With the number of phenomenal LGBTQ texts being published, there is no way to list every title.

Hostile Environment

This is a school or classroom environment in which there is no consciousness outside of the accepted societal norm for sexuality. When sexuality is broached in conversation, there is a heteronormative assumption or attitude, and there may even be a negative attitude or connotation brought toward deviation from the societal norm. In this context, sexual identity is seen as a choice that an individual makes, gender and sexuality are seen as synonymous, and demeaning language is often heard from both students and faculty.

The texts listed below in this category do not necessarily contain LGBTQ characters, but the conversations and language used invite discussion about language as manipulation, and as ways to assert power and control. For example, *The Chocolate War* is not an LGBTQ text, but it does have language that would indicate an issue with homosexuality. Jerry is called a "fag" repeatedly. What conversation could be had in the classroom that would explore the power of language, which is used to manipulate Jerry? Any text where you can disrupt the language use or the heteronormative assumptions being made on the part of the text or your students is a good place to start. This text also consists of mainly male characters; the few female characters are objectified, which can raise more questions. Each of the male characters plays a gendered role, and power is associated with that role. An examination of these roles can provide an interesting look at gender and power within our society.

Robert Cormier, *The Chocolate War* (1974)

Jerry Renault stands up to the biggest gang in his all-boys school through his refusal to sell chocolates in a school sale. Cormier makes constant social commentary throughout the novel, and he challenges readers to place themselves in the shoes of the characters, to determine what they would do and why.

Chris Crutcher, *Staying Fat for Sarah Byrnes* (1993)

Moby and Sarah are two teens who are used to being victimized. Moby, nicknamed based on his monstrous girth, attempts to stay overweight even as a competitive swimmer, so as not to isolate his best friend, Sarah. Sarah Byrnes, ironically named, has burn scars over a vast portion of her body from a mysterious childhood accident. Both teens attempt to confront big issues in life and the world, all while enduring bullying, adult resistance, and struggles with identity and self.

Nancy Garden, *The Year They Burned the Books* (1999)

An extremely controversial book, Garden's novel discusses sex education in schools, censorship, sexuality, and politics. Jamie discovers firsthand what it is like to operate in a world dictated by the politics of adults when she attempts to discuss certain controversial issues with the school newspaper as her vehicle, and she experiences censorship firsthand.

Jacqueline Woodson, *After Tupac and D Foster* (2008)

Three girls come of age in a close-knit African American community in Queens, at a time when Tupac Shakur is at the pinnacle of his musical career. Neeka and our unnamed narrator enfold D, a mysterious wandering foster child, into their long-standing friendship through their love of Tupac's music. As Tupac is shot and comes back stronger than ever, the three struggle to come to terms with their own issues. With the return of D's mysterious mother and Tupac's death, the friends are forced to say good-bye.

Ignorant/Open

This is an environment where there has been questioning and conversation, but there is still reluctance and often misunderstandings about sexuality and gender expression. In this environment there are questions, especially for students who are sitting in your classroom for whom the heteronormative view is not their reality, but these questions often go unanswered or do not approach disrupting the heteronormative view of the students in the classroom. This environment may have a Gay-Straight Alliance (GSA), or the idea has been raised by students or the administration but has not come to fruition. This could be an environment where faculty have had these conversations and are ready to work to create a safe atmosphere for LGBTQ students.

Stephen Chbosky, *The Perks of Being a Wallflower* (1999)

Charlie is an anxious boy attempting to find his way in the big high school setting. Told entirely through what the reader assumes are full-disclosure letters to an anonymous pen pal, Charlie endures many typical and a few atypical teen struggles. Through Charlie's eyes, the reader sees how nervous, introverted Charlie is able to come into his own with a select group of friends in the high school setting. Issues that are brought up include domestic abuse, drug use, sex, sexuality, and Charlie's molestation at the hands of a trusted adult.

Chris Crutcher, *Angry Management* (2009)

Several of Crutcher's most popular characters are placed together in an anger management group, and readers discover the tales of Angus Bethune and Sarah Byrnes, Montana West, and Matt Miller and Marcus James, as each struggles to come to terms with aspects of life outside of their control and searches for their identities.

David Levithan, *How They Met, and Other Stories* (2008)

In this exploration of ways in which people can meet and grow to love one another, Levithan adeptly shows love in all ages, sizes, genders, and sexualities, revealing to the reader that no two loves are exactly alike.

Carol Plum-Ucci, *What Happened to Lani Garver* (2002)

Lani's character brings gender and sexuality squarely into question. Throughout the text, Lani refuses to entertain questions about sexuality. Lani moves beyond the categories and stereotypes and just wants to exist—no questions, no stereotypes, no problems—just be. However, this is not acceptable to the school population, who consistently push to ascertain Lani's gender and sexual orientation. The ending leaves the reader questioning, not who Lani is and what gender or sexuality Lani would check on a college application, but rather why, and whether it really matters.

Ellen Wittlinger, *Hard Love* (1999)

John "Gio" meets Marisol Guzman while looking at zines in a record store. Throughout the text, John searches for his identity and struggles to come to terms with his parents' divorce, as Marisol insists that her sexual identity is fully formed and not open to John's advances. *Hard Love* was one of the earlier books with a lesbian main character.

Open/Accepting

This environment would probably have a GSA or ongoing discussion about a safe/open environment for all students. This might be a place where literature in the classrooms has been questioned, but the understanding is not on the level of accepting and discussing variation in characterization and approach to and around literature involving LGBTQ characters. This is where the idea of sexuality is still the main concern or question that arises from the text.

Nancy Garden, *Annie on My Mind* (1982)

Annie and Liza meet, fall in love, and remain together at the conclusion of the book, despite societal pressures forcing them apart. *Annie on My Mind* has withstood the test of time and remains a beautifully relevant text, richly depicting two women in a loving relationship.

John Green and David Levithan, *Will Grayson, Will Grayson* (2010)

Levithan and Green each wrote from the perspective of one Will Grayson character. The novel focuses on the individuality of one's sexuality and its place as only one aspect of a character's identity. Levithan and Green do an excellent job of creating multidimensional characters that are varied and highly relatable to teen readers.

James Howe, *The Misfits* (2001)

Four middle school students band together to form a group called the Misfits. Bobby, the narrator, moonlights as a tie salesman and finally becomes a hero by speaking out against name calling and bullying, while Addie, the politician, attempts to lead the student body toward greatness. Discussions in *The Misfits* center on life, careers, bullying, identity, and sexuality—all relevant conversations for teenagers.

David Levithan, *Love Is the Higher Law* (2009)

Claire, Jasper, and Peter are three very different teens in New York City who barely know one another. As the aftereffects of 9/11 permeate the lives of New Yorkers and Americans in general, they are forced to see a bigger picture for the first time. With the terrorist attacks in the foreground, the three teens struggle with making connections, establishing meaning, defining themselves, and finding purpose in a world that no longer makes sense to them.

Julie Anne Peters, *Far from Xanadu* (2005)

Michelle "Mike's" sexuality matters little in her small town. Only when Xanadu, an outsider with a mysterious history, arrives in town does Mike's identity and sexuality become an issue. Xanadu's arrival makes something that had previously gone unquestioned, a sudden object of curiosity.

Accepting

This would be an environment seen by students as accepting. This acceptance would move outside the boundaries of the school to the community in which the school is housed. This environment is where substantial conversation has been had about sexuality, possibly an environment already considered inclusive of LGBTQ literature and material. The texts below are considered in this category for two reasons: (1) because this is where a character's sexuality no longer defines the person, identity is seen as individual, and characters and readers are ready to address other issues and questions other than a character's sexuality; or (2) the text deals with issues that are still not accepted by a majority of society—bisexuality and transgender issues. Although lesbian and gay characters have seen increased acceptance, both in society and in young adult literature, bisexuality and transgendered characters are still fighting for that same acceptance.

Michael Cart (editor), *How Beautiful the Ordinary* (2009)

How Beautiful the Ordinary tells twelve wildly different tales of teens, adults, and sometimes even children struggling with identity. From Trev, the transgender elementary schooler, to Faroukh and his return to his original discovery of his homosexuality the summer after high school ends, this collection presents colorfully woven tales depicting multidimensional, relatable characters.

Julie Anne Peters, *Luna: A Novel* (2004)

Luna successfully captures the internal struggle that ensues when one's gender does not correspond exactly with one's sex. Reagan, Liam's younger sister, narrates this novel, as Liam transitions into Luna. Transgendered characters can pose an especially difficult time for teachers in the classroom. Teachers need to be ready and willing to answer a variety of questions, and so they need to be well read in the subject matter. Transgendered characters, like bisexual characters, are not seen as readily in YAL and may not be as accepted in a school or community as gay and lesbian characters. For this reason, both *Luna* and *Boyfriends with Girlfriends* are categorized in the "Open" category, since readers would need to be more open to their subject matter.

Julie Anne Peters, *Rage: A Love Story* (2009)

High school senior Johanna struggles with her attraction to fellow senior Reeve and is quickly drawn into the darkness of experiencing a first love with the person who hurts you the most. A powerful story that shows that domestic violence knows no boundaries, it also represents an interesting category of LGBTQ texts: the non-self-identified character. Johanna's best friend is an interesting study in a character who does not self-identify and the boundaries of categorization.

Alex Sanchez, *Boyfriends with Girlfriends* (2011)

Lance begins seeing Sergio, a bisexual boy who has only ever dated girls, as Allie finds herself inexplicably attracted to Kimiko, a Japanese American girl who struggles with her family over her own sexual identity. These four teens first begin to understand and come to terms with the fluid nature of sexuality in this groundbreaking novel about sexuality that is neither this nor that. While this is one of the first books to adequately address and explain bisexuality, texts with self-identified bisexual characters may be more difficult to bring into classrooms.

Whatever environment in which teachers find themselves teaching, there are serious questions to ask. Teachers should never teach based on assumption, and they should not assume they are teaching classes comprised entirely of heterosexual students. Along that same line, teachers should never assume that their students are automatically homophobic. Beginning with challenging the societal norm placed in front of our students on a daily basis, but without pigeonholing them as that "societal norm," is hard, but it is one way to combat the homophobic environments of our nation's schools. Teachers should work on incorporating LGBTQ texts into activities such as literature circles in the classroom, so that students have both the option to choose, and the option to enjoy reading and discussing on a more personal level. But it is not impossible! Remember that LGBTQ texts brought into the classroom should not be

- in response to a specific event that has occurred in the school or the media;
- a single unit where it is never discussed or seen again; it cannot be the token LGBTQ text; or

- a single book that covers all experiences. Just like not all white, middle-class males' experiences are the same, there are black, Jewish, Muslim, female/male, rich, poor, homeless, accepted, not accepted—there are various experiences! A character is a character first, not a sexual identity or gender expression.

CONCLUSION

English teachers know the power of literature. We know the power of seeing ourselves in a text, but we also understand the importance of seeing others, other ways of life, and other possibilities than those that surround us on a daily basis. We understand the need to question our surroundings, the environments in which we live, work, and breathe. But we also understand the need for our students to be safe—safe from the harm of being seen as different, and ignored.

Large populations of our students are not seen. They are not heard from because they are seen as different, as not acceptable, and as deviant. As teachers, we need to change that; we need to keep our students safe. The GLSEN survey shows that schools that have inclusive curricula are seen as safer environments for LGBTQ self-identified students. Bringing LGBTQ texts into the English classroom is not easy. It takes preparation and careful planning. It takes asking some hard questions. But isn't it worth it?

REFERENCES

Banks, W. P. (2009). Literacy, sexuality, and the value(s) of queer young adult literatures. *English Journal, 98*(4), 33–36.

Bargar, G. W. (1981). *What happened to Mr. Forster?* New York: Houghton Mifflin.

Bauer, M. D. (Ed.). (1994). *Am I blue? Coming out from the silence.* New York: HarperCollins.

Bishop, R. S. (1992). Multicultural literature for children: Making informed choices. In V. Harris (Ed.), *Teaching multicultural literature in grades K–8* (pp. 37–54). Norwood, MA: Christopher Gordon.

Blackburn, M. V., & Buckley, J. F. (2005). Teaching queer-inclusive English language arts. *Journal of Adolescent & Adult Literacy, 49*(3), 202–212.

Block, F. L. (1989). *Weetzie Bat.* New York: HarperTeen.

Burd, N. (2009). *The vast fields of ordinary.* New York: Dial.

Cady, J. (1995). American literature: Gay male, 1900–1969. In C. J. Summers (Ed.), *The gay and lesbian literary heritage* (pp. 30–39). New York: Holt.

Cart, M. (2004). What a wonderful world: Notes on the evolution of GLBTQ literature for young adults. *The ALAN Review, 31*(2), 46–52.

Cart, M. (Ed.). (2009). *How beautiful the ordinary: Twelve stories of identity.* New York: HarperTeen.

Cart, M., & Jenkins, C. A. (2006). *The heart has its reasons: Young adult literature with gay/lesbian/queer content, 1969–2004*. Lanham, MD: Scarecrow Press.
Chase, B., & Ressler, P. (2009). An LGBT/queer glossary. *English Journal, 98*(4), 23–24.
Chbosky, S. (1999). *The perks of being a wallflower*. New York: MTV Books.
Clark, C. T., & Blackburn, M. V. (2009). Reading LGBT-themed literature with young people: What's possible? *English Journal, 98*(4), 25–32.
Cormier, R. (1974). *The chocolate war*. New York: Knopf.
Crutcher, C. (1991). *Athletic shorts: Six short stories*. New York: Greenwillow.
Crutcher, C. (1993). *Staying fat for Sarah Byrnes*. New York: Greenwillow.
Crutcher, C. (2009). *Angry management*. New York: Greenwillow.
Daly, M. (1942). *Seventeenth summer*. New York: Putnam.
Donovan, J. (1969). *I'll get there. It better be worth the trip*. New York: Harper & Row.
Freymann-Weyr, G. (2002). *My heartbeat*. New York: Houghton Mifflin.
Garden, N. (1982). *Annie on my mind*. New York: Farrar, Straus & Giroux.
Garden, N. (1999). *The year they burned the books*. New York: Farrar, Straus & Giroux.
Gay, Lesbian, and Straight Education Network (GLSEN). (2009). *2009 School Climate Survey: Nearly nine out of ten LGBT students experience harassment in school*. Retrieved from http://glsen.org/cgi-bin/iowa/all/news/record/2624.html
Gay, Lesbian, and Straight Education Network (GLSEN). (2010). *Educators' guide to Ally Week*. Retrieved from http://voicebox.nwp.org/iwritethefuture/sites/default/files/files/4/oct/educators_guide_to_ally_week.pdf
Green, J., & Levithan, D. (2010). *Will Grayson, Will Grayson*. New York: Dutton.
Greenbaum, V. (1994). Literature out of the closet: Bringing gay and lesbian texts and subtexts out in high school English. *English Journal, 83*(5), 71–74.
Guy, R. (1976). *Ruby*. New York: Viking.
Hartinger, B. (2003). *Geography club*. New York: HarperTeen.
Hayn, J. A., & Hazlett, L. A. (2011). Hear us out! LGBTQ young adult literature wishes are answered! *The ALAN Review, 38*(2), 68–72.
Homes, A. M. (1989). *Jack*. New York: Simon & Schuster.
Howe, J. (2001). *The misfits*. New York: Atheneum.
Jago, C. (2000). *With rigor for all: Teaching classics to contemporary students*. Portsmouth, NH: Heinemann.
Johnson, M. (2004). *The Bermudez Triangle*. New York: Razorbill.
Katcher, B. (2009). *Almost perfect*. New York: Delacorte.
Kerr, M. E. (1986). *Night kites*. New York: Harper & Row.
Kerr, M. E. (1994). *Deliver us from Evie*. New York: HarperCollins.
Klein, N. (1980). *Breaking up*. New York: Knopf.
Kluger, S. (2008). *My most excellent year: A novel of love, Mary Poppins, and Fenway Park*. New York: Dial.
Koertge, R. (1988). *The Arizona kid*. New York: Joy Street Books.
Langner, J. (1995). *Envisioning literature: Literary understanding and literature instruction*. New York: Teachers College Press.
Levithan, D. (2003). *Boy meets boy*. New York: Random House.
Levithan, D. (2004). *The realm of possibility*. New York: Knopf.
Levithan, D. (2008). *How they met, and other stories*. New York: Knopf.
Levithan, D. (2009). *Love is the higher law*. New York: Random House.

Myracle, L. (2003). *Kissing Kate.* New York: Dutton.
Nelson, T. (1994). *Earthshine.* New York: Orchard Books.
Peters, J. A. (2004). *Luna: A novel.* New York: Little, Brown.
Peters, J. A. (2005). *Far from Xanadu.* New York: Little, Brown.
Peters, J. A. (2009). *Rage: A love story.* New York: Random House.
Plum-Ucci, C. (2002). *What happened to Lani Garver.* New York: Harcourt.
Probst, R. (2006). Sticks and stones may break my bones, but words, well, words can kill . . . *Voices from the Middle, 19*(2), 44–49.
Purves, A. C., Rogers, T., & Soter, A. O. (1990). *How porcupines make love II.* New York: Longman.
Ryan, S. (2007). *The rules for hearts.* New York: Viking.
Salinger, J. D. (1951). *The catcher in the rye.* Boston: Little, Brown.
Sanchez, A. (2011). *Boyfriends with girlfriends.* New York: Simon & Schuster.
Steffel, S., & Renzi-Keener, L. (2009). Breaking down the last taboo: LGBT young adult literature in the preservice classroom. *Language Arts Journal of Michigan, 24*(2), 29–36.
Weinberg, M. (2009). LGBT-inclusive language. *English Journal, 98*(4), 50–51.
Wilhelm, J. D. (1997). *"You gotta BE the book": Teaching engaged and reflective reading with adolescents.* New York: Teachers College Press.
Wittlinger, E. (1999). *Hard love.* New York: Simon & Schuster.
Wittlinger, E. (2007). *Parrotfish.* New York: Simon & Schuster.
Woodson, J. (1995). *From the notebooks of Melanin Sun.* New York: Scholastic.
Woodson, J. (2008). *After Tupac and D Foster.* New York: Putnam.

8

Multicultural Adolescent Literature: Finding the Balance

Judith A. Hayn and Sarah M. Burns

ESTABLISHING A RATIONALE

Multicultural literature, like the term itself, has multiple perspectives. Diverse perspectives from differing viewpoints provide a starting point on a definition. Any group that has been marginalized can be considered diverse or hold multicultural status, like race, gender, ethnicity, language of origin, ability, age, social class, religion, sexual orientation, and disabilities.

Nieto (2004) offers this support for multiculturism in the classroom:

> Multicultural education is not a remedy for social inequality, and it cannot guarantee academic success. At the same time, if one of the primary purposes of education is to teach young people the skills, knowledge, and critical awareness to become productive members of a diverse and democratic society, a broadly conceptualized multicultural education can have a decisive influence. (p. 390)

As English teachers, we bear the brunt for this inclusion through literature choice and selection, for myriad reasons. Literature is a major part of what we do with our curriculum, and much of our teaching focuses on text selection. The preponderance of the white, mainly male-produced canon mired in the past has been documented by Applebee, Burroughs, and Stevens (1994) in their analysis of high school required reading selections. These lists evolve from university and college reading requirements that were mandated more than a century ago. Remnants of that curriculum unfortunately still remain entrenched in schools all over the country.

Stallworth, Gibbons, and Fauber (2006) analyzed text choices by teachers in one Southern state to conclude that the 152 teachers surveyed continue to use the same selections year after year. Appearing on lists from the 2002–2003 and 2003–2004 school years were *To Kill a Mockingbird* by Harper Lee (1960), *The Crucible* by Arthur Miller (1953), *The Great Gatsby* by F. Scott Fitzgerald (1925), *The Adventures of Huckleberry Finn* by Mark Twain (1884), and *The Scarlet Letter* by Nathaniel Hawthorne (1850), plus the expected Shakespearean tragedies. The lack of diversity and relevance to contemporary adolescents is glaring.

Our classrooms reflect the society where we live. Woods (2009) makes a compelling argument in "Hearing the Voices: Multicultural Young Adult Literature as Authentic Cultural Experience." He utilizes the following definition:

> Culture is the dynamic of human interaction with the surrounding world, and the study of culture is a valuable endeavor that can bridge cultural divides by offering deeper more authentic understanding of cultures other than one's own. (p. 19)

We adopt this definition, and like Woods, we believe that the logical assumption extends to multicultural literature, which includes literature selections from all cultures. We intend to demonstrate that young adult literature is ready for the challenge.

As Fernandez (2003) reminds us, 80 percent of preservice teachers are white and middle-class, have never experienced any significant cultural oppression, and are unaware of how the practice of oppression continues today. Our teacher candidates enter the classroom sadly unprepared for the diverse nature of contemporary society. A brief examination of recently gathered statistical data reminds us of diversity's impact now and in the future.

- For the first time since census data has been released, the 2010 data shows that fewer than half of all the children (49.9 percent) in the youngest age group shown, three-year-olds, are white (Frey, 2011b).
- If immigration stopped tomorrow, we would achieve a national minority majority child population by 2050. This will occur by around 2023 if current immigration trends continue (Frey, 2011c).
- More than half of the growth in the total population of the United States between 2000 and 2010 was due to the increase in the Hispanic population, which grew by 43 percent, four times the growth of the total population at 10 percent (Albert, Ennis, & Rios-Vargas, 2011).
- Asian populations grew faster than any other major ethnic group between 2000 and 2010, increasing 43 percent (United States Census Bureau, 2010).
- No growth or a limited gain in the number of white children is projected for the future, but a sizable population gain is occurring among

"new" minorities, especially Hispanics but also Asians, those of mixed race, and other smaller groups (Frey, 2011a).

- More than half of all minority groups in large metro areas, including blacks, now reside in the suburbs. That number rose from 37 percent in 1990 to 44 percent in 2000, and to 51 percent in 2010. Higher shares of whites (78 percent), Asians (62 percent), and Hispanics (59 percent) in large metro areas now live in suburbs (Frey, 2011c).
- Surveys show that the percentage (about 76 percent) of American adults who claim to be Christian has been shrinking for a generation. At the same time, the percent of Americans who are Jewish, Muslim, Hindu, Buddhist, or members of other Eastern religions has doubled. About 25 percent of U.S. adults are not Christian, and our Christian population is steadily shrinking (Bascom, 2010).
- About 95 percent of six- to twenty-one-year-old students with disabilities are served in public school settings. These include students identified as having specific learning disabilities, speech or language impairments, mental retardation, emotional disturbance, multiple disabilities, hearing impairments, orthopedic impairment, other health impairments, visual impairments, autism, deaf-blindness, traumatic brain injury, and developmental delay (National Center for Education Statistics, 2010).

Thus, the changing faces, beliefs, and behaviors of Americans can be documented. For information about lesbian, gay, bisexual, transgender, and questioning (LGBTQ) youth, see chapter 7.

As Woods (2009) suggests, we, at the very least, ought to be engaged in introducing teachers to other cultures within the context of our shared academic interests and allowing those same teachers "to begin to truly hear the voices of others" (p. 22). While we have them captured in an adolescent literature class, a methods class, a conference session, in-service training, or on social networking sites, the following texts possess merit for facilitating this engagement. To counter the claim that there are no quality contemporary multicultural texts suitable for the classroom, publications during the last decade (2001–2011) are offered. For a discussion of texts prior to these dates, see "Diversity in Young Adult Literature" (Hazlett & Hayn, 2006) in *Using Young Adult Literature in the English Classroom*.

RACE AND ETHNICITY

Authors who write about the African American adolescent experience cover all genres, but most still focus on the coming-of-age novel set in urban areas. Walter Dean Myers reigns as the master storyteller for young men growing up in Harlem. However, in *Shooter* (2004), Myers tackles a school shooting set outside the city in fictional Madison High; the tragedy is revealed through various documents published after the event. *Harlem Summer* (2007) is historical fiction set in authentically researched 1926 Harlem, covering the story of sixteen-year-old Mark Purvis, who yearns to be a jazz musician. The powerful *Dope Sick* (2009) shows Lil J pursued by the police after a drug deal has gone wrong. He encounters a vagrant who forces him to examine his own life, becoming addicted to heroin and rapidly going out of control. More recently, in Myers's *Lockdown* (2010), the setting is Progress Center, a juvenile detention facility where thirteen-year old Reece earns a spot in a work release program.

One of the most popular historical fiction writers about the African American experience in the past twenty years is Christopher Paul Curtis, who burst on the YAL scene with *The Watsons Go to Birmingham—1963* (1995). His teen books have ties to his home in Flint, Michigan; *Bucking the Sarge* (2004) introduces budding philosopher Luther T. Farrell, who wants to escape Flint and his slumlord mother, the Sarge. *Elijah of Buxton* (2007) relates the story of the first free child born in a Canadian settlement of escaped slaves and is geared toward younger middle school readers. Rollicking humor and a likable protagonist characterize Curtis's works.

Another male author, Alan Lawrence Sitomer, writes of the adolescent African American urban experience as an outsider based on his experiences as a Los Angeles schoolteacher. His books include a series of portrayals of teens drawn from his classroom, beginning with *The Hoopster* (2006). Andre Anderson's dreams of a career in journalism are enhanced by his basketball skills; the future looks promising until he is beaten savagely by a gang of racists. *Hip-Hop High School* (2007a) introduces Teresa Anderson, Andre's street-savvy sister, who finds comfort in hip-hop music until she meets Devon, who inspires both of them to ace their SATs and get into top colleges; Dev's death in a street fight quashes her dreams. *Homeboyz* (2007b) ends the trilogy with Terry Anderson, whose younger sister Tina dies as a random victim of a drive-by shooting; Terry's attempts at revenge land him in jail and then under house arrest. Sitomer's novels are gritty and reflect streetwise authenticity as he chronicles urban youth who struggle just to survive.

A growing number of women chronicle the lives of urban youth. Sharon Draper finally ends her powerful Hazelwood High trilogy (*Tears of a Tiger*, 1996; *Forged by Fire*, 1998) in *Darkness before Dawn* (2002), where the characters are now seniors in high school, and Keisha is still grieving Andy's death. Another Draper trilogy, the Jericho series, begins with *Battle of Jericho* (2003), which focuses on peer pressure. Jericho Prescott, a junior at Frederick Douglass High School, is asked to pledge the most popular club at school; its reputation does not reflect its darker mission. In *November Blues* (2007), November Nelson's boyfriend Josh Prescott has been killed in a pledge stunt. Jericho also grieves the loss of his nephew, but discovers that Josh has left part of himself behind, as the two mourners rely on each other. The last book in the series, *Just Another Hero* (2009), presents Arielle Gresham, who is disliked and mistrusted by her classmates as she harbors a secret past. Draper uses her background as a Cincinnati, Ohio, high school English teacher to add authenticity to her characters, plot, and settings.

Sharon Flake leaped to prominence with her edgy short story collection, *Who Am I without Him? Short Stories about Girls and the Boys in Their Lives* (2004). Realistic dialect and authentic heroines pepper these tales of prejudice and poverty, which will resonate with teens. In *Bang!* (2005), Mann, at thirteen, copes with the death of his younger brother as violence continues to rip apart his community. Perhaps Flake's most evocative novel, *The Skin I'm In* (2007), relates the struggles of Maleeka Madison, who suffers daily from the taunts of the other kids in her class; they malign her homemade clothes, her good grades at school, and her dark, black skin—a deeper shade than any of theirs.

Another voice in female African American writers for teens belongs to Coe Booth, who uses her experiences as a New York City social worker for veracity. The first novel in the series, *Tyrell* (2005), follows a fifteen-year-old's quest for survival now that his father is in jail and his mother refuses to work; her welfare fraud has forced them into homelessness and life in a shelter. In *Kendra* (2008), the title character lives with her grandmother in Bronxwood while her young mother finishes school. Instead, Renée continues to abandon her daughter by making a life for herself without Kendra. *Bronxwood* (2011) continues Tyrell's story, as he returns to the Bronx and must decide whether his future will mimic his dad's career as a DJ or whether he will drift into the world of his drug dealer pals. All of Booth's novels are gritty, streetwise, and reflect the violence of life in the urban projects.

Yummy: The Last Day of Southside Shorty (2010) is based on a 1994 Southside Chicago gang-related incident. G. Neri frames the story of eleven-year-old Robert "Yummy" Sandifer, who shot and killed his fourteen-year-old neighbor Shavon Dean, through the eyes and voice of a fictional character, eleven-year-old Roger. Another historical fiction work, *Ninth Ward* by Jewell Parker Rhodes (2010), combines the drama of Hurricane Katrina with magical realism. Twelve-year-old Lanesha, who has a caul over her eyes, lives with Mama Ya-Ya in the Ninth Ward in New Orleans prior to the hurricane; Lanesha has second sight, which foretells catastrophe.

These authors focus on the urban experience, and while this is an important aspect of being young and black in America, the inclusion of African American teens in other settings needs addressing. Data mentioned above validates the need for this literature for suburban teens, but affirming the lives of all adolescents in rural areas and small towns could provide realistic books for those who are not urban.

Census data from 2010 documents the rising Hispanic population in this nation. Yet Gary Soto was for years the only male voice writing from this perspective. He has reduced his writing for teens in the past decade; however, *The Afterlife* (2003) tells Chuy's story. He is killed on the first pages of the novel when a stranger stabs him in a club bathroom over a misunderstanding. Now Chuy experiences an out-of-body self-exploration. In *Accidental Love* (2006), Marisa grabs the wrong cell phone and is soon involved with Rene, an unlikely match for her with his geeky status and focus on his studies.

Fortunately, Matt de la Peña has added his talents to YAL multicultural choices. However, his first novel, *Ball Don't Lie* (2007), focuses on a white boy living as a foster child in a culture other than his own. Sticky, seventeen, lived with his prostitute mother, was abused by pimps, was shifted from one foster home to another, and existed on the street between failed placements. Sticky has considerable basketball skills that have given him status among his mostly black peers. De la Peña's next book, *Mexican White Boy* (2008), shifts into the Hispanic community as biracial Danny Lopez doesn't fit in anywhere. He is an outsider with his Mexican father's family, where he is spending the summer, and at his mostly white school. He is a gifted pitcher but lacks control of his game, just like in his life. Miguel in *We Were Here* (2009) accepts guilt for a tragedy that destroys his family and the one-year sentence to a juvenile detention center, along with the requirement that he keep a journal. *I Will Save You* (2010) breaks into class and gender discord with Kidd's narration of his sad and violent life; he has escaped from a group home and lives on the beach, where he encounters characters who will either save or destroy him.

Coert Voorhees adds an authentic, humorous voice to the culture with Frankie's story in *The Brothers Torres* (2008). Frankie's brother Steve is more interested in partying all night than in securing the soccer scholarship coming his way. Their parents run a Mexican restaurant, which is about to be sold, while Frankie hides his brother's escapades from them. Voorhees's next young adult novel will be published in 2012.

Pam Muñoz Ryan has for many years spoken for young Hispanic girls. Her recent books begin with *Becoming Naomi León* (2004); Naomi León Soledad Outlaw, a shy and self-contained young girl, comes of age in the San Diego suburbs where she lives with her great-grandmother and younger brother. In *Paint the Wind* (2007), Maya is an orphan living in California with her strict grandmother. She imagines the life of a wild mustang in Wyoming as she yearns for connections and a sense of belonging. Chilean poet Pablo Neruda's childhood is lyrically revealed for young teens in *The Dreamer* (2010), and indeed Muñoz Ryan's books are undeniably appropriate for middle school classrooms.

Rita Williams-Garcia delivers *Jumped* (2009), whose heroine Leticia knows the outcome of girl fights in high schools, ugly and personal. Trina challenged tough girl athlete Dominique in the hallway, and violence is brewing in this three-person account of one school day. *One Crazy Summer* (2010) is for a younger audience and has an African American heroine in Delphine, who is eleven. She and her two younger sisters travel from Brooklyn to California to spend a month with their estranged mother, a poet who lives in Oakland amid the Black Panther movement of 1968.

Other female writers depicting the Hispanic experience include Nancy Osa, who relates Violeta Paz's attempts to reconcile her Cuban grandmother's expectations of a *quinceañera* with her own self-doubts and those of her mixed heritage in *Cuba 15* (2003). Julia Alvarez sets *Finding Miracles* (2004) in Vermont, where sixteen-year-old Milly Kaufman avoids considering her adoption in childhood from an unnamed Latin American dictatorship. When new student Pablo arrives from their native land, Milly tries to ignore him rather than face her past.

In Judith Ortiz Cofer's *Call Me María* (2006), the heroine is caught between two worlds: Puerto Rico, where she was born, and New York, where she now lives in a basement apartment in the barrio. While her mother remains on the island, María lives with her father, the maintenance man in their building. Ortiz Cofer's short story collection, *An Island like You: Stories from the Barrio* (1995), provides the springboard for Doris's story, *If I Could Fly* (2011). Doris is fifteen, and her life is falling apart when her mother returns to Puerto Rico for her health. Doris would like to fly away like the pigeons from all her problems but learns the value of confronting them and then moving forward.

The rapid growth of our Asian American population requires scrutiny of other books we might acquire for teaching and for our classroom libraries. Lisa Yee has created a series of four novels based at Rancho Rosetta Middle School. The saga begins with *Millicent Min, Girl Genius* (2003); Millicent is so smart she has finished her junior year of high school, but at eleven, she is a social outcast. In *Stanford Wong Flunks Big Time* (2005), Stanford finds that his summer school English tutor is his nemesis Millicent Min. His basketball eligibility depends on their relationship. *So Totally Emily Ebers* (2008) gives Emily a chance to tell her own story of that mismatched pair; she has just moved to California after her parents' divorce in New Jersey and analyzes the events from her viewpoint. Then in *Warp Speed* (2011), Marley Sandelski joins the hijinks. Geeky Marley attracts the school bully, while his speedy feet keep him temporarily safe. Yee's books are marked by humor and misadventure that appeals to middle school readers.

Laurence Yep takes a historical approach to the Chinese experience in his superb Golden Mountain Chronicles. *The Traitor* (2004) is the story of two teens growing up in Rock Springs, Wyoming, in 1885, when animosity between American and Chinese miners reached its peak. Born in the United States of Chinese parents, Joseph Young considers himself an American, but both communities see him as only Chinese. *Dragon Road* (2008) details the story of an itinerant basketball team in the late 1930s. Calvin (Flash) Chin and his friend Barney Young leave San Francisco and go on the road with four other Chinese American players. The last in this series is *Dragons of Silk* (2011), where silk weaving binds the lives of four girls from different generations. The story spans more than seventy-five years and is set in both China and America.

Cynthia Kadohata's Newbery Award–winning *Kira-Kira* (2004), which means "glittering," introduces Katie and Lynn Takeshima, whose family moves from an Iowa farm to southern Georgia where their ethnic appearance becomes an adjustment issue. Lynn's serious illness threatens the family structure, and younger sister Katie must find a way to unite them. *Weedflower* (2006) is the story of Sumiko, a young prisoner in the Japanese internment camps after Pearl Harbor; Sumiko's life before Pearl Harbor was happy and tranquil, when her parents operated a prosperous flower farm in California, but now that life is gone.

In *An Ocean Apart, A World Away* (2002), Chinese American author Lensey Namioka continues the story of *Ties That Bind, Ties That Break* (1999). This novel opens in 1921 in China, where the first book's protagonist Ailin is about to set sail for America. Her best friend Yanyan narrates the tale of her life as a medical student at Cornell. Namioka's *Mismatch* (2006) creates a modern-day Juliet in Suzanne Hua, a Chinese American, whose Romeo is Andy Suzuki, a Japanese American; they meet in their high school orchestra. Their ethnic roots may be Asian, but their cultural beliefs and biases are very different.

In *Nothing but the Truth (and a Few White Lies)* (2007), Justina Chen Headley introduces half-Taiwanese Patty Ho, who at fifteen is as uncomfortable at school as she is at home. Her overbearing mother enrolls her in Stanford Math Camp. To her surprise, she actually likes the brainy, spirited campers, who encourage her to celebrate her *hapa* (half-Asian) background. *Girl Overboard* (2009) tells Syrah Chen's story. Everybody thinks Syrah is the golden girl, but her life is not always what it seems, and her dreams of snowboarding championships fade after an accident. Syrah must rehab both her busted-up knee *and* her broken heart, and learn that she's worthwhile in her own right.

A major addition to Asian American young adult literature occurred with the publication of Gene Luen Yang's *American Born Chinese* (2006), the first graphic novel to win major children's book awards. Three parallel stories are intertwined in this mesmerizing story, beginning with Jin Wang, a Chinese American teenager, who is trying to fit in and win the girl of his dreams at his new school. Another outsider, the legendary Monkey King, has ruled for thousands of years but longs to be a god; his trouble-making antics prevent him from reaching his goal. Finally, Danny is popular and athletic until his cousin Chin-Kee arrives, bringing with him every Chinese stereotype possible. The three stories alternate throughout the book and unite in the climax.

Tanuja Desai Hidier's *Born Confused* (2002) introduces Dimple Lala, a New Jersey teen who has been confused about her identity as an Indian American and tries to blend in via her blue-eyed, blonde best friend, Gwyn. Dimple's parents introduce her to Karsh Kapoor for a possible relationship, but it is Gwyn who is smitten. Mitali Perkins's *Monsoon Summer* (2006) is Californian fifteen-year-old Jasmine's tale of a summer spent begrudgingly in Pune, India, volunteering at the orphanage where her mother was raised.

American Indian young adult literature received a boost with the publication of Sherman Alexie's *The Absolutely True Diary of a Part-Time Indian* (2007), which explores Indian and adolescent identity. The semiautobiographical account of fourteen-year-old Arnold "Junior" Spirit's life is told in wise-cracking narrative punctuated with cartoon illustrations. Poignant and moving, Junior's story engages and astounds young readers as they learn of life on a Spokane reservation and an American Indian's attempts to fit in at the all-white high school in an adjacent community.

Adult American Indian mystery writers, husband-and-wife team David and Aimee Thurlo set their young adult puzzler on the Navajo reservation in *The Spirit Line* (2004). Crystal Manyfeathers is preparing for her coming-of-age ceremony to please her father. When the traditional rug Crystal is weaving is stolen, she and her friend Junior seek the thief.

Joseph Bruchac, the prolific Abenaki writer, transfers elements of Native American legend into modern settings to create scary and intriguing mysteries for younger teens. Molly's immersion in her Mohawk heritage in *Skeleton Man* (2001) is something she takes for granted until she is kidnapped by the mysterious skeleton man of legend. In *The Return of Skeleton Man* (2008b), as Molly and her family try to forget the ordeal with a lavish vacation, she soon realizes the skeleton man is still pursuing them. *The Dark Pond* (2004) features Armie Katchatorian, who attends a private boarding school. Since he is only half-Indian, he feels alienated from his fellow students. He escapes to the woods, where he discovers a mysterious dark pond, which hides something sinister and dangerous. *Whisper in the Dark* (2005) introduces thirteen-year-old Maddie, who is the last descendant of a Narragansett chief. Her grandmother tells her about Whisperer in the Dark, the vampire-like creature who paralyzes his victims with fear. She and her best friend Roger are sure the Whisperer is after them.

For older readers, Bruchac's *Code Talker: A Novel about the Navajo Marines of World War II* (2006) follows young Ned Begay, who leaves his Navajo home as a small child for boarding school, where he learns the English language and American ways. At sixteen, he enlists in the Marines during World War II and is trained as a code talker. Now a grandfather, Ned relates his wartime experiences in the Pacific. *March toward the Thunder* (2008a) is the story of fifteen-year-old Louis, an Abenaki Indian from Canada, who enlists in the Union Army in 1864 and serves with New York's Irish Brigade. Basing the main character on his great-grandfather, Bruchac takes readers inside the Civil War soldier's reality.

Other cultures continue to arrive and settle in America, and YA authors write from their perspectives, too. For example, *Fresh Girl* (2002) by Jaira Placide traces the coming of age of fourteen-year-old Haitian American Mardi. Although her classmates taunt her for her differences and her poverty, Mardi harbors a shocking secret. While living in Haiti with her grandmother, she experienced a traumatizing event during the 1991 coup. Now reunited with her parents in New York, Mardi wants to forget and blend in with her American peers. Finding her voice to face the past adds power to the novel.

In *Tangled Threads: A Hmong Girl's Story* (2003), Pegi Deitz Shea introduces Mai, now thirteen, who lived with her grandmother in a crowded Thai refugee camp for ten years. When they arrive in Rhode Island to live with their Americanized relatives, confusion and isolation result, when little of their culture seems to matter. In *Abe in Arms* (2010), for older readers, the protagonist has been adopted by a loving, wealthy family. Abe is a senior in high school and heading for college when flashbacks begin to occur that remind him of his time as a young soldier in Liberia.

Ask Me No Questions (2007) by Marina Budhos is based on the government crackdown after 9/11. The Hossain family, immigrants from Bangladesh, has been living illegally in New York for years. For eighteen-year-old Aisha, this means the end of her dream of becoming a doctor. For fourteen-year-old Nadira, the narrator, it means emerging from behind the shadow of her perfect older sister to find her own strength and a way to reunite her shattered family.

OTHER CULTURES

Looking at the lives of teens who grow up outside the United States offers another way into appreciation and understanding of cultural differences and similarities for adolescents. Patricia McCormick's *Sold* (2006) has become a classroom staple. Lakshmi, thirteen, grew up in a small village in the Nepalese Himalayas. After it is destroyed by a monsoon, she thinks she has work as a maid in the city, so she can send money back home; instead, her stepfather has sold her into prostitution. She ends up in a brothel far across the border in the slums of Calcutta. Using free verse and first-person perspective, McCormick re-creates the brutality Lakshmi faces, along with the power of the human spirit.

Deborah Ellis writes the *Breadwinner* trilogy based on Afghan girlhood. In *Breadwinner* (2000), Parvana dresses as a boy to survive. In *Parvana's Journey* (2002), she wanders through war-torn Afghanistan looking for her mother and siblings, who disappeared after her father's death when the Taliban rose to power. The final book, *Mud City* (2004), is orphan refugee Shauzia's tale of leaving a Pakistani border camp and joining other homeless children on the streets of the city of Peshawar. She also survives by dressing as a boy. These stories offer realistic accounts of life in refugee camps and the toll constant warfare takes on children.

In *Secret Keeper* (2010), Mitali Perkins introduces Asha, who remains in her grandmother's household in Calcutta after her father goes to America to find a new job. Her new environment is restrictive, so Asha escapes to the rooftop to confide in her diary, the secret keeper.

A Little Piece of Ground (2003) is Elizabeth Laird's tale of Karim, a twelve-year-old Palestinian boy, who with two friends transforms an abandoned lot in Ramallah into a soccer field, a place to escape the trials of both family and life under Israeli occupation. *Oranges in No Man's Land* (2006) is the story of ten-year-old Ayesha's terrifying journey across no man's land in Lebanon during the civil war to reach a doctor in hostile territory as she seeks medicine for her dying grandmother.

Translated from the French, Valerie Zenatti's Romeo and Juliet story, *A Bottle in the Gaza Sea* (2008), begins when seventeen-year-old Tal, living in Tel Aviv, drops a bottle into the water; it contains a peace message with her e-mail address. Naïm, twenty, finds it on the Gaza beach, and replies. The two young people live just forty miles apart, but the distance between the two cultures is vast. The gap is covered through instant messaging, e-mails, and personal narratives to create a modern love story where disparate characters unite in their quest for peace.

Nigerian author Chimamanda Ngozi Adichie's *Purple Hibiscus* (2003) is fifteen-year-old Kambili's tale. She is the dutiful daughter of a rich man, a religious fanatic and domestic tyrant whose public image is that of a courageous newspaper publisher and philanthropist. The domestic terror he wields to control his household threatens to destroy Kambili and her family. Adichie's *Half of a Yellow Sun* (2006) introduces the Igbo people of eastern Nigeria, who seceded in 1967 to form the independent nation of Biafra. Ugwu, a thirteen-year-old peasant houseboy, and twin sisters Olanna and Kainene, from a wealthy and well-connected family, provide the lenses for this story of the bloody three-year civil war that followed.

As writers from other cultures have dealt with myth and legend to explore culture, Nnedi Okorafor in *Akata Witch* (2011) examines Nigerian folklore through their witches, called Leopard people. Sunny Nwazue was born in America, but her family returned to Nigeria when she was nine. She struggles to find acceptance, for she is an albino and maligned as an *asakata* (bush animal) witch by taunting classmates. As Sunny approaches her thirteenth birthday, she envisions the destruction of the world in a candle flame, an indication she may have spiritual powers.

Allan Stratton's award-winning novel, *Chanda's Secrets* (2004), illustrates the devastation of HIV/AIDS that threatens Africa. Chanda, sixteen, is a smart and determined South African girl on track to win a scholarship, but losing her sister to the deadly virus destroys that dream. Soon her mother's illness is impossible to hide, and a spirit doctor advises her to return to her home to lift the curse that is destroying them all. When Chanda discovers that her mother may have gone away to die, she leaves to seek her out and bring her home.

RELIGION

The data reminds us that religious diversity exists; young adult literature can help all readers understand the implications faith has for adolescents who struggle to fit into the world around them, regardless of faith or the lack of it.

Pete Hautman examines issues of doubt from a suburban boy's point of view in a National Book Award winner, *Godless* (2004). Jason, at fifteen, is an agnostic verging on atheism in a reaction to his father's devout Catholicism. He, his friend Shin, and classmate Henry create a new religion based on the town's local water tower, culminating in a midnight pilgrimage to the top. Conflicts exist with rivalry between Jason and Henry over local beauty Magda, with Jason's certainty that doing what he sees as right is more important than obeying his parents, and with Shin's continued belief in the church that has been debunked.

Deborah Ellis and Eric Walters team up in *Bifocal* (2007) to relate a tale of race prejudice that divides a high school after Azeem, a Muslim student, is arrested following a bomb plot. The story is told in alternating voices of two students, the academically inclined Haroon and Jay, a popular football player. As the trial progresses, vandalism and racial slurs escalate in the supposedly accepting school; the narrators are shocked by the actions and attitudes of people they thought they knew.

Buddha Boy (2004) by Kathe Koja is set in a rich, suburban high school, where the weird new kid who looks like a Buddhist monk and begs at lunch is ostracized. Justin, whose first-person narrative tells the story, is drawn to the stranger and defends him against vicious school bullies.

Although set in contemporary Damascus, Paula Jolin's *In the Name of God* (2008) presents an opportunity for discussion with this story of a Syrian teen who is drawn to Islamic fundamentalism. Seventeen-year-old Nadia, a devout Muslim, admires her cousin Fowzi for her hardline religious and political views. When Fowzi is arrested for criticizing the government, Nadia joins a radical group. When she is asked to become a suicide bomber, she agrees.

In Lisa Ann Sandell's *The Weight of the Sky* (2006), Sarah Green, sixteen, is one of only two Jewish students at her small Pennsylvania high school. She eagerly accepts her parents' offer to send her to Israel for a summer to live and work on a kibbutz. This free-verse narration outlines the shattering of Sarah's idealism as she gains a new sense of her Jewish identity.

Using a lighter approach, Melissa Schorr in *Goy Crazy* (2006) introduces Rachel Lowenstein, who hides her blonde, blue-eyed, non-Jewish boyfriend from her parents. As Rachel manipulates her dating life by using her Jewish neighbor Howard, she learns that Judaism may mean more to her than she thought and that having a boyfriend based on how he looks does not always work.

Finally, David Levithan produces *Wide Awake* (2006), where Jimmy and Duncan join other Americans who cheer the election of Abraham Stein, the first Jewish, gay president. Duncan is particularly thrilled as he is both gay and Jewish. However, the governor of Kansas is demanding a recount, so the two join other teens who travel to the state to prevent a corrupt election. Each character is struggling with personal issues, as well as the political ramifications of this history-making event.

DISABILITIES/CONDITIONS

If our preservice teachers feel inadequately prepared to deal with students from other cultures, this lack of knowledge might also extend to students who have special needs of varied kinds. Young adult literature authors provide ways into understanding and coping through realistic teen novels.

In Laurie Halse Anderson's tour de force *Speak* (2006), Melinda Sordino is mute after a savage rape at an end of summer party. Fear prevents her from speaking throughout her freshman year, until she gains the support and insight to overcome the trauma. In *Wintergirls* (2009), eighteen-year-old Lia faces her best friend's death from anorexia while struggling with the same disorder herself.

Dealing with weight issues continues with Maria Padian's *Jersey Tomatoes Are the Best* (2011). Fifteen-year-old Eva's chance at ballet camp success is hampered by her quest for the perfect dancer's body. Fourteen-year-old

Carmen's stress over her anorexic mother leads to bulimia in Julia Bell's *Massive* (2005). In *Purge* (2009), Sarah Darer Littman also deals with the ravages of bulimia. When her parents check sixteen-year-old Janie into a clinic to recover, she discovers she must discuss things she has never admitted, even to herself.

Marissa Walsh edits a collection of short stories about overweight teens in *Does This Book Make Me Look Fat?* (2008). Overweight fifteen-year-old Tristan lives unhappily with his divorced mother and her boyfriend Frank in Peter Marino's *Dough Boy* (2005). When Frank's daughter moves in, Tristan faces new insecurities regarding his weight.

Ellen Hopkins explores drug abuse in *Crank* (2004) and *Glass* (2007a), which feature Kristina Snow, whose story is based on Hopkins's daughter's struggles with addiction. Introduced to crystal meth (crank) during a visit to her father, the seventeen-year-old assumes an alter ego, Bree, whose risky lifestyle threatens to destroy her. In the sequel, Kristina returns home pregnant and goes back on speed after the baby is born in order to manage her weight. *Impulse* (2007b) features three teens who meet at a mental hospital after each has attempted suicide and connect with each other. *Fallout* (2010) is written in free verse and outlines the efforts of three teens trying to cope with the consequences of their mother's crystal meth addiction.

The Mealworm Diaries for younger readers (2009) by Anna Kerz features Jeremy, a troubled student, who is partnered with socially autistic Aaron for a science project dealing with mealworms. The stand-alone sequel, *Better than Weird* (2011), has twelve-year-old Aaron anxiously awaiting his father's return since his mother's death eight years earlier. Aaron is worried that his father—remarried with a pregnant wife—will not accept him. For older teens, R. P. and Wendy MacIntyre in *Apart* (2007) introduce Jessica, who, at sixteen, places a personal ad to locate her philandering, drug-dealer father. Jessica has been left with her devastated mother and the responsibility of caring for her autistic brother Timmy.

Beverly Brenna covers Asperger's syndrome in *Wild Orchid* (2005) and *Waiting for No One* (2011). Taylor is eighteen and hesitant to join her mother on a vacation as she narrates her fears of an unstructured world. The trip brings new understanding of her capabilities, and in the sequel, Taylor seeks more ways to be seen as a unique individual unrelated to her Asperger's. *Marcelo in the Real World* (2009) by Francisco X. Stork deals with a seventeen-year-old male's challenges with Asperger's when he goes to work in the mailroom of his father's corporate law firm.

In *Fade to Black* (2005), Alex Flinn tells the story of an attack on an HIV-positive high school student from three points of view: that of the victim, of the accused bigot, and of the only witness, a girl with Down syndrome. Thirteen-year-old Cynnie's life is grim in Catherine Ryan Hyde's *The Year of My Miraculous Reappearance* (2007), but caring for her brother Bill, who has

Down syndrome, gives it meaning. When her alcoholic mother sends him to her grandparents, Cynnie also turns to drinking for comfort.

Sixteen-year-old Lucy in Pete Hautman's *Sweetblood* (2003) has diabetes; after becoming involved with Goth culture, she begins losing control of school, her relationships, and her health. From another viewpoint, Susan Colebank's *Black Tuesday* (2007) deals with Jayne, who must help care for her diabetic sister, whose neediness sets Jayne up for disaster.

Several authors deal with the effects mental illness has on adolescent lives. Pete Hautman in *Invisible* (2005) provides an alternative look at the topic. Dougie, seventeen, has no social skills, interprets everything literally, and is a loner until he is befriended by a popular classmate. Tracy White's graphic novel *How I Made It to Eighteen: A Mostly True Story* (2010) is Stacy's story as she enters a hospital in an attempt to regain herself—whoever that is. In Julie Ann Peters's *By the Time You Read This I'll Be Dead* (2010), Daelyn has already attempted suicide and is now temporarily mute and in a neck brace. She finds an Internet suicide site and plans another attempt—until befriended by Santana.

For a complete discussion of literature dealing with disabled and ill students, see "Facilitating Inclusion: Young Adult Literature as a Tool" (Hayn & Hazlett, 2009).

CONCLUSION AND CHALLENGE

We encourage preservice teacher education that values where our students come from and who they are as a vehicle for building a program in which they will value all of their students' personal histories and allow the exploration of other cultures as well. We advocate young adult literature as a transformative tool to accomplish this challenge.

Hazel Rochman (1993) reminds us of the power of reading:

> Books can make a difference in dispelling prejudice and building community: not with role models and literal recipes, not with noble messages about the human family, but with enthralling stories that make us imagine the lives of others. A good story lets you know people as individuals in all their particularity and conflict; and once you see someone as a person—flawed, complex, striving—then you've reached beyond stereotype. Stories, writing them, telling them, sharing them, transforming them, enrich us and connect us and help us know each other. (p. 19)

Introducing our preservice teachers to multicultural literature is important not only because it is the socially just thing to do, but also because the percentage of students considered a minority continues to increase. The need for our teacher candidates to address diversity is more crucial than ever. We must introduce them to the importance of including multicultural literature in their curriculum and build their confidence in their ability to select appropriate high-quality texts. Barriers can disappear as teachers see themselves reflected in diverse cultures and recognize similarities across boundaries.

REFERENCES

Adichie, C. N. (2003). *Purple hibiscus*. Chapel Hill, NC: Algonquin Books of Chapel Hill.
Adichie, C. N. (2006). *Half of a yellow sun*. New York: Anchor Books.
Albert, N. G., Ennis, S. R., & Rios-Vargas, M. (2011). The Hispanic population: 2010. *2010 Census Briefs*. Retrieved from http://www.census.gov/prod/en2010briefs/c2010br-04.pdf
Alexie, S. (2007). *The absolutely true diary of a part-time Indian*. New York: Little, Brown.
Alvarez, J. (2004). *Finding miracles*. New York: Laurel-Leaf.
Anderson, L. H. (2006). *Speak*. New York: Farrar, Straus & Giroux.
Anderson, L. H. (2009). *Wintergirls*. New York: Viking.
Applebee, A., Burroughs, R., & Stevens, A. S. (1994). *Shaping conversation: A study of continuity and coherence in high school literacy curricula*. Albany, NY: National Research Center on Literature Teaching and Learning.
Bascom, T. (2010). The political challenge of religious diversity in America. (2010). Liberty Ledger. Retrieved from http://libertyledger.com/2010/08/22/the-political-challenge-of-religious-diversity/
Bell, J. (2002). *Massive*. New York: Macmillan.
Booth, C. (2005). *Tyrell*. New York: Push.
Booth, C. (2008). *Kendra*. New York: Push.
Booth, C. (2011). *Bronxwood*. New York: Push.
Brenna, B. (2005). *Wild orchid*. Markham, ON: Red Deer Press.
Brenna, B. (2011). *Waiting for no one*. Markham, ON: Red Deer Press.
Bruchac, J. (2001). *Skeleton man*. New York: HarperCollins.
Bruchac, J. (2004). *The dark pond*. New York: HarperCollins.
Bruchac, J. (2005). *Whisper in the dark*. New York: HarperCollins.
Bruchac, J. (2006). *Code talker: A novel about the Navajo Marines of World War II*. New York: Dial Books.
Bruchac, J. (2008a). *March toward the thunder*. New York: Dial.
Bruchac, J. (2008b). *The return of skeleton man*. New York: HarperCollins.
Budhos, M. T. (2007). *Ask me no questions*. New York: Atheneum.
Colebank, S. (2007). *Black Tuesday*. New York: Dutton.
Curtis, C. P. (1995). *The Watsons go to Birmingham—1963*. New York: Delacorte Press.
Curtis, C. P. (2004). *Bucking the sarge*. New York: Wendy Lamb Books.
Curtis, C. P. (2007). *Elijah of Buxton*. New York: Scholastic.
de la Peña, M. (2007). *Ball don't lie*. New York: Delacorte Press.
de la Peña, M. (2008). *Mexican white boy*. New York: Delacorte Press.

de la Peña, M. (2009). *We were here.* New York: Delacorte Press.
de la Peña, M. (2010). *I will save you.* New York: Delacorte Press.
Draper, S. (1996). *Tears of a tiger.* New York: Atheneum.
Draper, S. (1998). *Forged by fire.* New York: Atheneum.
Draper, S. (2002). *Darkness before dawn.* New York: Atheneum.
Draper, S. (2003). *Battle of Jericho.* New York: Atheneum.
Draper, S. (2007). *November blues.* New York: Atheneum.
Draper, S. (2009). *Just another hero.* New York: Atheneum.
Ellis, D. (2000). *Breadwinner.* Toronto: Douglas & McIntyre.
Ellis, D. (2002). *Parvana's journey.* Toronto: Groundwood Books.
Ellis, D. (2004). *Mud city.* Toronto: Groundwood Books.
Ellis, D., & Walters, E. (2007). *Bifocal.* Markham, ON: Fitzhenry & Whiteside.
Fernandez, A. (2003). Autobiography in multicultural, anti-racist education: Three case studies. *Teaching & Learning, 18*(2), 5–15.
Flake, S. (2004). *Who am I without him? Short stories about girls and the boys in their lives.* New York: Hyperion.
Flake, S. (2005). *Bang!* New York: Hyperion.
Flake, S. (2007). *The skin I'm in.* New York: Hyperion.
Flinn, A. (2005). *Fade to black.* New York: HarperTeen.
Frey, W. H. (2011a). America's diverse future: Initial glimpses at the U.S. child population from the 2010 Census. *State of Metropolitan America, 29.* Retrieved from http://www.brookings.edu/papers/2011/0406_census_diversity_frey
Frey, W. H. (2011b). A demographic tipping point among America's three-year-olds. *State of Metropolitan America, 26.* Retrieved from http://www.brookings.edu/opinions/2011/0207_population_frey.aspx
Frey, W. H. (2011c). Melting pot cities and suburbs: Racial and ethnic change in metro America in the 2000s. *State of Metropolitan America, 31.* Retrieved from http://www.brookings.edu/papers/2011/0406_censurs_ethnicity_frey
Hautman, P. (2003). *Sweetblood.* New York: Simon & Schuster.
Hautman, P. (2004). *Godless.* New York: Simon & Schuster.
Hautman, P. (2005). *Invisible.* New York: Simon & Schuster.
Hayn, J. A., & Hazlett, L. A. (2009, April). Facilitating inclusion: Young adult literature as a tool. *English Leadership Quarterly,* 8–11.
Hazlett, L., & Hayn, J. A. (2006). Diversity in young adult literature. In J. H. Bushman & K. P. Haas (Eds.), *Using young adult literature in the English classroom* (4th ed.). Upper Saddle River, NJ: Pearson Merrill Prentice-Hall.
Headley, J. C. (2007). *Nothing but the truth (and a few white lies).* New York: Little, Brown.
Headley, J. C. (2009). *Girl overboard.* New York: Little, Brown.
Hidier, T. D. (2002). *Born confused.* New York: Scholastic.
Hopkins, E. (2004). *Crank.* New York: Simon Pulse.
Hopkins, E. (2007a). *Glass.* New York: McElderberry.
Hopkins, E. (2007b). *Impulse.* New York: McElderberry.
Hopkins, E. (2010). *Fallout.* New York: McElderberry.
Hyde, C. R. (2007). *The year of my miraculous reappearance.* New York: Knopf.
Jolin, P. (2008). *In the name of God.* New Milford, CT: Roaring Brook Press.
Kadohata, C. (2004). *Kira-kira.* New York: Atheneum.

Kadohata, C. (2006). *Weedflower*. New York: Atheneum.
Kerz, A. (2009). *The mealworm diaries*. Victoria, BC: Orca.
Kerz, A. (2011). *Better than weird*. Victoria, BC: Orca.
Koja, K. (2004). *Buddha boy*. New York: Frances Foster Books.
Laird, E. (2003). *A little piece of ground*. London: Macmillan.
Laird, E. (2006). *Oranges in no man's land*. London: Macmillan.
Levithan, D. (2006). *Wide awake*. New York: Knopf.
Littman, S.D. (2009). *Purge*. New York: Scholastic.
MacIntyre, R. P., & MacIntyre, W. (2007). *Apart*. Toronto: Groundwood Books.
Marino, P. (2005). *Dough boy*. New York: Holiday House.
McCormick, P. (2006). *Sold*. New York: Hyperion.
Muñoz Ryan, P. (2004). *Becoming Naomi León*. New York: Scholastic.
Muñoz Ryan, P. (2007). *Paint the wind*. New York: Scholastic.
Muñoz Ryan, P. (2010). *The dreamer*. New York: Scholastic.
Myers, W. D. (2004). *Shooter*. New York: Harper Tempest.
Myers, W. D. (2007). *Harlem summer*. New York: Scholastic.
Myers, W. D. (2009). *Dope sick*. New York: HarperTeen.
Myers, W. D. (2010). *Lockdown*. New York: HarperTeen.
Namioka, L. (1999). *Ties that bind, ties that break*. New York: Puffin Books.
Namioka, L. (2002). *An ocean apart, a world away*. New York: Laurel-Leaf.
Namioka, L. (2006). *Mismatch*. New York: Delacorte Press.
National Center for Education Statistics. (2010). Percentage distribution of students 6 to 21 years old served under Individuals with Disabilities Education Act. (Data file). Retrieved from http://nces.ed.gov/fastfacts/display.asp?id=59
Neri, G. (2010). *Yummy: The last day of a Southside Shorty*. New York: Lee & Low Books.
Nieto, S. (2004). *Affirming diversity: The sociopolitical context of multicultural education, my lab book*. New York: Allyn & Bacon.
Okorafor, N. (2011). *Akata witch*. New York: Viking.
Ortiz Cofer, J. O. (1995). *An island like you: Stories from the barrio*. New York: Orchard Books.
Ortiz Cofer, J. O. (2006). *Call me María*. New York: Scholastic.
Ortiz Cofer, J. O. (2011). *If I could fly*. New York: Farrar, Straus & Giroux.
Osa, N. (2003). *Cuba 15*. New York: Delacorte Press.
Padian, M. (2011). *Jersey tomatoes are the best*. New York: Knopf.
Perkins, M. (2006). *Monsoon summer*. New York: Laurel-Leaf.
Perkins, M. (2010). *Secret keeper*. New York: Ember.
Peters, J. A. (2010). *By the time you read this I'll be dead*. New York: Hyperion.
Placide, J. (2002). *Fresh girl*. New York: Delacorte Press.
Rhodes, J. P. (2010). *Ninth ward*. New York: Little, Brown.
Rochman, H. (1993). *Against borders: Promoting books for a multicultural world*. Chicago: American Library Association.
Sandell, L. A. (2006). *The weight of the sky*. New York: Viking.
Schorr, M. (2006). *Goy crazy*. New York: Hyperion.
Shea, P. D. (2003). *Tangled threads: A Hmong girl's story*. New York: Clarion Books.
Shea, P. D. (2010). *Abe in arms*. Oakland, CA: PM Press.
Sitomer, A. L. (2006). *The hoopster*. New York: Hyperion.
Sitomer, A. L. (2007a). *Hip-hop high school*. New York: Hyperion.

Sitomer, A. L. (2007b). *Homeboyz*. New York: Hyperion.
Soto, G. (2003). *The afterlife*. Orlando, FL: Harcourt.
Soto, G. (2006). *Accidental love*. Orlando, FL: Harcourt.
Stallworth, B. J., Gibbons L., & Fauber, L. (2006). It's not on the list: An exploration of teachers' perspectives on using multicultural literature. *Journal of Adolescent & Adult Literacy* 49(8), 478–489.
Stork, F. X. (2009). *Marcelo in the real world*. New York: Arthur A. Levine Books.
Stratton, A. (2004). *Chanda's secrets*. Toronto: Annick Press.
Thurlo, D., & Thurlo, A. (2004). *The spirit line*. New York: Viking.
United States Census Bureau. (2010). 2010 census shows America's diversity. Retrieved from http://2010.census.gov/news/releases/operations/cb11-cn125.html
Voorhees, C. (2008). *The brothers Torres*. New York: Hyperion.
Walsh, M. (2008). *Does this book make me look fat?* New York: Clarion Books.
White, T. (2010). *How I made it to eighteen: A mostly true story*. New York: Roaring Book Press.
Williams-Garcia, R. (2009). *Jumped*. New York: HarperTeen.
Williams-Garcia, R. (2010). *One crazy summer*. New York: Amistad.
Woods, D. R. (2009). Hearing the voices: Multicultural young adult literature as authentic cultural experience. *Virginia English Bulletin, 58*(2), 15–30.
Yang, G. L. (2006). *American born Chinese*. New York: First Second.
Yee, L. (2003). *Millicent Min, girl genius*. New York: Arthur A. Levine Books.
Yee, L. (2005). *Stanford Wong flunks big time*. New York: Arthur A. Levine Books.
Yee, L. (2008). *So totally Emily Ebers*. New York: Arthur A. Levine Books.
Yee, L. (2011). *Warp speed*. New York: Arthur A. Levine Books.
Yep, L. (2004). *The traitor*. New York: HarperCollins.
Yep, L. (2008). *Dragon road*. New York: HarperCollins.
Yep, L. (2011). *Dragons of silk*. New York: HarperCollins.
Zenatti, V. (2008). *A bottle in the Gaza Sea* (A. Hunter, Trans.). New York: Bloomsbury.

9

Updating Young Adult Literature Reading Lists While Retaining Quality Titles

Lisa A. Hazlett

Canonical adult classical literature has its history, but young adult literature (YAL) also has a past, perhaps longer than commonly realized. S. E. Hinton's 1967 publication of *The Outsiders* (the initials "S. E." conveniently hiding her gender) is widely accepted as the genre's contemporary beginning, quickly followed by waves of equally significant titles: Robert Lipsyte's *The Contender* (1967), Paul Zindel's *The Pigman* and Ann Head's *Mr. and Mrs. Bo Jo Jones* (both 1968), or Bill and Vera Cleaver's 1969 *Where the Lilies Bloom* (Bushman & Haas, 2006; Nilsen & Donelson, 2009). These early works are now in their mid-forties and beyond; even Robert Cormier's venerable *The Chocolate War* (1974) is nearing its fortieth publication year.

The literary community's classification of adult canonical literature, succinctly summarized by Hipple (2000), is titles of literary quality, containing themes universal to human nature and common conditions faced, with their components—plots, stories/events, characters, and settings—vivid and forceful. They speak to readers over years, merit study and critique, and are reread.

Researchers of YAL (Blasingame, 2007; Bushman & Haas, 2006; Christenbury, 2006; Nilsen & Donelson, 2009) echo Hipple's standard definition. Herz and Gallo (2005) add that reading canonical texts allows entrance into the literary community, while Zitlow (2008) notes that these works influence subsequent titles. However, these authors also affirm this literature is intended for adults rather than adolescents.

Unfortunately, the above sentence has been virtually ignored; adult classics are firmly entrenched in English language arts (ELA) curricula. Applebee's 1989 survey of ELA titles taught showed classics as predominant, and nearly identical with a 1963 listing; Herz and Gallo (2005) also found the classics, with limited YAL, still reigning.

Adult classics remain due to politics, high-stakes testing, community desire, presence in anthologies and novels within schools, teacher education lacking YAL coursework, viewing YAL as lesser quality or for younger students, and the hoary "It's always been done this way." The latter is especially binding, as Iannaccone (1963) found; educators, regardless of schooling, teach as they were taught, and similarly to colleagues. Future educators study the classics in secondary school and then are employed where these texts are ELA staples; no wonder they are continually served.

Specialists in YAL (Blasingame, 2007; Bushman & Haas, 2006; Herz & Gallo, 2005; Lesesne, 2006; Nilsen and Donelson, 2009) similarly declare that this genre contains the same literary elements as the classics through consistent viewpoints, defined but not overly complicated plots, dynamic characterizations, important settings, genuine and spirited dialogue, and engaging styles.

Further, developmental theorists (Carlson, 1980; Havighurst, 1972; Piaget & Inhelder, 1969) state that YAL best fits adolescents' maturity and cognitive development. Bluntly summarized, a tenth-grade geometry textbook is obviously unsuitable for an ordinary second-grade student; likewise, much classical literature is similarly difficult for adolescents' comprehension—but unlike elementary educators, secondary teachers expect discernment of the classics.

How do educators teach novels that the majority of their students dislike and cannot understand? Perhaps the better question is why, but Herz and Gallo (2005) say classics are taught through guides, the triad of worksheet/quiz/test, and pre-planned, teacher-led discussions.

Christenbury (2000) agrees, including the fact that many students seek interpretations such as *Cliff's Notes* for understanding. This matches the reading habits compiled by Carlson and Sherrill (1988) from ELA educators, with the majority commenting they maintained their love of reading despite the classics and accompanying school assignments. As some of these educators state, gaining reading appreciation late in high school or afterward, such commentary of high schools' unhelpfulness regarding classics bodes ill for most students.

Young adult literature illustrates the many varied realities of contemporary adolescent life and portrays teens' dreams, worries, and problems through characters and their situations, obviously absent from adult classics. Perhaps most importantly, quality YAL assists in answering adolescents' universal questions of "Who am I?" and "Where do I fit in?" (Herz & Gallo, 2005).

Researchers (Blasingame, 2007; Bushman & Haas, 2006; Herz & Gallo, 2005; Hipple, 2000; Lesesne, 2006; Salvner, 2000) state their concerns with students leaving ELA classrooms without a love of literature. Some researchers (Christenbury, 2000; Herz & Gallo, 2005; Lesesne, 2006) particularly noted that educators commonly ignore or dismiss students' reactions to classics, listening instead for predetermined textual interpretations and answers, producing reading distaste.

This feared outcome was indeed found by the National Endowment for the Arts (2004) survey of literature (i.e., quality and/or canonical) read by adults; the percentage of adult readers has dropped dramatically over the past twenty years, with less than half of adults now reading literature—a loss of twenty million potential readers.

The decline in literary reading parallels the decline in total book reading, although literary reading is falling faster. The percentage of all adults reading any book within a year is 56 percent, with literature readers at 46 percent. Although higher education levels correlate to higher reading rates, reading among those of all education levels has also declined. The steepest decline is among the youngest age groups; those aged eighteen to thirty-four have moved from most likely to read literature to least likely (with an exception of those aged sixty-five and over). Moreover, as higher literary reading rates correlate to stronger participation and attendance in civic, cultural, volunteer, and athletic events, this decline foreshadows lessening participation.

These also correlate with increased participation in electronic media. While no single media activity is responsible for plunging reading rates, their overall presence and availability have increasingly drawn adults away from reading as entertainment.

If students are leaving school and gleefully tossing literary works aside with all other reading, this is hardly a testament to the use and teaching of literature in ELA classrooms.

Using only classics in ELA classrooms assures literature with which many students can neither develop appreciation nor make meaningful personal connection. As Bushman and Haas (2006) resolutely warned:

> This literary elitism encourages students to have an unhealthy, negative attitude toward their ability and, as a result, leads to nonreading when they leave school. If schools and teachers want students to understand what they read, to interact with the literature so that they can make connections to their own lives, to make critical judgments that will enhance their intellectual, emotional, and moral development, and, perhaps most important, to become lifelong readers, schools and teachers must evaluate the literature curriculum and make the necessary changes so that students can indeed achieve success in these areas. (p. 4)

However, YAL classroom use is growing (Blasingame, 2007; Cole, 2009; Herz & Gallo, 2005; Lesesne, 2006), with educators indicating that they do indeed desire increased classroom use (Hazlett, Beumer Johnson, & Hayn, 2009). Classics remain in classrooms, but they do not necessarily reign. The rationale for canonical selections has been stated above, but which YAL do educators continue using and recommending, and which not? Perhaps most importantly, how may educators best update their YAL reading lists while retaining quality titles?

EDUCATORS' RETENTION AND REJECTION OF YAL TITLES

The quality and popularity of YAL varies among educators, as preferences remain unique to individuals. However, personal preferences are only one of a myriad of factors determining classroom title selection. Titles widely considered preeminent, such as Robert Cormier's *The Chocolate War* (1974) or Lois Lowry's *The Giver* (1993), have longevity, but the majority of YAL fluctuates from prized to despised, causing vast variations of usage among secondary (i.e., middle and high school) educators. Selections are based upon more than quality, with the factors below certainly affecting educators' decisions.

Curricula

Major determiners of any novel's use are curricula and availability, but those afforded choices likely retain those previously used. Many YAL titles continually reappear because they are available and familiar with expansive resources; many educators, especially beginning ones, find it more convenient to use existing materials than create new ones (Iannaccone, 1963).

Of course, repeated use means overlooking that author's other works. For example, Robert Cormier is known for *The Chocolate War* (1974), but his novels also include *Tunes for Bears to Dance To* (1992) and *In the Middle of the Night* (1995), neither particularly popular or well known. Lois Lowry received a Newbery medal for both *Number the Stars* (1989) and *The Giver* (1993), but also authored *The Silent Boy* (2003) and *Gossamer* (2006). Likewise, Gary Paulsen is renowned for *Hatchet* (1987), but not for *Woodsong* (1990) or *Alida's Song* (1999). Some of these are impressive texts, but they are destined for relative anonymity if unused.

Regrettably, challenges, actual censorship, or fear of them are omnipresent. Most censorship episodes occur through public opinion rather than in courtrooms, although the majority of formal challenges are handled according to district procedure—with adherence and decisions varying. All, even the innocuous, are quickly broadcast, with the questioned novel soon becoming poisonous (Nilsen & Donelson, 2009).

Such episodes undoubtedly promote educator self-censorship by excising titles deemed potentially controversial to avoid protests. Not all parental concerns are censorious; many are simple questions, requests for rationales or reassurance, or a desire only that their child be exempt from reading a particular novel.

Educators seemingly believe self-censorship is not considered formal censorship, but aside from the same practice, it is as arbitrary and capricious as official censors' demands. Automatically expecting the worst leads to elimination of quality YAL, often resulting in narrower reading selections than if censors themselves had winnowed titles.

Individual Decisions

Educators as individuals must make decisions regarding titles, and disliking a particular novel or subject probably means that author or similar topics will remain unread. Likewise, author encounters—school visits, bookstore or convention talks and signings, online correspondence, chats, and interviews—range from fortunate to disastrous, with commensurate author opinions influencing their works' selection, more so as educators naturally share such encounters among themselves.

Educators must also make decisions regarding novels sharing similarities. There are scores of novels featuring World War II, the Civil War, colonial times, blank verse, and so on, and some may see few significant differences among them to warrant purchase. For example, retaining an older World War II title is simpler and less expensive than purchasing one more recent, but it results in a narrow cache of used titles and overlooked gems.

Established genre authors have a popularity advantage regarding selections, as those seeking titles in unfamiliar areas likely gravitate toward known authors. For example, Ann Rinaldi is synonymous with historical fiction, Jane Yolen and Tamora Pierce with fantasy, and Will Hobbs and Gary Paulsen with adventure—but using any other author for these genres might be rare.

Librarians are likely to face selection dilemmas with series titles, as sets by inexhaustible authors like Christopher Pike or R. L. Stein produce numerous works. Brian Jacques' *Redwall* series contains more than twenty titles; Phyllis Reynolds Naylor's *Alice* novels number some twenty-five. Nonsequential series authors also abound; the prolific Lurlene McDaniel shows more than sixty titles. Such books interest a niche audience, but their sheer number makes their teaching unlikely. Moreover, purchasing only one or two copies of a series for libraries seems unfulfilling, but entire collections are unaffordable. Exposure here is frequently word of mouth, from both educators and students.

Conversely, educators must also contend with authors underrepresented in YAL, as some primarily pen for younger teens, children, or adults, mainly marketing to those groups. Some educators may be unaware of their adolescent works; again, attention of some sort is often necessary for recognition of these authors.

Furthermore, authors may simply disappear. For example, the publisher's preface of Geoffrey Huntington's exciting and compelling *Sorcerers of the Nightwing* (2002) states that this novel marks the debut of a fantasy-horror series, with its cover promoting a themed website. *Demon Witch* (2003) continues this increasingly entertaining series, with its ending promising a sequel. As of this writing, there are no additional titles, with the originals out of print although available from various online sellers. These titles were unique and tantalizing but, oddly, abruptly stop at the second title, with additional information about the series seemingly unavailable.

Additionally, John Halliday's suspenseful *Shooting Monarchs* (2003) received acclaim, but apparently his only other novel is an out-of-print one for tweens. Brian Burks's *Soldier Boy* (1997) also received praise, but he too seems to have disappeared after three books, the latest dated 1999.

Although a good book remains a good book, authors who cease writing without explanation are, aside from being largely unfamiliar, almost certainly less likely to be considered or recommended by educators. Moreover, as these works age without others forthcoming, author information and supplemental materials will similarly be scant or nonexistent, all hardly conducive to selection.

Publishing Houses and Professional Organizations

Publishers keenly determine the influence of various YAL by establishing the type and amount of attention works will receive, as they both respond to and help create the book-buying audience. Publishers select novels to be heavily marketed, determine supporting materials' availability, and remove titles from print. Naturally, the most popular authors receive the most attention (Cole, 2009).

Like educators, publishers and authors are also inscrutable regarding selections; some will publish with one house, then be dropped or switched to another. Financial and other decisions rule, but gaps between novels affect selection. For example, Lois Ruby's *Soon to Be Free*, a companion work/sequel to her popular *Steal Away Home* (1994), did not see publication until 2000, with this six-year gap presumably resulting in the sequel's loss of the first title's audience.

Publisher representatives attend professional conventions and other venues, with those who are attentive and knowledgeable in attendance; they provide complementary materials, and follow-up naturally assists sales.

Unfortunately, while especially lavish YAL promotions occur at professional gatherings, those attending are likely post-secondary professionals familiar with the touted works. Although attendees share experiences, classroom use is likely unaffected.

Publishers also determine which novels will be included in professional publications that review and feature articles about YAL and its authors. The National Council of Teachers of English (NCTE) publishes *The ALAN Review* and the online *ALAN Picks*; *SIGNAL* serves the same purpose for the International Reading Association (IRA). *Voice of Youth Advocates* (VOYA) focuses on library media specialists and post-secondary YAL educators, and *Multicultural Review* includes titles featuring elements of diversity, with similar journals and reviews prolific.

Unfortunately, Hazlett, Beumer Johnson, and Hayn (2009) found that these journals' audience is composed almost exclusively of post-secondary educators. Secondary educators neither regularly read them nor hold the membership attached to the journals. Of course, membership does not assure readership, but Blasingame (2007) urged educators' familiarity and use of journals and YAL review for knowledgeable selections.

Journal editors must select titles for review from among the approximately three to four thousand YAL titles published yearly (L. Kurydala, personal communication, December 16, 2010); naturally, all cannot be reviewed. Editors eliminate those of poorest quality (reviewers are also allowed denial after editor permission), with remaining titles sent pro bono to trained, experienced reviewers. Ironically, of all venues, reviewing is almost certainly the least biased or influenced by other interests; unfortunately, novel reviews are read least by secondary educators (Hazlett, Beumer Johnson, & Hayn, 2009).

Technological Influences

A vital offering is technological sites, especially publishers' websites linked to those of individual authors. Contemporary educators expect attractive sites containing teaching materials, information such as awards received, author biographies, interviews, speaking information and fees, video clips, personal commentaries, e-mail and other contacts, and other eye-catching items. Popular authors' sites receive the most lavish information and assistance; for example, Scholastic's site featured a doomsday clock ticking the seconds until Collins's *Mockingjay* (2010) appeared, according to Cole (2009).

Herz and Gallo (2005) commend publishers for enticing teens to view sites by placing Internet addresses prominently on or in the novel that lead to teen-appealing sections, especially participatory ones such as blogs or chats. Cole's (2009) assertion that popularity equals attention again holds true, as publishers know teens share sites. Unfortunately, sites now contain trendy and often expensive merchandise such as T-shirts, posters, and mementos, enticing teen dollars while increasing site visitation and readership, all financially beneficial.

Conversely, Cole (2009) also laments the existence of sites that seem to receive less publisher attention; quality sites require time and technological proficiency, often a hardship. Unattractive, sparse sites reflect negatively upon the novel and author, and although publisher assistance arrives after a title's popularity increases, prior negative site visits may preclude future ones.

Booksellers' Role

Large chain bookstores and online-only sellers such as Amazon are hugely popular; both are influential regarding novel selection, using similar promotional tactics. Walk-in stores feature various eye-catching displays, like mystery novels during October, increasing purchase. Online sellers follow, placing popular titles on home pages, recommended lists, or offering special pricing as enticement.

Those less acquainted with YAL are more likely to purchase from these displays and lists, which often contain quality titles overshadowed by lesser titles with gory, flashy covers, classics (such as Jane Austen's *Pride and Prejudice,* 1813) for romance, or mass-produced series books. While such promotions lure purchasers, they also intimate that lower-quality books are representative of YAL (Herz & Gallo, 2005; Nilsen & Donelson, 2009).

Award-Winning and Popular Titles

Award-winning titles, with the Newbery most prominent, are certainly read and recommended, especially as their status and reputation generally assures a quality novel for those less familiar with YAL. Booksellers and publishers heavily promote authors and novels during their award year; however, an award novel's continual use also allows the writer's other titles to languish.

Interestingly, Newbery titles fade as quickly as they shine; their one glory year soon transfers to the subsequent recipient. Generally, only extraordinary Newbery recipients, such as Lois Lowry's *The Giver* (1993) or Karen Hesse's *Out of the Dust* (1997), remain strong; others are lumped among all other YAL, with awards tarnishing if featuring weaker quality.

Time's Passage

While deceased authors are a plus, not to mention a necessity, for adult classics, contemporary YAL authors' deaths are sadly occurring more frequently among YAL pioneers like Paula Danziger, Norma Klein, Norma Fox Mazer, Virginia Hamilton, and Paul Zindel. Young adult literature is especially locked in time due to its topical references; although meant to attract adolescents, they also date plots.

For example, Norma Klein's once immensely popular *Mom, the Wolf-Man and Me* (1974) featured a girl ashamed of her divorced mother wearing slacks—then a cringe-worthy problem, but quaint and surely irrelevant to contemporary teens. Paul Zindel's *My Darling, My Hamburger* (1969) was notorious for discussing abortion; while its subject remains contentious, current readers should find it far tamer and its late 1960s content unappealing.

While an author's death does not necessarily mean the same for his or her work, it does produce a peculiar feeling of resignation and perhaps a stigma, since no more titles will be forthcoming. Publishers hardly promote dated YAL from deceased authors over their new, popular works, and it is unlikely educators would select a deceased YAL author's novels unless canonical, with lesser-quality titles slowly forgotten.

THE ACTUALITY OF YOUNG ADULT LITERATURE SELECTION AND USE

There is no magic formula or single discernible reason for why some titles are used continually and others are not; the reality is that, aside from the rare canonical classic, no novel is assured of perpetual readership. Although the factors cited above affect readership, ultimately individual educators select the titles they wish to use.

Educators cannot possibly read, retain, or use the enormous number of published YAL; certain gems will always remain elusive. Often, young adult literature, like all others, is not canonical or even particularly memorable; only superlative titles remain popular after several decades, since readership slows as novels and adolescents age.

Individual young adult novels are static, but not time; although an educator may teach sophomores, each year brings different students to his or her classroom. Passing years continually produce teens seeking novels mirroring their present situations; only time will tell which of today's titles will be in tomorrow's classrooms or relegated to booklists.

LOCATING UNAVAILABLE TITLES

Few YAL novels are out of print and completely unavailable; those deemed lost are likely out of print with copies still available. Titles are in various school and community libraries for borrowing, even donation.

Technology assures Internet availability, albeit often expensive for hardbacks or original editions. Lower-tech options include used bookstores, Salvation Army–type stores, garage sales, or simply asking parents and students for titles. One can also have technology-savvy students search for titles, perhaps as an assignment.

Various events, such as an author or title receiving acclaim, otherwise newsworthy notice, or a movie based on a novel, can create a resurgence of popularity, with older works reappearing sporting updated covers. Novels may be revised, such as Judy Blume's *Forever* (1975, 2003), now containing information regarding sexually transmitted diseases and other contemporary issues, unwarranted nearly forty years ago.

Publishing houses and individual authors often retain copies, with many willing to donate or sell for nominal fees. Finally, there are businesses specializing in rare and/or out-of-print books; if an educator is creative and willing to search, nearly any previously unavailable title may be located. However, before beginning a possibly lengthy or expensive novel search, educators should read the reviews or other information likely available on the Internet. Novel titles can be confused; books long unread yet remembered fondly may not be as enjoyable upon another reading, especially as an adult.

BENEFITS OF OLDER AND CONTEMPORARY TITLES

A wealth of older YAL literature can benefit contemporary adolescents as teens discover their commonalities with them, reinforcing the concept that adult classics' timeless themes remain relevant to modern readers. The question of "Where am I in the story?" can connect any novel to teens. Educators should look beyond older YAL novels that were award recipients or especially popular, probing deeper to find hidden gems that received scant attention.

Still, if educators are seeking older YAL for the classroom, all should contain attributes of quality titles; "older" is not synonymous with exceptional. Of course, this should be the goal of all ELA educators when seeking titles—locating those that best meet their current students' needs at any given time. Added to the above purposes and qualities of YAL is that they, not adult canonical works, create lifelong readers.

REFERENCES

Applebee, A. (1989). *A study of book-length works taught in high school English courses.* Albany, NY: SUNY Press.
Austen, J. (1813/2007). *Pride and prejudice.* Cambridge, UK: Worth Press.
Blasingame, J. (2007). *Books that don't bore 'em.* New York: Scholastic.

Blume, J. (1975). *Forever.* New York: Simon & Schuster.
Blume, J. (2003). *Forever* (Rev. ed.). New York: Simon & Schuster.
Burks, B. (1997). *Soldier boy.* Orlando, FL: Harcourt Brace.
Bushman, J., & Haas, K. P. (2006). *Using young adult literature in the English classroom.* Upper Saddle River, NJ: Pearson Merrill Prentice Hall.
Carlson, R. (1980). *Books and the teen-age reader.* New York: Harper & Row.
Carlson, R., & Sherrill, A. (1988). *Voices of readers: How we come to love books.* Urbana, IL: National Council of Teachers of English.
Christenbury, L. (2000). Natural, necessary, and workable: The connection of young adult novels to the classics. In V. Monseau & G. M. Salvner (Eds.), *Reading their world: The young adult novel in the classroom* (pp. 15–30). Portsmouth, NH: Boynton/Cook–Heinemann.
Christenbury, L. (2006). *Making the journey: Being and becoming a teacher of English language arts.* Portsmouth, NH: Heinemann.
Cleaver, B., & Cleaver, V. (1969). *Where the lilies bloom.* New York: HarperCollins.
Cole, P. (2009). *Young adult literature in the 21st century.* New York: McGraw-Hill.
Collins, S. (2010). *Mockingjay.* New York: Scholastic.
Cormier, R. (1974). *The chocolate war.* New York: Dell.
Cormier, R. (1992). *Tunes for bears to dance to.* New York: Dell.
Cormier, R. (1995). *In the middle of the night.* New York: Dell.
Halliday, J. (2003). *Shooting monarchs.* New York: Simon & Schuster.
Havighurst, R. (1972). *Developmental tasks and education.* New York: David McKay.
Hazlett, L., Beumer Johnson, A., & Hayn, J. (2009). An almost young adult literature study. *The ALAN Review, 37,* 48–53.
Head, A. (1968). *Mr. and Mrs. Bo Jo Jones.* New York: Penguin.
Herz, S. K., & Gallo, D. R. (2005). *From Hinton to Hamlet.* Westport, CT: Greenwood Press.
Hesse, K. (1997). *Out of the dust.* New York: Scholastic.
Hinton, S. E. (1967). *The outsiders.* New York: Penguin.
Hipple, T. (2000). With themes for all: The universality of the young adult novel. In V. Monseau & G. M. Salvner (Eds.), *Reading their world: The young adult novel in the classroom* (pp. 1–14). Portsmouth, NH: Boynton/Cook–Heinemann.
Huntington, G. (2002). *Sorcerers of the nightwing.* New York: HarperCollins.
Huntington, G. (2003). *Demon witch.* New York: HarperCollins.
Iannaccone, L. (1963, April). Student teaching: A transitional state in the making of teachers. *Theory into Practice,* 73–80.
Klein, N. (1974). *Mom, the wolf-man, and me.* New York: Avon.
Lesesne, T. (2006). *Naked reading: Uncovering what tweens need to become lifelong readers.* Portland, ME: Stenhouse.
Lipsyte, R. (1967). *The contender.* New York: HarperCollins.
Lowry, L. (1989). *Number the stars.* New York: Houghton Mifflin.
Lowry, L. (1993). *The giver.* New York: Houghton Mifflin.
Lowry, L. (2003). *The silent boy.* New York: Random House.
Lowry, L. (2006). *Gossamer.* New York: Random House.
National Endowment for the Arts. (2004). *Reading at risk: A survey of literary reading in America.* Research Division Report No. 46. Retrieved from http://www.nea.gov/pub/readingatrisk.pdf

Nilsen, A. P., & Donelson, K. L. (2009). *Literature for today's young adults*. Boston: Pearson.
Paulsen, G. (1987). *Hatchet*. New York: Simon & Schuster.
Paulsen, G. (1990). *Woodsong*. New York: Simon & Schuster.
Paulsen, G. (1999). *Alida's Song*. New York: Delacorte.
Piaget, J., & Inhelder, B. (1969). *The psychology of the child*. New York: Basic Books.
Ruby, L. (1994). *Steal away home*. New York: Simon & Schuster.
Ruby, L. (2000). *Soon to be free*. New York: Simon & Schuster.
Salvner, G. (2000). Time and tradition: Transforming the secondary English class with young adult novels. In V. Monseau & G. M. Salvner (Eds.), *Reading their world: The young adult novel in the classroom* (pp. 85–99). Portsmouth, NH: Boynton/Cook–Heinemann.
Zindel, P. (1968). *The pigman*. New York: HarperCollins.
Zindel, P. (1969). *My darling, my hamburger*. New York: Bantam.
Zitlow, C. (2008). Twenty classic young adult novels. In P. Cole (Ed.). *Young adult literature in the 21st century* (pp. 51–57). New York: McGraw-Hill.

10

Crossing Boundaries

Genre-Blurring in Books for Young Adults

Barbara A. Ward, Terrell A. Young, and Deanna Day

Books for teens no longer consist solely of lines of text read from left to right, from the top of the page to the bottom. With the increasing popularity of verse novels, graphic novels, and multiple formats in books, today's teen readers are being called upon to use very different reading skills than they might have used a decade ago. They often need to attune their ears to different voices and perspectives in novels in verse, learn to read the illustrations and other graphic elements as well as the text, and draw inferences as their eyes move across the splashy colors that leap from today's teen-oriented graphic novels. At times, they must even shift back and forth from lines of print on a page to accompanying video clips on a Web page. In some cases, they need to alternate from pages of narrative to pages of factual information on the same topic, all within the same book. Clearly, literature for teens is changing at a rapid pace.

As the field of young adult literature continues to expand, authors eagerly push the envelope regarding the genres or literary categories in which they create their books, crossing genre boundaries in many different ways. Although teachers and librarians could once firmly point to a book and declare it to be poetry, for instance, today's books for teens may combine poetry and nonfiction; tell a story through traditional narrative supported by e-mail, brochures, and street signs; weave in several story lines on the same page; provide alternative versions of the same story; and even tell stories through text and video links. Today's teachers and students alike often struggle with the standard conventions of genres—wondering if a book should be considered fantasy, realistic, historical, or even something yet to be named. Seemingly defying classification since they are a mixture of two or more genres, many recently published trade books for adolescents often do not fit a traditional genre category.

Many of today's authors tell their stories through multiple genres, and as those genre lines are crossed, it's likely that more and more will overlap. Savvy teachers will recognize the enormous creative opportunity these changes offer, and immerse their students in many kinds of print and many types of literature. A genre study that pays tribute to the trend of blending genres can certainly fit in well in today's classroom. Analyzing different types of literature promotes cognitive development since students are able to apply similar skills and strategies, such as identifying themes discussed in one genre—fiction, for example—to other genres, such as poetry and drama. It stands to reason that the more experience students have in reading different genres, the more successful they could be writing in various genres.

Smith (2007) discusses reshuffling or reclassifying texts, as he and his students struggle with whether a book is fantasy or historical fiction. Since many recently published YA novels do not fit into a predictable genre category, he suggests these titles could be considered genre-busters or genre-blurring or genre-bending books. Literary scholars are fond of grouping literature into different categories for convenience and in order to note commonalities of the genre. But many young adult titles cause them puzzlement about how to classify books since they are both one thing and yet another, both historical fiction and magical realism. For instance, Megan Whalen Turner's *A Conspiracy of Kings* (2010) features a story set during the Middle Ages but with elements of magic. Donna Jo Napoli's *The Wager* (2010) retells a Sicilian fairy tale, but one that is filled with historical details. Smith proposes that the old habit of grouping reading materials according to genres is outdated and suggests that we redefine what genre looks like in the twenty-first century. In his view, the use of genre to classify books is now obsolete.

In this chapter, we highlight the work of four YA authors who blur genres. We examine the work of Patrick Carman, Gene Luen Yang, and Margarita Engle, describing the genre-blurring books these authors have created and providing snippets of author interviews we conducted by phone and through e-mail, as well as ideas for middle and high school educators. Additionally, we examine one book by the ever-popular and innovative Gary Paulsen that could live comfortably in both the historical fiction and nonfiction category.

PATRICK CARMAN ON TRANSMEDIA BOOKS

Digi-novels, transmedia, multimedia, or vooks (video-books) merge conventional print-bound text with a digital experience. These multiplatform books invite readers to log on to related websites to play video games such as in the *39 Clues* series by multiple authors—Rick Riordan wrote the first title in the series (*The Maze of Bones*, 2008)—decipher a puzzle as in *Spaceheadz* (Scieszka & Sedita, 2010a, 2010b) or watch videos as in *Trackers Book 1* (Carman, 2010b). Patrick Carman's *Skeleton Creek* series chronicles the adventures of teens Ryan McCray and Sarah Fincher as they investigate mysteries in and around their hometown. Sarah is a filmmaker who posts videos on the website sarafincher.com, which readers access using passwords. Ryan is a compulsive writer who keeps a journal of their adventures along with e-mails taped inside. These two friends provide a tag-team narrative of mystery, horror, and humor.

Groenke, Bell, Allen, and Maples (2011) note that young adolescents are definitely intrigued by the expanded media storytelling techniques. These teachers found that reading hybrid books, a mixture of text and digital, engaged their students, compelled them to keep reading, and inspired them to create their own digital novels.

In his most recent books, Carman has combined two artistic media, printed word and online video, something he is likely to do even more in the future (P. Carman, telephone interview, January 24, 2011). His inspiration for writing *Skeleton Creek* (Carman, 2009a) resulted from the fact that he is actually

> a traveling writer. I have been to over a thousand schools. The first time I toured schools, students did not have cell phones. Now 90 percent of middle school kids have cell phones, and even third and second graders have them. If I ask kids to give me a high five—"Did you watch TV, go on the Internet, play with an iPod, use a cell phone, or play a video game today?"—most kids will have five fingers up.

Over time, Carman says he began to see "major shifts in the amount of technology kids were using. Kids are part of a wired culture today. They are drawn to communication and entertainment technology."

As an author trying to predict the reactions to his books, Carman says that he kept asking himself, "How could I hook the most jaded readers?" He no longer likes some of the labels put on students who teachers think do not read. "I've abandoned the term 'reluctant reader.' If you go out and spend any time with kids in schools," he says, "it's not like they don't want to read; they are bored with it." Middle graders and teens are reading, he claims, but the kinds of texts they read avidly are not those typically associated with literacy. "They have a cell phone and are sending a thousand texts a month," he says. "Books are a tough sale when 75 percent are not reading or only reading when they have to. I can't put candy in a book. So I kept thinking that there has to be a way to lure kids to read. Mixing video with books was my answer."

He pitched his idea to Scholastic, thinking they wouldn't be interested; he was stunned to hear back from his editor, David Levithan, the same day. According to Carman, "Scholastic was already working on the *39 Clues* series internally, so my ideas for *Skeleton Creek* fit nicely into what they were doing. They were already beginning to do multimedia projects."

Clearly, there are differences between writing and creating videos. Carman says,

> When you write a book, it is just between you and your editor. That is hard work, yet a lonely pursuit. You are essentially doing it alone. What I love about these multimedia projects is getting the best of both worlds. I get to write these things, and I get to collaborate with others on the videos. I love working with creative people. Creating these projects is both challenging and a lot of fun.

Carman admits he had never written a screenplay before the *Skeleton Creek* series. Describing his creative process, he says, "I wrote the first book as one big document. Initially, I wrote the journal entries, and when I came to a part where a video was needed, I wrote that. I didn't write a screenplay; instead, it was a bunch of dialogue with what was happening." Scholastic gave Carman an advance that he used to hire a director, find a location, and employ all of the actors and actresses for the filmed portions of the book. "It was really hard at the beginning. I pretty much made the project twice," he says. "The first attempt didn't work to my satisfaction. I hired a whole new group of people. Now we get how to do it, and I have a core team of a half dozen people who are always involved."

Carman admits that he relied on his imagination rather than research for these multimedia texts. "I wouldn't say there was a lot of research with those books. Everything about those stories was made up," he says. The *Skeleton Creek* books have some intentional historical information in them so that they blur the lines between what is real and what is not real. The setting for the books is at a real dredge in Sumpter, Oregon, about which curious readers can learn more at the Friends of the Dredge website (http://www.friendsofthedredge.com/). Carman says he was able to use "archival data such as stories about people who worked on the dredge" to add to the stories' authenticity.

The third *Skeleton Creek* story, *The Crossbones* (2010a), contains puzzles and clues and is essentially a road trip of haunted spots across the United States. Carman explains, "The main character goes to places that have been reported to be haunted. For this book I went online and searched for all kinds of haunted places, and they are everywhere." Carman was able to be selective and used "the coolest ones with the most back story."

The fourth title in the *Skeleton Creek* series, *The Raven* (2011b), ties all the parts of the mystery together neatly, with more video clips from Sarah and journal entries and shots from his cell phone by Ryan, and could certainly be considered a homage of sorts to master of suspense Edgar Allan Poe.

All of the passwords used to access Sarah's videos online are completely by design. Some are characters from old gothic novels, while others are connected to classic scary films (Levithan, 2009). Carman describes their purpose: "The passwords did exactly what I hoped they would do. Kids watched the videos and then jumped online to find more information. The stories sparked curiosity and kids took action, searching the Internet to learn more."

Carman discusses two new projects. One that launches this year is 315stories.com. Each story requires three modes of response, according to Carman. To view the stories,

> young adolescents will listen, read, and watch. Students will purchase an app for an iPhone, iPad, iTouch, or Android. They will listen to an introduction and then read a short story for ten minutes. At the very end they will watch a spooky video. Kids will be able to get fifteen minutes of reading during the entire experience. Nine stories will come out over a nine-week period, with a total of nine per season.

He also has written a new novel titled *Dark Eden* (2011a):

> I am trying to meet every type of reader, so I wrote a traditional novel and a video experience. The idea was that there would be an entirely different story, nothing to do with the book, when children purchased the video app. Kids will go to the location of the story, click on numbers in the buildings and the borders. There are journal entries, video files, audio files, and pictures. The whole story is told in a collage format.

Digital Books

Carman, P. (2009a). *Skeleton Creek*. New York: Scholastic.

Carman, P. (2009b). *Skeleton Creek: Ghost in the machine*. New York: Scholastic.

Carman, P. (2010a). *Skeleton Creek: The crossbones*. New York: Scholastic.

Carman, P. (2010b). *Trackers, book 1*. New York: Scholastic.

Carman, P. (2011a). *Skeleton Creek: The raven*. New York: Scholastic.

Carman, P. (2011b). *Trackers, book 2: Shantorian*. New York: Scholastic.

DiTerlizzi, T. (2010). *The search for WondLa*. New York: Simon & Schuster.

Scieszka, J., & Sedita, F. (2010a). *Spaceheadz, book 1* (S. Prigmore, Illus.). New York: Simon & Schuster.

Scieszka, J., & Sedita, F. (2010b). *Spaceheadz, book 2* (S. Prigmore, Illus.). New York: Simon & Schuster.

Scieszka, J., Scieszka, C., & Weinberg, S. (2011). *Spaceheadz, book 3* (S. Prigmore, Illus.). New York: Simon & Schuster.

Two Carman novels, *Trackers Book 1* (2010b) and *Trackers Book 2: Shantorian* (2011c), are about five teenagers. Carman describes some of the challenges in creating the videos for these books:

> Working with an ensemble cast was interesting. We did a national talent search where thousands of kids tried out for the parts. We picked five teenage actors, and none of them were professional. We paid for each of them, along with a guardian, to come and live in a cast house for one month. Teenagers are teenagers. Getting it all to work was very challenging.

GENE LUEN YANG ON GRAPHIC NOVELS

Another popular trend in YA publishing is the graphic novel. These books blur the format boundaries between picture books and novels. Graphic novels can also be nonfiction, even though the term "graphic novel" leads many to believe the books will be fiction. The definition of graphic novels is somewhat elastic, as it is often difficult to make a distinction between comics and graphic novels (Ward & Young, 2011). There are some differences between the two, but the lines continue to blur as more graphic novels fill bookstore shelves. Typically, comic books have been characterized by their size and their format; they are usually twenty-eight pages in length and look similar to a magazine, only stapled, and they feature text and graphics that are enclosed in panels. The term "comic book" describes "any format that uses a combination of frames, words, and pictures to convey meaning and to tell a story. While all graphic novels are comics, not all comic books are graphic novels" (McTaggart, 2008, p. 31). In general, once a comic book has passed the fifty-page mark and is bound in soft or hard cover rather than being stapled, it is considered a graphic novel. However, it can still also be considered a comic book.

Printz Award–winning author Gene Luen Yang pushed the boundaries of young adult literature by blending three seemingly unrelated story lines in a graphic novel that neatly tied together all three stories in *American Born Chinese* (2006). Readers are often moved by the story of a Chinese American teen struggling to fit into his American classroom. The teen, Danny, has done such an effective job of hiding any traces of his cultural roots that he is embarrassed by the arrival of his cousin Chin-Kee, who epitomizes several stereotypes about Chinese Americans. Another storyline follows Jin's attempts to fit into his school and his avoidance of fellow immigrant Wei-Chen. Still another revolves around the Monkey King. Yang, who has spent some time as a teacher, had been drawing comics in a serious way for about five years prior to the publication of *American Born Chinese* (Gene Luen Yang, telephone interview, January 10, 2011). Admittedly, he says that even prior to that graphic novel, he was working on several stories that featured Asian American protagonists. "But their Asian American-ness did not play a huge part in the stories. It was almost inconsequential," he says.

> In my own life, my cultural heritage is such an important part of how I understand my place in the world so I wanted to write a story that addressed it head on. I came up with three ideas and decided as an intellectual exercise to see how I could weave them together into a single narrative.

The result of Yang's experiment or "intellectual exercise," as he calls it, was the first graphic novel ever awarded the Printz Award. Yang drew bits from his own life in writing *American Born Chinese* as well as reading translations of *Journey to the West* (Cheng'en, 2003), which is essentially the Monkey King's story. He also traveled to China and visited the Imperial Palace, allowing him to take "lots of pictures that found their way into the book panels."

There are different considerations when writing stories in book form and in graphic novel form, according to Yang. "When you are telling stories in comics you really have to think of the strengths and weaknesses of the two media," he says. "Each carries information to the reader differently. Readers respond differently to the text and drawings."

An avid reader of comics, Yang has been noting changes in comics and graphic novels over the years. In some respects, Yang is convinced that graphic novels are experiencing a renaissance of sorts, since so many of the most impressive stories to be told in this particular medium have been written during the past decade. "Interestingly," Yang points out, "many of the 'classic' graphic novels are still pretty new, and the people who created them are still fairly young." This leaves him hopeful for further creative efforts and pushing of the publishing and thematic boundaries for teen readers. There are several reasons for the youthfulness of this format, according to Yang, who notes that the comics medium "is a multimedia medium that combines two distinctive media—text and still images." Yang maintains that

> the developing online culture has acclimated people to dealing with a multimedia world. We are used to visiting sites that have text, pictures, and sound clips in a single document. Comics kind of feed into that because they are multimedia by nature. It is not a coincidence that as the Internet started up we started taking comics more and more seriously as a culture.

Although it seems clear that how we read is changing, Yang is undecided about which came first, the chicken or the egg. "I'm not sure if graphic novels are changing the way we read or if the way we read is changing and therefore we are more open to graphic novels," he says. "The borders between media are becoming blurrier and blurrier. You will have books that are very difficult to categorize. Comics blur the boundaries between media we watch and media we read."

Yang notes the abundance of YA novels nowadays that incorporate visual images. For instance, he finds it interesting to ponder whether Brian Selznick's *The Invention of Hugo Cabret* (2007) is actually a picture book or a YA novel. "It is kind of both," he says. Even in more traditional novels like Sherman Alexie's *The Absolutely True Diary of a Part-Time Indian* (2007), there are artistic elements that are just as important in their own way as the text. In novels from twenty to thirty years ago, according to Yang, "if you saw an illustration, it reinforced the information conveyed in the text." In Alexie's National Book Award–winning title, the illustrations actually do not reinforce information in the text so much as "presenting information that is vital to understanding the character. I think the trend will be toward more blurring in the genre lines," Yang says. "For instance, there are novels first released as podcasts before they are published in the print version. I think the trend will be the blurring of all boundaries."

Obviously, *American Born Chinese* is a graphic novel that fits the YA audience well, according to Yang. "I think YA itself is a blurry classification because some of the books are very adult and others are very childlike. Some even have chapters that vary from adult to childlike. Yes, even YA is a blurry category."

It may be that today's adolescent readers find it easier to read graphic novels than their parents might. "Reading comics and graphic novels does seem like a generational thing," Yang says. Younger readers often have more experience with hypertext and moving across the pages of graphic texts than their parents might have. Even so, Yang considers it "the responsibility of the cartoonist to create a comic that leads the eye flow because the reader's eyes should never be confused about where to go. It is really different reading graphic novels from reading prose."

In the case of comics, Yang is certain that younger readers are "much more familiar with the Japanese comic culture. They are used to the ways the Japanese tell stories and use the medium," he says. "Most of my students who read comics read either the Japanese comics or American comics that have incorporated that Japanese style."

Yang does not plan to leave the graphic novel format behind, since it allows him the creative freedom to tell the kinds of stories he wants to tell. He finds himself doing more research for the stories in his new books. "I'm writing and illustrating a book about the Boxer Rebellion, so I'm doing a lot of research for that one," he says. His research involves reading several books on the topic and visiting a photo archive "to get background for the visual images," he explains.

Exceptional Graphic Novels

Aristophane. (2010). *The Zambîme sisters.* New York: First Second.
Brosgol, V. (2011). *Anya's ghost.* New York: First Second.
Colbert, C. C., & Tantioc. (2010). *Booth: Actor, lover, idealist . . . assassin.* New York: First Second.
Hale, S., Hale, D., & Hale, N. (2010). *Calamity Jack.* New York: Bloomsbury.
Hinds, G. (Adaptor). (2010). *King Lear.* Somerville, MA: Candlewick Press.
Jablonski, C., & Purvis, L. (2010). *Resistance: Book 1.* New York: First Second.
Larson, H. (2008). *Chiggers.* New York: Atheneum.
Larson, H. (2010). *Mercury.* New York: Atheneum.
Lee, T. (2011). *Excalibur: The legend of King Arthur* (S. Hart, Illus.). Somerville, MA: Candlewick Press.
Satrapi, M. (2007). *The complete Persepolis.* New York: Pantheon.
Urrea, L. A., & Cardinale, C. (2010). *Mr. Mendoza's paintbrush.* El Paso, TX: Cinco Puntos Press.
Yang, G. L. (2007). *American born Chinese.* New York: First Second.
Yang, G. L. (2011). *Level up* (T. Pham, Illus.). New York: First Second.

MARGARITA ENGLE ON VERSE NOVELS

Like the graphic novel, the verse novel also crosses genres and is a very popular publishing trend today. Alexander (2005) defines the verse novel as a book in which "the entire story is told in the form of non-rhyming free verse. Very often, each section is less than a page in length and only rarely more than two or three pages" (p. 270). Letcher (2010) notes that "this is certainly not a new format, but within recent years, a number of authors have employed this approach to let their characters speak for themselves and about their experiences" (p. 87). Even though books such as Virginia Euwer Wolff's (1993) *Make Lemonade* are written in free verse, they are not considered poetry. *Make Lemonade* is classified as contemporary realistic fiction, while Marilyn Nelson's (2001) *Carver: A Life in Poems* is considered biography.

Margarita Engle is one of the authors whose novels in verse have been receiving considerable critical attention. Although she has only been writing books for young adults since 2006, Engle has already garnered numerous awards for her work: the 2009 Newbery Honor and Pura Belpre Award for *The Surrender Tree* (2008) and the 2011 Pura Belpre Award for *The Firefly Letters: A Suffragette's Journey to Cuba* (2010). In *The Firefly Letters,* Engle takes readers to Cuba as she follows the travels of Fredrika Bremer, a Swedish activist and feminist who visited the island and fell in love with its natural beauty and its inhabitants, while at the same time being horrified by the slavery that thrived in Cuba, forming the backbone for its economy. Engle has said that she drew inspiration from the verse novels of Karen Hesse for her own treatment of little-known aspects of history, because Hesse's books typically feature the voices of different narrators, allowing readers to explore different perspectives on historical events.

Engle notes that verse novels are often popular with teen readers (Margarita Engle, personal communication, April 26, 2011). "Young adult novels in verse are full-length books about mature topics, yet they can be read quickly. The pages aren't crowded, so for reluctant readers, they're not intimidating," she explains. Likewise, "novels in verse are simple, straightforward, and easy to read," according to Engle.

Verse novels seem to have a call for Engle. She says,

> As a child, I wrote poetry. Later, when I became an agronomist and botanist, most of my writing was scientific or journalistic. Eventually, after returning to Cuba in 1991, I tried short stories and prose novels for adults. Then, after reading Karen Hesse's multiple-voice verse novel *Witness*, I felt inspired to change my approach to writing *The Poet Slave of Cuba* [2006].

She had been struggling to write about Juan Francisco Manzano in prose, but she was unable to make the story work. "Perhaps because Manzano was a poet, I tried his story in free verse, and it felt as if I had found a home, after decades of wandering through different styles and forms," according to Engle.

Engle says that there are both advantages and disadvantages to writing verse novels. "The novel in verse form allows me to distill complex situations down to their emotional essence. There isn't room for every historical detail, so I have to decide what really matters to me. I have to choose. It's a wonderfully helpful exercise in simplicity," she says. One disadvantage she notes is that she has to substitute thoughts for dialogue. A second disadvantage is that she "rarely sees her books in chain stores, because they tend to treat poetry like some sort of plague to be avoided," she says ruefully.

Engle is eloquent concerning how she selects her subjects. "History is bursting with fascinating people," she says, "but for the sake of authenticity, I have to restrain myself, choosing topics that haunt me, but also ones that are familiar in some way." Her love of poetry drew her to tell Manzano's story. Regarding her other books, she recognizes personal connections as she conducts research and then creates her stories, explaining,

> In *The Surrender Tree* [2008], Rosa and I both love wilderness. In *Tropical Secrets* [2009], I love Cuban music and bird-watching. In *The Firefly Letters* [2010], Fredrika and I are two travelers in a suffering land, wondering how to help. In *Hurricane Dancers* [2011], I love horses, and there is also my own family history—I am the descendant of Ciboney Indians.

Assorted Novels in Verse

Adoff, J. (2004). *Names will never hurt me.* New York: Dutton.
Adoff, J. (2005). *Jimi and me.* New York: Hyperion.
Block, F. L. (2006). *Psyche in a dress.* New York: Joanna Cotler.
Brisson, P. (2010). *The best and hardest thing.* New York: Viking.
Bryant, J. (2005). *The trial.* New York: Yearling.
Bryant, J. (2008). *Ringside 1925: Views from the Scopes trial.* New York: Knopf.
Burg, A. E. (2009). *All the broken pieces.* New York: Scholastic.
Carvell, M. (2002). *Who will tell my brother?* New York: Hyperion.
Chaltas, T. (2009). *Because I am furniture.* New York: Viking.
Collins, P. L. (2003). *The fattening hut.* Boston: Houghton Mifflin.
Connor, L. (2005). *Dead on town line.* New York: Dial.
Crisler, C. (2007). *Tough boy sonatas* (F. Cooper, Illus.). Honesdale, PA: Boyds Mills Press.
Darrow, S. (2006). *Trash.* Somerville, MA: Candlewick Press.
Frost, H. (2007). *Keesha's house.* New York: Farrar, Straus & Giroux.
Frost, H. (2008). *The braid.* New York: Farrar, Straus & Giroux.
Frost, H. (2009). *Crossing stones.* New York: Farrar, Straus & Giroux.
Frost, H. (2011). *Hidden.* New York: Farrar, Straus & Giroux.
Glenn, M. (1997a). *Jump ball: A basketball season in poems.* New York: Dutton.
Glenn, M. (1997b). *Taking of Room 114: A hostage drama in poems.* New York: Dutton.
Glenn, M. (1999). *Who killed Mr. Chippendale? A mystery in poems.* New York: Puffin.
Glenn, M. (2000). *Split image: A story in poems.* New York: HarperCollins.
Grimes, N. (2000). *Jazmin's notebook.* New York: Puffin.
Grover, L. A. (2004). *On pointe.* New York: McElderry.
Hemphill, S. (2005). *Things left unsaid: A novel in poems.* New York: Hyperion.
Hemphill, S. (2007). *Your own, Sylvia: A verse portrait of Sylvia Plath.* New York: Knopf.
Hemphill, S. (2010). *Wicked girls: A novel of the Salem witch trials.* New York: HarperCollins.
Herrera, J. F. (1999). *Crash boom love: A novel in verse.* Albuquerque: University of New Mexico Press.
Herrick, S. (1996). *Kissing Annabel: Love, ghosts, and facial hair.* New York: Simon & Schuster.
Herrick, S. (1998). *A place like this.* New York: Simon & Schuster.
Herrick, S. (2004). *The simple gift: A novel.* New York: Simon Pulse.
Hesse, K. (1997). *Out of the dust.* New York: Scholastic.
Hesse, K. (2001). *Witness.* New York: Scholastic.
Hopkins, E. (2004). *Crank.* New York: Simon Pulse.
Hopkins, E. (2006). *Burned.* New York: McElderry.

(*continued*)

Assorted Novels in Verse (*continued*)

Hopkins, E. (2007). *Impulse.* New York: McElderry
Hopkins, E. (2008). *Identical.* New York: McElderry.
Hopkins, E. (2009). *Tricks.* New York: McElderry.
Hopkins, E. (2010). *Fallout.* New York: McElderry.
Jenkins, A. M. (2006). *Beating heart: A ghost story.* New York: HarperTeen.
Koertge, R. (2003). *Shakespeare bats clean-up.* Cambridge, MA: Candlewick Press.
Koertge, R. (2004). *The Brimstone journals.* Cambridge, MA: Candlewick Press.
Koertge, R. (2010). *Shakespeare makes the playoffs.* Cambridge, MA: Candlewick Press.
Myers, W. D. (2007). *Street love.* New York: Amistad.
Ostow, M. (2011). *Family.* New York: Egmont.
Richards, J. (2010). *Three rivers rising: A novel of the Johnstown flood.* New York: Knopf.
Rosenberg, L. (2002). *Seventeen: A novel in prose poems.* Chicago: Cricket Books.
Rylant, C. (2003). *God went to beauty school.* New York: HarperTeen.
Rylant, C. (2006). *Ludie's life.* San Diego: Harcourt.
Sandell, L. A. (2006). *The weight of the sky.* New York: Viking.
Sandell, L. A. (2007). *Song of the sparrow.* New York: Scholastic.
Schroder, L. (2010). *Chasing Brooklyn.* New York: Simon Pulse.
Smith, C. R. (2007). *Hoop kings.* Cambridge, MA: Candlewick Press.
Sones, S. (2003). *What my mother doesn't know.* New York: Simon & Schuster.
Sones, S. (2005). *One of those hideous books where the mother dies.* New York: Simon & Schuster.
Sones, S. (2008). *What my girlfriend doesn't know.* New York: Simon & Schuster.
Wayland, A. (2002). *Girl coming in for a landing.* New York: Knopf.
Wolff, V. E. (1993). *Make lemonade.* New York: Holt.
Wolff, V. E. (2001). *True believer.* New York: Atheneum.
Woodson, J. (2002). *Locomotion.* New York: Speak.
Woodson, J. (2009). *Peace, Locomotion.* New York: Putnam.

Her stories and research are also products of her travels. "In college, I began a lifelong habit of traveling to remote corners of Latin America by bus, train, dugout canoe, and borrowed donkey," Engle notes.

> Each book takes a year of research and a year of writing. While researching *The Firefly Letters,* I was fortunate to have interlibrary loan access to Bremer's diaries and letters, published in both English and Spanish. While writing *The Firefly Letters,* I was already beginning to research *Hurricane Dancers.* I manage this schedule by writing in the mornings and reading in the afternoons.

Once Engle has chosen her topic, she reads, reads, and reads even more, immersing herself in the time period she is living through vicariously. Not only does she read current history books and journal articles, but she also uses interlibrary loan to borrow rare, antique references:

> I search the bibliographies of old books, finding older and older references, hoping to eventually reach first-person narratives, such as diaries and letters. Once I have a first-person account, as I did with *The Poet Slave of Cuba* and *The Firefly Letters,* I try to retain the spirit of those autobiographical notes.

Engle says she is often asked about why she included so much cruelty and violence in *The Poet Slave of Cuba.* "I did it because Manzano wrote about his own childhood, describing the suffering. If he didn't keep it secret, who am I to soften images of slavery that come directly from his own honest memories?" she asks. However, violence was not a part of *The Firefly Letters.* Engle explains, "Fredrika Bremer, on the other hand, was an outsider. She wrote about slavery in Cuba without having experienced violence, so I followed her example."

OTHER WAYS OF BLURRING GENRES

Graphic novels and novels in verse are two popular ways that YA literature continues to blur genres and puzzle librarians trying to classify the books. However, there are other innovative approaches to creating books for teen readers that draw from many types of texts with which teens will be familiar. For instance, Saci Lloyd's *The Carbon Diaries 2015* (2009) and *The Carbon Diaries 2017* (2010) contain song lyrics, advertisements, e-mails, bills, flyers, application forms, school correspondence, and an illustration of a car tagged with a message—all layered around musician Laura's journal entries.

In these books with a green message, the author blends the important issue of global warming and the impact of the carbon footprint of humans with music and a family struggling with its own identity. Laura Brown, sixteen, lives in London, where the environment has gone haywire due to the lack of the warm air of the Gulf Stream. While rehearsing with her eco-friendly band the Dirty Angels and enduring increasingly irrelevant school days, Laura curbs her own consumption of energy while the rest of her family copes in different ways, some not so well. The second title reveals the condition of London after the worst has possibly happened.

Another fresh approach to storytelling that confuses genre lines consists of basing a graphic novel on a short story that is, in turn, adapted from a screenplay, as in the case of Danica Novgorodoff's *Refresh/Refresh* (2009). When three Marine Reservist fathers leave the Oregon countryside for Iraq, their absence is felt, particularly by their three sons, Josh, Cody, and Gordon. To fill the empty hours, they stage boxing matches in the backyard and visit local bars that serve them alcohol although they're underage. Throughout the day, though, they keep checking for e-mail news from their fathers. When tragedy strikes, the boys react from their hearts and not their heads, and their actions change all of their lives forever.

Walter Dean Myers, whose *Monster* (1999) included parts of a screenplay and interior monologues and won the very first Printz Award in 2000, could be considered one of the originators of all this genre shifting. His *Riot* (2009) is also innovative in its blending of history and fiction. Using a screenplay format, Myers stretches the boundaries of historical fiction as he tells the little-known story of the New York Draft Riots of 1863. Wealthy young men avoided military service by paying someone else to take their place. The daughter of an Irish mother and black father, Claire, comprises the heart of this book, which describes the prejudices of Irish immigrants and emancipated blacks competing for the same jobs. Myers includes useful back matter such as photographs, maps, and illustrations from periodicals.

More recently, Myers has given a modern spin to the classic opera *Carmen,* setting the story of love gone wrong in New York's Spanish Harlem in his own *Carmen* (2011). Meg Cabot and Michelle Ray have brought the past into the present as well, writing *Abandon* (2011) and *Falling for Hamlet* (2011), respectively. *Abandon* tells the story of Persephone—only in this version she is called Pierce, while *Falling for Hamlet,* told from the point of view of Ophelia, is set in modern-day Denmark, complete with text messages, newspaper clippings, a talk show appearance, and interviews with the Denmark Department of Investigation.

Gary Paulsen's *Woods Runner* (2010) is yet another book that crosses genre boundaries, almost defying categorization. This historical novel introduces readers to Samuel, a thirteen-year-old boy who typically spends his days in the woods finding food for his family. The story's setting is Pennsylvania in 1776. Samuel and his family hear rumors of the war. Later, he learns that his parents have been captured by British soldiers and Iroquois. Samuel experiences the brutality and horrors of war when he tries to rescue his mother and father. Paulsen skillfully weaves short nonfiction segments between chapters to provide the background information needed so readers can fully understand the historical story. Thus, Paulsen has blended informational nonfiction with historical fiction.

There was never any doubt about how he would tell his story, according to Paulsen, who envisioned his book "as a combination of nonfiction and fiction from the very start" (Gary Paulsen, personal communication, June 23, 2011). He says he never even considered telling the story simply as a linear narrative. "I knew I could do more with the story if I set it between facts, and I believed the facts would seem more vital in the context of fiction written from a young person's point of view," he explains. While there was the possibility that the nonfiction pieces might overwhelm the story being told rather than supporting it, Paulsen's editor Wendy Lamb made sure that didn't happen, trimming parts of it to make sure the story remained preeminent. Initially, Paulsen says, he had written "much longer historical sections in the book, actually three pretty lengthy portions." Those portions eventually were shortened and scattered between the chapters so that "they provide relevancy to Sam's story without distraction," according to Paulsen.

While Paulsen recognizes that books for middle graders and teens seem to be changing in content and in format, he maintains that "reading becomes attractive to kids when options are given to them, I think. Authors and teachers should give kids as many books as possible and then things will work out fine. At least that's what I hope." Despite the fact that some regard historical fiction as lacking appeal for middle grade and teen readers, Paulsen contends that "if the story is told right, I think readers will respond. Again, at least that's what I hope each time I sit down in front of my computer."

The prolific writer notes that he writes and revises his books "until the hair on the back of my neck stands up; I figure if I can do that, I've got a pretty good shot at reaching my audience." After all, according to Paulsen, "a story is a story, and we've been telling each other stories since cavemen danced around the fire and told what the hunt was like."

Although some might think that books such as *Woods Runner* that intersperse the narrative with factual vignettes require much explanation before being read, Paulsen trusts his young readers and thinks no guidance is needed. "Learning is a self-correcting experience," he says. "The only thing I ever say about reading is this: Read like a wolf eats."

Paulsen fans can expect more books similar to *Woods Runner*, according to the author. "I'm always reading history," he says. "I had a great time researching and writing the book."

CONCLUSION

Readers of *Woods Runner*, *The Firefly Letters*, *Skeleton Creek*, or *American Born Chinese* might need some guidance since the books are different from the texts typically read in English classes. In the case of his books, Carman has this advice for teachers: "Read aloud the first chapter of a *Skeleton Creek* novel and show the first video. This will hook kids into reading the remainder of the book. I have found that they are very viral books." However, it is more likely that the adolescents in teachers' classrooms may lead the way in understanding these genre-blurring texts, even helping their teachers understand the nuances of reading graphic novels and novels in verse, for instance.

In a nod to the wonderful innovations in technology, students are likely to enjoy creating podcasts; social media narratives using iMovie, Movie Maker, and Garage Band; and Web graphic novels using Make Beliefs Comix (http://www.makebeliefscomix.com) or Comic Master (http://www.comicmaster.org.uk). Young adolescents would also certainly enjoy writing social media narratives, Web graphic novels, or digital stories through websites such as Story Jumper (http://www.storyjumper.com), MeMoov (http://memoov.com), or Zooburst (http://www.zooburst.com/index.php). Students could make book trailers using free video creator websites such as Animoto, Jay Cut, or Photo Peach. Comics and graphic novels could be formed at Beliefs Comix or Comic Master Young.

Whether today's teachers choose to incorporate novels in verse that offer fresh perspectives on historical events such as *Wicked Girls: A Novel of the Salem Witch Trials* (Hemphill, 2010); address social issues through the saga of the effects of addiction on one family, as in the case of Ellen Hopkins's 672-pager *Fallout* (2010); look for books with accompanying Internet components such as *The Search for WondLa* (DiTerlizzi, 2010); or turn to graphic novels that highlight a troubled life cut short on Chicago's streets such as *Yummy: The Last Days of a Southside Shorty* by G. Neri (2010), the English teacher's literacy toolkit is certain to be more practical with the inclusion of these offerings that blur the border lines of genre and format.

REFERENCES

Alexander, J. (2005). The verse-novel: A new genre. *Children's Literature in Education, 36*(3), 269–283.
Alexie, S. (2007). *The absolutely true diary of a part-time Indian*. New York: Little, Brown.
Cabot, M. (2011). *Abandon*. New York: Scholastic.
Carman, P. (2009a). *Skeleton Creek*. New York: Scholastic.
Carman, P. (2009b). *Skeleton Creek: Ghost in the machine*. New York: Scholastic.
Carman, P. (2010a). *Skeleton Creek: The crossbones*. New York: Scholastic.
Carman, P. (2010b). *Trackers, book 1*. New York: Scholastic.
Carman, P. (2011a). *Dark Eden*. New York: HarperCollins.
Carman, P. (2011b). *Skeleton Creek: The raven*. New York: Scholastic.
Carman, P. (2011c). *Trackers, book 2: Shantorian*. New York: Scholastic.
Cheng'en, W. (2003). *Journey to the West*. Beijing: Foreign Language Press.
DiTerlizzi, T. (2010). *The search for WondLa*. New York: Simon & Schuster.
Engle, M. (2006). *The poet slave of Cuba: A biography of Juan Francisco Manzano*. New York: Holt.
Engle, M. (2008). *The surrender tree*. New York: Holt.
Engle, M. (2009). *Tropical secrets: Holocaust refugees in Cuba*. New York: Holt.
Engle, M. (2010). *The firefly letters: A suffragette's journey to Cuba*. New York: Holt.
Engle, M. (2011). *Hurricane dancers: The first Caribbean pirate shipwreck*. New York: Holt.

Groenke, S., Bell, R., Allen, E., & Maples J. (2011). "What is this thing called a vook?" Using *Skeleton Creek* to transform students' reading experiences in (and out of) school. *English Journal, 100*(3), 105–108.
Hemphill, S. (2010). *Wicked girls: A novel of the Salem witch trials*. New York: HarperCollins.
Hopkins, E. (2010). *Fallout*. New York: McElderry.
Letcher, M. (2010). Off the shelves: Poetry and verse novels for young adults. *English Journal, 99*(3), 87–90.
Levithan, D. (2009). A conversation with Patrick Carman. Scholastic. Retrieved from http://www.patrickcarman.com/media-kit/skeleton-creek/
Lloyd, S. (2009). *The carbon diaries 2015*. New York: Holiday House.
Lloyd, S. (2010). *The carbon diaries 2017*. New York: Holiday House.
McTaggart, J. (2008). Graphic novels: The good, the bad, and the ugly. In N. Frey & D. B. Fisher (Eds.), *Teaching visual literacy: Using comic books, graphic novels, anime, cartoons, and more to develop comprehension and thinking skills* (pp. 27–46). Thousand Oaks, CA: Corwin Press.
Myers, W. D. (1999). *Monster*. New York: HarperCollins.
Myers, W. D. (2009). *Riot*. New York: Egmont.
Myers, W. D. (2011). *Carmen*. New York: Egmont.
Napoli, D. J. (2010). *The wager*. New York: Holt.
Nelson, M. (2001). *Carver: A life in poems*. Honesdale, PA: Front Street/Boyds Mills Press.
Neri, G. (2010). *Yummy: The last days of a Southside Shorty*. New York: Lee & Low Books.
Novgorodoff, D. (2009). *Refresh/Refresh*. Based on the short story by B. Percy. Adapted from the screenplay by J. Ponsolt. New York: First Second.
Paulsen, G. (2010). *Woods runner*. New York: Random House.
Ray, M. (2011). *Falling for Hamlet*. New York: Little, Brown.
Riordan, R. (2008). *The maze of bones: 39 clues, book 1*. New York: Scholastic.
Scieszka, J., & Sedita, F. (2010a). *Spaceheadz*. New York: Simon & Schuster.
Scieszka, J., & Sedita, F. (2010b). *Spaceheadz, book 2*. New York: Simon & Schuster.
Scieszka, J., Sciezka, C., & Weinberg, S. (2011). *Spaceheadz, book 3*. New York: Simon & Schuster.
Selznick, B. (2007). *The invention of Hugo Cabret*. New York: Scholastic.
Smith, S. (2007). The death of genre: Why the best YA fiction often defies classification. *The ALAN Review, 35*(1), 43–50.
Turner, M. W. (2010). *A conspiracy of kings*. New York: HarperCollins.
Ward, B. A., & Young, T. A. (2011). Reading graphically: Comics and graphic novels for readers from kindergarten through high school. *Reading Horizons, 50*(4), 283–295.
Wolff, V. E. (1993). *Make lemonade*. New York: Holt.
Yang, G. L. (2004). *Loyola Chin and the San Peligran Order*. San Jose, CA: SLG Publishing.
Yang, G. L. (2006). *American born Chinese*. New York: First Second.
Yang, G. L. (2009). *The eternal smile: Three stories* (D. K. Kim, Illus.). New York: First Second.
Yang, G. L. (2010). *Animal crackers: A Gene Yang collection*. San Jose, CA: SLG Publishing.

11

The Best-Selling Adult Novelist and Young Adult Fiction

Steven T. Bickmore

I am not sure when, exactly, I transferred from reading juvenile books to the books in the library's "grown-up" section. I checked out *Moby Dick* (Melville, 1851) several times before I finished it in college. I knew it was an adult book, a book with weight that serious readers discussed. Instead of reading the classics during secondary school, I drifted toward adult best-sellers. By "adult" I don't mean racy, hide-under-your-mattress books. I mean books intentionally meant for adults. I read L'Amour and Brand, Stewart and White, Uris and Michener, MacDonald and Chandler, and Tolkien and Burroughs, but I didn't select the classics for my own reading until college. I was clearly a reader. If my teachers bored me, I read in class. My Spanish teacher, Mrs. Trapletti, took *Topaz* (Uris, 1967) and I never finished it—there were too many other books I wanted to read.

How do we reach readers and guide them to quality works of young adult (YA) literature on their way to classics, or for that matter, to whatever they want to read as adults? How did I miss the classics or other books directed at me as a voracious reader? I read, but I was absolutely an undirected reader. I graduated high school in 1973 and missed the beginning wave of YA novels—*The Contender* (Lipsyte, 1967), *The Chocolate War* (Cormier, 1974), *The Outsiders* (Hinton, 1967) or *The Pigman* (Zindel, 1968)—in the schools I attended. Should students be directed to novels written for them and about their concerns? Maybe yes and maybe no. I loved drifting into best-selling fiction. As for the classics, I was behind my college peers, but I had read widely and the books I read were not without connections to the classics.

People are still reading fiction. Best-seller lists influence bookstores and libraries. Serious writers make their way in the world. They work as university professors, teachers, salesmen, doctors, insurance executives, and stay-at-home writers, until suddenly someone discovers them—as if they hadn't been writing for years. Take McCarthy, for example, an excellent writer who, while mainly unknown, worked persistently at his craft, until the Coen brothers recognized the brilliance of *No Country for Old Men* (McCarthy, 2005) and produced the film (Coen & Coen, 2007). While excellent writers struggle on, most English language arts (ELA) classes continue to teach books primarily written by dead white males. We need more options on the table.

This chapter examines a phenomenon in the publishing world—adult authors in two groups, best-sellers and literati, who now write for adolescents. What does this trend suggest?

THE TREND AND WHAT IT MIGHT MEAN FOR YOUNG ADULT LITERATURE

Series fiction aimed at adolescent readers has a long history. Quick examples are Nancy Drew, Trixie Belden, the Hardy Boys, Cherry Ames, Sue Barton, Chip Hilton, and John R. Tunis. More recently, we find series originally marketed to adults being created for adolescent audiences. Some examples are Young Bond, Young Sherlock Holmes, and others spinning off from movies (Young Indiana Jones and *Star Trek* novels). There might be many reasons why authors and publishers want to market to adolescents; capitalizing on economic opportunity is probably the primary reason. J. K. Rowling and Stephenie Meyer top the best-seller lists with books written directly for children and young adults. While overall book sales diminish, the market share captured by YA fiction rises. With the success of *Harry Potter,* beginning in 1997, and *Twilight,* starting in 2005, it is no wonder that series like *Diary of a Wimpy Kid* (Kinney, 2007), Percy Jackson, Lemony Snicket's books, the Sisterhood of the Traveling Pants, and Suzanne Collins's *The Hunger Games* trilogy have emerged. Obviously, other writers want access to adolescent readers. At least two groups of adult novelists are entering the fray since the beginning of the century. The first consists of best-selling authors—those whose novels repeatedly reach the top of the *New York Times* best-seller list. Many of their novels I consider pulp fiction or, as a colleague once suggested, "mind candy." Regardless of what English teachers might infer, people read and enjoy these books. My vacations are incomplete without the latest novels by Robert Crais, Elmore Leonard, or Lee Child in tow. The second group includes writers of critical acclaim. As expected, many more novelists from the first group produce YA novels. The market opportunities are too big to ignore. The second group interests me more. They might be categorized as part of the group that disdains young adult literature, a group that often fails to acknowledge the literary merit of YA fiction. Why would writers with lofty reputations want to write adolescent fiction, with its cloudy reputation among keepers of the literary flame?

The notion of an adult best-selling novelist turning to YA literature might have seemed incongruous several years ago. However, James Patterson has merged the two quite successfully. What does his success suggest for the future of YAL? This chapter hopes to capture a partial picture of YA fiction as represented by how successful adult novelists have migrated, at least in part, to YA fiction. The chapter looks at six authors in two classifications who, after establishing reputations as novelists, write novels for YA audiences. James Patterson, Ridley Pearson, and Carl Hiaasen are the first group; they are best-selling authors for adult audiences. Sherman Alexie, Michael Chabon, and Joyce Carol Oates are the second group and represent authors who have achieved literary acclaim. In addition, all three have experienced marketing successes. At the same time, Oates has won the National Book Award and is considered an important living literary figure. An examination of the sales of the YA novels by authors in both of these categories might lead to speculation about whether or not other adult novelists might join the fray.

WRITERS OF BEST-SELLERS OR PULP FICTION RETURN TO SCHOOL

The first half of this chapter focuses on three novelists with notoriety or financial success achieved through books written for adults. These are writers who would generally be considered authors of best-selling novels, as opposed to writers of "literature." Whether or not their novels represent literature is a debate for another day. What does matter is that their works are widely available; people buy and read them. There are more than three best-selling authors who have tried their hand at writing a children's book or an adolescent novel. For example, C. S. Lewis is more famous for the Chronicles of Narnia than for his adult fiction or scholarship. I have chosen Patterson because I heard him speak at a National Council of Teachers of English (NCTE) convention, and I frequently read Pearson's and Hiaasen's works.

James Patterson

It is sometimes difficult to determine the rationale for the NCTE convention keynote speaker. It isn't always based on literary reputation. For example, Julie Andrews is a lovely actress, but her literary fame is not the same as her acting fame. With similar wonderings, I heard James Patterson speak several years ago. I knew the name, but I had never read his novels or considered them for my students' summer reading list. I was out of the loop. People do read Patterson's books. Early on the day of his keynote speech, a large group had already gathered. His message was engaging; he powerfully emphasized how teachers connect with their students. He highlighted the crucial role teachers have in their students' reading lives. I also learned that Patterson had published a novel for adolescents. I read *The Angel Experiment* (2005), the first novel in the *Maximum Ride* series, on the airplane home. I wasn't overly impressed, but I was intrigued. The plot moved well and was a blend of science fiction and fantasy bound to attract young readers. I read the sequel and my interest waned; nevertheless, I continued to follow the series. During my next beach trip, I read one of his adult novels—interesting, but not exactly my brand of crime fiction.

The essential question is this: Why would such an established, successful, and prolific writer like Patterson produce novels for adolescents? He is so busy that most of his recent titles share authorship with someone else. Since 2005, Patterson has authored fourteen YA novels, not including graphic novels or manga based on his three YA series. Patterson seems the prime example of an author who understands advertising and marketing. He is a former ad man who remembered his roots when he became a successful novelist. Several of his adult novels are successful movies, and film versions of his adolescent novels will appear soon. I am all for getting kids to read and, if Patterson pulls it off, more power to him.

Maximum Ride Series (2005–2011)

The impulse for the *Maximum Ride* series is ripped from the headlines surrounding stem cell research and the genome project. What happens with unbridled scientific research? What if scientists figure out how to merge chromosomes from one species to another? This is the stuff of science fiction; we can go back to Dr. Jekyll and Mr. Hyde. Movies like *The Fly* (Cronenberg, 1986; Neumann, 1958) and *Swamp Thing* (Craven, 1982) suggest genetic mutations. After World War II, movie audiences were treated to Japanese films with a variety of mutated monsters. Patterson starts with a flock of children who can fly. The story begins *in media res* as several children, led by Max, search for their origins as avian children. The biggest obstacle is another genetic mix of human-lupines who are vicious and aggressive.

The series has seven novels, and the eighth novel will end the series. While the plots are fast paced, these novels are long by young adult literature norms. Three are over four hundred pages and only one is under three hundred pages. The themes are similar to those in mainstream adolescent fiction: absent parents, alienation, coming-of-age discoveries, and conflicts with rules and adult control. While exploring these, Patterson continues to discuss the ethical issues of scientific research that thread through the novels. Government conspiracy and global warming complicate the plot, as Max and her friends try to survive and save the world. Patterson has capitalized on a market niche that seems rewarding.

Daniel X Series (2008–2011)

With the *Daniel X* series, Patterson creates a hero of intergalactic proportions. Reminiscent of *Men in Black* (Sonnenfeld, 1997), aliens are everywhere and in every guise. The protector, however, is not a member of a secret government agency, but another alien. Never fear, as a good alien he assumed his father's role as the Earth's protector after his parents' assassination when he was three. Now, twelve years later, Daniel has super speed, super strength, and super mental powers that allow him to shape-shift as he destroys one intrusive alien after another. In addition to his ability to shape-shift, he can create and manipulate objects. There are some limitations, or Daniel wouldn't have a flaw to overcome while protecting Earth. Daniel's home planet, Alpar Nok, is also in peril. He must protect Earth by vanquishing the evil aliens, who also have designs on his planet.

Patterson and coauthors have three novels in this series, as well as a graphic novel and manga version of the first book. His rate of production keeps pace with the rest of Patterson's publishing empire. The series is similar to comic book heroes painted with broad strokes of good and evil. The good guys are very good, and the bad guys are very bad. The books are action driven rather than displaying subtle developments of character or theme.

Witch and Wizard Series (2009–2011)

James Patterson has little fear of censors. Complaints about magic haven't noticeably slowed the success of Harry Potter, and Patterson steps right in with the *Witch and Wizard* series. The series capitalizes on the dystopian trend in YA fiction represented by *Unwind* (Shusterman, 2007), *Feed* (Anderson, 2002), *The House of the Scorpion* (Farmer, 2002), and *The Hunger Games* (Collins, 2008). Whit and Wisty, a brother and sister with magical powers, team up with other lost adolescents to oppose the New Order. The New Order is a totalitarian government seeking to control adolescents with magical power or any others who disrupt the authority of the Ones. Overwhelmingly, magic is a force for good in this world. The adolescent witches and wizards are forces that fight against a centralized undemocratic government.

As with the *Daniel X* series, Patterson's *Witch and Wizard* series is plot driven and weak on character development or thematic concerns. Patterson pushes past magic and into the realm of science fiction. For example, portals exist that allow characters to travel to Shadowland, a liminal existence on the edge of the known world. Shadowland is home to half-lights, dead beings with the ability to communicate with the living. The world of *Witch and Wizard* is a dystopia full of adolescent resistance fighters. The normal laws of nature are suspended in this world, as Patterson creates new devices, abilities, or conveniences to drive the plot.

It would be easy for a teacher to dismiss Patterson's work for adolescents. If we do, we are missing the point. Patterson seems driven to get kids to read. His website is accessible, full of trailers, advance notices, and links to every social networking tool. Perhaps the most important link on the home page is to Read Kiddo Read. Patterson greets parents, teachers, and librarians dedicated to the reading future of kids. He promises that if you get kids to read some of the titles linked to the website, they will become readers. His efforts seem genuinely directed at reluctant readers, the ones who haven't found it easy to finish a book. Getting kids to read is a worthy goal that most ELA teachers share and work to achieve. His website links to books listed by age group. He also links to an educator page with lesson plans for books as diverse as *How I Became a Pirate* (Long & Shannon, 2003) and *The Catcher in the Rye* (Salinger, 1951). The resources are abundant and encourage adults to engage kids with reading activities.

Ridley Pearson

Pearson's primary series focuses on nine detective novels featuring Seattle police lieutenant Lou Boldt. Pearson's police procedurals are gritty and suspenseful. He provides readers with novels that create atmosphere, as he displays an understanding of police practices. Since 1988, he has published twenty-five adult novels: sixteen novels divided into three series and nine stand-alone suspense novels. Pearson was the first American to receive the Raymond Chandler Fulbright Fellowship in Detective Fiction from Oxford University. In 2004, he teamed up with Dave Barry and joined the wave of writers producing YA fiction. They have eight books, including one stand-alone novel and two series building on the Peter Pan myth. Alone, Pearson has written six novels in two series. One focuses on a mystical world that exists in Disney World after closing. The other highlights the adventures of adolescent spy Steven "Steel" Trapp. Pearson's YA books are light-hearted adventure stories capitalizing on established icons that adolescents identify immediately—Peter Pan and Disney villains. The potential for mass marketing and a transition to movies and television seems obvious.

Starcatchers Series (2004–2009)

The *Starcatchers* series features Peter Pan before the time frame created by J. M. Barrie. Pearson and Barry create a series of pre-adventures for Peter before he meets Wendy and before being rediscovered in *Hook* (Spielberg, 1991). Who knew that Wendy, Michael, and John's mother, Molly, shared adventures with Peter? Their exploits range from Never Land to the shipping ports of nineteenth-century England. The first book explores the magical powers of a secret dust. The next two books move directly to explore Lord Ombra's attempts at destroying the world. True to the swashbuckling spirit of its inspiration, the books are full of captures, escapes, cliffhangers, and daring deeds. The fourth book returns to the original setting, as Wendy and her brothers join forces with James, one of Peter's Lost Boys, in order to save Prince Albert Edward from evil.

Never Land Series (2006–2008)

For their next series, Barry and Pearson explore Never Land while Peter is away. In these three novels, there are new adventures that the Lost Boys have never quite noticed before. The authors also introduce Little Scallop, a princess of the Mollusk tribe, who is also easily bored. Why should the boys have all the fun? The young female inhabitants of Never Land have their share of danger even without Peter's guidance. Barry and Pearson capitalize on existing cultural icons while expanding them for their own purposes. Surprise earthquakes, mysterious caves, strange ships in the distance, and Captain Hook all cause trouble for the Mollusk tribe, the Lost Boys, and the mermaids.

Science Fair (2008)

This stand-alone novel foreshadows the tone of the Hiaasen novels. *Star Wars* memorabilia collections, rogue government agents, and science geeks combine to make a science fair more interesting than you might recall. Barry and Pearson combine their ironic sense of humors to create adolescent characters that frustrate the terrorist antics of agents from a fictionalized Soviet bloc nation. A few spoiled rich kids plan to commission a science project rather than create their own. Toby and his friends seek to disrupt the cheaters' plans so their work will be appreciated. However, they aren't quite prepared for floating frogs, owls with laser eyes, and bumbling spies.

Kingdom Keepers Series (2005–2010)

The *Kingdom Keepers* series blends science fiction and fantasy as it imagines holographic images as adolescent guides throughout Disney World.

The adventures begin as Disney World selects five unknown teenage actors and finishes mapping their actions so that computers can control their holographs. It's a great job—good pay and lifetime passes for you and your family. Things roll along fine until all five actors discover that their dreams are real. At night, they become their holographic images and roam Disney World. In their transitional state, they can see and interact with the Disney characters as they come to life. Especially dangerous are the witches, who seek to control the park's power.

The main character, Finn, is instructed by Wayne, an old Disney Imagineer, who tells him that, together, the guides can fight the evil that threatens the park. They synchronize their sleep in order to arrive in the park together. Pirates come alive, dolls in *It's a Small World* run amok, and witches cast spells to thwart our heroes' quest for the secrets of the Magic Kingdom. The first book's action is in Disney World, and the second takes place in Disney's Animal Kingdom. The third bounces from Hollywood Studios to Epcot. The conflict in all three books and into the fourth is between the teens and the Overtakers. If the Disney Imagineers can create remarkable holographic technology, can the evil Disney characters learn the skills and combat the efforts of Finn and his crew of protectors? Pearson has teamed up with Disney World to produce a Kingdom Keepers Quest in the Magic Kingdom that began in April 2011 (see http://www.ridleypearson.com/YA/index.php). Is a movie far behind?

Steel Trapp Series (2008–2010)

In the next series, Pearson returns to his roots as a crime writer. Steven "Steel" Trapp gets his nickname when an elementary school teacher discovers his photographic memory. On a trip to a science fair, Steel inadvertently interrupts a briefcase exchange. Unwittingly, he attempts to return a briefcase that was dropped for another agent. Complications ensue when the courier denies it; the Marshall Service wants it; the intended receiver is intent on recovering it; the FBI is interrupting; and Steel strives to keep it concealed—all while traveling on a train. Steel doesn't know how closely his life is connected to the underworld, and he has no intention of saving the world. Unfortunately, he knows what he knows, and his persistent curiosity leads him into trouble. Luckily, he joins forces with Kaileigh, another precocious adolescent on the run, to solve the problem. The second novel continues when Steel and Kaileigh find that they both have been invited to a special school. What kind of school has blow-gun training, underground passages, and secret doorways from the bathrooms to the chapel? Of course, if Steel sees it, he remembers it, and his curiosity pulls him and Kaileigh into another adventure.

Carl Hiaasen

Hiaasen's crime novels are driven by comic mania embedded in Florida's environmental issues. Hiaasen has honed the word choices (few, if any swear words) for his adolescent eco-mysteries, but the tone remains humorous. Readers can expect a few dumb-as-a-brick crooks, greedy entrepreneurs, and, of course, a clever protagonist. Even though environmental issues drive the plot, contextual circumstances follow the expected formulas for adolescent novels—new kid in town, absent parents, and a general sense of awkwardness that sets the characters apart. These novels are perfect additions to cross-curriculum middle grade units between science and English classes with shared students. Just as Rick Riordan has rejuvenated the classics with Percy Jackson, maybe Hiaasen can spark environmental activism. Unlike the series novels produced by Patterson and Pearson, Hiaasen's novels stand alone. While formulaic in many ways, they engage the reader in interesting environmental issues.

Hoot (2002)

Hoot (2002) tells the story of three unlikely adolescent friends who fight to save a habitat for small burrowing owls from becoming a pancake house. One character, Mullet Fingers, is an adolescent on the fringe. He is, however, dedicated to continually disrupting the construction plans by systematically removing stakes and tampering with equipment. As the plot progresses, Roy begins to help Mullet, even though they are unacquainted. Roy understands Mullet's quest, and through an uneasy alliance with Beatrice, Roy helps Mullet undermine the construction. The novel has a variety of twists and turns that keep the reader moving through the narrative. While *Hoot* (2002) is clearly an eco-mystery, it is also a character's journey into self-discovery.

Flush (2005)

While Noah's father can't prove that the casino boat is flushing sewage into the harbor, maybe Noah and his motley assembly of friends can. Hiaasen's second adolescent novel allows teenagers to take over where adults have failed. Noah is upset, not by his father's radical environmentalism, but that his father's activism is tearing apart his family. *Flush* is another eco-mystery, but in this case, Hiaasen develops more complex adolescent characters. While *Hoot* (2002) was almost purely plot driven, *Flush* (2005) becomes a character study of Noah as he works to solve the mystery and to save his family.

Scat (2009)

Hiaasen claims that *Scat* (2009), the third novel, was not planned. He was inspired by the enthusiastic responses of young readers to the first two novels, which convinced him that an audience existed. "More than anything, the letters I received from kids were so touching and funny and smart that it made me want to do another book" (Hiaasen, 2011). In *Scat*, Hiaasen has created an even more complex plot—more bad guys, more good guys, and intricate twists and turns. *Scat* is more reminiscent of Hiaasen's fast-paced adult capers.

Can an oil company drill in one of the only remaining habitats for the Florida panther? In order to take action, Nick, Marta, and Smoke need clear evidence (scat, if you will) that proves the panther's existence. The last thing they expect is help from their overbearing science teacher, Mrs. Starch. When an unexplained brush fire starts during a science field trip to the swamp, people assume a student caused the damage. In reality, the crooks started the fire to draw the students away from a wildcat oil drill on state land. Independently, both Smoke and Mrs. Starch understand that the fire needs investigation, especially when they both glimpse a panther running from the fire.

WRITERS WITH LITERARY ACCOLADES

Choosing to teach young adult literature does not mean selecting works of inferior quality (Bickmore, 2008). Teachers should read widely and select texts demonstrating quality craftsmanship. During this renaissance of YAL, we should look closely at novelists with critical acclaim who now write for adolescents. Three novelists quickly surface: Sherman Alexie, Michael Chabon, and Joyce Carol Oates.

Even though I read more young adult fiction than I can track, I still read the classics, detective fiction, and the winners of literary awards. As an English teacher, I tried to stay current. Inevitably, some students asked what was worth reading that was current. This is an important question, but it needs context. Students have legitimate questions: What is worth reading today if they want entertainment? If they want to relax? If they want to stay current with literary trends? If they want to become lifelong readers? If we want to help, we need to read widely ourselves. I am saner and easier to live with if I am reading a good novel; maybe our students need as many options as we do.

During graduate school I read Alexie's *Indian Killer* (1996) with other graduate students. We struggled with postmodern language, shifting identities, and the difficulty of representation. Discussing *Indian Killer* became an exercise in postmodern literary analysis and identity representation.

Michael Chabon came to my attention through another group of readers. For years, Michael Moore from Georgia Southern University has hosted an informal book group at the NCTE convention. Readers gather to discuss their recent discoveries. One year, someone mentioned the *The Yiddish Policemen's Union* (Chabon, 2007). It was a perfect fit for my addiction to detective fiction.

As an English major in the 1970s, I knew of Joyce Carol Oates's growing reputation. She won the National Book Award in 1970 for *Them* (Oates, 1969). It seemed everyone referenced her, but no one taught her works. I was genuinely puzzled, but I didn't read one of her novels until I found *Black Water* (Oates, 1992). Twenty years later, this novel remains a dominant example of haunting narratives and a disruptive point of view. Her adolescent novels are also built on provocative narrative structures. In each novel, Oates uses short, direct chapters to shape the narrative. They roll by like pictures in a scrapbook, exposing events and points of view along the arc of the plot. When Oates slows down the narrative with a longer chapter, the reader sees how the quick glimpses come together to unify the events and their consequences.

All three writers are eclectic in their production. Each has written novels, short stories, essays, and now YA novels. Alexie and Oates are published poets. Chabon has written comics; Oates, dramas and children's books. Alexie has also worked in films as both a writer and director. Each has literary contributions worth considering. Their work demands attention and is analyzed and studied. They are important contributors to a growing canon of quality literature. Perhaps their YA fiction can link adolescent readers to classical contemporary literature.

Sherman Alexie

Alexie is the premier Native American writer in the United States. While intensely personal, his work captures a unique perspective of the American Indian experience. Alexie believes that "we belong to a lot of tribes; culturally, ethnically, and racially" (Nygren, 2005, p. 152). Alienation, marginalization, isolation, and humiliation are universal themes apparent in his *Reservation Blues* (1995) and *Indian Killer* (1996). Without exception, these are thematic concerns that appeal to adolescent readers.

Alexie's YA novel *The Absolutely True Diary of a Part-Time Indian* (2007) won the National Book Award for young adult literature. Adolescents who read this book will find a compelling comic narrative and an engaging misfit who struggles for personal acceptance in the face of despair. Adolescents will find a form of racism that few witness firsthand, which remains at the root of American history. Questions of poverty, education, and opportunity weigh heavily on a narrative that, initially, seems too light. The humorous first-person point of view allows the serious nature of the text to sneak up on the reader. Alexie's first YA novel engages young readers and moves them to complicated themes. Adolescents do have lives that are complex and problematic. At its finest, YAL acknowledges this and allows readers to sort through issues that are close to them or to vicariously experience others more distant from their everyday experiences. Alexie has produced a postcolonial text. Arnold, his protagonist, is a shy but gifted boy who fights against poverty, racism, and alcoholism produced by invaders. The novel is both the story of an individual struggling for meaning in his life and a broader statement about a subjugated people.

Michael Chabon

Chabon's novels have gathered praise. *The Amazing Adventures of Kavalier and Clay* (2000) won the Pulitzer Prize for fiction. *The Yiddish Policemen's Union* (2007) is a detective novel set in an alternate history; it won the Nebula, the Hugo, and the Sidewise Award for Alternative History. His adolescent novel *Summerland* (2002) won the Mythopoeic Fantasy Award for children's literature. It is hardly a child's book but instead a well-crafted fantasy novel for adolescent readers. Critics might compare Chabon to the luminaries of magical realism (Marquez, Morrison, or Singer) or of fantasy (Tolkien, Lewis, or Brooks); for me, he also hints of the best of Bellow, Roth, and Malamud. Chabon is a serious writer with vision and ambition.

Even though *Summerland* won a fantasy award, the initial reviewers, Maslin (2002) and Lipstye (2002), offered a lukewarm reception to Chabon's baseball fantasy. When I first discovered *Summerland*, I had a similar reaction. But once I was familiar with the characters, the various worlds, and the underlying mythology, I was engaged with the mythic journey and hung on every pitch. Chabon presents a YA fantasy novel with common adolescent themes—lost parents, isolation, and growing pains. If you believe in baseball in its pure state as it captures the romance of American possibility, then this novel is for you.

Joyce Carol Oates

Few living writers have a more significant body of work. Beyond her numerous novels, she has written poetry, plays, short stories, essays, and criticism. She has had five nominations for the National Book Award and won the award in 1970. In addition, she is a three-time finalist for the Pulitzer Prize. Her short fiction won the O. Henry Award and the PEN Malamud Award. She is frequently on the short list for the Nobel Prize for Literature.

Her turn to the adolescent novel is an interesting nod to an important reading audience. In my estimation, not enough attention has been given to her four adolescent novels: *Big Mouth & Ugly Girl* (2002), *Freaky Green Eyes* (2003), *Sexy* (2005), and *After the Wreck, I Picked Myself Up, Spread My Wings, and Flew Away* (2006). They share stylistic similarities—short, fast-paced chapters; interesting characters; and subtle use of symbols and imagery. Each novel's theme is unique and directed at teen readers. They are intelligent works of art written for adolescents without talking down to them. Her novels await bright readers who are ready to think deeply.

Big Mouth & Ugly Girl (2002)

If you were teaching in 1999, you remember that the impact of the Columbine shootings was tremendous. School safety, bullying, alienated students, and inclusive climates were the topics of the day. *Big Mouth & Ugly Girl* (Oates, 2002) addresses these issues directly, with remarkable insight into the interactions of teens. Oates captures their tentative confidence mixed with self-doubt. She demonstrates the importance of technology in their lives, and much of the character development depends on e-mail.

It is important in a school to notice the unusual and the dangerous, but what if we are wrong? What if the big mouth boy is just a loud, dramatic boy figuring out when to perform and when to shut up? What if his only witness is a self-proclaimed ugly girl, who feels too tall, too athletic, and too mature for the stupidity of school? Oates creates a riveting novel. How do schools ensure safety while honoring individuality and self-expression? Oates explores the possibility of friendship in the midst of teen angst. Matt and Ursula are characters that teachers will recognize, and adolescent readers will look over their shoulders to see if they are in the room.

Freaky Green Eyes (2003)

In this next novel, Oates tackles two serious issues: divorce and abuse. Too many students experience one or the other; lamentably, some experience both. The green-eyed monster rears its ugly head in this riveting novel. Franky, the novel's protagonist, initially believes that her mother has needlessly abandoned the family through selfishness. She slips from naive, selfish concerns to a confrontation with evil and violence hiding barely under the surface within people she loves.

Sexy (2005)

In Oates's next novel for teens, adolescence equals discovery and exploration. In *Sexy* (2005), Oates explores the power of labels to define us, even apparently flattering ones, and how they affect teens. Darren wonders about his position in the school's social structure. He is on the school's swim team, an average student, and one of the poor kids. When his body changes before his junior year, he discovers he is "sexy." Sexy is a descriptor that he doesn't understand. He is confused by vivid sexual thoughts when "he's talking to someone, a girl, a teacher, his own mother" (p. 4).

The plot gets complicated. A popular male teacher is kind to Darren. He encourages him to be a better student and gives him generous grades. Mr. Tracy offers him a ride, a simple ride home, when Darren is stranded in the snow after swim practice. Nothing happens, no sexual advances, but Darren is confused by the attention. At the end of the semester, one of the swimmers fails Mr. Tracy's class for plagiarism and becomes ineligible to continue on the swim team. Typical of a teenager's response, the consequences for his actions couldn't be based on his own culpability.

In an act of vengeance, several boys (but not Darren) begin to accuse Mr. Tracy of homosexual activity. Darren is aware of their actions, but he doesn't participate. Can one sit on the margins of a crime? Oates builds ambiguity. Darren remains frozen, incapable of acting; he is, after all, sexy, and people are attracted to him. Was he also attracted to Mr. Tracy? Oates creates a dynamic narrative of sexual self-identity.

After the Wreck, I Picked Myself Up, Spread My Wings, and Flew Away (2006)

We always remember the first time we lose a loved one. For adolescents especially, this is a traumatic experience; it brings an awareness of their own mortality. Naturally, the event is intensified if a parent is the one who dies. Now, imagine the isolation if the surviving child is an only child, and the other parent is estranged and lives across the country. This is the setting for Oates's fourth YA novel, almost. The plot begins when Jenna is in the car when her mother dies, and she thinks it is her fault.

Oates delivers a tour de force. She presents a case study of a young girl who struggles through grief, guilt, and suicidal tendencies. Jenna must recover from her own injuries as she remembers and reconstructs the accident. In her isolation, Jenna begins a new life with her aunt's family, including attending a new school—filled with all sorts of possibilities. Oates surrounds Jenna with supporting characters who serve as foils, companions, and guides. Jenna's most important relationship is with Crow, an outsider with his own secrets. As Oates asks indirectly, what can a biker from the wrong side of the tracks have in common with this now wounded rich kid?

Readers who are familiar with Oates's work will not be surprised by the novel's craftsmanship. She weaves a narrative of discovery through flashbacks and real-time events that reconstruct the accident as Jenna attempts to piece together her life. Even though flying is suggested in the title, Oates's use of birds and flight as symbols throughout the text is subtle. She is an author who, at the height of her career, offers adolescent readers another sophisticated text that ushers them into a reading experience that doesn't insult their intelligence, but rather expects them to tackle difficult issues without sentimentality or the promise of easy answers.

One final distinction between Oates's books for adolescents compared with what she writes for an adult audience is most important, though. As I read her novels, I ask myself, "Is every novel with an adolescent protagonist young adult literature? And if not, why not?" Young adult literature is a genre with a range of novels that meet readers where they are. Too often, the critics of YAL accuse the field of being too light, too easy to read, or they suggest that while important themes are covered, the books are just not weighty. They will not prepare the best and the brightest students for important reading at higher levels. These critics haven't considered the adolescent novels of Joyce Carol Oates. These four works are sophisticated novels unapologetically written directly to bright, engaged adolescents. These novels will remind readers of the best of two of young adult literature's premier novelists, Robert Cormier and Chris Crutcher, as Oates's novels capture adolescents in crisis; in addition, they suggest hints of the darkness and brooding nature of classic authors like Melville and Hawthorne.

IMPLICATIONS AND CONCLUSION

This chapter is a quick overview of six writers for adult audiences who have written YA novels. To be sure, there are others, and this analysis should encourage teachers, English educators, and librarians to examine their favorite writers and see if they are trying YAL. There are implications connected to this trend. For example, while book sales decline, these six authors have produced thirty-seven adolescent novels in a ten-year period. This is an impressive number, and despite their success with teens, these writers remain engaged in projects for adult readers. These writers seem aware of market demands and produce series fiction as fast as readers pick them up. Patterson and Pearson lead the way. Patterson has fourteen books over three series and Pearson has fourteen books over four series, plus one standalone novel. Pearson's website (http://www.ridleypearson.com) points in two directions—one for his adult books and one for adolescent novels. Pearson understands that his Web presence needs to be accessible to both audiences. Hiaasen, too, has produced three young adult novels that are true to his adult works in terms of tone, style, and theme.

All three writers in the best-seller category focus on the strengths that they bring to their adult fiction. Patterson and Pearson capitalize on interesting characters surrounded by a supporting cast that helps drive their plots. Pearson's *Steel Trapp* series is a satisfactory surprise that deserves an audience. Hiaasen keeps with an environmental agenda in his young adult fiction. His novels suggest a perfect pairing for a unit between a middle-level science teacher and her English teacher counterpart. Inquiry-based science education through YA fiction is a cross-curriculum dream come true.

The writers in the second group have a smaller output. Alexie and Chabon have one novel each; both novels have won awards. Oates has been more productive, but then again, she has always been one of America's prolific writers. Since 2002, she has four YA novels and fourteen adult novels. Her YA novels stand out from the others reviewed here. The writing is excellent, demonstrating craftsmanship that is subtle and unobtrusive.

While I enjoyed and recommend the work of the best-selling authors, the work of Alexie, Chabon, and Oates is superior in almost every aspect. It is perhaps difficult to create what critics call "literature" using primarily the stock devices of series fiction—well-known major characters, predictable bad guys, fast-paced narratives, and plots that advance through twists and turns—rather than the development of character, symbols, and theme. Alexie, Chabon, and Oates create complex narratives that invite adolescents to think deeply. While Alexie's presentation of Junior may initially seem comic, no reader leaves the novel without a deeper understanding of racial inequality. Chabon not only weaves a superb fantasy tale but also builds a narrative around baseball, one of America's great metaphors for a nostalgic vision of the past. Oates's novels should erase the doubt about the quality of YA fiction. They are equal to the best of realistic YA fiction. She does what the best writers always do. They retain their own voice and style as they unapologetically write novels that directly investigate the issues and concerns of real kids, whether or not those issues are easy to hear or are politically correct.

These authors' YA fiction is a welcome addition to the field. Some researchers might question their motives—money, recruiting new audiences for already published novels, or keeping market share. We should, however, consider how these novels compare to the novels currently promoted by teachers, librarians, and booksellers. What books do teachers value for whole class discussions, literary circle selections, or independent self-selected reading? At the very least, we should remember that YAL is probably not so different from adult fiction. Both have their divisions and categories. Both have a place for the best-selling author and the author writing more literary fare. Perhaps our biggest task as educators, in any setting, is helping our students attain the skills necessary to argue about the difference.

REFERENCES

Alexie, S. (1995). *Reservation blues*. New York: Atlantic Monthly Press.

Alexie, S. (1996). *Indian killer*. New York: Atlantic Monthly Press.

Alexie, S. (2007). *The absolutely true diary of a part-time Indian*. New York: Little, Brown.

Anderson, M. T. (2002). *Feed*. Cambridge, MA: Candlewick Press.

Barry, D., & Pearson, R. (2005). *The missing mermaid: A Never Land book*. New York: Disney Editions/Hyperion.

Barry, D., & Pearson, R. (2007a). *Cave of the dark wind: A Never Land book*. New York: Disney Editions/Hyperion.
Barry, D., & Pearson, R. (2007b). *Peter and the secret of Rundoon*. New York: Disney Editions/Hyperion.
Barry, D., & Pearson, R. (2008a). *Blood Tide: A Never Land book*. New York: Disney Editions.
Barry, D., & Pearson, R. (2008b). *Science fair: A story of mystery, danger, international suspense, and a very nervous frog*. New York: Disney Editions.
Barry, D., Pearson, R., & Call, G. (2004). *Peter and the Starcatchers*. New York: Disney Editions/Hyperion.
Barry, D., Pearson, R., & Call, G. (2006). *Peter and the shadow thieves*. New York: Disney Editions/Hyperion.
Bickmore, S. T. (2008). It is inexcusable to deny *Inexcusable* a place in the classroom. *The ALAN Review, 35*(2), 75–83.
Chabon, M. (2000). *The amazing adventures of Kavalier and Clay*. New York: Random House.
Chabon, M. (2002). *Summerland*. New York: Miramax/Hyperion.
Chabon, M. (2007). *The Yiddish policemen's union*. New York: HarperCollins.
Coen, J., & Coen, E. (Directors). (2007). *No country for old men* [Motion picture]. United States: Miramax Films.
Collins, S. (2008). *The hunger games*. New York: Scholastic.
Cormier, R. (1974). *The chocolate war*. New York: Pantheon Books.
Craven, W. (Producer/Director). (1982). *Swamp thing* [Motion picture]. United States: Swampfilms.
Cronenberg, D. (Director). (1986). *The fly* [Motion picture]. United States: 20th Century Fox.
Farmer, N. (2002). *The house of the scorpion*. New York: Atheneum.
Hiaasen, C. (2002). *Hoot*. New York: Knopf.
Hiaasen, C. (2005). *Flush*. New York: Knopf.
Hiaasen, C. (2009). *Scat*. New York: Knopf.
Hiaasen, C. (2011). Frequently asked questions. Retrieved from http://www.carlhiaasen.com/faq/faq-scat.shtml
Hinton, S. E. (1967). *The outsiders*. New York: Viking Press.
Kinney, J. (2007). *Diary of a wimpy kid* (3rd ed.). New York: Amulet.
Lipsyte, R. (1967). *The contender*. New York: Harper & Row.
Lipsyte, R. (2002, November 7). Children's books: Field of really strange dreams. *New York Times*. Retrieved from http://www.nytimes.com
Long, M., & Shannon, D. (2003). *How I became a pirate*. San Diego, CA: Harcourt.
Maslin, J. (2002, September 16). Books of the Times: In Tolkien territory, but with baseball and a Saab. *New York Times*. Retrieved from http://www.nytimes.com
McCarthy, C. (2005). *No country for old men*. New York: Knopf.
Melville, H. (1851). *Moby Dick*. London: Richard Bentley.
Neumann, K. (Director). (1958). *The fly* [Motion picture]. United States: 20th Century Fox.
Nygren, Å. (2005). A world of story-smoke: A conversation with Sherman Alexie. *MELUS, 30*(4), 149–169.

Oates, J. C. (1969). *Them*. New York: Vanguard Press.
Oates, J. C. (1992). *Black water*. New York: Dutton.
Oates, J. C. (2002). *Big Mouth & Ugly Girl*. New York: HarperCollins.
Oates, J. C. (2003). *Freaky green eyes*. New York: HarperCollins.
Oates, J. C. (2005). *Sexy*. New York: HarperCollins.
Oates, J. C. (2006). *After the wreck, I picked myself up, spread my wings, and flew away*. New York: HarperCollins.
Patterson, J. (2005). *The angel experiment*. New York: TimeWarner.
Pearson, R. (2005). *Kingdom keepers*. New York: Disney Editions.
Pearson, R. (2008a). *Kingdom keepers II: Disney at dawn*. New York: Disney Editions.
Pearson, R. (2008b). *Steel Trapp: The challenge*. New York: Disney Editions.
Pearson, R. (2010). *Steel Trapp: Academy*. New York: Disney Editions.
Pearson, R. (2011a). *Kingdom keepers III: Disney in the Shadow*. New York: Disney Editions/Hyperion.
Pearson, R. (2011b). *Kingdom keepers IV*. New York: Disney Editions/Hyperion.
Salinger, J. D. (1951). *The catcher in the rye*. Boston: Little, Brown.
Shusterman, N. (2007). *Unwind*. New York: Simon & Schuster.
Sonnenfeld, B. (Director). (1997). *Men in black* [Motion picture]. United States: Columbia Pictures.
Spielberg, S. (Director). (1991). *Hook* [Motion picture]. United States: TriStar Pictures.
Uris, L. (1967). *Topaz: A novel*. London: Kimber.
Zindel, P. (1968). *The pigman: A novel*. New York: Harper & Row.

12

Young Adult Literature as a Call to Social Activism

Lois T. Stover and Jacqueline Bach

> Katie entered her student teaching experience wanting her students to think about how they could make a difference in the world by engaging in acts of community service. For her, the decision to use young adult literature as a vehicle for moving students into service-learning was clear—if students relate better to protagonists who are undergoing similar experiences, shouldn't they be inspired and encouraged to make a difference by reading about young adults engaged in such activities? Using a young adult novel as the centerpiece for a unit on community service, Katie sought to create experiences for her students in which they sought out possible volunteer outlets for their skills and interests. Because her students were already required to complete fifteen hours of community service each year, she hoped that her students would become lifelong contributors to important causes.

> An eighth-grade English class in New York City voted to explore gay rights issues as part of their annual service project. They read both young adult literature and other kinds of texts and then decided to raise awareness of the continued struggles of the lesbian, gay, bisexual, and transgender (LGBT) community to win legal and social equality by exploring the history of those fights. The actual project included teams of students investigating significant places in New York City at which important events happened; then they moved about the city, standing at each site and videotaping each other as they outlined what had happened at each place, talking to any passers-by as they did so, and then posted their video to the school website.

These two anecdotes demonstrate the ways in which activism and service-learning, partnered with the use of young adult literature, can become part of the secondary English language arts (ELA) classroom and connect in-class learning with out-of-classroom experiences. The idea of using literature, especially young adult literature, as a means for introducing students to social justice issues has produced a wealth of rich resources (Alsup, 2003; Eppert, Etheridge, & Bach, 2007; George, 2001; Glasgow, 2001). Also notable are those efforts by college composition instructors to incorporate service-learning into their curricula—they create courses that contain what Bringle and Hatcher (1995) describe as educational experiences in which students participate in organized acts that address community needs. Those engagements, they argue, can further foster an understanding of the discipline. We hope to demonstrate how young adult literature might serve as a catalyst for community service and activism and enhance student learning. In this chapter, we focus on the use of young adult literature in conjunction with a variety of strategies that all fall under the umbrella of a larger "activism" concept that, for us, includes service-learning (courses that require students to spend time volunteering for a cause and incorporating those experiences into the content of the course), community service (often hours of service students complete volunteering as part of their school experience), and activism itself (which includes taking action to support a cause, such as participating or organizing a group of people who want to raise awareness about a social issue). We've identified five topics that are all of importance in society today and will discuss at least two books, with lists of other possible titles, and suggest ancillary activities that result in students taking action in issues relevant to them.

WHY YOUNG ADULT LITERATURE?

The English classroom—in particular, at the university level—has a long history with service-learning and activism. Whether those endeavors take the form of tutoring (for example, Clark, 2002) or secondary students raising awareness of environmental issues in their community (Cortez-Riggio, 2011) the significance of students utilizing their skills and interests in real-world scenarios is invaluable. The position statement by the National Council of Teachers of English (NCTE) on twenty-first-century skills recognizes that our students will need writing and reading skills that will enable them to design, create, synthesize, share, evaluate, and create in complex technological environments (NCTE, 2008). This notion of disseminating information for global audiences points to the increasing importance of online communities in our students' futures. Furthermore, the NCTE's policy research brief on adolescent literacy (Gere et al., 2007) cites research that shows

> the literacies adolescents bring to school are valuable resources, but they should not be reduced to stereotypical assumptions about predictable re-

> sponses from specific populations of students; adolescents are successful when they understand that texts are written in social settings and for social purposes; adolescents need bridges between everyday literacy practices and classroom communities, including online, non-book-based communities. (p. 4)

In a year-long world literature course, Singer and Shagoury (2005) focused on the theme of social activism in order to "explore issues of activism and progressive social change" (p. 319). Singer, their classroom teacher, made sure her tenth graders had plenty of opportunities to self-select literature to read alongside the required texts. They began the year by reading biographies and autobiographies of activists and ended the year by educating their peers on social issues that they felt were important. Their unit provides excellent ideas and steps for teaching about activism that incorporate reading and writing using a variety of methods including technology—such as creating music CDs and engaging multimedia presentations.

In his article "What's the Big Idea? Integrating Young Adult Literature in the Middle School," George (2001) studied middle school teachers who use young adult literature to teach their students about "big ideas" such as responsibility, equity, and injustice. Like Singer and Shagoury (2005), he finds that the core reading of texts should be supplemented with independently chosen selections and that young adult literature offers a large number of high-quality engaging choices. It is our belief that while reading these books facilitates a connection of the heart and mind that leads to a desire to facilitate change, when they are paired with reflective acts of service, there might exist a transformative power that surpasses the mere reading of these texts.

DECIDING ON A CAUSE

We often read or hear phrases encouraging us to "help us fight intolerance," "join the fight against world hunger," "save the wetlands," or "end deforestation" from the many worthwhile organizations dedicated to making our world a better place. As with selecting any piece of literature or theme to incorporate into the classroom, units are at their most successful when students play a role in the direction they take. Convincing some students to become interested in a social issue, especially one that is removed from their day-to-day experiences, might present a challenge, as students might not first think about their community needs and instead latch onto a more abstract issue. Projects like Schultz's (2008) "Project Citizen" unit, in which his students decided to renovate their school, show the amazing transformations that can occur when students focus on causes that are in their immediate surroundings and can see the impact of their actions. Young adult narratives featuring protagonists who are successful in enacting transformation might also serve as motivating factors for students to take action in their worlds.

Therefore, we offer the following suggestions when deciding on a unit designed to instigate activism or service-learning opportunities:

1. Consider asking students what social issues they are interested in—and have a selection of texts, including poetry and drama, that deal with those issues.
2. Use novels that invite interdisciplinary cooperation. For example, work with the earth science teacher, the social studies teacher, or the computer teacher in order to delegate the number of tasks that can be involved with some of these units. Certainly, these approaches also encourage the participation of community stakeholders—from a local grocery store to a local nonprofit organization.
3. Employ resources from a number of organizations dedicated to activism and service-learning when considering a unit of this type. Of particular usefulness are the National Service-Learning Cooperative's "Eleven Essential Elements of Service Learning," which point out the need for ongoing assessments and student voice (cited in Billig, 2000), as well as the information on how to use social media to get one's message out found at the Learn and Serve: America's National Service-Learning Clearinghouse's website (2008).

Each of the following sections will provide an overview of an issue, possible texts, and how to frame activities and units around them. These are not meant to represent all possible issues—just ones we are familiar with through our own experience and research.

RAISING AWARENESS OF ENVIRONMENTAL ISSUES: PAMPHLETS, PLANTING, AND PAPER BAGS

When we use the term *environmental issues,* we refer to a wide variety of topics—pollution, sustainability, natural resources, health, food supply, ecosystems—all of which have ties to community and culture. Proponents of including more environmental-related movements in schools point out that its ultimate importance is in preparing our children to inherit a world with depleting resources, loss of biodiversity, controversies concerning genetically altered food, and natural disasters like catastrophic hurricanes and oil spills (Orr, 1992; Stone, 2009). These efforts almost always include efforts from the entire community; thereby, there exists a valuable opportunity for students to work with adults. Young adult literature can complement or even spur these efforts when readers see protagonists like themselves make changes, maybe even subtle ones, in their surroundings.

The young adult novels by Carl Hiaasen do just that. *Flush*, like his other works, is set in the Florida Keys and its characters are closely connected with the status of their ecosystem. In *Flush*, brother and sister, Noah and Abbey, take up their father's cause after he gets caught sabotaging a casino boat that has been dumping sewage into their local waterway in the Florida Keys. This text serves as a model for students to think about identifying the needs in their local communities alongside global ones. The novel poses questions such as these: What responsibility do we have to our environment? How far should one go to protect the environment? What actions can young adults take to make a difference in their communities? Teachers can also use the novel's theme to encourage their students to examine their ecosystems and identify actions that they can take to protect or sustain their surroundings.

One culminating activity for units dealing with environmental issues might be the creation of informational pamphlets. In this activity, students identify a cause to support—perhaps something local like the adoption of a section of a highway to keep clean or a global cause such as promoting renewable energy sources. Students then research their cause and create a pamphlet meant not only to inform readers about their cause but also to suggest ways in which they can become involved.

Teachers and students might also consider using this activity with more traditional novels such as Henry David Thoreau's *Walden* (1854/2004). Two other possible considerations are Mark Kurlansky's *Cod: A Biography of the Fish That Changed the World* (2008), a title suggested in an early version of the national core curriculum, and Phillip Hoose's *The Race to Save the Lord God Bird* (2004). These two nonfiction texts examine the role of humans' responsibility to the world's wildlife.

While the pamphlet assignment promotes individual causes, a schoolwide project like the creation of a community garden can involve not only most of the school but also parents and members of the community. A natural pairing with the creation of a school garden is Paul Fleischman's *Seedfolks* (1997). *Seedfolks* is the story of an urban community coming together to build a local garden; the story is told through the voices of thirteen different narrators. The novel raises issues such as what is one's responsibility to one's neighbors and neighborhoods, how cultural and ethnic identities influence one's way of life, and what are the rewards of helping others. The increasingly popular endeavor of starting school gardens can be enhanced through the incorporation of interdisciplinary efforts among content area teachers and supported by the ELA classroom with the reading of a young adult novel. The details of creating and maintaining a community garden are too detailed to outline here, so we direct readers to these useful sources:

The Edible Schoolyard: A Universal Idea (Waters, 2008), *Ecological Literacy: Educating Our Children for a Sustainable World* (Orr, 1992), and *Place-Based Education: Connecting Classrooms and Communities* (Sobel, 2006).

For teachers and students interested in inspiring people to make a difference, but who don't have a lot of time for the week-long pamphlet or the long-term commitment to a school garden, they might consider having students write inspirational slogans on grocery-store paper bags as a venue for their enviromental messages. In *The Gospel according to Larry* (Tashjian, 2001), Larry starts an anonymous blog that encourages people to change the world, by denouncing their materialistic and celebrity-obsessed ways. This novel features a young adult addressing his peers through an authentic voice as Josh (the real person behind Larry) struggles with being an outsider and disgusted with what he sees in society. As social networking continues to boom among young people, we see this venue as an ideal one for learning and documenting a class service-learning project or a way to raise awareness about an issue.

A novel and low-tech twist to blogging is the paper bag campaign. (Incidentally, the person responsible for getting Larry's book published was handed it by him in a grocery-store paper bag.) In this activity, students could include pithy statements from the novel and perhaps a companion text that reflects the lines from these texts that are meaningful to them. It's another way of sharing their thoughts in a very tangible and immediate way and asks them to look closely at the texts they read.

STORY AS A WAY OF KNOWING: ORAL HISTORIES AND NARRATIVES

As a young psychologist, Robert Coles was having difficulty understanding and connecting with patients whose lived experiences were very different from his own. In *The Call of Stories* (1989), he recounts with great poignancy the first time he decided to stop talking and just *listen* to a patient. Once he did, he found that he had a great deal more to offer those he was attempting to help—and found, too, that in the process of making their stories more concrete through having an audience, they gained confidence and awareness, which also supported their treatment. As Bloom tells us, being willing to listen to the stories of others—in the school, community, state, nation, or the world—is the first step in building empathy and moving toward not just tolerance of, but appreciation for, the diversity that is the mosaic of our global community (cited in Woolfolk, 2010, p. 460). Young adult narratives that highlight oral history projects might spark similar endeavors in their readers including recording, documenting, and sharing the experiences of community members.

For example, in Carolyn Meyer's *Rio Grande Stories* (1994), a group of junior high students attending a magnet school decide to sell a volume of stories as a fund-raising project to support the principal, who wants to purchase a sculpture for the front lawn of the school that will symbolize the rich ways in which the Rio Grande brings the community together. The student voices in *Rio Grande Stories* are diverse, representing Native American, African American, Hispanic, and Anglo perspectives. Each chapter includes a student's essay, prefaced by the narrative of how that author came to write his or her contribution. One future teacher attending college in southern Maryland who read the volume commented, "I love the idea of kids investigating their own communities, of finding the stories that bring them together."

In conducting similar kinds of research in their local community as a way to experience from the inside out the kinds of service-learning activities they might do with their future secondary students, these future teachers learned that mulberry trees, not native to the area, were brought there in an attempt to start a silk industry in the mid-1800s. They learned more about the history of racial segregation that led to the current establishment of the "Salt and Pepper" breakfast: One wise black man and one wise white man came together to share their perspectives over breakfast once a month. They each decided to ask one more person to join them—and those individuals each asked one more, until now there is a vibrant informal interracial dialogue that undergirds the local political structure. The future teachers now hope to model this practice in their own schools with their future students.

News headlines make a perfect "way in" to the concept of listening to others' stories as a way to build empathy and then work toward social action. *Return to Sender* (2009) by Julia Alvarez and *Crossing the Wire* (2006) by Will Hobbs both make concrete and real the issues faced by the children of illegal immigrants to the United States.

In *Crossing the Wire*, Hobbs is eloquent in describing the reasons behind the often desperate attempts individuals make to cross the border and in making tangible and real the terrors of such crossings. In this action-filled survival tale, Hobbs chronicles the story of Victor, who, at fifteen, has been supporting his family since his father's death. When corn prices bottom out and it is not even worthwhile to plant, Victor decides he has to go to El Norte; lacking money for a guide, he is forced to take his chances waiting at a border town, where he is able to hear others' stories about how best to make his moves. As he makes successive attempts, he unwittingly becomes involved with drug traffickers and faces mountainous and desert terrain, thieves, and, of course, the Border Patrol. One of the strengths of the novel is the way Hobbs is able to weave in a great deal of information about geography, politics, and local customs while asking, "Who is a hero?"

In Alvarez's book, the father of thirteen-year-old Tyler is injured in a farm accident and so needs help to cope with the workload; he turns to undocumented farm workers, making an empty trailer on the farm available for the Cruz family. At first Tyler resents their presence, but he gradually befriends Mari, in a relationship forged over their common love of stargazing. Tyler learns Maria's mother is missing and comes to understand the family's fear of immigration officers. When coyotes contact Mari's family, saying her mother is being held for ransom, Tyler lends Mr. Cruz his savings. The novel is told in chapters that alternate Tyler's voice with heart-rending letters Mari writes to her mother coupled with entries from Mari's diary.

In particular, students respond to the ways in which families can be torn apart by the actions of "la migra" (Homeland Security); children of illegal immigrants born in the United States have U.S. citizenship and are not deported with their parents. So the parents lie low and do not do anything to call attention to themselves, which makes it difficult for a child of "undocumenteds" to receive special services in the event that these are needed—or even to receive translation services for school newsletters, report card comments, or field trip permission forms. While not every curriculum affords the time and space for a teacher to conduct the kind of extensive community service story-collection project exemplified in Meyer's book, students studying Spanish can offer their services as translators, volunteering to create the Spanish versions of parent newsletters and other forms or documents for school systems and teachers strapped for resources. And both Hobbs and Alvarez pave the way for in-class discussions about how, in general, people arrived in this country and what hardships they were fleeing as they made their way here, relating our national history of displacement of Indians to that of migrant workers today, or the story of the Underground Railroad. Having students create a wiki about these issues is a way for them to collaboratively share their research and growing collective understanding of the issues.

MENTAL HEALTH ISSUES: BRINGING THE COMMUNITY INTO SCHOOL

The National Institute for Mental Health (2009) reported:

> In 2006, suicide was the third leading cause of death for young people ages 15–24. Of every 100,000 young people in each age group, the following number died by suicide: Children ages 10–14—1.3 per 100,000; Adolescents ages 15–19—8.2 per 100,000; Young adults ages 20–24—12.5 per 100,000.

Of course, not all young adults who experience mental health issues attempt suicide explicitly; some develop eating disorders, such as anorexia or bulimia; others engage in self-injury behaviors, such as cutting; and others attempt to escape their mental anguish by self-medicating with alcohol or drugs. And then there are those adolescents who cope on a daily basis with autism or serious learning disabilities that make their lives difficult both in school and out.

Reading books in school in which there are major characters dealing with mental health disorders and learning disabilities is a way to heighten awareness of these problems, and a way of bringing the community into the school with a common goal of increasing understanding of those who suffer from these ailments so that we can make appropriate referrals and provide appropriate support.

Thus a unit on mental health and learning disabilities that allows individual students to select a title of interest and appropriate readability level, investigate the topic at the center of the text, and then invite community and school system professionals into the classroom for a panel discussion of "fact versus fiction" and suggestions about how to best support their friends who may be suffering in silence is a great option, bridging the disciplines of English, health, and social studies in the process. Using books about characters with mental health disorders or learning disabilities who are authentically portrayed can be a safe way to provide insight into their emotional landscape and therefore to discuss how best to respond to individuals wrestling with such special needs. The unit can begin by having students work in small groups to brainstorm what they already know, or think they know, and what they want to learn about the following issues: depression, anorexia, borderline personality disorder (of which cutting is a symptom), anxiety/panic disorder, obsessive-compulsive disorder, autism, or learning disabilities. Ask them, too, to discuss how these terms can be both a help and a hindrance to everyone involved in supporting individuals dealing with these issues. The question here is "Is labeling disabling?"

Two notable books for a unit such as this are Ellen Hopkins's *Impulse* (2008) and Laurie Halse Anderson's *Wintergirls* (2010). *Impulse* by Ellen Hopkins deals with depression. In this novel in verse, three teens—Vanessa, Tony, and Conner—alternately tell their stories about how they have come to be hospitalized after attempting suicide. The complexities of their family situations and the ways in which their depression manifested itself as it spiraled out of control are presented with powerful imagery and humor. They form friendships that are tested, as one of them just can't seem to cope with the thought of the family realities that await after treatment ends, leaving the other two to pick up the pieces as they gain strength and do manage to move forward with their lives even in the wake of their loss.

Wintergirls by Laurie Halse Anderson contains characters who suffer from anorexia/bulimia. Cassie and Lia have been best friends forever, but each has developed an eating disorder. As seniors, they are no longer friends, which is why Lia refuses to answer the phone the night Cassie calls her over thirty times—the night Cassie dies. The book follows Lia as she comes to understand Cassie and herself, and begins to work toward a fragile but developing desire to live, rather than following Cassie into the darkness. Like *Impulse,* the sense of voice and the amazing imagery bring readers directly into Lia's world of subterfuge, loss, and pain.

Other titles and issues include *Cut* by Patricia McCormick (2002). In *Cut,* Callie is a "guest" at Sea Pines, nicknamed "Sick Pines" by its other residents. She's been sent there because she's been cutting herself with sharp objects and has stopped speaking. As she gradually begins to open up to the therapist and other girls, the reader travels along the journey to a hard-won recovery, triggered by the beginnings of self-understanding, with her in this moving depiction of adolescent angst. *I Don't Want to be Crazy* by Samantha Schutz (2007) is her memoir of the debilitating panic attacks that begin as she moves into her college years, unfolded in free verse. The passages in which she describes how the anxiety begins, how it feels as it gains momentum, and how it brings her to her knees and takes her out of circulation convey the absolute terror she experiences—terror exacerbated by her growing recognition that she has to redefine herself as an individual with a serious mental health disorder. Other quality texts are *Joey Pigza Loses Control* by Jack Gantos (2002; ADHD), *Rules* by Cynthia Lord (2008; autism), and *Kissing Doorknobs* by Terry Spencer Hesser (1999; OCD).

After learning about these various mental health issues through reading and discussing these books, students can examine collectively questions such as "What *is* normal?" "When is labeling useful and when can it hurt?" "What are our responsibilities if a friend or classmate is suffering from what we suspect may be an undiagnosed mental health problem?" "What is true, and what is false, about the ways individuals with mental health problems are presented in the media?"

To help answer the latter question, students can do library research on a particular mental health problem. Then they can invite a panel of representatives of the various resources and agencies involved in supporting individuals with mental health issues to talk about their roles and responsibilities. Someone from the guidance department, a school psychologist for the school district, a special educator, the school nurse, a family practitioner, licensed social worker, and a psychiatrist would all be helpful members of such a panel. It is also possible that a student with a sibling or other personal experience navigating the use of such support systems might volunteer to speak. Students should have questions prepared, based on the novels they have read and the research they have conducted, that will help them use the panel members to better understand whether or not their readings provided a true depiction of the various problems experienced by their characters.

In *Dramatizing the Content with Curriculum-Based Readers Theater, Grades 6–12* (2007), Flynn describes how to guide students in the creation of readers' theater texts that go beyond the use of an existing literary work, incorporating other material and curricular content to provide context for the literature. As a culminating activity, students can work in jigsaw groups to create readers' theater scripts that bring the various characters about whom they have read into conversation with one another—and with the more factual material they gathered from their research and from the panel presentation. A group of English future teachers who had read several of the titles from the list above shared their final products with their colleagues intending to teach other subject areas at the secondary level and also with a high school health class, as a way to take their developing understanding of these issues public in true service-learning fashion. High school students could perform for other classmates, but given the sensitivity of the subject matter, it might be easier for them to perform for the PTA, groups of future teachers, or for teachers during in-service workshops in order to share their developing knowledge and understanding in ways that cement their learning and make a difference in the larger community.

See Black and Stave (2007), Brinda (2008), and Shepard (2010) for additional guidance on using readers' theater in the classroom.

ABUSE: "BEING THERE"— SOMETIMES THAT REALLY IS ALL IT TAKES

Abuse—physical and sexual—is, like mental illness, often an unseen problem, and difficult to discuss. It's hard for those who have not ever had to fear the wrath or advances of a parent or other trusted adult to even imagine how victims of sexual and physical abuse feel, why they cannot seem to find their way out of abusive relationships, and what they must do to cope and protect themselves. Young people have few avenues of legal recourse open to them, and those who care about individuals who are experiencing abuse are also hampered by a lack of true power to *do* something. But service-learning projects centered on supporting existing community resources can provide powerful mechanisms for heightening awareness and introducing secondary students to the network of support structures that exist in the community for those dealing with abuse of all sorts. In teacher education programs, such projects are valuable for introducing future teachers to ways in which school systems can interact with other community support structures to best serve students.

Woodson tells how her powerful novel *I Hadn't Meant to Tell You This* (1995) began when she heard the main character, Lena, speaking to her, saying the line, "Black, white, it shouldn't make no difference. We all just people here" (p. 59). Before Lena actually says this line in the book, we meet Marie, good student, good friend, popular girl, daughter of a fairly well-off African American academic who is grieving, with Marie, because her mother has decided, after battling depression for quite some time, to just take off, leaving her family behind. Lena shows up at Marie's middle school; Marie senses something in Lena's eyes that make her think Lena, too, knows about loss. Asked by her teacher to show Lena around the school, Marie risks ostracism by the popular crowd with whom she usually hangs by actually befriending Lena, whose mother, she tells Marie, died of cancer. In his grief, her father has been unable to hold a job, and Lena and her sister, as a result, are labeled "poor white trash," given where they live and what they wear. Yet Marie and Lena, from very different worlds, understand each other's longing for what's missing in their lives—although Marie's father has trouble accepting Lena because of her lower socioeconomic status. It takes a while, but almost without thinking, Lena finally lets Marie in on what she perceives to be her dirty secret: her father has been abusing her, which is why she refuses to make herself look attractive, to comb her hair or even wash. When Lena realizes her father is turning his attention to her younger sister, she decides her only way out is to take Dion and run away to find her mother's people.

Woodson tells how she thought that, having gotten the sisters out of their father's clutches, she was ending the book on a note of hope, but her readers had other ideas (Stover, 2003, p. 52). The problem is, of course, that the world is not a hospitable place for two young girls on their own. Eventually, Woodson caved in to pressure from her readers and gave us *Lena* (2006a), in which Marie finally realizes the perils facing Lena and Dion—and realizes, as well, that this is a situation that calls for adult intervention. By the end of *Lena*, Marie's father has not only faced some of his own socioeconomic prejudices but also helped organize a search. When Lena calls Marie, Marie gives her the remarkable news that (a) Lena's father has taken off without a trace, and (b) Marie's father wants Lena and Dion to live with them. He truly wants to give them a home—and in so doing, to make his house more of the home Marie has been lacking since her mother's departure.

In this pair of novels, readers are introduced to several different kinds of abuse: physical abuse, sexual abuse, the abuse of abandonment, and the abuse of the bullies/students in power who thrive on making those who do not fit the norm feel invisible, despised, and unwanted. David Klass's *You Don't Know Me* (2002) and Stephen Chbosky's *The Perks of Being a Wallflower* (1999) both explore the theme of abuse and the ways in which it permeates the heart and soul of two males who experience it. Charlie—introspective, very bright, a geek—is the wallflower of the Chbosky title who gradually comes to realize what his beloved Aunt Helen did to him as a child as he works his way through grief over a friend's suicide, and has his first encounters with drugs and sex. John, also very bright, funny, and insightful, has been the recipient of physical violence at the hands of his mother's boyfriend, "the man who is not my father," for quite some time. In both cases, the boys manage to find adults who help them recognize they are not to blame for their victimized status and who help them find some measure of equilibrium at school and at home. Readers learn from these quirky, likable young men the reality that abuse victims often go underground, psychologically speaking—and, like Lena, how important it is to have a friend, someone who can (as Marie does) just listen, who can just "be" with them. That's a powerful message for readers who may feel helpless knowing their friends are being victimized.

However, Eric from *Staying Fat for Sarah Byrns* by Chris Crutcher (2003) finally feels compelled to go beyond just "being" there for Sarah. Friends since childhood, Eric and Sarah were drawn together by their misfit status—he because of his obesity, she because she's been horribly burned and disfigured by an "accident." Now in high school, Eric is slimming down due to his workouts on the swim team, but he remains faithful to Sarah, whose caustic sense of humor has long been her defense against the world. But something has pushed Sarah over the edge; she has stopped talking and is committed to the psych ward of a local hospital. Eric is torn—he continues to visit Sarah, to "be" there for her and with her, but he feels it is time to break his vow of silence about Sarah's situation, though he knows that in doing so, he risks their friendship. He ultimately realizes he cannot face Sarah's father, who stalks Eric and attempts to stab him, on his own, and he eventually gets support from individuals he would not have expected to have much to offer, including his own mother's boyfriend, whom Eric has always viewed as wimpy. In this case, just being there isn't enough, and that's an important message for readers to hear, too.

Tish, of Cynthia Voigt's older but very powerful *When She Hollers* (1996), provides yet a different kind of role model for young adults who are being abused. The novel spans just one day in Tish's life—the day she leans across the breakfast table, knife in hand, to tell Tonnie, her stepfather, that he will never sexually abuse her again. Her totally vulnerable mother has not been able to protect Tish, and while Tish has tried more reasonable strategies in the past, nothing has worked. So on this day, she takes charge. Leaving the house armed with the knife, she goes to school as though nothing is wrong, but she can't keep up the facade forever, and she does eventually find someone who can help her. This is a tautly drawn, no-holds-barred examination of the lived experience of a victim of abuse.

While the circumstances are rather different, Melinda of Laurie Halse Anderson's *Speak* (2006) also eventually learns that the young man who has raped her does not have power over the entirety of her existence. Like Sarah,

Melinda goes mute during her first year of high school; her throat is always sore, her lips dry, and when she tries to talk, it's as though she's been hit by sudden laryngitis. Of course, nobody at school is speaking to her because she called the cops to the site of an end-of-summer party. And her parents don't speak a great deal either; they tend to write messages on sticky notes instead. But eventually, through the freedom of expression she is afforded in her art class, Melinda begins to understand—and the readers with her—that her silence has been caused by her state of victimization, and that she needs to speak out in order to prevent the rapist from controlling her life.

What we learn from all of these stories is the importance of seeing behind the walls of humorous deflection or invisibility the victims raise, of listening beyond the silence that victims of abuse feel in the face of betrayal at the hands of those with power, who often are those from whom they should have naturally expected protection. And the other important message is that there are times when breaking silence is mandatory; regardless of the vow of friendship, true friends help those being victimized by finding adults with authority to limit the power and threats of the victimizer.

For young adults reading these books—or those more classic texts that also deal with issues of abuse of all kinds (physical, emotional, and sexual)—learning how to just sit with a victim in acceptance is crucial. Woodson's Lena is eloquent about the need to feel real and visible. From Audre Lorde's *Cancer Journals* (1980), Lena and Marie learn that battling despair means "teaching, surviving, and fighting with the most important resource I have, myself, and taking joy in that battle" (p. 102). They learn, too, that battling despair is contingent upon "knowing . . . my life and my love and my work has particular power and meaning relative to others" (p. 103). They give each other a sense of having been seen, which is crucial in their development as individuals who can face down abusers.

But it is also critical for students to learn about community resources and individuals who can be counted on to intervene when a victim cannot stand up for herself or himself. In terms of "being there," secondary students can prepare story time or arts and crafts activities that they can implement at a shelter for battered women in their community that they choose to adopt.

Perhaps even more important, they can take their learning about issues of abuse and victims' rights public by creating pamphlets or fliers that they can distribute around schools, parks and recreation sites, playgrounds, the mall—places where victims might find them and learn more about their options. In the process of creating such products, they can research California's "Megan's Law," which requires convicted sex offenders to be publicly registered; debate whether or not "sexting" between "consenting" teens should or should not be prosecuted under existing laws; look at the ways bullying has exploded into cyberspace; and work to create a bill of rights for their school population. While holding bake sales, talent shows, car washes, or spaghetti dinners to raise money for their particular cause (see more about hosting events in the next section), students can disseminate the results of their research and use examples from the various books they read to give voice to the voiceless as they create their reference materials. In the process of engaging in such activities, they are pairing fiction and nonfiction texts to create a richer perspective on the issue of abuse, developing empathy for those who have experienced abuse, and collaborating to provide resources of value to both individuals and the school communities, while writing for real audiences with a real sense of purpose.

One important resource for teachers to tap in searching for books specifically about abuse related to bullying are the two books by C. J. Bott, *The Bully in the Book and in the Classroom* (2004) and *More Bullies in More Books* (2009). She provides a wealth of information about the scope of the bullying problem in the United States today, and she annotates many, many novels for a variety of ability/grade levels that deal with the topic from multiple perspectives. Using these references is a very helpful way for teachers to awaken to the role they can and must play in helping both victims and bullies find other ways of interacting.

IT'S ABOUT MORE THAN JUST COLLECTING PENNIES, OR EVEN SWEATERS: HOSTING EVENTS AND ADOPTING SCHOOLS

Almost half the world's population, more than 3.3 billion people, live on less than $2.50 a day (Shah, 2010). According to 2008 statistics from the U.S. Census Bureau, 39.8 million people, 13.2 percent of the population of the United States, were below the poverty level, the highest since 1997. Among those under eighteen, 19 percent, or 14.1 million, lived below the poverty level (U.S. Bureau of the Census, 2009). In an effort to convey to his sixth-grade students the fact that most people on the continent of Africa are incredibly poor, much more poverty stricken than those in their local community (something his students were unaware of for the most part), a student teacher created a unit that culminated in a fund-raising event. He had the students do research on their area, creating math charts that compared what they found about median income, housing prices, and FARM statistics at the school with any statistics they could find about specific African countries. Then they hosted a spaghetti dinner to raise money—they had to do all the cooking and figuring out of ingredients and prices, and also publicity—at which they shared their results, and turned the money they raised over to the local United Way campaign.

A number of books depict young adult protagonists who find themselves suddenly poor or homeless through tragic circumstances. Jacqueline Woodson's *Miracle's Boys* (2006b) depicts an African American family who after losing both of their parents struggle to stay together. The oldest brother, Ty'ree, sacrifices his college scholarship and assumes the role of breadwinner for his two brothers, Lafayette and Charlie, in this story of urban poverty and family devotion.

In Leslie Connor's *Waiting for Normal* (2010), twelve-year-old Addie literally waits for her mom to come home. While doing so, Addie finds herself rationing her food and money and longing for a normal life. In Sharon Flake's *Money Hungry* (2001) and its sequel *Begging for Change* (2004), thirteen-year-old Raspberry Hill sells candy and does odd jobs in an effort to keep her family from having to live in their car again. These three novels depict the many tracks to poverty in the United States and help dispel the myths sometimes portrayed by the media.

Nonfiction texts about individuals making a difference can also inspire students and show them the possibilities of helping those in poverty here in the United States and worldwide. The stories in Phillip Hoose's *It's Our World, Too! Young People Who Are Making a Difference* (2002) describe young adults helping the homeless and those in need. A sort of how-to book, this collection of stories ends with questions and resources on identifying actions one can take, including writing petitions and starting organizations.

In our experience, students have long engaged in fund-raising efforts to assist those living in poor countries or devastated by natural disasters. However, their understanding of poverty may be largely based on images from the media or classroom discussions, and they may oversimplfy what it means to be poor. Reading texts that feature young adults who are or become poor for a number of reasons is a way for them to begin to make sense of what poverty is. One way is Sardone and Devlin-Scherer's (2010) "blending of technology and nonfiction texts that can assist students in understanding contemporary social issues that deserve critical attention" (p. 61). In this unit, students read political cartoons, and in the culminating activity, students play as refugees struggling for survival in a Darfur refugee camp. The game ends, like Hoose's book, with a "Take Action" section that provides several approaches students can take to increase awareness of this issue. Sardone and Devlin-Scherer also provide several other ideas for enhancing the teaching of nonfiction texts with technology.

UNICEF's (2010) website also provides a place, Voices of Youth, where students can read about and reach out to each other. They feature video diaries of children from around the world, as well as social networking sites. They, too, have computer games intended for youth to learn more about social issues such as poverty and HIV/AIDS.

CONCLUSION

One of the most infuriating acts for Justin that Jinsen, a.k.a. the Buddha Boy in Kathe Koja's (2003) book of the same name, undertakes is to begin begging during school lunch. Justin has a difficult time rencociling why someone would expose himself to ridicule by asking for money, if he didn't have to. Koja's book does not focus just on poverty and almsgiving but more on the philosophy of nonviolence; therefore, Jinsen's act in the novel that causes so much teasing from his peers is his not-acting. *Act* is at the beginning of the term *activism* and at the very core of its meaning. We hope that we have shown in this chapter the ways in which engaging students in "acts," no matter the course, can further the ways in which young adult literature can help students continue to discover their roles in the world. As educators, we need to model service-learning in teacher education so that our future teachers have that inside-out experience with true service-learning that will nurture their disposition and ability to engage their own students in service-learning, activism, and community engagement as well.

REFERENCES

Alsup, J. (2003). Politicizing young adult literature: Reading Anderson's *Speak* as a critical text. *Journal of Adolescent and Adult Literacy, 47*(2), 158–167.

Alvarez, J. (2009). *Return to sender.* New York: Knopf.

Anderson, L. H. (2006). *Speak.* New York: Penguin.

Anderson, L. H. (2010). *Wintergirls.* New York: Penguin.

Billig, S. H. (2000). Research on K–12 school-based service-learning: The evidence builds. *Phi Delta Kappan, 81*(9), 658–664.

Black, A., & Stave, A. M. (2007). *A comprehensive guide to readers theatre: Enhancing fluency and comprehension in middle school and beyond.* Newark, DE: International Reading Association.

Bott, C. J. (2004). *The bully in the book and in the classroom.* Lanhan, MD: Scarecrow Press.

Bott, C. J. (2009). *More bullies in more books.* Lanham, MD: Scarecrow Press.

Brinda, W. (2008). Engaging aliterate students: A literacy/theater project helps students comprehend, visualize, and enjoy literature. *Journal of Adolescent & Adult Literacy, 51*(6), 488–497.

Bringle, R., & Hatcher, J. A. (1995). A service-learning curriculum for faculty. *Michigan Journal of Community Service Learning 2,* 112–122.

Chbosky, S. (1999). *The perks of being a wallflower.* New York: MTV/Pocket Books.

Clark, C. T. (2002). Unfolding narratives of service learning: Reflections on teaching, literacy, and positioning in service relationships. *Journal of Adolescent & Adult Literacy, 46*(4), 288–298.

Coles, R. (1989). *The call of stories: Teaching and the moral imagination.* Boston: Houghton Mifflin.

Connor, L. (2010). *Waiting for normal.* New York: Turtleback.

Cortez-Riggio, K.-M. (2011). The Green footprint project: How middle school students inspired their community and raised their self-worth. *English Journal, 100*(3), 39–43.

Crutcher, C. (2003). *Staying fat for Sarah Byrnes.* New York: HarperCollins.

Eppert, C., Ethridge, K., & Bach, J. (2007). Bridging the gap: Using young adult literature to teach a just and sustainable world. *Talking Points, 19*(1), 10–20.

Flake, S. (2001). *Money hungry.* New York: Hyperion.

Flake, S. (2004). *Begging for change.* New York: Hyperion.

Fleischman, P. (1997). *Seedfolks.* New York: HarperCollins.

Flynn, R. M. (2007). *Dramatizing the content with curriculum-based readers theater, grades 6–12.* Newark, DE: International Reading Association.

Gantos, J. (2002). *Joey Pigza loses control.* New York: HarperCollins.

George, M. A. (2001). What's the big idea? Integrating young adult literature in the middle school. *English Journal, 90*(3), 74–81.

Gere, A. R., et al. (2007). *NCTE Principles of Adolescent Literacy Reform: A Policy Research Brief Produced by the National Council of Teachers of English.* Urbana, IL: National Council of Teachers of English.

Glasgow, J. N. (2001). Teaching social justice through young adult literature. *English Journal. 90*(6), 54–61.

Hesser, T. S. (1999). *Kissing doorknobs.* New York: Laurel-Leaf.

Hiaasen, C. (2005). *Flush.* New York: Random House.

Hobbs, W. (2006). *Crossing the wire.* New York: HarperCollins.

Hoose, P. M. (2004). *The race to save the Lord God Bird.* New York: Farrar, Straus & Giroux.

Hoose, P. M. (2002). *It's our world, too! Young people who are making a difference.* New York: Farrar, Straus & Giroux.

Hopkins, E. (2008). *Impulse.* New York: McElderry.

Klass, D. (2002). *You don't know me.* New York: HarperTeen.

Koja, K. (2003). *Buddha boy.* New York: Farrar, Straus & Giroux.

Kurlansky, M. (1998). *Cod: A biography of the fish that changed the world.* New York: Penguin.

Learn and Serve: America's National Service-Learning Clearinghouse. (2008, March). Retrieved July 20, 2010, from http://www.servicelearning.org/instant_info/marketing_101

Lord, C. (2008). *Rules.* New York: Scholastic.

Lorde, A. (1980). *Cancer journals.* San Francisco: Spinster/Aunt Lute.

McCormick, P. (2002). *Cut.* New York: Scholastic.

Meyer, C. (1994). *Rio Grande stories.* New York: Harcourt Brace.

National Council of Teachers of English. (2008). The NCTE definition of twenty-first century literacies. Retrieved from http://www.ncte.org/positions/statements/21stcentdefinition

National Institute for Mental Health. (2009). Retrieved June 6, 2010, from http://www.nimh.nih.gov/health/publications/suicide-in-the-us-statistics-and-prevention/index.shtml

Orr, D. W. (1992). *Ecological literacy: Educating our children for a sustainable world*. Albany: SUNY Press.
Sardone, N. B., & Devlin-Scherer, R. (2010). Keeping it current: Using technology to teach about social issues. *English Journal, 99*(4), 61–64.
Schultz, B. D. (2008). *Spectacular things happen along the way: Lessons from an urban classroom*. New York: Teachers College Press.
Schutz, S. (2007). *I don't want to be crazy*. New York: Scholastic.
Shah, Anup. (2010). Poverty facts and stats. Retrieved from Global Issues website: http://www.globalissues.org/article/26/poverty-facts-and-stats
Shepard, A. (2010). What is reader's theater? Retrieved June 15, 2010, from http://www.aaronshep.com/rt/whatis.html
Singer, J., & Shagoury, R. (2005). Stirring up justice: Adolescents reading, writing, and changing the world. *Journal of Adolescent & Adult Literacy, 49*(4), 318–339.
Sobel, D. (2006). *Place-based education: Connecting classrooms and communities*. Great Barrington, MA: The Orion Society.
Stone, M. K. (2009). *Smart by nature: Schooling for sustainability*. Healdsburg, CA: Watershed Media.
Stover, L. (2003). *Jacqueline Woodson: "The real thing."* Lanham, MD: Scarecrow Press.
Tashjian, J. (2001). *The gospel according to Larry*. New York: Holt.
Thoreau, H. D. (1854/2004). *Walden*. Introduction and annotations by Bill McKibben. Boston: Beacon.
UNICEF. (2010). Voices of youth. Retrieved July 20, 2010, from http://www.unicef.org/voy/
U.S. Bureau of the Census. (2009). *Income, poverty, and health insurance coverage in the United States: 2008*. Report P60-236, Table B-2, pp. 50–55. Retrieved from http://www.census.gov/prod/2009pubs/p60-236.pdf
Voigt, C. (1996). *When she hollers*. New York: Scholastic.
Waters, A. (2008). *The edible schoolyard: A universal idea*. San Francisco: Chronicle Books.
Woodson, J. (1995). *I hadn't meant to tell you this*. New York: Laurel-Leaf.
Woodson, J. (2006a). *Lena*. New York: Penguin.
Woodson, J. (2006b). *Miracle's boys*. New York: Perfection Learning.
Woolfolk, A. (2010). *Educational psychology* (11th ed.). Upper Saddle River, NJ: Merrill.

ADDITIONAL NOVELS

Abuse/Bullying

Avasthi, S. (2010). *Split*. New York: Knopf.
Knowles, J. (2009). *Lessons from a dead girl*. Cambridge, MA: Candlewick Press.
Koertge, R. (2004). *The Brimstone journals*. Cambridge, MA: Candlewick Press.
Mazer, N. F. (2000). *When she was good*. New York: Scholastic.
Peters, J. A. (2010). *By the time you read this, I'll be dead*. New York: Hyperion.

Environmental Issues

Hiaasen, C. (2002). *Hoot.* New York: Random House.
Hiaasen, C. (2006). *Nature girl.* New York: Random House.
Spinelli, J. (1988). *Night of the whale.* New York: Dell.

Immigration Issues

Blohm, J., & Lapinski, T. (2006). *Kids like me: Voices from the immigrant experience.* Yarmouth, ME: Intercultural Press.
Carlson, L. (1995). *Cool salsa.* New York: Fawcett.
Cisneros, S. (1994). *The house on Mango Street.* New York: Knopf.
Crews, L. (1991). *Children of the river.* New York: Laurel-Leaf.
Gallo, D. (2007). *First crossings: Stories about teen immigrants.* Cambridge, MA: Candlewick Press.
Lahiri, J. (2004). *The namesake.* Boston: Houghton Mifflin.
Namioka, L. (2007). *April and the dragon lady.* Boston: Houghton Mifflin.
Yoo, P. (2008). *Good enough.* New York: HarperTeen.

Mental Health and Learning Issues

Adler, C. (1986). *Kiss the clown* (ADHD). New York: Houghton-Mifflin.
Kephart, B. (2010). *The heart is not a size* (anorexia). New York: HarperTeen.
Walters, E. (2009). *Special Edward* (dyslexia). Victoria, BC: Orca.
Wolff, V. E. (2002). *Probably still Nick Swanson* (intellectual disabilities). New York: Pulse.

Poverty Issues

Armstrong, W. H. (1969/2004). *Sounder.* New York: HarperCollins.
de la Peña, M. (2005). *Ball don't lie.* New York: Delacorte.
Dickens, C. (1837/1998). *Oliver Twist.* New York: Tor Classics.
Martinez, Victor. (1996). *Parrot in the oven: Mi vida.* New York: HarperCollins.

Section III

WHERE IS YAL GOING?

13

Beyond the Language Arts Classroom

The Dynamic Intersection of Young Adult Literature and Technological, Pedagogical, and Content Knowledge

Colleen T. Sheehy and Karina R. Clemmons

It was the day he had anticipated for the last three and a half years: the beginning of student teaching internship. Drew landed a coveted placement; he specifically requested to work at Metropolitan Middle and High School (MMHS), the area's only school with a unique arrangement of middle school and high school on the same campus. The first week of the placement was aimed at observing teachers all over campus to get a sense of the school culture, while also witnessing a range of instructional approaches utilized by the dynamic faculty at MMHS.

Drew, anxious to get out and observe, asked his cooperating teacher, Ms. Tezano, to help him see what literacy across the curriculum looked like. This was a critical component in Drew's teacher education preparation, yet he had never had the opportunity to see this in practice. An elated Ms. Tezano directed Drew to classrooms all over the school that week, classrooms where she knew the teacher promoted the active and engaging use of technology while incorporating literature in inventive and inspiring ways. What he saw opened his eyes to the power of literacy, particularly through the use of young adult literature and effective technology integration.

The use of young adult literature (YAL) in all content area classrooms opens a powerful avenue to probe difficult concepts, investigate challenging ideas, and generate knowledge of the subject matter while seamlessly using various technologies to support this learning. In an education climate of accountability, standards, benchmarks, and high-stakes testing, combining contemporary YAL and technology provides an innovative and engaging way to teach curriculum standards across *all* areas of study, not simply in the English language arts (ELA) classroom. The Common Core Standards, adopted by the vast majority of states, push students, teachers, and districts to include both critical analysis and media production in all classrooms, not simply ELA. YAL is a resource for teachers of all subjects; it appeals to adolescents and teenagers in many ways through timely topics; dynamic, first-person narration; innovative formatting; and imaginative story lines. Young adults enjoy reading fiction more than nonfiction, especially when the fictional stories revolve around the coming of age of their characters (Furi-Perry, 2003). This enjoyment is grounded in strong connections between the characters and the reader and strong parallels between the story line and life of the reader. Moreover, technology has a ubiquitous presence in the lives of young adults today. The future of YAL must include its integration into *all* content areas through engaging projects that challenge students to integrate literacy, critical thinking, content, and technology. This chapter continues to follow Drew and Ms. Tezano to illustrate a dynamic future for YAL.

A RESOURCE FOR ALL CONTENT AREAS

> After the first day of classroom observations, Drew remained impressed, yet he found it interesting that teachers besides ELA teachers were using YAL. One question he posed to Ms. Tezano was "It's unique to see students reading novels in math, science, and even music class. Why so much attention to YAL?"

YAL has typically been seen as a resource for only ELA classrooms, yet using multiple texts in other content areas helps expand students' thinking and comprehension processes and provides a foundation for students to further synthesize varied and complex concepts (Hynd, 1999). Reading and building literacy skills is central to learning. As students move from elementary to secondary, the focus of instruction moves from *learning to read* to *reading to learn*. As students enter middle school, they are faced with more and more expository writing and expectations to learn content-specific vocabulary and concepts from this writing. Many misconceptions exist related to reading in the secondary school: that teaching reading is a responsibility of the elementary school, that teaching reading is a separate task from teaching subject matter, and that reading needs at the secondary level can only be helped by remediation, to name a few. However, literacy and reading skills encompass a synergy of multimodal aspects that help a reader develop; the fluidity of today's literacy continues to change as technology enhances and develops. If teachers and districts want to develop and foster literate students, it is imperative that educators broaden the definition of literacy to include this amalgam of skills and motivation. Examples follow of effective ways to integrate YAL and to embrace the very media that so successfully grasp our students' attention.

MATH EDUCATION

In *The Number Devil: A Mathematical Adventure* by Hans Magnus Enzensberger (2005), twelve-year-old Robert is confused and disengaged by his math class, or so he thinks. When Robert dreams, he is visited every night by a mysterious Number Devil, who presents mathematical concepts like prime numbers, square roots, and infinity in unusual, intriguing, and sometimes humorous ways that actually make sense. The Number Devil uses strange oddities for examples, and by the end of the adventure, Robert is interested in math and becomes a Number Apprentice to the surreal apparition in his dreams.

The Number Devil offers potential to engage students in math content and technology through a collaborative analysis project in which students work together to critically analyze the book and the math content in order to electronically storyboard their own graphic novel version of each dream. After reading and thoroughly discussing the book as a class, small groups of students are assigned one of Robert's dreams found within the book. Students work collaboratively to select potential scenes, conflicts, turning points, and dialogue to include in an electronic storyboard for their group's assigned dream. After the initial selection phase, students use various electronic presentation or movie-making technologies to create a storyboard of each dream. Student projects are then combined to create a class electronic graphic novel of the book.

A dynamic project inspired by *The Number Devil* gives readers a chance to connect dynamic and relevant math content with critical analysis and technology in a collaborative setting, illustrating the power of YAL to engage students across content areas.

MUSIC EDUCATION

In K. L. Going's *Fat Kid Rules the World* (2004), the main character struggles to develop self-esteem. At the beginning of the book, Troy is an overweight seventeen-year-old contemplating suicide by jumping in front of a train. He is interrupted by Curt, a musically talented and charming high school dropout. Curt connects with and befriends Troy, and he convinces Troy to be the drummer in his band. As the story unfolds, Troy imagines all the events in his life connected to facetious newspaper headlines, always related to his weight. Connected by their love of music, Troy and Curt's friendship develops when they experience adventures and gain life lessons, and they end up helping each other through life in a time of mutual need.

The themes of self-esteem, friendship, and music in *Fat Kid Rules the World* create multiple opportunities for students to analyze the universal effects of music on the human experience as they deconstruct Troy and Curt's experiences and ultimately create an autobiographical soundtrack for an important year of their own life. After reading and discussing the book, students analyze the importance of music to the main characters' development. Building on their analysis of music's influence on the development of the characters in the book, students then introspectively analyze their own lives in relation to music. Students use their analysis to develop a timeline for an important year of their life that reflects how music has impacted their lives and why. Students use multimedia technology such as presentation software, audio software, or movie-making programs to create a soundtrack of their life, narrated by fictional headlines used as captions.

Fat Kid Rules the World offers students a chance to connect YAL, music content, technology, and analysis skills in a creative, engaging project that highlights the importance of music to the human experience.

MEETING ACADEMIC STANDARDS AND STUDENT NEEDS

> Between class observations on Drew's second day he asked Ms. Tezano, "How on earth are teachers able to cover all the standards when they are reading YAL in all of their classes? Even more, how does reading YAL keep students interested all the time?"

The authentic voice of a charismatic teenaged character connects with the readers, and current societal issues are critically tackled in engaging, age-appropriate ways (Herz & Gallo, 1996). In addition to highlighting timely social issues, meaningful YAL has inherent capabilities to draw attention to various concepts in history, science, math, social sciences, the arts, health sciences, business, and a variety of other specific content areas (Readence, Bean, & Baldwin, 2004). Alvermann, Moon, and Hagood (1999) and O'Brien (2003) assert that understanding more popular media texts that engage student interest can help educators not only understand their students but also motivate them. The use of YAL in content area classrooms gives teachers the ability to reach more standards and, many times, cover more content with greater depth. The examples that follow illustrate how YAL is an invaluable resource to help teachers connect back to standards and cover more content through connecting to students' lives on a deeper level.

SCIENCE EDUCATION

The *Carbon Diaries 2015* by Saci Lloyd (2010), appropriate for ninth to twelfth graders, specifically addresses environmental consciousness. The novel, written from the perspective of sixteen-year-old Laura, is set in the future in London in a world confronted with the environmental consequences of global warming. In her diary, Laura describes huge storms brought about by climate change and the impact of the new carbon rationing that Britain has required of all its citizens. With the limited amount of carbon each person is allowed to produce each month, Laura details how hard daily life has become: It is difficult to heat one's house, shower, travel by car or airplane, use a cell phone, or even buy food that has been transported long distances. In between required lectures on reducing energy consumption, Laura tries to find comfort in her music and her friends and family, but the stress continues to grow with the increasing pressures of adapting to the environmental changes.

As many of the connections to science in the book are related to the environmental consequences of excessive carbon emissions, assign students to keep a list of all the activities in their own daily lives that leave a carbon footprint. From this list, have students work cooperatively to compile and analyze their lists and order the activities and products from most to least carbon impact. Big-picture concepts are then taken down to an individual level to inform a critical class discussion of why and how climate change occurs and possible solutions. In order to apply previously learned knowledge, students break into groups to brainstorm and investigate different potential solutions for individual components creating climate change. Students expand on current knowledge and research online to investigate an assigned country's or region's carbon emissions related to its population. With the use of word processing, spreadsheet, and presentation software, students create charts, tables, reports, and presentations reporting the results of their research and analysis. Students apply their research knowledge and present, using computer programs that generate graphs and charts of changes over time, possible solutions for climate change on an individual, country, and global level.

The Carbon Diaries 2015 offers the potential to engage students in a comprehensive project that connects science content related to environmental consciousness through YAL, technology, and the critical thinking skill of application.

ENGLISH LANGUAGE ARTS EDUCATION

In the fantasy adventure *Going Bovine* by Libba Bray (2010), Cameron, a sixteen-year-old slacker from a dysfunctional family, is diagnosed with Creutzfeldt-Jakob ("mad cow") disease. When Cameron is hospitalized for treatment, the reader is led into the world of his imagination and hallucinations, never quite knowing when reality begins and ends as Cameron follows his quest for a cure and his hope to meaningfully reconnect with his family. As Cameron goes in and out of reality, he has to battle evil forces of wizards, giants, and a happiness cult as he searches for the missing Dr. X, the only one who can cure Cameron and save the world.

Going Bovine offers ELA students a chance to evaluate the concept of reality and fantasy. After reading and discussing the book, students analyze how a writer effectively uses language to create fantasy worlds through topic choice, vocabulary usage, spelling, and syntax. Students draw on their evaluation of the author's use of language to create Cameron's real and imagined world, transfer the content knowledge, and practice the techniques through their own writing. Each student is assigned to choose and ultimately describe another situation that bends reality, such as an escapist daydream, what it might be like living with a psychological disorder, or even the reality of an elderly relative afflicted with Alzheimer's. Students then create a narrative blog that represents the daily entries of the character being described over the course of a specified time. Students focus on using language to create their narratives, and an electronic blog is an ideal medium; it allows an informal setting for experimenting with stream-of-consciousness writing, as well as the ability to add multimedia effects to enhance their blogs.

As Cameron was motivated to go on a metaphorical journey, so, too, will students as they evaluate their own writing on the blog to ensure they are using topic, tone, vocabulary, and syntax to effectively illustrate the stream of consciousness one experiences throughout an experience of altered reality. The project effectively merges YAL, ELA curriculum, technology, and critical thinking in an engaging project that allows students to hone their knowledge of the writer's craft.

WORLD LANGUAGES EDUCATION (SPANISH)

In Ann Jaramillo's novel *La Línea* (2008), readers experience one side of the issue of illegal immigration from the point of view of two adolescents who cross the border and forever change the course of their lives. Brother and sister Miguel and Elena trek from Mexico to the United States after their parents, who successfully crossed the border themselves some time before. *La Línea* offers rich opportunities to learn history, culture, and language, while connecting with adolescents through themes of stubbornness, fear, and determination.

This book connects students with Spanish content by helping them learn many Spanish phrases in an authentic context throughout the story. The book also spotlights some aspects of Mexican culture, such as how birthday parties are celebrated and the typical customs of a weeknight dinner. Most importantly, the book offers opportunities to discuss and evaluate the many sides of the issue of immigration. To combine content knowledge with technology and with the events in the story, students choose a character from the book, evaluate that character's motivations and resources, and create a website that documents an escape journey from Mexico across the border to the United States. Students are assigned to locate multiple links that include a motivation for escape, an evaluation of the best route, potential resources available, and possible dangers. The multiple sections of each character's website call on students to connect with their Spanish content knowledge of language and culture, as well as to evaluate multiple research sources. For example, students complete online research on weather conditions and research communities rich with Hispanic resources, in order to highlight five advantageous stops along the characters' hypothetical journey. A website allows students to integrate graphics, photo galleries, and music to enrich their projects. Depending on student proficiency in Spanish, some or all components of the project may be required to be written in Spanish.

A research project building on *La Línea* encourages students to develop evaluation strategies, to connect with multiple aspects of Spanish content through the YAL selection, and to use engaging website technology.

SEAMLESS TECHNOLOGY INTEGRATION

> Drew had noticed many teachers' effective use of technology in lessons, but he felt daunted by the prospect of having to add "one more thing" to his lesson plans. The next time they met, Drew asked Ms. Tezano, "Why is technology integration so important to our lessons, and how can I make technology an integral and natural component of lessons, rather than an artificial add-on?"

Technology is and will continue to be central to the lives of students. For many students, *doing* is more important than *knowing*, and learning is accomplished through trial and error, rather than by a rule-based approach. Students today have different expectations for learning, given their comfort with technology of all kinds. The constructivist theory of learning describes meaningful knowledge as constructed rather than acquired. Further, the root of Vygotsky's (1978) educational theory is the understanding of human cognition and learning as social and cultural rather than individual phenomena (Kozulin, Gindis, Ageyev, & Miller, 2003). Kozulin et al. (2003) explained that Vygotsky saw the development of intellect in terms of tools, like language, that are constructed by experience and exposure. The use of a wiki, blog, video, and social networking technology is exactly this: constructing knowledge together. Richardson (2006) points out that students who use a wiki and other interactive Web 2.0 technologies tap into a part of the Web that has now become a conversation and no longer a lecture. The following are examples that illustrate how to seamlessly integrate technology into content lessons using YAL.

SOCIAL STUDIES EDUCATION

In the novel *Hot, Sour, Salty, Sweet* (2009) by Sherri Smith, fourteen-year-old Ana Shen has a Chinese American father and an African American mother. As she prepares for her eighth-grade graduation, both sets of grandparents come to town to help with the festivities. When it's time to make food for the party, Ana's grandmothers can't agree on much, and Ana tries to figure out how all the different "flavors" of her family, now together in the kitchen, can fit together perfectly. Ana's multicultural family exemplifies the difference in cultures that exists within the United States. The stories her grandparents tell of their childhoods make connections to geography and world history in a first-person view, as well as providing insight into other cultures. Grandmother Nai Nai speaks often about Grandfather Ye Ye's childhood during the First Sino War and having to eat moldy corn because the Japanese soldiers burned the Chinese crop fields. These stories help explain Nai Nai and Ye Ye's current personalities, including Nai Nai's feelings toward not wasting any food and even using scraps for a meal. Grandpa and Grandma White represent a different subculture of the United States with a different history. Their stories are particularly interesting because they represent not only the history of American people, but also that of the African American people. Grandpa White's story of his experience in the Korean War is also a valuable connection to world history and ties into multiple standards regarding cultural conflict with Koreans and Americans. Geography is also represented in his descriptions of the terrain and how geographical boundaries can change as a result of war and conflict.

Students in a middle school social studies classroom can work in collaborative groups within a wiki to represent different cultures and associated opinions and experiences with war. Each group of three or four students is assigned to create a two-page newspaper/journal about an assigned event from the viewpoint of their assigned cultural group. For example, the burning of China's crops during the Sino War can be explored from the Chinese perspective, the Japanese perspective, and other nations' perspectives. Or students can evaluate the events of the Korean War from the perspective of African Americans, North Koreans, and South Koreans. The news/journal article can be written in the time period of the event, with particular attention to how the media can represent the same facts in different ways to different audiences to evoke different meanings and emotions. Students' assignments might include requirements such as one major story, an additional opinion or personal story, newspaper name, article titles, and a minimum number of accompanying pictures. The use of a wiki helps students stay in communication with each other about the project even outside of class and provides a place for each group's notes and brainstorming. Further, by putting accountability on each group, feedback among groups can be provided in the wiki through clear expectations of each student's commenting on at least one other group's wiki page at the end of every class.

Hot, Sour, Salty, Sweet is an excellent YAL selection that students can connect to. The book, combined with the wiki project, helps students evaluate complex social studies content in context.

HEALTH SCIENCES EDUCATION

In *Wintergirls*, Laurie Halse Anderson (2010) tells the story of Lia and Cassie, two friends who have known each other since elementary school. Through adolescence, they grow apart, and each girl develops a self-destructive eating disorder. Even though their friendship has drifted, Cassie calls Lia multiple times on the night Cassie commits suicide, but Lia doesn't answer the phone. After Cassie's death, Lia struggles with guilt in addition to her irrational need to be thin. In this dark, realistic world of low self-esteem and self-torture, Lia begins cutting herself as she fails several times to recover from her anorexia and her guilt. Lia's search for acceptance and even her very survival is the backdrop of this engaging novel that opens a dialogue about body image issues facing many young people.

After a thorough book study of *Wintergirls*, students can draw on their health sciences content knowledge to work collaboratively to create a public service announcement (PSA) informing young people about the health dangers of various self-destructive behaviors. Multiple technologies can be effective for this project, such as various presentation and video software. After deciding on the unhealthy behavior they will address, students can work to plan the facts, images, sounds, and text they will use in the creation of their PSA. In order to use their projects to help a larger audience, students can share their PSA with the class and even with the larger school community.

The use of multimedia technologies allows students a motivating platform through which to connect their reading of Anderson's *Wintergirls* with their health content knowledge in order to create a PSA with an empowering message for their peers.

TPACK: BRIDGING THEORY AND PRACTICE

In his internship meetings with his mentor in his teacher education program, Drew was called upon to write several reflections on the emerging framework known as TPACK (Technological, Pedagogical, and Content Knowledge). After turning in his assignment, Drew wondered just how to effectively integrate TPACK in the classroom. The next time he met with Ms. Tezano, Drew asked her, "TPACK seems like a good idea, but how can I take the theory and apply it in the classroom on a daily basis?"

The emerging framework of Technological, Pedagogical, and Content Knowledge (TPACK) is an extension of Schulman's (1986) work with pedagogical content knowledge (PCK). For example, science teachers can use a particular pedagogical approach to teaching a science lab. However, the approach used in a science classroom may not be as effective for teaching a lesson in a world language course. On the other hand, the use of a language lab demonstrates a specific pedagogical approach to language acquisition that would not be as effective in a science lab. That is, each content area has specific pedagogy for best practice. Koehler and Mishra (2008) built onto the PCK construct by adding technology knowledge to create a complex interaction among these bodies of teacher knowledge. This synergistic relationship is now referred to as TPACK.

According to Koehler and Mishra (2008), within the context of TPACK, each body of knowledge is specifically defined: Technology knowledge is inherently fluid and continually evolving; pedagogical knowledge characterizes detailed methods and strategies used in the classroom to deliver instruction; content knowledge describes the subject matter learned and taught within the specific field, including theories, processes, and established practices. In the P–12 setting, content is dictated by district and state level benchmarks and standards. The following examples show how YAL, combined with TPACK, supports the essential intersection of these bodies of knowledge as the place where effective instruction occurs.

BUSINESS EDUCATION

In M. T. Anderson's futuristic, yet remarkably realistic, novel *Feed* (2004), teenaged Titus and his high school peers all have a microchip in their head, known as a feed, that constantly uploads information. The feeds influence what the teenagers want to buy, eat, wear, and even do on a daily basis. Life goes along smoothly in conformity until Titus meets a girl named Violet, who helps him see life in a completely different way. Violet is different; she didn't have the feed installed into her head until she was seven years old, causing her to have malfunctions when she tries to not let the feed influence her. While the essence of marketing and advertising is to make a product or service look good to a target audience, Anderson's *Feed* presents a biting commentary on how corporations market products to target audiences through technology such as television and the Internet. The feed finds things that companies and organizations know the teenagers in the story will want because of their age. Inherently, the feed brainwashes them so they will buy the products.

As a summative project in a business education course, students can apply their prior knowledge of marketing and advertising with their new experience reading *Feed*. Using movie-making software or publishing software, students can be assigned to create their own advertisement to promote Anderson's book or another YAL title. Using this technique, students are called upon to apply prior business content knowledge related to marketing, as well as promotion variables such as advertising, public relations, selling, message, media, and budgeting, and thus students can effectively engage in a project that promotes a book. The project offers much choice in how the final advertisement looks and, more importantly, students are called on to apply their previously learned business content knowledge.

Feed is an excellent YAL selection that motivates students to participate in a discussion of the importance of marketing and the positive and negative effects it can have on people. The project offers a chance for students to engage with YAL and apply business content knowledge in a fresh way using technology.

ART EDUCATION

Chasing Vermeer by Blue Balliett (2005) is a mystery that engages young readers in a mysterious art heist of a valuable Vermeer painting. The fast-paced action involves Petra and Calder, two middle school students, piecing together a mystery of stolen Vermeer paintings through patterns, puzzles, codes, and fact-checking. Petra and Calder's friendship is strengthened as they work together to put the pieces of the puzzle together clue by clue and plan their next move. They have to rely on their collaboration, problem-solving skills, analysis, and knowledge of Vermeer. The author threads the language of artwork throughout the book and has even hidden puzzles within the book for decoding.

The background and events in *Chasing Vermeer* make this YAL selection an ideal springboard for a project in which students apply their knowledge of art elements and themes to the analysis of a well-known artist's work. After first reading and discussing the book, students are then assigned to conduct research on a specific artist by visiting multiple examples of the artist's work in various museums that offer online components of their collections. Virtual tours available online allow students to access art resources beyond their local community, enabling them to see artwork from around the world. The research component can spur students to apply critical thinking skills to evaluate the validity and reliability of their sources. In addition, students can compare and contrast multiple examples of an artist's work by analyzing the artwork for repeated elements before selecting a representative sample of the artist's work displaying the targeted themes. In the culmination of the project, students are challenged to apply their research to their own mystery as they present their findings and possibly create their own puzzle based on the artist's work.

A project utilizing Balliett's *Chasing Vermeer* offers students the opportunity to connect art content with technology, employ their critical thinking skills, and engage in application by applying their research to explore intriguing components of art history and art production beyond the examples given in the book.

THEATER ARTS EDUCATION

In Walter Dean Myers's captivating story *Monster* (2001), Steve, a young protagonist accused of murder and on trial for his life, is forced to think about his actions, thoughts, and moral decisions while grappling with the ongoing question "Am I a monster?" This book connects seamlessly with teaching the theater arts. Steve, an aspiring filmmaker, processes his thoughts and experiences through a movie script and journal format.

The reader has a front-row seat when witnessing this adolescent caught in the circumstances of an adult world. This is a cautionary tale of small, daily decisions that eventually lead to larger consequences, something extremely pertinent to the lives of adolescents. Also inherent in this tale is a value of the theater craft, as the first-person point of view bounces between movie script and journal writing. Through this novel, Myers illustrates a clear significance of performance art as a means to process and learn from emotional experiences.

So, is Steve a monster? The prosecution thinks so. What do students who read this book think? To incorporate technology and theater arts content into an authentic, summative project, students can grapple with the same question as they choose scenes from the book to reenact, record on video, edit, and create a short movie trailer. After reading, studying, and discussing the book, the important next step is to have students brainstorm their answers to the question "Is Steve a monster?" During this critical phase of the creative process, students can use the text as evidence to carefully select the scenes from the book that represent the sum of their judgment. Once students have a clear answer to the question, they can create a storyboard, or sequence of sketches, that depict their answer to the question. In doing this, students choose images, scenes, music, and dialogue to support their thesis.

Next in the creative process, students can physically act out their ideas and capture them on video. When the video has been collected, students can then import the footage through movie-making software and begin to edit. The editing phase is where the answer to the question comes to life. Students can deliberately select what to include and what to omit in their movies, and once they are satisfied with their product, they are ready to publish.

Myers's novel *Monster* gives readers the chance to be juror and witness of Steve's life. This creative movie trailer project gives students the chance to use critical thinking skills by generating their own product to answer an open-ended question. Technology, pedagogy, and content merge in a new way so students can bring the book to life on the silver screen.

A DYNAMIC FUTURE FOR YAL

> As the time drew near to complete his internship at MMHS, Drew reflected on the wealth of knowledge he had gained from Ms. Tezano and his students. He was finally able to take his preparation from theory to practice. He had a whole new insight into the value of YAL to help him integrate effective pedagogy with content instruction and technology across the curriculum. He wondered, "How can I mentor other teachers to see the amazing opportunities within YAL?"

Interactive Web 2.0 technologies, combined with the wealth of motivational potential and meaningful messages inherent in YAL, offer an essential resource to further engage students in a learning conversation across *all* content areas, not simply in ELA. Alvermann and Hagood (2000) argued that if educators want students to perform well on academic assessments and in challenges of the world outside of school, students will need to develop a critical understanding of how all texts (both print and nonprint) position them as readers and viewers within different social, cultural, and historical contexts.

Meaningful learning occurs when students are engaged in the learning process; the use of technology and YAL not only involves students but also provides inherent motivation and engagement to the topic. Using YAL with technology is a pedagogical approach for encouraging meaningful learning as teachers use the book's authentic experiences to elaborate on prior connections of what the students know about themselves, the subject matter in all content areas, and the world around them.

The specific examples elaborated in this chapter illustrate how seamlessly YAL can be integrated into TPACK and promote critical thinking skills. The future of YAL includes a necessary integration of these components. Critical thinking has long been recognized as essential in all content areas, and literacy and competence in technology are beginning to be recognized as skills that should be developed in all content areas as well. YAL offers opportunities to build literacy, develop critical thinking, connect with technology, and explore many challenging topics.

In short, YAL is too powerful a resource to be seen as strictly for ELA classrooms. YAL and technology offer a wealth of motivational potential for students, regardless of which classroom they find themselves in (see appendix). Though YAL titles and technologies may change, the need to engage students in critical thinking, technology, and essential content standards remains critical. The future of YAL contains a call to action for all teachers. YAL is an essential resource that teachers across all content areas should incorporate into their instruction as they prepare students for the varied demands and modern literacy of our changing world.

APPENDIX

Book Title	Author	Topic/Issue
Art Education		
Masterpiece	Elise Broach	Reproduction art
Business Education		
Lawn Boy	Gary Paulsen	Small business
How to Hook a Hottie	Tina Ferraro	Small business
Leaving Simplicity	Claire Carmichael	Advertising
Audrey, Wait!	Robin Benway	Branding, sudden fame
English Language Arts		
Schooled	Gordon Korman	Homeschooled boy adjusting
Hunger Games series	Suzanne Collins	Science fiction thriller
Fancy White Trash	Marjetta Geerling	Modern family dynamics
The Book Thief	Markus Zusak	Death as narrator
Health Sciences		
Gym Candy	Carl Deuker	Human growth hormone
Speak	Laurie Halse Anderson	Date rape
Deadline	Cris Crutcher	Living life after terminal diagnosis
Mathematics Education		
The Fractal Murders	Mark Cohen	Mystery; mathematical clues

Sir Cumference series	Cindy Neuschwander	Geometry
Do the Math: Secrets, Lies, and Algebra	Wendy Lichtman	How math concepts are all around us; coming of age
Music Education		
A Little Wanting Song	Kath Crowley	Singing; Australia, coming of age
A Song for Ba	Paul Yee	Singing; Chinese opera
Rock Star Super Star	Nelson Blake	High school and professional bands
Science Education		
Rampant	Diana Peterfreund	Chemistry
Flush	Carl Hiaasen	Biology/environment
Charles and Emma	Deborah Heiligman	Darwin
Compromised	Heidi Ayarbe	Hypotheses; scientific approach to life
Social Studies Education		
Chains	Laure Halse Anderson	American Revolution
Nation	Terry Pratchett	Tsunami survival
Elephant Run	Roland Smith	World War II; London, Burma
Fire from the Rock	Sharon Draper	Central High School and the Little Rock Nine
Theater Arts Education		
Eyes like Stars: Theatre Illuminata, Act 1	Lisa Mantchav	Magical world of theater
World Languages Education		
Mexican Whiteboy	Matt de la Peña	Self-identity as a mixed-race teenager
The Red Necklace: A Story of the French Revolution	Sally Gardner	Class relations during the French Revolution

REFERENCES

Alvermann, D., & Hagood, M. (2000). Critical media literacy: Research, theories, and practices in "new times." *Journal of Education Research, 93*, 193–205.

Alvermann, D. E., Moon, J. S., & Hagood, M. C. (1999). *Popular culture in the classroom: Teaching and researching critical media literacy.* Newark, DE: International Reading Association.

Anderson, L. H. (2010). *Wintergirls.* New York: Viking.

Anderson, M. T. (2004). *Feed.* Cambridge, MA: Candlewick.

Balliett, B. (2005). *Chasing Vermeer.* New York: Scholastic.

Bray, L. (2010). *Going bovine.* New York: Delacorte.

Enzensberger, H. M. (2005). *The number devil: A mathematical adventure.* New York: Holt.

Furi-Perry, U. (2003). "Dude, that book was cool": The reading habits of young adults. *Reading Today, 20*(2).

Going, K. L. (2004). *Fat kid rules the world.* New York: Puffin.

Herz, S. K., & Gallo, D. R. (1996). *From Hinton to Hamlet: Building bridges between young adult literature and the classics.* Westport, CT: Greenwood Press.

Hynd, C. (1999). Teaching students to think critically using multiple texts in history. *Journal of Adolescent & Adult Literacy, 42*(6), 428–436.

Jaramillo, A. (2008). *La línea.* New Milford, CT: Roaring Brook Press.

Koehler, M. J., & Mishra, P. (2008). Introducing technological pedagogical content knowledge. In AACTE Committee on Innovation and Technology (Ed.), *The Handbook of Technological Pedagogical Content Knowledge for Educators* (pp. 1–29). New York: Routledge/Taylor & Francis.

Kozulin, A, Gindis, B., Ageyev, V. S., & Miller, S. (Eds.). (2003). *Vygotsky's educational theory in cultural context.* New York: Cambridge University Press.

Lloyd, S. (2010). *The carbon diaries 2015.* New York: Holiday House.

Myers, W. D. (2001). *Monster.* New York: HarperCollins.

O'Brien, D. (2003). Juxtaposing traditional and intermedial literacies to redefine the competence of struggling adolescents. *Reading Online, 6*(7). Retrieved June 8, 2004, from http://www.readingonline.org/newliteracies/lit_index.asp?HREF=obrien2/

Readence, J. E., Bean, T. W., & Baldwin, R. S. (2004). *Content area literacy: An integrated approach* (8th ed.). Dubuque, IA: Kendall/Hunt.

Richardson, W. (2006). *Blogs, wikis, podcasts, and other powerful Web tools for classrooms.* Thousand Oaks, CA: Corwin Press.

Schulman, L. (1986). Those who understand: Knowledge growth in teaching. *Educational Researcher, 15*(2), 4–14.

Smith, S. L. (2009). *Hot, sour, salty, sweet.* New York: Delacorte Press.

Vygotsky, L. (1978). *Mind in society: The development of higher psychological processes.* Cambridge, MA: Harvard University Press.

14

Reading with Blurred Boundaries

The Influence of Digital and Visual Culture on Young Adult Novels

Linda T. Parsons and Melanie Hundley

> Being digital is different. We are not waiting on any invention. It is here. It is now. It is almost genetic in its nature, in that each generation will become more digital than the preceding one.
>
> —Nicholas Negroponte (1995, p. 231)

The digital generation, those contemporary young adult readers who have grown up surrounded by digital media, consume stories and narrative in a variety of ways (e.g., YouTube videos, online games, audiobooks, fan fiction, television, movies, graphic novels), as well as traditional print books. These readers are "so bathed in bits that they think it is part of the natural landscape" (Tapscott, 1998, p. 1). Today's media-savvy adolescents utilize multimodal literacy skills in informal writing that plays an integral role in their lives; a reported 85 percent of adolescents communicate through some form of digital writing (Reich, 2008). The landscape of their textual world situates story in a broad, connected environment in which traditional forms of text are only a small part. Keith,[1] a fifteen-year-old in an afterschool book group, explained, "It's a digital world. . . . I don't want just a book. I want more. I want to read it and then play it and then see it. I like it when books have movies and games and websites."

1. Keith (pseudonym), Mya (pseudonym), Keeley (pseudonym), and Sam (pseudonym) were participants in one of three afterschool book discussion groups; the book groups occurred between 2006 and 2010. Participation in the book groups was voluntary and included discussions of both the books and the students' experiences with reading the books. The participants in the group selected the books they read within established parameters: The books had to be books they had not read before, published within the past two years, and include some use of digital technology.

Adolescent readers see movies-of-the-week based on stories featured on the evening news or as newspaper headlines and Internet articles. Popular books, television shows, and movies have websites that encourage fan interaction in the forms of fan fiction, character blogs, print texts, and other tie-ins. Fans can play the games, participate in discussion boards, chat with other fans around the world, read and write fan fiction, buy the merchandise, and create YouTube smash-ups. The boundaries between media blur and print texts exist in a web of interconnected, often interactive, media experiences. The click-and-go ease of the Internet allows fluid movement between various digital story forms and social networks.

The culture in which they learn to read and interact shapes readers' expectations of text. Hill and Mehlenbacher (1996) contend that "readers who grow up in a world of hypertext and discussion groups will have different expectations of text than our generation does, and writers will have a different set of constraints and opportunities than writers do now" (p. 264). Readers' and writers' expectations will be reshaped in a context in which digital technologies increasingly mediate interactions with print text. The textual expectations of readers accustomed to the click-and-go of online reading and the click-and-choose of video games often include nonlinearity, immediacy, collaboration, and integrated images. The textual world of young adult literature (YAL) is influenced by elements of digital and visual culture. Interactivity, connectivity, linking, and immediate access to information (elements of digital media) and jump cuts, montage, juxtaposition of scenes, characters, or points of view (elements of visual media) have contributed to the development of readers who synthesize across multiple texts and multiple sources to negotiate multilayered, nonlinear narratives.

To respond to these changes, many young adult authors utilize the affordances of digital media—nonlinearity, lack of closure, narrative dispersed across multiple genres, disrupted narrative flow, and images that carry narrative weight—to situate their texts in larger digital contexts and create spaces for readers' social networking. These authors recognize that adolescents expect interactivity in their reading and engagement with texts; they situate texts in multimodal spaces or incorporate multimodality in texts to appeal to media-savvy adolescents.

In this chapter, we will discuss YAL that responds to the changing expectations of digital generation readers and have chosen texts we believe serve as exemplars.

EXPANDING THE EXPERIENCE: OPPORTUNITIES FOR INTERACTIVITY IN YAL

Mya, a fifteen-year-old girl in an afterschool reading group, stated, "I like to read but I don't want to just do it from a book. I want a book that has more. I want to go online and discover something that the book doesn't have. I want a book that moves and lets me read and play." Implicit in Mya's description of what she wants from a book is the view that the book should exist in multiple formats; she wants to read, play, and view the text. Conceptually, then, the world of the book is larger than its traditional form and exists in three-dimensional space.

Carson (2000), in discussing the ways a particular "world" is created in theme parks, argues that "the story element is infused into the physical space a guest walks or rides through. It is the physical space that does much of the work of conveying the story the designers are trying to tell" (n.p.). While the story worlds of YAL may not actually exist in a form readers may walk through, the novels often exist in forms that allow readers to "move" virtually through the story world, explore particular characters or events in more depth, see renderings of relevant objects or locations, or interact with additional texts or play related games. Elements from the story—whether character, additional dialogue, deleted scenes, or images—are infused in the novel's online world, extending it and permitting a level of interactive participation not possible prior to the advent of digital technologies. For Carson (2000), theme park story worlds worked in part because the physical space played upon "memories and expectations to heighten the thrill of venturing into your created universe" (n.p.). For the virtual worlds of young adult novels to be successful, they too must build on readers' memories and expectations, while simultaneously creating a virtual space that connects with the world of the text and builds an imagined space that allows for different media interactions.

YAL authors are beginning to use the space of the Internet as a tool to connect with their readers. In Jodi Lynn Anderson's *Loser/Queen* (2010), Cammy, a "loser" in the school hierarchy, follows the directions from an anonymous texter and destroys a "queen." *Loser/Queen* is the print version of a novel that began as an interactive online serial. Each week, the author posted chapters and asked readers to vote on various elements of the plot and incorporated winning choices into subsequent chapters. This use of reader input in the development of the story pushes the boundaries of reader co-construction to a new level. The author's role is challenged and changed by this visible and active reader participation, representing the shifting and evolving relationship between author and reader (Hill & Mehlenbacher, 1996; Miskec, 2007). This level of author/reader collaboration compels writers to relinquish authorial control.

The collaboration between author and reader in *Loser/Queen* (Anderson, 2010) forges a new level of connection between character and reader. The idea of voting on something, expressing an opinion, and seeing who and how many people respond similarly is an aspect of digital culture that occurs in both Facebook and Twitter. Facebook readers can click and share their "likes" for all to see; Twitter followers forward favorite postings to others by re-tweeting. Anderson's serial readers who voted for the most interesting plot twists continued and extended a practice developed in social media.

While *Loser/Queen* (Anderson, 2010) requires readers fluent in digital technology, novels such as *The Lightning Thief* (Riordan, 2005), *Trackers* (Carman, 2010), and *The Softwire: Virus on Orbis 1* (Haarsma, 2006) connect the reader with online worlds. Keeley, an eleven-year-old book club participant, discussed her reading practices and explained, "Before I even start a book, I google it to see if there is a website. . . . If I have two books to read and one has stuff to do online but the other one doesn't, then I will read the one that does first." Many young adult authors extend their book worlds through author or fan websites.

Rick Riordan, author of *The Lightning Thief* (2005), a traditional print text that brings the Greek gods into a modern setting, has created an online presence for the novel with games, interactive maps, information on the Greek gods, and an author blog. The interactive opportunities on the site extend the possibilities offered by the print novel alone. Sam, a sixth grader reading the novel for class, said, "I got really excited about *The Lightning Thief* when [my teacher] introduced it by showing us the author's web page. I got to see a map of the Underworld and Camp Halfblood before I got to the book." The novel exists in a media field that includes its online presence. Both Keeley and Sam interact with the text of the novel and the novel's Web presence. In addition, they can interact with other fans of the novel through message boards, fan fiction, and blogs.

Like *The Lightning Thief* (Riordan, 2005), *Trackers* (Carman, 2010), a novel about young computer hackers, has an active online presence. However, *Trackers* is a multiplatform novel that exists in print and online. Readers begin with the print text of the novel, and at a certain point in the text, they are given a Web address and password. The novel continues in the online environment using the affordances of digital media to provide image, text, video, and click-and-go options for readers. The narrative is dispersed throughout the print and digital forms of the novel, with each form providing information not available in the other (Rowsell & Burke, 2009).

The multiplatform novel requires readers who can synthesize across multiple genres as well as multiple media forms. The online world of the novel provides videos, clues for the codes, and additional images. Like a video game, this novel provides additional levels of action and involvement for its readers. Online site interaction necessitates navigating multiple options and engaging with images and videos that share the narrative weight of storytelling with the print text. While it is possible to read the text without visiting the online sites, readers lose context, depth of characterization, and ways in which juxtaposition of print, image, and video develop the complex narrative. The narrative is shaped and reshaped based on readers' choices and is therefore nonsequential and nonlinear. The readers construct the narrative from their choices, combining the digital text with the print text to create a story that does not exist in a single media format.

Unlike *Trackers* (Carman, 2010), a novel told in two platforms, and *The Lightning Thief* (Riordan, 2005), a novel extended by its website, *The Softwire: Virus on Orbis 1* (Haarsma, 2006) creates the world of the novel and invites readers to play in it. *The Softwire: Virus on Orbis 1*, a novel about a boy with the ability to communicate telepathically with computers, has a video game component to accompany the novel series. The video game cannot be separated from the novel, for without the world of the print novel and the clues it provides, readers would be unable to participate in the online experience. Simon, a seventh grader, discussed the experience of reading *The Softwire: Virus on Orbis 1* and then playing the game, explaining, "The game made me read better because I needed to know certain things to play. I didn't want to have to go back to the book to move on in the game so I had to really pay attention when I was reading the book." While *The Softwire: Virus on Orbis 1* in print form stands on its own, it is not possible to play the game successfully without information from the print text. The online world is both an extension of the novel and a space in which the novel is enacted. Like the physical space of theme parks, the game needs the memory of the novel to exist.

The interactive, multimedia experiences of these novels realize the possibilities of interactive narratives and media texts and exemplify a "synergistic aesthetic reading experience" (Dresang & Kotrla, 2009, p. 94). Adolescents mediate much of their world through experiences with digital media, and these authors use formats with which readers are intimately familiar to enhance their engagement. The shifting "movement from book to screen promises a metamorphosis" (Lanham, 1993, p. x) of what is possible for storytelling. Much as the three-dimensional spaces of theme parks rely on their participants' immersion in the created worlds of the park, the authors of these texts rely on readers' immersion in the multiple narrative formats of the novels building connections between and across textual forms to create an immersive narrative experience. As the narrative storytelling possibilities of digital technologies develop further, so will the readers' aesthetic expectations for texts.

MAKING IT WORK: THE FUNCTIONS OF TECHNOLOGY IN YAL

Digital technologies alter the relationships between reader and text and between author and craft (Hill & Mehlenbacher, 1996). Breaking a long tradition of "showing" through the medium of words, authors experiment with ways of "showing" through textual and visual representations that mimic the messiness of online interactions. This fundamental conceptual shift in storytelling options reflect the nuanced ways adolescents maintain relationships, create and re-create identity, and make meaning in the world. Authors create hybrid texts that blur the boundaries between page and screen and deconstruct the stability of traditional narrative. Thus, digital media become a trope for authors to use.

Contemporary characters in YAL would be inauthentic if they did not use or resist forms of social networking. Miskec (2007) argues that adolescents have a "distinct way of knowing the world because of their connection to technology—a very different experience than that of the generations that preceded them" (p. 7). Adolescents presume they can communicate with others through social media, and authors use social media as a tool to connect characters, reveal information, or bring a sense of immediacy and gossip to character interactions. In this sense, the technology is a tool without which the action of the story could not occur.

Technology as a Literary Trope: Telling Stories Multimodally

Authors are creating books with little or no traditional prose narrative—hybrid texts—choosing to tell stories through e-mails, IMs, blogs, playbills, handwritten letters, and journal entries. Each genre within this multimodal story construction conveys potential meanings unique to that form and not offered through any other (Rowsell & Burke, 2009). This reflects new literacy practices associated with digital technologies that differ in substantive ways from those connected with print-based books (Dresang & Kotrla, 2009; Lam, 2009). These multimodal, hybrid texts also reflect adolescents' "perceived comfort with chaos and disorderliness" (Miskec, 2007, p. 11). The interplay of the texts' complex discourses calls upon adolescents' ways of making meaning of and seeing the world.

In *An Order of Amelie, Hold the Fries* (Schindler, 2004), Tim becomes infatuated with a young woman he passes on the street but then begins to correspond with the wrong girl. The narrative is carried entirely through communications between various characters as relationships are forged, maintained, and negotiated through e-mails, IMs, handwritten letters, postcards, and notes written on surfaces from toilet paper to hotel stationery, as well as shopping lists and other personal reminders. The trajectory of the reading path in traditional narratives is linear, but the path in this text must be actively constructed, because seemingly innocuous images are crucial to understanding the story line. The side-by-side placement of images without traditional transitions and the use of multiple genres and social media place demands on readers that go beyond the demands of familiar, traditional narrative forms. Readers construct meaning across the multiple genres in ways that mimic the demands of social media.

Another hybrid text is *My Most Excellent Year: A Novel of Love, Mary Poppins, and Fenway Park* (Kluger, 2008). Three friends separately recount their freshman year in high school as they write compositions titled "My Most Excellent Year" for their junior English class. Readers must piece together the multiple narratives and perspectives to form a cohesive whole. In addition to excerpts from the characters' compositions, the story line is carried through IMs, handwritten letters and notes, baseball stats, e-mails, Web pages, newspaper reviews, and diary entries. The mix of genres that layer and interrupt each other heightens the sense of the characters' dynamic participation in social networks that are part of their daily lives (Koss & Tucker-Raymond, 2010). The various means of communication that convey the narrative emphasize that adolescents create and negotiate their identity through digital media.

Claire, in Elizabeth Rudnick's *Tweet Heart* (2010), is fully engaged in her online life on Twitter. She is delighted when the boy she has a crush on begins "following" her and their relationship develops offline as well as online. Readers must be fluent in the language and structural requirements/limitations of Twitter as well as the abbreviations common to instant messaging. The narrative is carried across tweets, e-mails, blog entries, and Claire's advice column. A reader unfamiliar with Twitter might not realize that postings are limited to 140 characters, meaning that a story may be spread across multiple tweets. This results in interruptions to the story being relayed. A fluent Twitter reader can follow the original tweet as well as the interrupting comments. In this format, there can be multiple conversations going on at once, often weaving in and out of each other. Characters who exhibit the ability to manage multiple, simultaneous conversations reflect adolescents' real-world interactivity (Lam, 2009). Fully developed stories with all the important details are often saved for e-mails, blogs, or face-to-face conversations. Groenke and Maples (2010) argue that when "media platforms converge, the varying platforms provide opportunities to tell different parts of a story in different ways" (p. 40). Elizabeth Rudnick weaves together several media platforms to tell Claire's story and relies on readers' experiences with these platforms.

Technology as Narrative Tool: Developing Identities and Relationships

Adolescents rely on social networking affordances to maintain relationships, and their online lives typically extend their offline lives (Koss & Tucker-Raymond, 2010). This extension is evident in YAL, as is the building of unlikely relationships across space. Complications of distance, social class, and/or culture are moot in online environments, where characters whose paths would never cross can and do meet. Character development occurs through dialogue, as the author relinquishes the voice of the omniscient narrator in favor of an immediate first-person narrative. Readers learn about characters through their personal digital compositions or what other characters reveal. Adolescent characters construct identity through online networks, presenting themselves as they hope to be perceived in that moment: authentically, fluidly, and sometimes deceptively (Koss & Tucker-Raymond, 2010). Adolescent characters mimic adolescents' use of digital media and social networking for relationship maintenance and identity construction.

In *ChaseR: A Novel in E-mails* (Rosen, 2002), Chase adjusts to the culture shock of moving from a metropolitan to a rural area. He relies on digital technology to maintain relationships and express his creativity, and readers could not know him in the same way through any other narrative form. There is no countervoice to balance his naïveté as he wrestles with the morality, or immorality, of hunting, so his voice becomes "ultimately unassailable" (Cadden, 2000, p. 148). Readers know about the advice he gets from others solely through his responses to them, which necessarily reflect his interpretation of what was said. Readers assume "the fully sympathetic part of the ideal listener" (Wyile, 1999, p. 192) in response to Chase's e-mails and e-newsletters. Chase's voice is omnipresent in the narrative and heard only through digital communication.

The computer serves as a medium for his creative talents as well as his journalistic skills. Chase designs smileys for the people he e-mails: Jeremy is -õ∫ô- (Rosen, 2002, p. 10) until he gets new glasses, and Chase redesigns his smiley as - Û∫Ù- (p. 129). Readers are privy to Chase's sense of humor through his own observations about his smileys and his self-deprecating comments. When he offers several smileys for his sister to "pick her very own," he suggests # (: ¬ { }) as a "bad hair day, lots of lipstick" (p. 45). He uses computer symbols and icons to create aesthetic forms that he embeds in e-mails and e-newsletters. Chase exemplifies Miskec's (2007) recognition of the "distinct convergence of [adolescents'] selves and technology as a combined, inextricable thing" (p. 16). Chase is who he is, and who he tells us he is, in large part because of his use of technology and its integration in the novel.

Adolescent characters use technology to forge relationships that might not be possible due to cultural and spatial distances in *A Bottle in the Gaza Sea* (Zenatti, 2008). After a café bombing, Tal decides to put a note in a bottle and set the bottle adrift in the Gaza Sea. Naïm Al-Farjouk (a.k.a. Gazaman) finds the bottle and her note, and they correspond online, hoping to bridge the divide between their warring peoples. The relationship between Tal and Naïm is possible because of technology that allows their relationship to be "disembedded from their locations" and relocated in "virtual space" (McLean, 2010, p. 15). Both of these characters are empowered by their performance of self as they control what they reveal and conceal. As adolescent characters negotiate issues of identity presentation and re-presentation in online social networks and in correspondences such as e-mails and IMs, honesty or deception are often difficult to discern.

The plot of *Will Grayson, Will Grayson* (Green & Levithan, 2010) turns on issues of honesty and deception in identity construction and online meetings. For over a year, Will Grayson develops an online relationship with Isaac as they correspond through private IM conversations. As they become increasingly involved, Will reflects on the limitations of a relationship positioned solely in virtual space. Using digital media, the characters create, present, and re-present their identities to different people for different reasons (Koss & Tucker-Raymond, 2010). The dangers and pitfalls of online relationships become clear when Will learns that "Isaac" does not exist but is simply a profile his friend invented. Will's relationship with Isaac reflects adolescents' abilities to "respond to virtual and mediated reality in intense, personal, and specific ways" (Miskec, 2007, p. 8). Although Will goes on to form face-to-face relationships with other boys, he does not feel as connected to any of them as he felt to Isaac.

Just as Will forms intense online connections, so too does Serafina67 in Susie Day's *serafina67*urgently requires life** (2008). Serafina67 constructs and reconstructs her identity in her blog, the structure of which demonstrates her newness at blogging, her chattiness, and her willingness to talk about private issues in a semipublic space. Serafina67 engages in multiple identity constructs and "tries on" different aspects of her identity (princess, witch, and girl); even Serafina67 is a construct and not exactly her real name. This awareness that a user can play with how she presents herself to the world in an online environment is part of the understanding of online communications. Serafina67's blogging, like the writing that adolescents do in online environments, "does not always follow traditional conventions, featuring instead images . . . and a form of shorthand in which vowels and punctuation are irrelevant and time-consuming to use" (Sweeney, 2010, p. 121). Furthermore, characters often make visible what Alvermann (2008) acknowledges as "the centrality of audience as a major contributor to adolescents' fascination with self-created online content" (p. 10). Serafina67 demonstrates this fascination as she constructs herself in her blog and refers to her readers as her audience.

READING THE IMAGE: THE USE OF VISUAL ELEMENTS IN YAL

Whether it is the use of photos, artwork, or other graphic elements, the role of the visual is expanding. Authors use images as visual cues, as visual shorthand, and as a communicative element. Visual cues such as font or color changes signal speaker or genre changes, while visual shorthand such as the use of avatars or IM boxes signal the unique ways readers are expected to engage with the text. Readers must recognize visual changes in text structure and apply the rules of reading in online worlds to reading print texts. The visual shorthand identifies a shift in reading expectations.

Novels in Lauren Myracle's *Internet Girls* series, for example, use different fonts and font colors to indicate the speaker. The visual elements in *ttyl* (Myracle, 2004), *ttfn* (2006), and *l8r g8r* (2008) are used as visual shorthand. Rather than tell the reader that the dialogue is going to occur in an online environment, the author re-creates the visual elements of the online environment. The pages look like screen shots of instant message chats and require readers' fluencies in both the language and characteristics of instant messaging. These communications incorporate short sentences and abbreviations. The assumption is that both characters and readers are familiar with the characteristics of this medium and are able to recognize its elements and limitations (Sweeney, 2010). The readers see only the communications between the characters, so any character or plot development occurs in those interactions. To connote action, the author uses IM conventions—for example, *chortle chortle* as one character's laughing response to a text message. The reported physical action helps develop the scene and the characters' personalities and moves the narrative forward.

What's Your Status? (Finn, 2010) visually connects readers to social media through the authentic representations of Twitter pages. Madison introduces herself through a social profile on FriendVERSE. She tells the reader what she is doing, what she hearts (loves), and warns that she updates her status a lot. The tweets in *What's Your Status?* use the visual elements of tweets and include a picture or avatar of the speaker with the text. The author both frames and interrupts the traditional chapters of the text with tweets. This visual framing mimics the ways adolescents incorporate their online worlds into their daily lives, serving as a visual reminder of the way online engagement happens in concentrated chunks of time that frame or interrupt a school day.

CONSIDERATIONS AND CONCLUSIONS

Authors of YAL blur the boundaries between page and screen to create texts that feature the variability and instability of digital technologies. Simultaneously, researchers recognize the importance and interplay of transliteracies: reading, writing, and interacting across modalities. Hybrid texts make demands on readers that reflect new literacy practices necessitated by making meaning across multiple media (Hull & Stornaiuolo, 2010). Adolescents bring sophisticated and complex literacy skills to bear as they meet the unique demands of multimodal or hybrid texts. When novels integrate popular digital media, readers must use their knowledge of and facility with the conventions and norms of digital environments to negotiate these texts. YAL is increasingly situated in larger digital contexts, allowing adolescents to move beyond the text itself to connect with authors and other readers through social networking or to expand the text through online affordances. Today's adolescents increasingly expect the interactivity and interconnectivity of handheld text and online world.

A gulf exists between media-savvy adolescents and many of those who teach them. Prensky (2001) distinguishes between digital natives and digital immigrants. Immigrants are those of us born before the digital age who had to consciously learn, adopt, and adapt to this new language. For adolescent readers, however, the various languages of digital media are native languages—they were "born" to them. Digital immigrants typically have little appreciation of or respect for, indeed little understanding of, the sophisticated skills digital natives use competently. These competencies include interpreting graphic information, making meaning across multiple platforms, negotiating nonlinear and complex reading paths, adhering to the conventions of social networks, and switching codes and voice according to audience (Dresang & Kotrla, 2009; Lewis & Fabos, 2005). Young adult novels that blur the boundaries between digital and visual media may be a venue through which teachers who are not Internet savvy can experience multimodal texts using a traditional handheld book (Gardner, 2007). These novels may be a preliminary way to bridge the divide between natives and immigrants.

A risk authors take when they integrate popular digital formats relates to the changing technological landscape as media become dated and outdated rapidly. Another risk is that adults writing as adolescents necessarily do so as they perceive adolescents to be. For example, several adolescents who read *An Order of Amelie, Hold the Fries* (Schindler, 2004) stated that they always spell words completely when texting or IMing. Marcy[2] said, "Adults just think we write that way. They don't really know what we do." Research supports her observation that adults are guided by their perceptions of who adolescents are and by their aspirations for who they want them to be (Dresang & Kotrla, 2009; Lewis & Fabos, 2005).

Authors who create story worlds using multiple media platforms are "pushing against the limits of what can be accomplished in a printed text and thus their works fare badly against aesthethic standards defined around classically constructed novels" (Jenkins, 2004, p. 122). This "faring badly" is not to say that the works are not well crafted; rather, it is to argue that there is no aesthetic standard by which to judge them. Readers develop separate expectations for the print, online, or game components of a text. Currently, there are no guidelines for evaluating multiplatform

2. Marcy (pseudonym) was an adolescent reader in a book group reading *An Order of Amelie, Hold the Fries* (Schindler, 2004). Two high school English teachers, a group of volunteer high school students, and a university professor participated in a summer reading program in 2010. Their readings focused on books that integrated and imitated online communications.

novels. Similarly, evaluating understanding of hybrid texts presents unique challenges beyond those presented when reading traditional narratives. While reader response theories stress each reader's unique transaction with any given text, the design elements of multimodal or hybrid texts result in "weaving together a story or experience arguably unique to the individual reader" (Dresang & Kotrla, 2009, p. 99).

As teachers and researchers advocate for the expansion of the definition of "literacy" to "literacies," the discrepancies between formal and informal literacies become ever more evident. Kress, Jewitt, and Tsatsarelis (2000) note that adolescents' interactions and engagements with digital technologies feature multiplicity, performativity, flexibility, and adaptability. These characteristics stand in contrast to the stability of formal literacies and traditional narratives. As we move toward recognition of and regard for adolescents' competencies with digital language and technology, we hope to see a concurrent recognition of and regard for the reflection of these competencies and technologies in young adult novels.

APPENDIX

Blogs

Bell, C. D. (2010). *Little blog on the prairie.* New York: Bloomsbury.
Clairday, R. (2005). *Confessions of a boyfriend stealer.* New York: Delacorte.
Day, S. (2008). *serafina67*urgently requires life*.* New York: Scholastic.
Dellasega, C. (2007). *Nugrl90 (Sadie).* Tarrytown, NY: Marshall Cavendish.
Dellasega, C. (2009). *Sistrsic92 (Meg).* Tarrytown, NY: Marshall Cavendish.
Goldschmidt, J. (2005a). *Raisin Rodriguez and the big-time smooch.* New York: Razorbill.
Goldschmidt, J. (2005b). *The secret blog of Raisin Rodriguez.* New York: Razorbill.
Goldschmidt, J. (2007). *Will the real Raisin Rodriguez please stand up.* New York: Razorbill.
le Vann, K. (2010). *Things I know about love.* New York: Egmont.
Mackler, C. (2010). *Tangled.* New York: HarperTeen.
Myracle, L. (2009). *Luv ya bunches.* New York: Amulet.
Myracle, L. (2010). *Violet in bloom.* New York: Amulet.
Noel, A. (2007). *Kiss and blog.* New York: St. Martin's Press.
Norris, S. (2008). *Something to blog about.* New York: Amulet.
Scandiffio, L. (2010). *Crusades* (T. Holcroft, Illus.). Toronto: Annick.
Sloan, B. (2006). *Tale of two summers.* New York: Simon & Schuster.
Tashjian, J. (2001). *The gospel according to Larry.* New York: Holt.

E-mails

Amato, M. (2003). *The naked mole-rat letters* (H. Saundes, Illus.). New York: Holiday House.
Colasanti, S. (2008). *Take me there.* New York: Viking.

Danziger, P., & Martin, A. M. (2000). *Snail mail no more.* New York: Scholastic.
d'Lacey, C., and Newbery, L. (2004). *From e to you.* London: Barn Owl Books.
Freitas, D. (2008). *The possibilities of sainthood.* New York: Farrar, Straus & Giroux.
Freitas, D. (2010). *This gorgeous game.* New York: Farrar, Straus & Giroux.
Gauthier, G. (2003). *Saving the planet and stuff.* New York: Putnam.
Honey, E. (2002). *Remote man.* New York: Knopf.
Hrdlitschka, S. (2005). *Sun signs.* New York: Orca.
Ishizaki, H. (2007). *Chain mail: Addicted to you.* Scranton, PA: Tokyopop.
Klinger, S. (2008). *Kingdom of strange.* Tarrytown, NY: Marshall Cavendish.
Koertge, R. (2010). *Shakespeare makes the playoffs.* Somerville, MA: Candlewick Press.
Lockhart, E. (2008). *The disreputable history of Frankie Landau-Banks.* New York: Hyperion.
Mackler, C. (2003). *The earth, my butt, and other big round things.* Cambridge, MA: Candlewick Press.
Moriarty, J. (2005). *Year of secret assignments.* New York: Scholastic.
Moriarty, J. (2006). *The murder of Bindy Mackenzie.* New York: Arthur A. Levine.
Moriarty, J. (2010). *The ghosts of Ashbury High.* New York: Arthur A. Levine.
Myracle, L. (2004). *ttyl.* New York: Amulet.
Myracle, L. (2006). *ttfn.* New York: Amulet.
Myracle, L. (2008). *l8r g8r.* New York: Amulet.
Myracle, L. (2009). *Luv ya bunches.* New York: Amulet.
Myracle, L. (2010). *Violet in bloom.* New York: Amulet.
Rosen, M. (2002). *ChaseR: A novel in emails.* Cambridge, MA: Candlewick Press.
Schindler, N. (2004). *An order of Amelie, hold the fries.* Buffalo, NY: Firefly.
Siebold, J. (2002). *Doing time online.* Morton Grove, IL: Albert Whitman.
Wittlinger, E. (2004). *Heart on my sleeve.* New York: Simon & Schuster.
Zenatti, V. (2008). *A bottle in the Gaza Sea.* New York: Bloomsbury.

Facebook

Griffin, A. (2010). *The Julian game.* New York: Putnam.

Gaming

Doctorow, C. (2010). *For the win.* New York: Tor Teen.
Haarsma, P. J. (2006). *The softwire: Virus on Orbis 1.* Somerville, MA: Candlewick Press.
Haarsma, P. J. (2008). *The softwire: Betrayal on Orbis 2.* Somerville, MA: Candlewick Press.
Haarsma, P. J. (2010). *The softwire: Wormhole pirates on Orbis 3.* Somerville, MA: Candlewick Press.
Haarsma, P. J. (2010). *The softwire: Awakening on Orbis 4.* Somerville, MA: Candlewick Press.
Mancuso, M. (2010). *Gamer girl.* New York: Speak.

Instant Messaging and Texting

Bell, C. D. (2010). *Little blog on the prairie.* New York: Bloomsbury.
Colasanti, S. (2008). *Take me there.* New York: Viking.
Day, S. (2008). *serafina67*urgently requires life*.* New York: Scholastic.

DeMatteis, J. M. (2010). *Imaginalis*. New York: HarperCollins.
Freitas, D. (2008). *The possibilities of sainthood*. New York: Farrar, Straus & Giroux.
Freitas, D. (2010). *This gorgeous game*. New York: Farrar, Straus & Giroux.
Gauthier, G. (2003). *Saving the planet and stuff*. New York: Putnam.
Lyga, B. (2006). *The astonishing adventures of Fanboy and Goth Girl*. Boston: Houghton Mifflin.
Moriarty, J. (2010). *The ghosts of Ashbury High*. New York: Arthur A. Levine.
Papademetriou, L., & Tebbetts, C. (2005). *M or F?* New York: Razorbill.
Schindler, N. (2004). *An order of Amelie, hold the fries*. Buffalo, NY: Firefly.
Wilhelm, D. (2003). *The revealers*. New York: Farrar, Straus & Giroux.
Wittlinger, E. (2004). *Heart on my sleeve*. New York: Simon & Schuster.
Zenatti, V. (2008). *A bottle in the Gaza Sea*. New York: Bloomsbury.

Multi-Format/Hybrid Texts

Anderson, J. L. (2010). *Loser/queen* (B. Lee, Illus.). New York: Simon & Schuster.
Black, B. (2010). *iDrakula*. Naperville, IL: Sourcebooks Fire.
Carman, P. (2009). *Skeleton Creek*. New York: Scholastic.
Carman, P. (2010). *Trackers*. New York: Scholastic.
Klise, K. (2004). *Regarding the sink: Where, oh where, did waters go?* (M. S. Klise, Illus.). San Diego, CA: Harcourt.
Klise, K. (2005). *Regarding the trees: A splintered saga rooted in secrets* (M. S. Klise, Illus.). San Diego, CA: Harcourt.
Klise, K. (2006). *Regarding the bathrooms: A privy to the past* (M. S. Klise, Illus.). San Diego, CA: Harcourt.
Klise, K. (2007). *Regarding the bees: A lesson, in letters, on honey, dating, and other sticky subjects*. San Diego, CA: Harcourt.
Kluger, S. (2008). *My most excellent year: A novel of love, Mary Poppins, and Fenway Park*. New York: Dial.
Schindler, N. (2004). *An order of Amelie, hold the fries*. Buffalo, NY: Firefly.

Online Sites

Bateson, C. (2010). *Magenta McPhee*. New York: Holiday.
Petersen, P. J., & Ruckman, I. (2004). *rob&sara.com*. New York: Laurel-Leaf.
Vega, D. (2005). *Click here (to find out how I survived seventh grade)*. New York: Little, Brown.
Wilhelm, D. (2003). *The revealers*. New York: Farrar, Straus & Giroux.

Twitter

Finn, K. (2010). *What's your status?* New York: Scholastic.
Rudnick, E. (2010) *Tweet heart*. New York: Disney/Hyperion.

REFERENCES

Alvermann, D. (2008). Why bother theorizing adolescents' online literacies for classroom practice and research? *Journal of Adolescent & Adult Literacy, 52*(1), 8–19.

Anderson, J. L. (2010). *Loser/queen* (B. Lee, Illus.). New York: Simon & Schuster.
Cadden, M. (2000). The irony of narration in the young adult novel. *Children's Literature Association Quarterly, 25*(3), 146–202.
Carman, P. (2010). *Trackers*. New York: Scholastic.
Carson, D. (2000). Environmental storytelling: Creating immersive 3D worlds using lessons learned from the theme park industry. Retrieved from the Gamustra website: http://www.gamasutra.com/view/feature/3186/environmental_storytelling_.php?print=1
Day, S. (2008). *serafina67*urgently requires life**. New York: Scholastic.
Dresang, E., & Kotrla, B. (2009). Radical change theory and synergistic reading for digital age youth. *Journal of Aesthetic Education, 43*(2), 92–107.
Finn, K. (2010). *What's your status?* New York: Scholastic.
Gardner, T. (2007). Bold books for teenagers: Internet literature for media-savvy students. *English Journal, 96*(6), 93–96.
Green, J., & Levithan, D. (2010). *Will Grayson, Will Grayson*. New York: Dutton.
Groenke, S. L., & Maples, J. (2010). Young adult literature goes digital: Will teen reading ever be the same? *The ALAN Review, 37*(3), 38–44.
Haarsma, P. J. (2006). *The softwire: Virus on Orbis 1*. Somerville, MA: Candlewick Press.
Hill, C. A., & Mehlenbacher, B. (1996). *Readers' expectation and writers' goals in the late age of print*. Paper presented at the ACM Special Interest Group for Design of Communications Research, Triangle Park, NC.
Hull, G., & Stornaiuolo, A. (2010). Literate arts in a global world: Reframing social networking as cosmopolitan practice. *Journal of Adolescent & Adult Literacy, 54*(2), 85–97.
Jenkins, H. (2004). Game design as narrative architecture. In N. Waldrip-Fruin & P. Harrington (Eds.), *First person: New media as story, performance, and game* (pp. 117–130). Cambridge, MA: MIT Press.
Kluger, K. (2008). *My most excellent year: A novel of love, Mary Poppins, and Fenway Park*. New York: Dial.
Koss, M., & Tucker-Raymond, R. (2010). Representations of digital communication: Science fiction as social commentary. *The ALAN Review, 38*(2), 43–52.
Kress, G., Jewitt, C., & Tsatsarelis, C. (2000). Knowledge, identity, pedagogy, pedagogic discourse, and the representational environments of education in late modernity. *Linguistics and Education, 11*(1), 7–30.
Lam, W. S. E. (2009). Multiliteracies on instant messaging in negotiating local, translocal, and transnational affiliations: A case of an adolescent immigrant. *Reading Research Quarterly, 44*(4), 377–397.
Lanham, R. (1993). *The electronic word: Democracy, technology, and the arts*. Chicago: University of Chicago Press.
Lewis, C., & Fabos, B. (2005). Instant messaging, literacies, and social identities. *Reading Research Quarterly, 40*(4), 470–501.
McLean, C. (2010). A space called home: An immigrant adolescent's digital literacy practices. *Journal of Adolescent & Adult Literacy, 54*(1), 13–22.
Miskec, J. (2007). YA by Generation Y: New writers for new readers. *The ALAN Review, 35*(3), 7–14.
Myracle, L. (2004). *ttyl*. New York: Amulet.
Myracle, L. (2006). *ttfn*. New York: Amulet.
Myracle, L. (2008). *l8r g8r*. New York: Amulet.

Negroponte, N. (1995). *Being digital.* New York: Knopf.
Prensky, M. (2001). Digital natives, digital immigrants. *On the Horizon, 9*(5).
Reich, J. (2008, May 13). Turn teen texting toward better writing. *Christian Science Monitor,* p. 9.
Riordan, R. (2005). *The lightning thief.* New York: Scholastic.
Rosen, M. (2002). *ChaseR: A novel in emails.* Cambridge, MA: Candlewick Press.
Rowsell, J., & Burke, A. (2009). Reading by design: Two case studies of digital reading practices. *Journal of Adolescent & Adult Literacy, 53*(2), 106–118.
Rudnick, E. (2010). *Tweet Heart.* New York: Disney/Hyperion.
Schindler, N. (2004). *An order of Amelie, hold the fries.* Buffalo, NY: Firefly.
Sweeney, S. M. (2010). Writing for the instant messaging and text messaging generation: Using new literacies to support writing instruction. *Journal of Adolescent & Adult Literacy, 54*(2), 121–130.
Tapscott, D. (1998). *Growing up digital: The rise of the net generation.* New York: McGraw-Hill.
Wyile, A. S. (1999). Expanding the view of first-person narration. *Children's Literature in Education, 30*(3), 185–202.
Zenatti, V. (2008). *A bottle in the Gaza Sea.* New York: Bloomsbury.

15

YAL in Cyberspace: How Teachers Are Following Their Students into New Literacies

James Blasingame

LIFE IN THE TIME OF SCREENAGERS

How can books possibly compete with video games like World of Warcraft, social networking sites like Facebook and Twitter, fansites like Twilight Lexicon, or infinite shopping possibilities, from eBay to dEliAs.com, for the hearts and minds of young people? Perhaps they don't need to compete after all but can, instead, take advantage of all these new literacies to enhance the reading experience of adolescents by following them into digital regions they already inhabit. Teachers around the country are finding ways to use blogs, Skype, YouTube, video games, wikis, Facebook, and fansites to improve their students' reading experiences and to bring technology into the classroom as a powerful tool for learning.

Admittedly, for many parents and teachers the amount of time young people are spending in front of a computer or other electronic device has become a very real concern, one which led to the term "screenagers," first coined by Douglas Rushkoff in his 1997 work *Playing the Future*, to refer to young people for whom accessing information and interacting socially on a computer screen is all they have ever known. As technology improves, prices of computers and smartphones continue to come down, and affordability brings more and more young people online on some form of computer screen, from iPad to Android. At the same time, high-quality graphics, programs, and "apps" (applications) continue to evolve at a startling rate, tempting young people to join the fun and social interaction. Reporting on a 2010 study from the Kaiser Family Foundation, *New York Times* reporter Tamara Lewin explains that kids eight to eighteen spend the majority of their time outside of school "using a smart phone, computer, television or other electronic device," for an average total of 7.5 hours a day (Lewin, 2010).

Not only are kids using electronic devices to communicate with peers and entertain themselves for the majority of their free time, but it is a majority of kids who are doing it. The Pew Research Center's (2008) Internet and American Life Project found that 97 percent of the kids in their sample of 1,102 play video games. Nearly half of the sampled population played games on cell phones, which are also increasing in use at a breakneck pace. Alex Mindlin (2010), also writing for the *New York Times*, reports on another study, this one from the Mediamark Research and Intelligence marketing firm, that kids' cell phone possession nearly doubled between 2005 and 2010 and boys have almost closed the gap with girls in ownership. Boys are also more likely to "perform data-intensive activities with their phones, like downloading games and browsing the Web," according to Anne Marie Kelly, an executive with Mediamark Research and Intelligence (Mindlin, 2010).

And has this been at the expense of reading? *Reading at Risk*, a report from the National Endowment for the Arts (2004), found a serious decline in literary reading, especially among young adults and even more so among people who watched television (p. vii). Ironically, World of Warcraft, the most commonly played Massively Multiplayer Online Role Playing Game (MMORPG), was released that same year, and by October 2010, twelve million players would be subscribed to what has come to be known as WoW.

VIDEO GAMING

Gaming has definitely become a part of life for teens, with 99 percent of boys and 94 percent of girls playing them at some time, according to the Pew Study. Younger boys play on a daily basis twice as often as younger girls, followed by older boys and older girls, the study showed. Playing video games is more likely to be a social experience than a solitary one; in fact, 65 percent of them play with others who are physically present in the room with them, while 27 percent play with people they only know on the Internet (National Endowment for the Arts, 2004, p. iii).

For young people, whose attention spans are short and whose expectations for quick gratification are high, the appeal of video games lies in the ingenious structure built in by successful game designers. As new literacies expert James Gee (2007) explains, successful video games establish "what the psychologist Eric Erickson has called a *psychosocial moratorium*—that is, a learning space in which the learner can take risks where real-world consequences are lowered" (p. 59). As game designers have come to understand, players find just the right amount of challenge rewarding. In addition, the challenge needs to escalate as the players have more experience and improve, so that they can rise to higher levels of play and become experts. Higher levels of challenge mean higher rewards in the game and a built-in acknowledgement of higher ability. A challenge that is too hard, too soon, or fails to reward the player proportionately to the challenge may disrupt what researchers have termed "flow" and frustrate the player enough to end play. As the coiner of the term "flow," Mihaly Csikszentmihalyi (1999) explains:

> Another universal condition for the flow experience is that the person feels his or her abilities to act match the opportunities for action. If the challenges are too great for the person's skill, anxiety is likely to ensue; if the skills are greater than the challenges, one feels bored. When challenges are in balance with skills, one becomes lost in the activity and flow is likely to result. (p. 825)

When game players are experiencing flow, according to Csikszentmihalyi, they likely experience a "sense of having stepped into a different reality [which] can be induced by environmental cues" (p. 825). Needless to say, good graphics help make a video game appealing; what are called "first-person shooter games," such as Halo 3, look and feel so much more realistic, yet otherworldly, than the early games, such as Space Invaders or Donkey Kong. As players become lost in the flow of the game, Csikszentmihalyi (1996) tells us, "You lose your sense of time, you're completely enraptured, you are completely caught up in what you're doing" (p. 121). This euphoria is heightened by immediacy of feedback, which happens in the split second a player makes a good or bad move. Players may stop an enemy in his tracks with their weapon of choice, or they may fail and face the ultimate consequence—only to come back in the next round with a little bit more information about how to avoid repeating that consequence. Failure, or risk taking, is actually a good thing!

The best of video games engage the players in an evolving story, however, and good stories are what young adult literature (YAL) is all about. What happens when a great young adult book is used to create a game, embedding the story of the book into the game? What happens is that the flow felt by video game players in the height of their playing experience serves as an entry point into reading for many teens, especially boys, who have been notoriously anti-reading for decades. An example of this entry point is illustrated by the *Softwire* science fiction series, written by P. J. Haarsma, which includes not only four books with fast-paced plots but also a free online video game based on the books, which allows players to choose an identity and step into the story as full-fledged participants who make choices and control their own destinies.

ENTER *THE SOFTWIRE*: VIDEO GAMING MEETS ENGAGING SCIENCE FICTION STORY

When Haarsma began writing his first science fiction book, *The Softwire: Virus on Orbis 1* (2006), he was already an experienced video game player; in fact, he and his friends, actors Nathan Fillion and Alan Tudyk, had a weekly tradition of playing Halo 1, Halo 2, and then Halo 3, at the Haarsma residence on Sunday evenings (P. J. Haarsma, personal communication, November 20, 2010). Nathan and Alan were such well-known aficionados of the game that they accepted the invitation to provide voices for characters in the most up-to-date version, Halo 3. As a former movie and advertising video producer and director for his own company, Redbear Productions, Haarsma had a keen understanding of flow in screenplay writing and the perfect pacing to keep viewers engaged with a message. Coupled with his affinity for video games, this video production experience proved an invaluable asset for plot construction in the *Softwire* series. Critical reviewing publications such as *Booklist* have described the book's appeal: "A fast-moving plot filled with kids fighting against the odds; bizarre creatures both devious and noble; real messages about civilization, barbarity, ethics, and freedom; and a healthy dose of alien gore make this a strong science-fiction read for the younger teen set" (Koelling, n.d.).

When Candlewick Press sent Haarsma on book tour, he discovered a readership composed of teen readers, many of whom were boys, who loved the same things he did: Comic Cons (gigantic conventions held in Chicago, Phoenix, and San Diego for aficionados of comic books, graphic novels, and science fiction movies, such as *Star Wars* and *Star Trek*), video games, science fiction books and movies, the possibility of alien visitors to the planet Earth, and the science of space travel.

When he experienced the traditional snail's pace of the publishing process from manuscript to book sales, he was determined to provide readers with a way to continue their *Softwire* experience immediately, one in which they could take an active rather than passive role. And so he created the Rings of Orbis video game, complete with every plot, setting, and character detail from the book and much more. As they played the game with others around the world, participants would be creating their own stories based on the creatures and places in his imagination.

The video game was a big hit, but more than this, the book–video game combination was an even bigger hit. As Haarsma explained in an interview with *New York Times* feature reporter Motoko Rich, "'You can't just make a book anymore.' . . . Pairing a video game with a novel for young readers, he added, 'brings the book into their world, as opposed to going the other way around'" (Rich, 2008).

In the lingo of video gaming ("their world"), the Rings of Orbis is an RPG, a role-playing game. This allows the players to enter the plot line with the same identity every time they log in to play and to return to the circumstance they created for themselves in past bursts of play as they amass wealth, buy and accessorize a spaceship, build a workforce and maintain it, maintain their own physical and spiritual health, and interact with players from around the world, many of whom they come to know—albeit in their *Softwire* identities only. Players who play enough and with the highest level of success will even be accepted onto the Rings of Orbis Trading Council, the group that holds sway over the rules of the game.

Upon venturing into the literary/fictional Rings of Orbis, the setting for the *Softwire* series, we find that the story revolves around Johnny Turnbull, or JT, as his friends call him. JT and his friends arrive at an intergalactic trading post, the Rings of Orbis, an artificial set of rings surrounding a black hole, populated by a range of sentient beings with a variety of abilities and prejudices. The earthlings had been awakened in deep space during a two-hundred-year journey to the Rings of Orbis when a malfunction caused the death of their parents. As JT and the other young people arrive without their parents to earn a living, they find they are bound as indentured servants who must do the bidding of their new masters to fulfill the contracted obligations of their parents.

When the residents of the Rings of Orbis discover that JT is a Softwire, a being who can control any electronic device with his mind, including computers, he becomes a very dangerous yet desired possession for the greedier inhabitants. The Rings of Orbis are controlled by a giant supercomputer, and when things start going wrong, everyone suspects that JT is involved

Secrets abound across the four-novel series, and each new book has taken readers in a new and unexpected direction. Understanding the books is crucial to playing the game to its full potential, which has players scrambling to read and read carefully. Inside the game, players "will not suffer a [non-reading] fool." Haarsma himself, playing with his own chosen identity, reports on an incident in which a player asked those in the game at that time for information to help him succeed: "They flamed him immediately. 'Dude!' they said, 'you gotta read the books! Go find out and come back!'" (P. J. Haarsma, personal communication, November 20, 2010). Prizes, information, and book trailers can be accessed on the *Softwire* website as well, but only after successfully answering detailed and somewhat difficult questions about the plot.

The effects of the game on reading have been captured in surveys within the game. Players are randomly given opportunities to answer survey questions, the results of which are found online at the Rings of Orbis game website. Of a sampling of 314 players who answered the question "After playing this game, how likely are you to buy the new books in the series as they come out?" 84.1 percent reported that they were "very likely," 12.4 percent reported that they were "somewhat likely," and 3.5 percent reported that they were "not likely" (Rings of Orbis, n.d.). This totals 96.5 percent of the players as reporting they were likely, in varying degrees, to read the new books as they came out, a very strong testimony to the effects of the game on reading attitudes, at least toward the *Softwire* series. Interestingly enough, when asked "Do/Did you like the books you had to read in school?" 53.8 percent of the respondents said they "loved them," 30.8 percent said they "hated them," and 15.4 percent said they "didn't care" (Rings of Orbis, n.d.). Perhaps the most likely conclusion that can be drawn from intersecting these two sets of survey responses is that the book itself makes a difference, but a video game companion to the book accelerates the growth of a reading fan base for the series.

The *Softwire* series is nothing if not a story of immigration and ethnic conflict. The various races of beings that inhabit the Rings of Orbis have various levels of social status and power. The protagonists, JT and his friends, are what are called knudniks (indentured servants), the bottom of the social ladder, and they encounter prejudice at school on the Rings from other students who believe that only the earlier inhabitants, those who own property, should be allowed to attend school or play in competitive sports. They also do not believe in the right of all creatures to earn citizenship. As players participate in their own self-created story within the Rings of Orbis game, they are put into situations—sometimes at random, sometimes as a programmed function of the game—in which they have to act according to a real or appropriated set of values about the basic worth and rights of living creatures, especially sentient ones.

Interestingly enough, research has been done on "pro-social and anti-social behavior while gaming" (Pew Research Center, Pew Internet and American Life Project, 2008, p. iv). Sixty-three percent of teens encountered "people being mean and overly aggressive while playing," including 49 percent who experienced "people being hateful, racist, or sexist" in the game, but nearly 75 percent reported that "another player responded by asking the aggressor to stop." Eighty-five percent of teen players reported experiencing other players who were "generous or helpful while playing." One of the benefits of reading espoused by noted authors of young adult literature is that young readers encounter and learn to deal with the problems of the world from the safe distance of a book, helping prepare them for what to do when they encounter it in the real world. As Chris Crutcher (1992), multiple award-winning author, puts it, "Stories can help teenagers look at their feelings or come to emotional resolution, from a safe distance" (p. 39). Katherine Paterson also praises what reading can do to prepare young people for life: "That's what books do for you. They give you practice in doing the difficult things in life" ("Katherine Paterson bio," n.d.). Surely, video games can do the same, albeit with a lot more autonomy on the part of the player.

SOCIAL NETWORKING AND COLLABORATIVE KNOWLEDGE BUILDING: WIKIS, TWITTER, FACEBOOK, AND FANSITES

New literacies involve more than just video gaming, however. In video gaming, students can cocreate new plot lines and interact within the imaginary universe originally created in an author's imagination, but what about the handling of factual information in cyberspace? In its *21st-Century Literacies: A Policy Research Brief*, the National Council of Teachers of English (2007) insists, "Effective instruction in 21st-century literacies takes an integrated approach, helping students understand how to access, evaluate, synthesize, and contribute to information" (p. 5). The policy brief goes on to recommend that students and their classmates "use a wiki to develop a multimodal reader's guide to a class text" (p. 5).

Wikis are websites with a very democratic philosophy on providing information. According to the website wiki.org:

> Wiki is a piece of server software that allows users to freely create and edit Web page content using any Web browser. Wiki supports hyperlinks and has a simple text syntax for creating new pages and crosslinks between internal pages on the fly.
>
> Wiki is unusual among group communication mechanisms in that it allows the organization of contributions to be edited in addition to the content itself. (Cunningham, 2002)

The term *wiki* may have come from the name of a Hawaiian airport shuttle bus, the Wiki-Wiki Shuttle, *wiki* being a Hawaiian word meaning "quick." Ward Cunningham bought the domain name for WikiWikiWeb in 1994, claiming that he wanted to emphasize the speed of his website (Cunningham, 2002). A wiki is a website that allows users to add content. The website, or wiki, can be set up to allow everyone who logs onto it to enter content or to allow only authorized users to add content. Editing can also be done by anyone or only by people authorized by the wiki creator. User-friendly wiki sites are available free online through a number of websites, including Wetpaint.com and Wikispaces, which also provide wiki sites with more sophisticated capabilities for a price.

Students may be accustomed to using the wiki format in their experiences with affinity groups, groups of individuals who share a common interest in something and share ownership in a website that revolves around the object of their interest. These wikis could be about a rock star, an actor, a movie, a genre of literature, a hobby, anything. The speed of the wiki format provides the same immediacy as video gaming. In some cases, information can be added in the moment on the wiki. Depending on how it is set up, participants may have to wait for editors to check their information before it posts. In many cases, the affinity group members have chosen editors who check the citations of "facts" posted on the wiki and take down pieces of information whose sources don't stack up.

Young people put up wikis on a variety of topics just for the love of the subject matter, but there is also a thrill in creating one's own authoritative site on the subject. Sometimes wikis are noticed by higher authorities who provide even greater opportunities, if the wiki is a good one. In 2009, high school students volunteering to participate in a wiki based on Haarsma's *Softwire* series received a surprising honor when the books' publisher, Candlewick Press, contracted with the students to reprint a portion of the wiki they had created in the paperback version of *The Softwire: Wormhole Pirates of Orbis 3*.

Using a Wetpaint.com platform, students at Basha High School in Chandler, Arizona, created a sophisticated wiki that included a lexicon of alien species and words that spread across several screens. Under the guidance of Basha teachers Devon Adams, Keri Matthew, and Lindsay Palbykin, students did exactly as the National Council of Teachers of English (2007) recommended and used "a wiki to develop a multimodal reader's guide to a class text" (p. 5). The pages that can now be found in the 2010 printing of *The Softwire: Wormhole Pirates of Orbis 3* reflect only a small fraction of the information the students placed on the wiki. In addition to the lexicon of names and terms, their definitions, and—if helpful—their scientific explanations, the students posted numerous video clips of the author explaining the science of his imaginary universe, the challenges of intergalactic travel, the technology of creating talking aliens for a website, and tips for playing and winning at the Rings of Orbis. The wiki has discussion threads that allow entry at any time on interesting topics from the book series and game, and room for members of the class to start new components. This wiki was set up so that only class members could add information, and a small number of ambitious students volunteered to act as editors of the site, checking facts and judging appropriateness.

The wiki includes a link to Haarsma's personal Facebook page, where information about his family, daily adventures, and interesting details about the books and his friends in the literary, movie, and comic book industries can be found. In addition, Rings of Orbis has a Facebook group with 510 members; the *Softwire* series also has its own Facebook page, currently with 188 "likes." Haarsma's Facebook page has no fewer than 1,028 friends. A quick perusal of Facebook shows that Haarsma is typical of young adult authors today, the majority of whom seem to have Facebook pages, and discussion postings they use to communicate with readers and keep them apprised of what is happening in their lives, from book tours to new manuscripts. Lisa McMann, for example, has 4,989 friends; David Levithan has 4,842 friends; Laurie Halse Anderson has 4,900 friends; and Ellen Hopkins has 4,887 friends. Since Facebook limits the number of friends a page holder can have to 5,000, it is easily surmised that the top young adult authors quickly top out and hover around the limit as people drop off of the social network and others apply for friend status. Many young adult authors also have a Twitter account, through which fans who want to "follow" them can get the latest news from their lives posted in 140-character "tweets." Tweeting (using the Twitter format) can be a means for young writers to learn to be concise in their composition.

The Basha High School *Softwire* wiki also includes discussion threads in which participants can post their opinions on a topic, such as who should play JT if a movie were to be made in the near future. Young people are accustomed to participating in these online conversations, most commonly on fansites, websites created by aficionados of a movie, a story, an actor, an author—fans of almost any person or thing imaginable that has a following.

At last count, there were over a hundred fansites for the *Twilight* vampire–gothic romance series of young adult novels written by Stephenie Meyer. These Twilight fansites are in countries all over the world and in various languages, each fansite placing its own particular spin on illuminating the books and movie adaptations. Fansites, such as Twilight Lexicon (http://www.twilightlexicon.com) include anything and everything newsworthy about the four books, the four movies, the writer, the actors, related Hollywood events, and a lot of speculation about the characters and stories beyond where the author actually took them. In particular, one form of speculation, called fanfiction, involves writers other than the author of the books writing to extend the characters' lives and the novels' story lines. A visit to www.twilightlexicon.com yields links to a variety of fanfiction sites, including one called Twilight Fanfiction and Fan Art, which has 6,068 members, among whom are 217 writers who create poetry, short stories, and novels all based on the *Twilight* series. Another 2,269 write reviews of the fanfiction, and the remainder of the membership can be assumed to read and enjoy what their fellow Twilight fans have produced.

Discussion on this website abounds; in fact, the Twilight Lexicon Forum has sets of discussion forums, such as one titled "The Cullen Basement," which has forty-nine separate discussion threads going on and more than 125,000 participants. Another set called "In the Meadow" includes a discussion forum called "Sparkling in the Sun," which is described as a "character discussion forum" and has 21,064 posts on eighty-four subjects. Questions on this forum ask for opinions and often some degree of connection to the story, as in the question "With which character do you most identify?" Teachers around the world are accepting participation in these discussion forums and in fanfiction as legitimate writing tasks and giving credit for posting stories and poems and participating in discussions. Assignments of this nature harness young writers' intrinsic motivation to connect to an audience of peers. As writing teachers know, an authentic writing assignment is one in which the student writes to a real audience in hopes of a real outcome. The outcome a student experiences in posting a fanfiction story or a discussion thread opinion (and arguments/illustrations in proof of that opinion), in addition to class credit, is similar to the outcome in video gaming: immediate feedback. Not only does the student not have to wait for the teacher to take papers home over the weekend and return them when they're graded, but the student also gets meaningful feedback online from peers the student cares about, who share informed opinions about the topic in which they have a common interest.

One of the interesting nuances of fanfiction is the high cognitive level it demands from participants. In Bloom's revised hierarchy of cognitive taxonomy, "synthesizing" has bumped "evaluating" from the top of the list (Anderson & Krathwohl, 2001). In fanfiction, writers must synthesize all they know, not only about the art of fiction or poetry but also about the author and books the fansite revolves around. In fansite terminology, the act of writing fanfiction that stays true to the original author's style, theme, and ideas is known as staying "canon." Reviewers of fanfiction, reading and writing their reviews from all over the world, will quickly criticize a piece of writing that is not canon—in other words, a piece that doesn't show insight into the beloved author's craft, characters, and story. Writing so as to remain faithful to the original works is difficult to do, but again, the payoff is grand because students can luxuriate in the posted reviews of their peers who find the work to be canon—high praise from those in the know.

BLOGGING: STUDENTS HOST THEIR OWN INTERNET TALK SHOW

Another means for carrying on conversations about beloved topics in cyberspace is through the blog (a blend of "Web log"). A blog is a website on which someone posts thoughts and feelings on a regular basis. Blog sites can be acquired for free at locations like www.blogger.com (all that is required is a Google membership), but any website can serve as a blog provided that the blogger has autonomy over what is posted. Generally, the blogger posts his or her writing on a topic which is much on his or her mind that day, and then followers of the blog site send in responses, which the blogger chooses to accept or reject for posting. Teachers around the country are harnessing the blogging energy of their students by giving them license to blog for class, especially on their favorite young adult novels. Like fansite discussion forums and fanfiction, blogs give immediate feedback from an audience the writer cares about. The Internet is already home to scores of teenager blogs about young adult books, and some of these blogs are so well done and have such a large following that authors are consenting to online interviews by e-mail.

Dr. Stephanie Knight, a seventh- and eighth-grade English teacher at Tesseract School in Phoenix, Arizona, uses blogging as a required feature of thematic units for literature study. In 2010–2011, Knight chose the theme of totalitarianism for her eighth graders and gave the unit the backdrop of World War II and the topic of the Holocaust, and students chose from available young adult novels, including *Milkweed, Soldier Boys, Night, Boy in the Striped Pajamas, The Book Thief,* and *If I Should Die Before I Wake.* Seventh graders did an all-class reading of *Chains,* a Revolutionary War slave narrative by Laurie Halse Anderson, and then students chose an individual book about the Civil War. In both grades, students were required to maintain a blog about their reading. These blogs were required to combine fact with opinion. In addition, opinions about or examples from the book had to have MLA citations. An interesting feature of Knight's use of the blog was that students were not only required to blog, but they also were required to post replies to each other's blogs, one reply for every blog post. Knight herself logged onto all the blogs once a week and also posted a response. In addition, students were required to post the words from their reading of which they did not know the meanings. These words became the basis for a vocabulary test every other week.

Knowing that students already live in a blogging world of their own, Knight harnessed their motivation to talk with peers about their favorite books by using the teachable moment and modeled both how to write a blog post and how to write a response that reflects "careful development and depth of thought" (S. Knight, personal communication, March 31, 2011). In addition, she modeled online responding that "showed respect and welcomed further discussion" (S. Knight, personal communication, March 31, 2011). Knight reports:

> The students LOVED the blogging aspect. There's freedom in blogging in that the students have a timeline to complete their blogs. They have a chance to think out their blog before they write. The standards were set high due to modeling. Then, in terms of reply, they had to add to the discussion. I wanted them to give insightful comments, alternative viewpoints, and probing questions that would move the discussions forward. (S. Knight, personal communication, March 31, 2011)

Knight's students completed guided response items on Fridays, for which they could use their notes, their books, and their blog posts and responses.

YOUTUBE: VIEWING, ANALYZING AND CREATING VIDEOS

YouTube is another location in cyberspace frequently inhabited by students. Almost anything and everything has been captured on video and placed on YouTube, from the silly to the sublime. Young people are both consumers and creators of YouTube videos, using a range of equipment from sophisticated cameras and computer editing programs to smartphones and software that enables them to upload videos directly to the YouTube website as a function of the editing program. With new technology comes new skills or literacies. Teachers around the country are teaching their students to evaluate YouTube videos for content quality, for bias, for technique, and for accuracy. In addition, they are empowering their students to place their own YouTube videos on the Internet as the students apply artistic license to works of literature.

Gary Paulsen's young adult novel *Hatchet* (1987) is in almost every school curriculum in the United States, usually somewhere between fifth and eighth grade. A quick perusal of YouTube shows a nearly endless list of student book trailers and adaptations of *Hatchet*, some with fairly advanced computer-generated animation. From Volvo station wagons with airplane cockpit instrument printouts taped to the dash to clips of very real plane crashes inserted between live action from student's backyards, these videos are inventive attempts to capture conflict, characterization, and setting.

Dr. Mary Powell's students at North High School (NHS) in Phoenix, Arizona, used everything from toy planes and action figures to backyard swimming pools in order to portray the initiating incident in *Hatchet*, a plane crash that leaves Paulsen's protagonist, Brian Robeson, stranded in the Canadian wilderness. The NHS students acted out some scenes, sometimes using dialogue directly from the book but more often using a script/screenplay they had written to convey the book's main conflict in the much shorter time that video requires as a medium. Writing skills, speaking skills, and presenting skills all came into play, but only after reading and analyzing the book for its most essential elements. Adapting a book to the screen is difficult and motivates students to read for the writer's craft. This can also be a reading strategy for readers who have a hard time visualizing what they read. Moving back and forth from text to video and asking students to interpret their reading through this visual medium will help those readers to see a sort of movie in their minds as they read, something that good readers are already adept at. In the case of these NHS students, creating a YouTube video was not required but was among choices of how students might demonstrate their level of engagement with the novel. Powell explains:

> As a language arts teacher in the twenty-first century, I know how important it is to allow students to use the virtual world to interpret the texts that we read.

> Thus, I afforded my ninth graders the opportunity to use YouTube in a young adult literature project. . . .
>
> YouTube allows my students to take the books that we read and transform them into film, displaying their work in a global, public forum that can be viewed by their peers. According to one student, "I made a video of *Hatchet* because I like to act. This gave me an opportunity to do so. Also, I am a visual learner so putting the book into something I could watch made it easier for me to understand the book. . . . I thought the class would have a better time watching my video than listening to me read something off of a paper." When we encourage students to read texts that resonate with their experiences and transform them into a technological, artistic creation, we build a bridge between students' interests and the subjects that we teach. (M. Powell, personal communication, April 1, 2011)

Powell's assertion that her students need to be publishing in "a global forum" is an interesting one. Students participating in fansites, Facebook, Twitter, wikis, blogs, and YouTube are accustomed to interacting with peers from around the world. How different is this from having the teacher as the only consumer of their products? Even group work or publishing pieces in a school collection do not have the cachet of finding oneself with a global audience of followers interested in reading your next blog. Surely, there could be no more appealing audience than the whole world.

What if equipment is a problem? Many schools can barely scrape together the funds to put one set of thirty desktop computers in the library and keep them operating, let alone provide iPads, laptops, camcorders and so on. One teacher literally followed her students into cyberspace, in a sense, when she asked them to do a digital storytelling project. Dr. Corrine Gordon at Horizon School in Phoenix, Arizona, attended a summer workshop on digital storytelling and was excited to share this technique with her students. The cost of the equipment required was prohibitive, however, for her to share this, at the time, cutting-edge approach to narrative wedded to technology. Her students were ahead of her, however: "Miss, we can use our phones for the taping," they exclaimed, flipping open their advanced cell phones (C. Gordon, personal communication, November 10, 2010).

Analyzing YouTube videos adapted from YAL that students have already read or are reading is another way to get them reading for craft and evaluating the quality of what they view rather than accepting it at face value. Jennifer Wermes at Explorer Middle School in Paradise Valley, Arizona, uses iPads, iPod touches, and Mac laptops with her students to search for videos of texts they have read and evaluate them using a rubric. Wermes trains students on the use of a rubric for evaluating various aspects of a YouTube clip and comparing it to the book from which it has been adapted. "We want to be sure our students are intelligent consumers of technology," Wermes explains, "and not passive recipients of everything they see on a screen."

Wermes's students learn to analyze YouTube videos depicting scenes from literature, scenes in which the video creators may have taken great license in interpretation:

> The actors in the YouTube video could be Lego figures or teens in steampunk costumes; nevertheless, there are qualities that students learn to evaluate the videos on in the visual realm along with the usual elements of literature, including seven items on a rubric: (1) collateral additions to the scene (such as props and backdrops), (2) characters' costuming/clothing and how this contributes to the overall effect of the scene, (3) setting, (4) the portrayal of events from the plot, (5) differentiate between minor and major events in the scene and explain their relationships, (6) evaluate the acting (does the actor convey the characteristics of the person being played as they were developed in the book?), and (7) adaptations to modern culture. (J. Wermes, personal interview, February 18, 2011)

TEACHING A TECHNOLOGY-ENHANCED CURRICULUM

Explorer Middle School was selected to pilot the Paradise Valley School District technology program. The school has equipment that many schools don't have currently but are likely to have in the future. In addition to the iPads and iPod touches, every group of four teachers shares a laptop cart with thirty-two Mac laptop computers that use Google Chrome as the Internet browsing engine rather than the typical Explorer or Mozilla Foxfire used by most schools. Google (2009) Chrome claims to be superior to other browsers in speed, security, individuality (the user designs the physical appearance), anti-tab-crash effects, usability (additional searching can be done from the same box), and anonymity (browsing is "incognito"—no one can see what the user looked at online). Explorer Middle School also has flip cameras, relatively inexpensive and simple video camcorders that are easy to use. In general, Wermes describes the Explorer technology arsenal as "enough technology for the kids to enjoy learning" (J. Wermes, personal interview, February 18, 2011).

Wermes also points out that

> Kids want to get their hands on technology. With each new application, kids want to try it. They don't really learn it if they don't get to use it, so we always include hands-on time, time for kids to use the technology themselves. We have double periods for English, which provides for the longer hands-on time needed. (J. Wermes, personal interview, February 18, 2011)

Explorer is also a school that practices inclusion and succeeds very well at adapting instruction to students' needs. Wermes explains:

> The use of technology is tremendously effective in differentiating instruction. Students have control of their learning, work at their own pace, can zoom ahead if they understand something quickly, like the use of Prezi (the next generation of computer-generated presentation programs), or editing videos for YouTube. With literature, they can access the text at the level they are comfortable with rather than being lost if the class activity is too far above their reading comprehension level or bored if it is below their level. (J. Wermes, personal interview, February 18, 2011)

Many students are primarily visual learners, and the hands-on activities technology affords them are of great benefit. English language learners find instructional advantages with technology as well, in that it enables them to repeat experiences until they are ready to move forward without feeling self-conscious in front of the class. Wermes continues:

> If a student is viewing a YouTube video, they can press pause and ask their group members for clarification, or they can press rewind and view/listen as many times as they need to before moving on. Otherwise, they may fall farther and farther behind. Control over the visual and auditory elements really helps ELL students who might flounder if they were restricted to written text. (J. Wermes, personal interview, February 18, 2011)

This may also be helpful to students who may have elements of Attention Deficit Hyperactivity Disorder.

Students in Wermes's class also have the nearly infinite choice provided by the Internet. Searching for YouTube videos depicting a certain book, creating a game, looking for fansites/fanfiction, blogging and looking for blogs, and so on all put the learner in position to search the depth and breadth of cyberspace and choose the places that best fit the searcher's interests. They also have twenty-four-hour access to class material, because Wermes creates website-based units for most of their learning. They can access these websites at any time of the day or night, complete tasks, research online, and e-mail questions to Wermes or their peers as needed.

INTO THE FUTURE

Video gaming, blogging, fansites, fanfiction, Twitter, YouTube, smartphones, and Facebook: Who knows what will come next? What we do know for sure is that young people are likely to continue riding the crest of the technology wave, and schools can either find a way to position teaching and learning side by side with their students on the wave or have it roll over them unceremoniously, drowning educational hopes and dreams. In addition, these new literacies truly are that—literacies—and all literacies need certain skills to go hand in hand with them, such as critical thinking and purposefulness. No one questioned the teaching of drivers' education in twentieth-century schools—why question the teaching of young adult literature through the harnessing of the latest in technology in the twenty-first century? Or, as a recent tweet said, "A million great conversations about books are whizzing past our heads, unseen in cyberspace! Why not join in all the fun? Log on now!"

REFERENCES

Anderson, L. W., & Krathwohl, D. R. (Eds.). (2001). *A taxonomy for learning, teaching, and assessing: A revision of Bloom's taxonomy of educational objectives*. Boston: Allyn & Bacon.

Crutcher, C. (1992). Healing through literature. In D. Gallo (Ed.), *Author's insights: Turning teenagers into readers and writers* (pp. 33–40). Portsmouth, NH: Boynton/Cook.

Csikszentmihalyi, M. (1996). *Creativity: Flow and the psychology of discovery and invention*. New York: HarperCollins.

Csikszentmihalyi, M. (1999). "If we are so rich, why aren't we happy?" *American Psychologist, 54*(10), 821–827.

Cunningham, W. (2002). What is wiki. Retrieved from http://www.wiki.org/wiki.cgi?WhatIsWiki

Gee, J. P. (2007). *What video games have to teach us about learning and literacy* (Rev. ed.). New York: Palgrave Macmillan.

Google. (2009). Chromefeatures. Retrieved from http://www.youtube.com/watch?v=SC-2VGBHFQI&annotation_id=annotation_749979&feature=iv

Haarsma, P. J. (2006). *The softwire: Virus on Orbis 1*. Somerville, MA: Candlewick Press.

Haarsma, P. J. (2010). *The softwire: Wormhole pirates on Orbis 3*. Somerville, MA: Candlewick Press.

Katherine Paterson bio. (n.d.). Retrieved from Scholastic, http://www2.scholastic.com/browse/contributor.jsp?id=3555

Koelling, H. (n.d.). Review of *The softwire: Virus on Orbis 1*. From *Booklist* as quoted on Amazon.com. Retrieved from http://www.amazon.com/Softwire-Betrayal-Orbis-ebook/dp/B003EINO08

Lewin, T. (2010, January 20). If your kids are awake, they're probably online. *New York Times*. Retrieved from http://www.nytimes.com/2010/01/20/education/20wired.html

Mindlin, Alex. (2010, March 7). Drilling down: Rapid rise of children with cellphones. *New York Times*. Retrieved from http://www.nytimes.com/2010/03/08/technology/08drill.html

National Council of Teachers of English. (2007). *21st-century literacies: A policy research brief*. Retrieved from http://www.ncte.org/library/NCTEFiles/Resources/PolicyResearch/21stCenturyResearchBrief.pdf

National Endowment for the Arts. (2004). *Reading at risk: A survey of literary reading in America*, Research Division Report 46. Retrieved from http://www.nea.gov/pub/ReadingAtRisk.pdf

Paulsen, G. (1987). *Hatchet*. New York: Simon & Schuster.
Pew Research Center. Pew Internet and American Life Project. (2008). Teens, video games, and civics. Retrieved from http://www.cbsnews.com/htdocs/pdf/PIP_Teens_Games_and_Civics_Report_FINAL.pdf
Rich, M. (2008, October 5). Using video games as bait to hook readers. *New York Times*. Retrieved from http://www.nytimes.com/2008/10/06/books/06games.html?pagewanted=1&_r=3&adxnnlx=1301180786-NV8yBXuW8MiHNy661jDYwQRings of Orbis
Rings of Orbis game website. (n.d.). Retrieved from http://www.ringsoforbis.com/docs/info_desk/surverys/reading_surveys.php?action=results&poll_ident=48

Index

About the Contributors

Jacqueline Bach, a former high school English teacher, is assistant professor of English education and curriculum theory at Louisiana State University in Baton Rouge. Her scholarship, which has appeared in *Changing English, English Journal*, and *Journal of Curriculum Theorizing*, examines how young adult literature engages teachers and students in conversations about social issues and the ways in which popular culture informs pedagogy. She is coeditor of *The ALAN Review*, a journal dedicated to the study and teaching of young adult literature. She is currently studying the role of service-learning in young adult literature courses and recently coauthored an issue of *Theory into Practice*.

Steven T. Bickmore has taught high school English at every ability level from ninth through twelfth grades. He is currently assistant professor of English education at Louisiana State University, with a joint appointment in the Department of Educational Theory, Policy, and Practice and in the English Department. He is a coeditor (2009–2014) of *The ALAN Review*, a journal dedicated to the research, teaching, and promotion of young adult literature. His research interests include the teaching and preparation of English methods courses, the induction experiences of new English teachers, and how and why English teachers use young adult literature in their classrooms.

James Blasingame, director of English education at Arizona State University, is former coeditor of *The ALAN Review* and past president (2010) of the Assembly on Literature for Adolescents of the National Council of Teachers of English (NCTE). He creates the Books for Adolescents pages for the

International Reading Association's *Journal of Adolescent & Adult Literacy* and coauthors the annual *English Journal* honor list of young adult literature. He is coauthor of *Literature for Today's Young Adults* (ninth edition) and author of *Books That Don't Bore 'Em: Young Adult Books That Speak to This Generation* and *Gary Paulsen (Teen Reads: Student Companions to Young Adult Literature)*. He serves as chairman of the board for Kids Need to Read Foundation.

Kelly Byrne Bull, assistant professor of education at Notre Dame of Maryland University, centers her scholarship and service on connecting teachers and young adults with engaging books. Bull has written for *English Journal, Theory Into Practice,* and *ALAN Picks*. Serving as the Assembly on Literature for Adolescents (ALAN) state representative for Maryland, she recruits new members and presents at local, state, and national conferences on adolescent literacy and young adult literature. Bull serves on NCTE's Conference on English Education Commission on the Study and Teaching of Adolescent Literature, the State of Maryland International Reading Association's (SoMIRAC) higher education committee, and the Baltimore City Reading Council. Bull volunteers with public libraries to host writing workshops and literacy events for teens.

Sarah M. Burns is a graduate research assistant for teacher education at the University of Arkansas at Little Rock. She was an assistant language teacher with the Japan Exchange and Teaching Program (JET). She taught English to Japanese students in grades K–9 in rural Japan, where she was involved in grassroots internationalization. She was the director of a high school international exchange program, where she worked with students from Asia, Europe, and Latin America, before deciding to pursue a masters in secondary education for English language arts.

Karina R. Clemmons is assistant professor of secondary education at the University of Arkansas at Little Rock. Dr. Clemmons has taught English as a Second Language in middle school, high school, and adult settings in the United States and abroad. Her research interests include technology in education, second language acquisition, teacher preparation, and young adult literature as a means to improve content area literacy.

Deanna Day teaches undergraduate and graduate literacy courses for Washington State University, Vancouver. Previously she was a classroom teacher in Arizona for fifteen years. One of her goals as a teacher was to help students become lifelong readers and to critically think about what they were reading. She has continued this goal as a professor, helping teachers become readers and pass their love of literacy into their classrooms. Her scholarly interests have centered on children's and young adult literature, including interviewing authors and illustrators, critically examining books, and researching literature circles in different settings. Her professional work has appeared in several literacy journals, including *Dragon Lode, Journal of Children's Literature, Language Arts,* and *Reading Horizons.*

Susan E. Elliott-Johns is a former elementary school teacher, language and literacy consultant, and school principal (JK–8). She is currently tenured assistant professor of literacy teacher education in the Schulich School of Education at Nipissing University in North Bay, Ontario, Canada. Her research interests include literacy teacher education, multimodal responses to literature, and the effective integration of young adult literature in language arts programs for contemporary classrooms.

Judith A. Hayn is a former middle and high school English language arts teacher and is currently associate professor of English education at the University of Arkansas at Little Rock. Hayn is the chair of the NCTE Conference on English Education Commission on the Study and Teaching of Adolescent Literature and of SIGNAL, IRA's Special Interest Group Network on Adolescent Literature. She has published numerous young adult book reviews and articles in the field. She recently coedited a themed issue on young adult literature for *Theory into Practice.*

Lisa A. Hazlett is professor of secondary education at The University of South Dakota, where she teaches courses in middle/secondary English language arts education and specializes in young adult literature. She served as an ALAN board member and is active with both the Conference on English Education's Commission of Young Adult Literature and South Dakota Council of Teachers of English. A regular presenter for NCTE and ALAN, she has also published numerous book chapters, brochures, and journal articles, all incorporating young adult literature. However, her preference and expertise is reviewing; she regularly reviews manuscripts, novels, and textbooks for *Voice of Youth Advocates, Journal of Adolescent & Adult Literacy, Multicultural Review, SIGNAL, The ALAN Review, ALAN Picks, WILLA Journal,* and for various publishing houses.

Crag Hill, after eighteen years teaching English language arts, grades 9–12, is currently assistant professor of English education at Washington State University, Pullman, where he has been instrumental in integrating young adult literature and graphic novels into the curriculum. He was a major contributor to the project *Rationales for Teaching Graphic Novels,* writing 10 of the 108 rationales, including rationales for *V for Vendetta, The Sandman:*

Preludes and Nocturnes, Pride of Baghdad, Safe Area Gorazde, and *The Adventures of Jimmie Corrigan,* and he has published articles in *The ALAN Review, Signal, English Journal,* and other journals.

Melanie Hundley is a former middle and high school English language arts teacher and is currently assistant professor in the practice at Vanderbilt University in Nashville, Tennessee. Hundley is the coeditor of *The ALAN Review,* a journal that promotes the teaching and research of young adult literature. She has published numerous young adult literature book reviews and several articles and book chapters in the field.

Jeffrey S. Kaplan is a former middle and high school English language arts teacher and is currently associate professor of English education at the University of Central Florida, Orlando. Kaplan is a member of the NCTE Conference on English Education Commission on the Study of Teaching of Adolescent Literature and of SIGNAL, the Special Interest Group Network on Adolescent Literature for the International Reading Association. He is also the Research Connections editor for *The ALAN Review,* a leading peer-reviewed journal on the study and teaching of young adult literature. Author of numerous articles and book reviews on teaching and learning, he recently coauthored an article on research and writing about the study of young adult literature for *Theory into Practice.* He is the president-elect for the Assembly on Adolescent Literature of the National Council of Teachers of English.

Michelle J. Kelley is a former elementary school teacher and is currently associate professor of reading education at the University of Central Florida. Kelley is actively involved in the International Reading Association in a variety of roles. Additionally, she serves as coeditor of *Literacy Research and Instruction,* the journal of the Association of Literacy Educators and Researchers. She has published numerous articles and two professional resources in the field of literacy, specializing in the areas of motivation and comprehension.

Melanie D. Koss is assistant professor of children's and young adult literature and literacy at Northern Illinois University. She specializes in the teaching and research of children's and young adult literature. Her research interests include looking at young adult novels with multiple narrative perspectives, representations of digital communication technology in children's and young adult literature, and representations of special needs characters in children's and young adult texts. In addition to her research, she has published articles in journals including *The ALAN Review, SIGNAL,* and *The Journal of Adolescent & Adult Literacy (JAAL).* She serves on the editorial board of both *The Journal of Children's Literature* and *JAAL*. She is an advocate of the authentic use of children's literature in the classroom and believes that children's literature spans the education, English, and library information science (LIS) disciplines.

Mark Letcher is currently assistant professor of English education at Purdue University Calumet. He is an active participant in the field of young adult literature, through various committees in NCTE and IRA, as well as through the column he edits for NCTE's *English Journal*. He has presented and published in the area of LGBTQ-themed young adult literature.

Kristen Miraglia lives just outside of Philadelphia, Pennsylvania. She graduated from West Chester University with a BSEd in English. She loves teaching, reading, writing, and learning. Currently she is pursuing a teaching career in high school English. She most looks forward to the prospect of continuing her research in the areas of teacher education and equal rights for all genders, races, and sexualities.

Amanda L. Nolen is associate professor of educational psychology at the University of Arkansas at Little Rock. She is the former chief operating officer for the Holmes Partnership, a national educational reform consortium. Nolen has published widely on topics such as emerging research methods, educational psychology, and teacher education reform.

Linda T. Parsons is assistant professor at The Ohio State University at Marion in the College of Education and Human Ecology, School of Teaching and Learning, where she teaches courses in middle childhood literacy and children's and young adult literature. Her research interests include the analysis of children's and young adult literature, interrogating single novels and text sets as repositories that reinforce and/or challenge established cultural norms. She also explores children's and adolescents' engagement with and response to literature. She is an active member of the National Council of Teachers of English, the International Reading Association, and the American Library Association.

Laura A. Renzi is a former middle and high school English and history teacher and is currently assistant professor of English at West Chester University in West Chester, Pennsylvania. Renzi is a cochair of the NCTE Conference on English Education Commission on the Study of English Methods, and she serves on the LGBT Advisory Council for NCTE.

Colleen T. Sheehy is assistant professor of secondary education at the University of Indianapolis. She is a former middle and high school English language arts teacher and is nationally board certified in the area of adolescent–young adult English language arts. Her research interests include media literacy education, young adult literature across the content areas, and technology in education.

Lois T. Stover is a former middle and high school teacher of English and drama who currently serves as professor and chair of educational studies at St. Mary's College of Maryland. She teaches courses in children's and young adult literature, educational psychology, and teaching methodology. A past president of the Assembly on Literature for Adolescents of NCTE, she is the author of *Young Adult Literature: The Heart of the Middle School Curriculum, Presenting Phyllis Reynolds Naylor, Jacqueline Woodson: The Real Thing,* and numerous book chapters and articles on young adult literature. She coedited the thirteenth edition of NCTE's annotated bibliography for high school readers, *Books for You.* Her most recent book, *Teaching the Selected Works of Katherine Paterson,* on which she collaborated with former students and county teachers, was published in 2008.

Barbara A. Ward, formerly a middle and high school English language arts teacher, is currently assistant professor of literacy at Washington State University, Pullman, where she teaches children's literature and young adult literature. Ward is the chair of the NCTE Excellence in Poetry for Children Award Committee and the president-elect of the Children's Literature and Reading Special Interest Group of IRA. She served for three years on the Amelia Elizabeth Walden Award Committee of ALAN and enjoys writing book reviews and journal articles about young adult literature.

Nance S. Wilson is associate professor and director of middle childhood education at Lourdes University in Sylvania, Ohio. She studies adolescent literature and teaching and learning of the language arts.

Terrell A. Young is professor of children's literature and literacy at Brigham Young University in Provo, Utah. Young's articles have been published in *Reading Teacher, Language Arts, Childhood Education, Reading Psychology, Journal of Children's Literature, Dragon Lode,* and *Book Links.* He is the coauthor or editor of seven books. Young served as president of the Washington Organization for Reading Development, the IRA Children's Literature and Reading Special Interest Group, and the NCTE Children's Literature Assembly. From 2009 to 2012, he has served as a member of the IRA board of directors. Young is a recipient of the IRA Outstanding Teacher Educator in Reading Award.

CPSIA information can be obtained at www.ICGtesting.com
Printed in the USA
BVOW020800020412

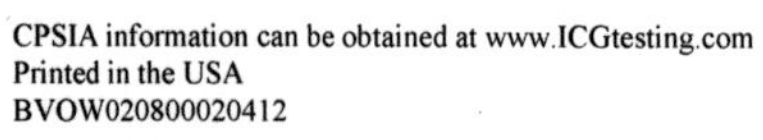